Applying Quality of Life Research

Best Practices

This book series focuses on best practices in specialty areas of Quality of Life research, including among others potentially: community development, quality of work life, marketing, healthcare and public sector management. In today's world, governments, organizations and individuals alike are paying increasingly more attention to how their activities impact on quality of life at the regional, national and global levels. Whether as a way to tackle global resource shortages, changing environmental circumstances, political conditions, competition, technology or otherwise, the far-reaching impact of decisions made in these and other areas can have a significant impact on populations regardless of their level of development. Many lessons have been learned; yet many are still to be realized. Across a number of volumes on diverse themes, this book series will address key issues that are of significant importance to decision makers and participants across all sectors. The series will be invaluable to anyone with an interest in applying quality of life knowledge in contemporary society.

More information about this series at http://www.springer.com/series/8364

M. Mercedes Galan-Ladero • Reynaldo G. Rivera
Editors

Applied Social Marketing and Quality of Life

Case Studies from an International Perspective

Springer

Editors
M. Mercedes Galan-Ladero
University of Extremadura
Badajoz, Spain

Reynaldo G. Rivera
Austral University
Buenos Aires, Argentina

ISSN 2213-994X ISSN 2213-9958 (electronic)
Applying Quality of Life Research
ISBN 978-3-030-83285-8 ISBN 978-3-030-83286-5 (eBook)
https://doi.org/10.1007/978-3-030-83286-5

This Springer imprint is published by the registered company Springer Nature Switzerland AG.
The registered company address is: Gewerbestrasse 11, 6330 Cham, Switzerland

To all the people and organizations who work to make a better world, to help other people to improve their quality of life.

Preface

In the age of globalization and digitalization, societies face important challenges related to public health, education, the environment, etc., which can be addressed and solved by social marketing, and which have a great influence on people's quality of life.

Thus, social marketing has become a key tool to promote, modify, discourage, or even abandon certain ideas, values, attitudes, and/or social behaviors.

The aim of this book is to describe different cases about the application of social marketing in different areas, in different countries, and by different organizations (public and nonprofit organizations mainly but also businesses), and which have an impact on the quality of life of their target audiences. Thereby, this book approaches social marketing from quality-of-life (QOL) marketing philosophy in an international context, including case studies from different regions around the world.

Therefore, this book is structured as follows:

- A theoretical initial chapter, to introduce the concepts of social marketing, quality of life, and the link between these two terms.
- 25 case studies: they are brief but sufficiently complete, so that readers can understand the initial problem and see how the social marketing campaign was developed.

  These cases have been grouped into several thematic sections, focused on:

  - Health: Disease Prevention and Risk Behavior. This section includes cases related to the prevention of diseases and risk behaviors.
  - Safe and Healthy Lifestyles. This section includes cases related to promoting better lifestyles (exercise, sustainable food, recycling, etc.)
  - Inclusion and Interpersonal Relationships. This section refers to cases related to inclusive education and labor inclusion (people with disabilities, refugees, family orientation, and community-based actions for social change).

Within their diversity, a similar organization of all the chapters has been sought:

- An introduction to the topic
- The development of the case

- Conclusions
- Discussion questions (to be discussed in class, or outside the classroom)
- Teaching notes: with the possible solutions to the questions, or guidelines for working and discussing them (when they are personal opinions and do not have correct/incorrect answers).

This book is aimed at undergraduate and graduate students in marketing courses in general, and social marketing in particular. It is also intended for social marketers and practitioners who work in this discipline, so that they know different experiences of social marketing campaigns carried out in other countries and see the different results obtained. Thus, they can compare them and/or take them as a reference, improving their ability to design and implement new social marketing campaigns and strategies in their specific contexts.

As editors, we would like to especially thank the work of all the authors who, with their cases, have made this book possible. Their availability and collaboration in these difficult months of lockdown in practically all the countries due to the global COVID-19 pandemic have been key to bringing this project to fruition. We have been able to verify firsthand the effect of social marketing campaigns on our attitudes and behaviors (e.g., those that wanted us to "stay at home". or "use the mask") with different results depending on the countries, and how much they have affected our quality of life.

Finally, we would also like to thank the International Association of Public and Non-Profit Marketing (AIMPN - IAPNM), its members, and participants in its conferences, for the support they have given us, collaborating as authors in many of the case studies and/or helping to spread the call for chapters of this book.

We hope this book will be useful and enjoyable for readers, and will help to highlight the importance of social marketing around the world. And we also hope that it will encourage more research and work in this field, to spread the benefits that social marketing can provide, especially in improving people's quality of life worldwide.

We invite readers to contact us if they wish, to send us their comments or make suggestions for improvements for future editions of this book.

Badajoz, Spain
Buenos Aires, Argentina
November, 2020

M. Mercedes Galan-Ladero
Reynaldo G. Rivera

Contents

Contributors

Madalena Abreu Coimbra Business School–ISCAC, Coimbra, Portugal

Ogechi Adeola Lagos Business School, Pan-Atlantic University, Lagos, Nigeria

Filipa Almeida Coimbra Business School–ISCAC, Coimbra, Portugal

Helena Alves University of Beira Interior, Covilha, Portugal

María Amérigo University of Castilla La Mancha, Toledo, Spain

Pierre Arwidson Santé Publique France, Saint-Maurice, France

Justine Avenel-Roux Santé Publique France, Saint-Maurice, France

Natacha Beltrán National University of Cordoba, Cordoba, Argentina

Hina Y. Bhatti Riphah International University, Lahore, Pakistan
University of Extremadura, Badajoz, Spain

Enrique Bianchi National University of Cordoba, Cordoba, Argentina

Aurélie Blanc Santé Publique France, Saint-Maurice, France

Jose M. Bodoque University of Castilla La Mancha, Toledo, Spain

Edy L. Burbano University of San Buenaventura Cali, Cali, Colombia

Vanessa Burgal Lagos Business School, Pan-Atlantic University, Lagos, Nigeria

Nuno Cadete Coimbra Business School–ISCAC, Coimbra, Portugal

Pablo Cardona-Soriano International University of La Rioja, Logroño, Spain

Ana Cardoso University of Minho, Braga, Portugal

M. Victoria Carrillo-Durán University of Extremadura, Badajoz, Spain

Beatriz Casáis University of Minho, Braga, Portugal

Luis M. Cerdá-Suárez International University of La Rioja, Logroño, Spain

Patricia Correa Catholic University of Uruguay, Montevideo, Uruguay

Juliana Correia Universidade Católica Portuguesa, Porto, Portugal

Marco A. Cruz-Morato University of Malaga, Malaga, Spain

Félicie David Santé Publique France, Saint-Maurice, France

Jennifer Davies Santé Publique France, Saint-Maurice, France

Estela M. Díaz ICADE, Faculty of Economics and Business Administration, Department of Management, Madrid, Spain

Andrss Diez-Herrero IGME, CSIC, Geological Survey of Spain, Madrid, Spain

Auriane Djian Santé Publique France, Saint-Maurice, France

Paulo Duarte University of Beira Interior, Covilha, Portugal

Carmen Dueñas-Zambrana University of Malaga, Malaga, Spain

Joao Fins Ascendi–IPAM, Porto, Portugal

Daniela Fontana National University of Cordoba, Cordoba, Argentina

Dolores Frías-Jamilena University of Granada, Granada, Spain

M. Mercedes Galan-Ladero University of Extremadura, Badajoz, Spain

Clementina Galera-Casquet University of Extremadura, Badajoz, Spain

Araceli Galiano-Coronil University of Cadiz, Jerez de la Frontera, Spain

Karine Gallopel-Morvan EHESP School of Public Health, Rennes, France

Iñaki García-Arrizabalaga University of Deusto, Donostia/San Sebastian, Spain

María García-García University of Extremadura, Badajoz, Spain

Juan A. Garcia University of Castilla La Mancha, Talavera de la Reina, Spain

Purificación García-Miguélez University of León, Leon, Spain

Juan José Gibaja-Martíns University of Deusto, Donostia/San Sebastian, Spain

Romain Guignard Santé Publique France, Saint-Maurice, France

Pilar A. Huerta-Zavala University of Burgos, Burgos, Spain

Oserere Ibelegbu Lagos Business School, Pan-Atlantic University, Lagos, Nigeria

Nora Lado University Carlos III, Madrid, Spain

Óscar Licandro CLAEH University, Montevideo, Uruguay

Carlota López-Aza Complutense University of Madrid, Madrid, Spain

David F. Martín-García ICADE, Faculty of Economics and Business Administration, Department of Marketing, Madrid, Spain

Rafael Fabricio Matos-Cámara La Salle University Cancun, Cancun, Mexico

Filipe Melao Ascendi, Porto, Portugal

Mariana Mendoza National University of Cordoba, Cordoba, Argentina

Alazne Mujika-Alberdi University of Deusto, Donostia/San Sebastian, Spain

Viêt Nguyen-Thanh Santé Publique France, Saint-Maurice, France

Jazmín Nogaró Austral University, Buenos Aires, Argentina

Magda Lizet Ochoa-Hernández Autonomous University of Tamaulipas, Tampico, Mexico

M. Elena Ordóñez Y Revuelta Universidad Empresarial Siglo 21, Cordoba, Argentina

Manuela Ortega-Gil University of Cadiz, Algeciras, Spain

Romina Paiaro National University of Cordoba, Cordoba, Argentina

Anne Pasquereau Santé Publique France, Saint-Maurice, France

Francisco Peco-Torres University of Granada, Granada, Spain

Bryan F. Peñaranda-Casablanca Latin American Social Interaction Observer "LASIO", La Paz, Bolivia

Teresa Pintado-Blanco Complutense University of Madrid, Madrid, Spain

Susete Pires Ascendi, Porto, Portugal

Ana Isabel Polo-Peña University of Granada, Granada, Spain

João F. Proença University of Porto, Porto, Portugal
University of Lisbon, Lisbon, Portugal

Guillemette Quatremére Santé Publique France, Saint-Maurice, France

Marta Rey-García University of A Coruña, A Coruña, Spain

Reynaldo G. Rivera Austral University, Buenos Aires, Argentina

Daniela Nicole Rodríguez-Mincey Austral University, Buenos Aires, Argentina

Belén Ruiz University of Castilla La Mancha, Talavera de la Reina, Spain

Joaquin Sánchez-Herrera Complutense University of Madrid, Madrid, Spain

Susana Silva Universidade Católica Portuguesa, Porto, Portugal

Olivier Smadja Santé Publique France, Saint-Maurice, France

Bruno Sousa Polytechnic Institute of Cavado and Ave–IPCA, Braga, Portugal

Juan Luis Tato-Jiménez University of Extremadura, Badajoz, Spain

José Luis Vázquez-Burguete University of León, Leon, Spain

Stefanía Yapor Catholic University of Uruguay, Montevideo, Uruguay

Part I
Health: Disease Prevention and Risk Behavior

Chapter 1
Theoretical Background: Social Marketing and Quality of Life

Helena Alves, M. Mercedes Galan-Ladero, and Reynaldo G. Rivera

Abstract Nowadays, social marketing is a key tool for accepting, promoting, encouraging, changing, modifying, discouraging, rejecting, or abandoning ideas, values, attitudes, conducts, or behaviors.

Although it was initially used by public and non-profit organizations, currently businesses are also implementing social marketing. Since it can affect people's quality of life (QOL), it is applied in different areas, such as public health and welfare, education, governance, or environment issues.

Simultaneously, the quality of life approach would provide new insights to marketing strategies and better understanding of the audiences, as well as improving organizations' strategies, programs' effectiveness and results (financial, social and environmental).

In this theoretical chapter, some definitions and core concepts about social marketing approaches and strategies from quality of life perspective are considered. The main steps of a social marketing program are also explained. Ethical and cultural issues that influence social marketing are also referred to.

Keywords Social marketing (SM) · Quality of life (QOL) · Ideas · Attitudes · Behaviors · Social interventions

---

H. Alves
University of Beira Interior, Covilhã, Portugal
e-mail: halves@ubi.pt

M. M. Galan-Ladero (✉)
University of Extremadura, Badajoz, Spain
e-mail: mgalan@unex.es

R. G. Rivera
Austral University, Buenos Aires, Argentina
e-mail: rrivera@austral.edu.ar

M. M. Galan-Ladero, R. G. Rivera (eds.), *Applied Social Marketing and Quality of Life*, Applying Quality of Life Research,
https://doi.org/10.1007/978-3-030-83286-5_1

Introduction

The twenty-first century society is volatile, uncertain, complex and ambiguous (Mack et al. 2015). Endogenous and exogenous factors change, sometimes at a fast pace, the objective and subjective conditions of people's lives. Crisis like COVID-19 pandemic and technological shifts like the massive introduction of artificial intelligence are dramatically changing people's quality of life. Therefore, public and private organizations search and design programs that would improve it through positive changes and processes.

Social marketing has been used to respond to social problems in different areas like health, environment, citizen participation, education, employment, among many others. These areas constitute people's quality of life (QOL) dimensions and therefore it is clear the impact that social marketing campaigns have on people's quality of life.

In the following sections, we introduce the main theoretical concepts that will help to understand how marketing, looking for the solution of social problems and needs, would be oriented by a quality-of-life (QOL) paradigm.

Social Marketing

In a globalized world, *social marketing*, also called *marketing of social causes,* or *marketing of ideas*, has become essential to solve problems related to public health, global warming, education, social issues, traffic safety, etc. Thus, social marketing has become a key tool for all types of organizations (public and nonprofit organizations, but also businesses[1])—Galan-Ladero and Alves (2019).

Definitions and Core Concepts: Some Areas for Its Application

The first academic definition of *social marketing* was published in 1971 by Kotler and Zaltman, who considered it as "*the design, implementation and control of programs calculated to influence the acceptance of social ideas and implies considerations of product planning, price, communication, distribution and marketing research*" (Kotler and Zaltman 1971: 5). This definition "*was very innovative at that time, because it meant transferring the marketing mix scheme (the 4 Ps) to a new type of products*": ideas (Alves and Galan-Ladero 2019: 3). Later, social marketing was also defined as "*the use of marketing techniques and principles to influence a*

---

[1]In this latter case, authors such as Kotler and Lee (2005) prefer to call it "Corporate Social Marketing". e.g. when a company encourages physical exercise, healthy eating, or recycling.

Table 1.1 Other definitions about social marketing

Authors	Definitions
Moliner Tena (1998: 27)	Social marketing is an extension of marketing that studies the relation of exchange that arises when the product is an idea or social cause
Weinreich (2006)	Social marketing is the use of marketing techniques to promote the adoption of healthy or pro-social behaviors
Santesmases (2007: 1036)	Social marketing is a part or aspect of marketing . . . whose purpose is to stimulate and facilitate the acceptance of ideas or social behaviors that are considered beneficial to society, or to stop or discourage those other ideas that are considered harmful
French and Russell-Bennett (2015: 142)	Social marketing is a multidisciplinary branch of marketing. Social marketing is concerned with the social marketplace and making a significant contribution to solving social challenges. Social marketing seeks to make this contribution through the application of marketing principles, methods and systems to influence not only the behavior of citizens but also the behavior of social service providers, policymakers, politicians, and other stakeholders associated with particular social issues including the for-profit sector, the not-for-profit sector, and the media sector. Social marketing is defined by its central focus on social value creation using exchange, relationship building, and the provision of social offerings to influence behavior that will result in positive social change
Newton-Ward (2016: 1)	It is a systematic way to understand the determinants of health and social problems, and to address these causes with an array of interventions—in a way that makes change "fun, easy, and popular"
Basil (2019: 23)	Social marketing is the application of commercial marketing and other principles to influence behavior for the good of the individual and society

Source: own elaboration, from the cited authors

specific public that voluntarily accepts, rejects, modifies or abandons behavior for the benefit of individuals, groups or society as a whole" (Kotler and Lee 2005: 115). Finally, the Boards of the International Social Marketing Association, European Social Marketing Association, and Australian Association of Social Marketing also defined it (Morgan 2017), and established that "*Social Marketing seeks to develop and integrate marketing concepts with other approaches to influence behaviors that benefit individuals and communities for the greater social good. Social Marketing practice is guided by ethical principles. It seeks to integrate research, best practice, theory, audience and partnership insight, to inform the delivery of competition sensitive and segmented social change programs that are effective, efficient, equitable and sustainable*". Other definitions are included on Table 1.1.

However, *social marketing* is frequently confused with other communication strategies and socially responsible initiatives, such as *cause promotion, cause-related marketing*, *corporate social responsibility*, *health marketing, nonprofit marketing, social advertising, social communication, social media marketing, social propaganda, socially responsible marketing, or societal marketing* (Table 1.2).

Thus, differently to other communication strategies and socially responsible initiatives, social marketing focuses on accepting, influencing, modifying, changing, discouraging, or abandoning ideas, beliefs, attitudes, values, practices, and behaviors (Andreasen 1994), to "*benefit the individual, their community, or the environment, achieving an individual and societal well-being*" (Basil 2019: 4). Targeted publics' needs and quality of life are top priorities in social marketing.

To sum up, social marketing tries to "encourage a certain social behavior, foster a specific value, promote a specific attitude, facilitate a behavior or try to accept a certain idea, all of which are considered beneficial for society, or for a part of it. Or, on the contrary, it can also try to discourage or stop that behavior, attitude or idea that is not socially desirable, because it is considered harmful (Galan-Ladero and Galera-Casquet 2019). Some areas where social marketing has been applied are summarized in Table 1.3.

How the Quality-of-Life Paradigm Can Guide Social Marketing

Quality of life (QOL) surpluses economic well-being: it is "*the perception each individual has of his/her position in life, within the cultural context and system of values in which he/she lives, in relation to his/her expectations, interests and achievements*" (Tonon 2020: 2). From that approach, marketing is an organizational function that produces, prices, promotes, and distributes value that maximizes target audiences' quality of life. This goal requires consumers' well-being improvement, reduction of negative side effects or non-maleficence towards potential stakeholders and long-term social and environmental profitability (Alves and Vazquez 2013; Sirgy 1996).

Sometimes, QOL is confused with other terms that, although related, are not synonymous: living conditions, health conditions, welfare, well-being, happiness, sustainability, or human flourishing (see Table 1.4).

QOL is conditioned by the social structure (socio-demographic features), cultural traits, psycho-social characteristics of the community, and its private and public institutions operating within that context (Tonon 2020: 1). On the other hand, QOL is influenced by two types of forces (Tonon 2020: 1–2):

- Endogenous: it includes an individual's mental, emotional, spiritual, and psychological responses to his/her living conditions and socio-cultural context.
- Exogenous: it refers to the social structure, relational and cultural influences of the communities where the individuals live.

Table 1.2 Other concepts related, but different, to social marketing

Concepts	Definitions
Cause promotion	"It is a CSR initiative whose objective is to build awareness and concern for social causes. The core element of the effort is promotional in nature. Persuasive communications are usually used" (Kotler and Lee 2005: 80)
Cause-related marketing	"It is a CSR initiative that consists of an agreement between a company and an NGO to collaborate in a social cause and obtain a mutual benefit. The company's commitment is focused on contributing (financially or in kind) to the cause based on the sales or transactions made (the donation will depend, therefore, consumer behavior). Normally, the campaign is carried out for a specific product, for a specific period and with a particular NGO" (Galan-Ladero 2011: 97; Kotler and Lee 2005: 23; Santesmases 1999: 1004)
Corporate social responsibility	"It is a commitment to improve community well-being through discretionary business practices and contributions of corporate resources" (Kotler and Lee 2005: 3). "It is a concept whereby companies integrate social and environmental concerns in their business operations and in their interaction with their stakeholders on a voluntary basis. CSR concerns actions by companies over and above their legal obligations towards society and the environment" (Commission of the European Communities 2001)
Health marketing	It is a multidisciplinary area of public health practice that promotes the use of marketing research to educate, motivate and inform the public on health messages (CDC 2011)
Nonprofit marketing	It is the marketing that aims to improve the exchange activities of all non-profit institutions, although with more restrictive criteria this name is reserved for private NPOs or NGOs (Santesmases 1999: 899–902)
Social advertising	"It consists of applying the techniques and methods of commercial advertising to social causes" (Quintanilla et al. 1988: 140)
Social communication	"It is the use of language in social contexts. It encompasses social interaction, social cognition, pragmatics, and language processing" (ASHA 2020)
Social media marketing ("social marketing")	"Marketing via online tools and platforms that people use to share information with each other, such as blogs, social networking sites, wikis, podcasts, and shared media sites" (Weinreich 2006)
Social propaganda	It deals only with strengthening of beliefs and is entirely didactic in nature (O'Shaughnessy 1996)
Socially responsible marketing	It is a marketing philosophy where the company should take into consideration the best interest of society in the long term
Societal marketing	It is a marketing concept that holds that a company should make marketing decisions not only by considering consumers' wants, the company's requirements, but also consumers' and society's long-term interests (Kotler et al. 2000: 921)

Source: own elaboration, from cited authors

Table 1.3 Some areas where social marketing has been applied

Areas	Examples
Health and Welfare	To avoid health problems (obesity, diabetes, cholesterol, high blood pressure, heart attack, ictus, etc.): – Promotion of healthy food consumption – Promotion of fat, sugar, and/or sodium reduction – Promotion of physical activity and healthy habits – Promotion mandatory social distance and isolation in the pandemics To reduce child mortality: – Prenatal care – Breastfeeding promotion – Implementation of hygienic measures – Vaccination promotion – Improvement of potable water access To reduce maternal mortality (during the pregnancy or the birth): – Prenatal care – Avoidance of child marriage To prevent diseases (such as cancer, HIV infection, measles, etc.), or detect it on an early stage: – Promotion of periodic revisions and tests – Vaccination – Social distance and isolation To save lives: – Encouragement of blood donation – Promotion of organ donation – Awareness about antibiotics use, to avoid becoming ineffective – Reduction of smoking, drinking, or drug use
Governance	Citizenship: – To promote civic participation – To enforce democratic attitudes and behaviors – To improve safety and reduce street violence – To implement mobility restrictions (e.g. lockdowns in pandemics) Cities: – To promote green and sustainable urban planning – To foster smart cities models Social Responsibility: – To encourage social entrepreneurship – To implement social responsibility in public administrations
Education	Vial education (road safety): – To use the seat belt – To respect speed limits – To promote sustainable social behaviors – Not to drink or use drugs when driving – To rest from time to time – Not to use mobile phones when driving – To use a child protection chair – To improve cyclist security – To enhance pedestrian security Desirable social values: – Full inclusion of diverse and migrant people – Full inclusion of people with disabilities (encouragement of social and labor integration; awareness of the need of correct accessibility to buildings and other

(continued)

Table 1.3 (continued)

Areas	Examples
	spaces; etc.) – Gender equality (to avoid gender violence, gender discrimination in the work, opportunities in the labor market, . . .) Traditions and cultural practices: – To avoid child marriage – To stop female genital mutilation – To stop persecution against religions Consumer protection and rights: – Information about consumer rights and awareness of consumer protection – Tax payment (VAT) Tax payment: – To avoid tax evasion Preservation of the natural environment: – Recycling and reuse – Avoidance of animal mistreatment and pet abandonment – Responsible use of water and other natural resources – Reducing consumerism that impacts on economic wealth (e.g. consumption of electricity)
Environment	To protect and preserve the environment: – To protect forests – To stop desertification – To diminish consumption of natural resources – To increase recycling and reuse – To fight against climate change To reduce pollution: – To reduce waste – To reduce plastic use – To improve air, water and soil quality – To encourage the use of clean, renewable and/or sustainable energy

Source: Adapted from Alves and Galan-Ladero (2019)

Therefore, social marketing is a framework for the planning and implementation of social change, which seeks to achieve a greater degree of well-being in people and in their quality of life. Thus, it can occur in four levels (Quintanilla et al. 1988: 142):

- A cognitive change (beliefs): understanding of something concrete, by the target audience.
- A change of action: specific actions to be carried out by the target audience.
- A behavior change: creating a new pattern of behavior in the target audience.
- A change in values: trying to alter some type of belief or value deeply ingrained in the target audience.

As an approach to social change and innovation, social marketing strategies are not ruled by market demand and economic value (Sirgy et al. 1985). Contrary to other types of marketing, ideas or causes could be controversial, painful for the public, but beneficial to their quality of life in the long term. From this point of view, marketing helps people to discover new ways of doing and flourishing. It requires a

Table 1.4 Other terms related to QOL

Term	Definition
Happiness	State of pleasant spiritual and physical satisfaction (RAE 2020). It is a component of QOL (Guardiola 2020: 194)
Health conditions	Health is "a state of complete physical, mental, and social well-being and not merely the absence of disease or infirmity" (WHO 1948) Thus, health conditions means "the status of a resident's physical, mental, and psychosocial well-being" (Law Insider 2020). Health conditions affect people's ability to function or enjoy life
Human flourishing	A critical and broad concept which includes many dimensions of physical, mental, social, relational, and spiritual well-being. It indicates growth, resilience, happiness, development and, mainly, thriving in human life (Archer 2017). In fact, "... the higher purpose of marketing is welfare in terms of well-being and prosperity, or human flourishing" (Varey 2013)
Living conditions	"The circumstances affecting the way in which people live, especially with regard to their well-being" (Oxford Dictionary on Lexico 2020)
Sustainability	"Quality that can be maintained for a long time (e.g. without depleting resources or causing serious damage to the environment)"—RAE (2020). It is a component of QOL (Guardiola 2020: 194)
Welfare	"The health, happiness, and fortunes of a person or group" (Oxford Dictionary on Lexico 2020)
Well-being	"The state of being comfortable, healthy, or happy" (Oxford Dictionary on Lexico 2020) It is a subject area in philosophy. It is the investigation of what determines how good or bad a life is for the one living it (Weijers 2020: 15). It is usually considered synonymous with welfare, prudential value, and the prudential good life (Weijers 2020: 16)

Source: Own elaboration, from the cited authors

marketer interested in transcendent motives, able to manage a proposal that has a price that does not match the demand, and a communication which is not propaganda but dialogue and cooperation towards shared goals.

QOL theory offers, to social marketing, a guide for designing and implementing strategies that do not search to maximize return on investments, but "*. . . an end state which is to be defined in terms of people's needs, preferences, satisfactions, and well-being. The objective is then to maximize individuals' well-being*" (Sirgy et al. 1985: 221). From that perspective, social marketing is not about exchanges that produce short-term satisfactory emotional states, but moral goods or values (directly related to publics' needs, affects and culture) that facilitate human flourishing in the long-term.

An organization applying QOL social marketing should design and deliver ideas that increase physical, psychological and spiritual growth; establishing a price that is both affordable for the target and sustainable for society and environment; distributing the value in an inclusive way through promotional decisions that are simultaneously respectful and positive for targets and stakeholders identities.[2]

[2]For a complete analysis, see Alves and Vazquez (2013), and Lee and Sirgy (2004).

Social marketing guided by QOL principles generates trust, commitment, satisfaction and long-term relationships with publics (Alves and Vazquez 2013; Lee and Sirgy 2004). Those consequences require a clear ethical orientation in the organization implementing the strategy. Its purpose should be guided by an allocentric orientation rather than an egocentric one. While the latter is focused on the organization's economic value, the former recognizes the value of the entire organizational network and socio-cultural system (Sull and Ruelas-Gossi 2010).

In consequence, QOL marketing performance and effectiveness cannot be measured exclusively from the marketer's point of view and interests, but should analyze the strategies impact on subjective and objective life dimensions like: overall happiness with life, health, work, family satisfaction, housing, transportation, education, employment, personal security, spiritual or religious beliefs, participation in cultural activities, environment, values, social support, economic and political stability and welfare (Alves and Vazquez 2013:10; Tonon 2016).

QOL social marketing perspective requires a different kind of research and planning processes, which are not focused on "the market" needs and desires, but on the beneficiaries' culture, goals, social and personal purpose in life and the means to achieve them.

Rather than focusing on resources and economic goals, QOL social marketing is based on a stakeholders-based view, which requires a shift in terms of strategies design but also results and impact evaluation. A quality-of-life philosophy requires that social marketing strategies should:

- Define the problem in terms of quality-of-life and long-term life satisfaction.
- Conduct situation analysis considering publics' physical, social and psychological characteristics (which include dimensions like culture, affects, spirituality, traditions, etc.).
- Consider the influence of relational, transcendent and moral dimensions on human and social behavior.
- Select target, objectives and goals accordingly with actual and potential quality of life levels.
- Understand the diversity of targets' experiences, needs and expectations.
- Identify means influencing positive personal and social development that do not clash with other non-marketing quality of life means (e.g. healthy behaviors, altruistic attitudes, political participation, etc.).
- Develop a set of indicators to estimate the marketing program contribution to QOL. Those indicators should capture (through quantitative and qualitative methods) targets experiences with product "... acquisition, preparation, consumption, possession, maintenance, and disposal ... reflecting both individual and societal welfare" (Alves and Vazquez 2013: 11).
- Define objective, goals, positioning statement and marketing mix strategies considering the social and ecological context where they will be implemented.

Although a large part of marketing impact evaluations are based on quantitative metrics, QOL marketing requires to adopt mixed methods approaches, with a particular interest for qualitative studies. "*The importance of the use of qualitative methodology in quality of life studies is related with the importance of considering people's perceptions, opinions, feelings, ideas and interpretations. This kind of approach is essential to the understanding of people's experiences of wellbeing and to the discovery of new issues related with the quality of life field*" (Tonon 2015: 4).

Applied studies on QOL analyze the material, psycho-social and emotional conditions of the people and how they respond towards their living contextual conditions. That means that in a world where change, complexity, sustainability and connectivity are conditioning the way organizations and individuals are taking decisions, QOL philosophy provides a framework that really puts the people and their interests at the center.

The relevance of the field is clear from its impact in social progress: QOL is vital for achieving UN sustainable development goals (SDGs). In fact, in 2011 the OECD launched the Better Life Initiative[3] that, focused on the aspects that shape people's lives, contributes to understanding current distance to the SDG targets and offers a framework and methodology to improve the measurement of well-being. Accordingly with OECD (2017), individual well-being dimensions include material conditions (income and wealth, jobs and earnings, housing) and quality of life (health status, work and life balance, education and skills, social connections, civic engagement and governance, environmental quality, personal security and subjective well-being).

Consequently, QOL definition combines and integrates two dimensions (Martinez 2020: 210):

- Objective: QOL is usually measured by using indicators that represent observable and measurable conditions (e.g. durable housing, adequate water provision, availability of green areas, and accessibility to schools).
- Subjective: QOL sometimes requires some sort of subjective judgement (e.g. different standards may exist to consider a dwelling inadequate).

Thus, QOL incorporates two main approaches (Tonon 2020: 1):

- Quantitative—objective approach: what people have and can be observed directly.
- Qualitative—subjective approach: what people feel and can be observed indirectly.

From that perspective, QOL philosophy allows social marketers to guide their decision-making processes not only by transactional and relational approaches, but also by a holistic and ethical perspective, which includes a wide spectrum of objective and subjective personal and socio-cultural dimensions. Therefore, an effective QOL social marketing strategy should increase specific targets' well-being and create social value for a wide set of potential stakeholders, including the

[3]OECD Better Life Initiative website: http://www.oecd.org/statistics/better-life-initiative.htm

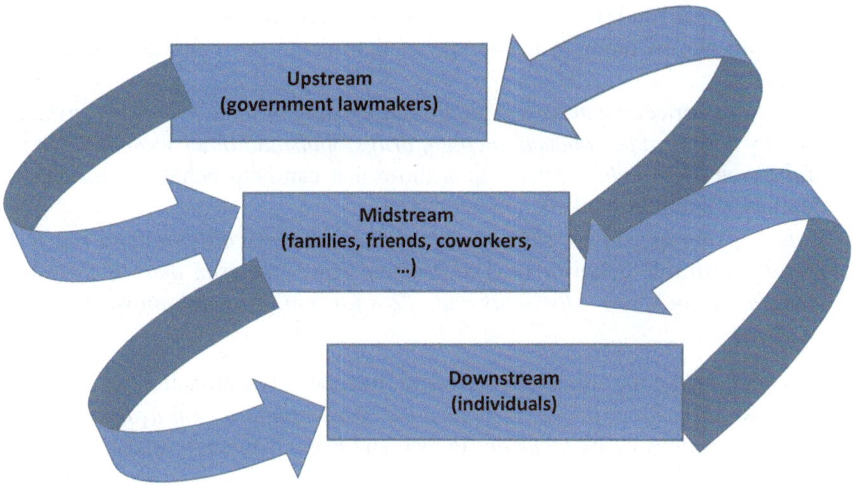

Fig. 1.1 Three streams in social marketing. Source: Own elaboration

environment. In this way, QOL social marketing represents a powerful tool for human development and flourish societies.

Social Marketing Streams

Donovan and Henley (2010) propose that "*the goal of social marketing is not just to encourage individual voluntary behavior and modify the environments that facilitate such changes, but also trying to influence and transform the social structures that will facilitate individual changes*". This will mean "*targeting the individuals that have the power to change policies and legislation*" (Alves and Galan-Ladero 2019: 3). To achieve that, a combination of three approaches is advisable (Donovan and Henley 2010; Basil et al. 2019)—(Fig. 1.1):

- *Downstream approaches*: addressing the problem by facilitating access to solutions, influencing the behavior of individuals directly. That is, efforts are focused on those individuals whose behavior is wanted to be directly influenced (Basil et al. 2019: 3).

  E.g. smoking, drinking, over eating, sedentary lifestyle, water and energy consumption, etc. Informational and educational programs for these target individuals might be useful.
- *Upstream approaches*: identifying and acting upon the main causes of the problem, by "*influencing social and environmental policies, structures, and decision makers that can help to alleviate the problem*" (Basil et al. 2019: 12). That is, efforts are focused on those who can influence the system within which the behavior occurs (e.g. decision makers, politicians, [local, regional, national,

or international] authorities, and others whose decisions could influence the social environment), in order to encourage or discourage the behavior (Basil et al. 2019: 3).

E.g. to restrict or ban the sale and/or advertising of some products considered socially undesirable (tobacco, alcohol, drugs; guns and other weapons; etc.).

- *Midstream approaches*: acting upon those that can help behavior change, like families, friends, coworkers, among others.

  E.g. giving incentives, subsidies, grants, etc. if they collaborate to reach the socially desirable behavior (e.g. to promote family tourism, there is the family tourism seal in Spain—discounts and offers for families going on vacation with children).

A social marketing intervention could include a combination of all these approaches. *Thus, for example, to reduce the consumption of soft drinks with high sugar levels, actions could focus on (*French and Russell-Bennett 2015*):*

- *Manufacturers (to make healthier products).*
- *Politicians (to regulate the sugar level of these products, by law; or its advertising; or the places of sale—e.g. to ban the sale of soft drinks in vending machines in schools; or to increase taxes for these products).*
- *Families (to reduce the consumption of these soft drinks at home, replacing them with healthier products).*
- *Individuals/Consumers (to be aware of the health risks that its consumption implies).*

In order for social marketing to become effective, four dimensions must be present (Hastings and Domegan 2014):

- *"Customer" (citizen) orientation*: identification of people's needs, aspirations, values, and priorities. To be effective, "*marketers first must understand the elements that determine people's current behaviors*" (Basil et al. 2019: 9): the demographic, economic, social, environmental, technological, legal, cultural, historical, and political forces that influence individuals' behavior. But also the barriers to behavior change (to identify, reduce, or eliminate them).
- *Creative orientation*: finding imaginative ways to engage people (target audience).
- *Collective orientation*: recognizing that social and cultural context matters.
- *Competitive orientation*: critically addressing the competition while reducing the efforts (price) that target has to afford.

Scholars and practitioners "*have been supporting these orientations, in their practice and research, with the useful insights of several theories and models of behavior change*" (Donovan and Henley 2010; Hastings and Domegan 2014; Basil et al. 2019), namely, the Health Belief Model, Stages of Change or the Transtheoretical Model, Community Readiness Model, Extended Parallel Process Model, Hierarchy of Effects and AIDA Model; the Protection Motivation Theory, the Social Learning Theory, the Theory of Reasoned Action, the Theory of Planned

Behavior, the Theory of Trying, the Theory of Interpersonal Behavior, the Exchange Theory, the Social Cognitive Theory, and the Social Capital Theory, Product Differentiation Theory, Consumer choice Theory, Diffusion of Innovation Theory, Involvement Theory, Co-creation Theory, Self-efficacy Theory, Social Norms Theory, Utility Theory, among many others. All these models and theories contribute to understanding the influences on behavior and hence provide a framework to develop the strategy and campaigns to fight social problems (Alves and Galan-Ladero 2019: 3–4). They arise from a variety of fields including marketing, psychology, and sociology (Basil et al. 2019: 72).

Social Marketing Approaches and Strategies

Social marketing is characterized by the coordination of different complementary approaches, to achieve the realization or modification of ideas, attitudes, or behaviors (Santesmases 1999; Rivera et al. 2016; Alves and Galan-Ladero 2019: 5): *a legal approach* (based on regulations, sanctions, rules, laws, etc.), *a technological approach* (using innovations to facilitate the desired behavior), *an economic approach* (reducing the cost of carrying out the desired behavior, or increasing the price to discourage unwanted behavior), *an informational approach* (focused, above all, on persuasive information), and a *relational approach* (based on interpersonal interactions and the impact of social behaviors and experiences).

*E.g. to reduce the tobacco consumption, many governments have banned smoking in public places, the sale of cigarettes to minors, or any kind or tobacco advertising (**legal approach**), promote non-smoking lifestyle among teens who can influence their peers (**relational approach**), medicines have been created (e.g. nicotine gum, nicotine patches, pills, . . .; which are, in some cases, subsidized, and included in the National Health System)—**technological approach**, and many persuasive information has been offered, also in the cigarette packs (warning labels, fear-appeal messages, cancer images, . . .)—**informational approach**. And the price has also increased (**economic approach**).*

*E.g. To reduce plastic pollution, some governments have banned single-use plastic bags and others have mandated, by law, that each bag be charged (**legal approach**); new recyclable and/or reusable plastic bags have also been created, as well as new materials (e.g. potato starch) that are less harmful to the environment, in addition to the traditional ones made of paper or cloth (**technological approach**); information on the damage that plastic bags cause to nature (**informative approach**); it is segmented according to the reference groups (**relational approach**); and the cost of the plastic bags (they are no longer free, to discourage their use) - **economic approach**.*

*E.g. To avoid the spread of COVID-19, the governments of many countries decreed a state of alarm and the lockdown of the population, restricting the mobility, and also making the use of masks and social distance mandatory (**legal approach**);*

hydroalcoholic soaps, gels and sprays, PCR tests, new drugs, vaccines, as well as mobile applications to track population demographic movements and, using big data, artificial intelligence and geolocation, defining the spread patterns of the virus and evaluating the effects of the lockdown measures imposed (to review and, consequently, relax or tighten quarantine orders), would represent the ***technological approach****; official and expert information on prevention measures and the correct use of masks, as well as the benefits of wearing them (****informative approach****); responsibility towards one's family, friends, coworkers, and/or fellow students (****relational approach****); and the regulation of the price of gloves, hydro-alcoholic products, and masks (with fixed prices to avoid speculation and facilitate access to them by everyone; and even being free, in some cases, for vulnerable people and/or without resources)—****economic approach****—was promoted.*

Consequently, different strategies can be applied in social marketing, depending on the purpose sought (Santesmases 1999; Alves and Galan-Ladero 2019: 6–7; Penelas-Leguía et al. 2012):

- To reinforce ideas, attitudes and/or behaviors: *a reinforcement strategy* (e.g. using awards, rewards, social recognition, economic incentives, legal norms, training programs, educational activities, information reports, etc.).

  E.g. public recognition and awards for people with the highest number of blood and bone marrow donations.
- To induce the accomplishment of a desirable behavior: *an induction strategy* (e.g. establishing social controls, facilitating material and human means to carry out desired behavior, providing economic incentives, legal regulations, etc.).

  E.g. some UK councils give free special bags to citizens for organic garbage.
- To generate a change in attitude (when it is negative toward a desirable social behavior, although it is practiced): *a rationalization strategy* (e.g. giving more information, trying to persuade with controls, advertising, etc.).

  E.g. in some countries where some vaccines are compulsory (parents should vaccinate their children to maintain high rate of population's immunization), experts can make parents aware of the benefits that their children will have if they are protected against some diseases, such as measles (and not only to lose public economic support—e.g. Australia -, or avoid fines—e.g. Italy).
- To generate a change in attitude and behavior: *a confrontation strategy* (e.g. applying economic sanctions, using coercive actions, or persuasive information).

  E.g. persuasive and/or fear-appeal information, fines, and even jail sentences, for drivers that do not respect traffic laws and rules (e.g. exceeding speed limits, parking in double row, or in prohibited areas, drunk driving, not wearing seatbelt, etc.).

  E.g. in some countries, garbage is not collected if it is not correctly classified for recycling, and even can be given fines if it is not removed from the street in a determined period of time (e.g. Germany).

Marketing Mix Strategies (The 4 Ps)

Similar to profit marketing, social marketing also applies the marketing mix strategies (the Four Ps)[4]:

First P: Product
The core product is intangible: an idea, cause, attitude, or behavior. But it can also involve supporting products (e.g. a tangible support—goods—, or even another intangible support—services).

E.g. to adopt healthy habits (core product), healthy food (for example, fruit) is given to the children, so they can have breakfast at school; and, as physical exercise is recommended, councils can offer garden areas for walking, bikes for rent, and sports facilities.

The product should be clearly defined (Basil et al. 2019: 23). Marketing research is essential for this, and to understand what benefits the target audience values most (Grier and Bryant 2005), and adopt a holistic orientation (including a stakeholder orientation in general, and a "customer" orientation in particular).

Second P: Price
Price can be monetary (the costs for the promised benefits—although many times they are offered for free or subsidized), and/or non-monetary (e.g. waste of time, effort, sacrifice, embarrassment, diminished pleasure, psychological hassle or psychic discomfort, etc.) in social marketing, for achieving the wanted behavior, or changing or abandoning the behavior. That is, there can be monetary and non-monetary incentives and disincentives.

It is important to identify all of the costs that the target audience perceives regarding the behavior (Basil et al. 2019: 32). In any case, the required considerations must be reduced to the maximum, so that the desired attitude or behavior is carried out (Alves and Galan-Ladero 2019: 8)—reducing barriers (that is, try to minimize price—Basil et al. 2019: 23). On the other hand, using barriers could be necessary to discourage unwanted attitude or behavior to be carried out. That is, "*that the rewards of a behavior are always higher than the cost or effort to be made*" (Quintanilla et al. 1988: 146).

E.g. In countries such as Spain, no money is paid to donors of blood, marrow or organs. On the contrary, donors, in exchange for showing solidarity and gratitude for their donation, "pay" a non-monetary price, such as the discomfort caused by the puncture or the extraction process, as well as a certain subsequent discomfort, and even the risk of suffering a complication or contracting an

[4]The Four Ps (Product, Price, Place, Promotion), proposed by McCarthy in 1960, is the most common model used to analyze the marketing strategy, also in social marketing. Authors, like Kotler and Lauterborn, have proposed similar models but including other components (like people, processes, programs and performance; customers, convenience, cost, communication). For a review, see e.g. Constantinides (2006).

infection when donating. However, sometimes they receive a consideration: a soft drink and/or snack (or sandwich) after donating blood, a small gift (a keychain, a pen), or even a plaque or medal to recognize the work and commitment of the big donors.

A common feature in social marketing is that there is rarely an immediate, explicit payback to target audiences in return for their adoption of the desired behavior (Grier and Bryant 2005).

Third P: Place

Place focuses on providing appropriate distribution and response channels to transform motivations into actions (e.g., physical location where achieving the desired behavior—Alves and Galan-Ladero 2019: to consider its location, accessibility, comfort, operating days and hours, decoration, cleaning, among others).

As social marketers must make the behavior change as easy as possible for the target audience (Basil et al. 2019: 33), sometimes social marketing can involve efforts to increase the availability of items that encourage to achieve the desired behavior and benefit social welfare.

E.g. To recycle, it is necessary that there are differentiated containers and collection points close to homes, to facilitate this action. It is also important that these collection points are safe and do not give off bad odors.

Channels can be direct or indirect (if intermediaries are needed to facilitate the behavior change)—Alves and Galan-Ladero (2019: 8). In the latter case, the channels can be short (with one intermediary) or long (with several intermediaries).

E.g. Sometimes the Administration subcontracts or gives certain services to an NGO to reach the target audience. Thus, to prevent the homeless from sleeping on the street or spending the coldest winter nights in the open, or for the treatment and rehabilitation of drug addicts, organizations such as Caritas or the Red Cross take care of them.

Fourth P: Promotion

Promotion is the most visible part of the marketing mix (Alves and Galan-Ladero 2019: 8). Communication with the audience is essential in order to encourage them to adopt the desired behavior, or to persuade them to change or abandon it.

Social advertising (similar to commercial advertising) is emphasized, above all (Alves and Galan-Ladero 2019: 8). But the other elements of the communication mix should be also considered (such as public relations, promotional activities, personal [face-to-face] attendance, and direct marketing, among others). Internet, social networks, and mobile phones Apps, can help to achieve larger audiences, sharing quickly the social marketing campaigns (Alves and Galan-Ladero 2019: 8). Thus, selecting communication channels is a key decision for the success of a social marketing campaign.

Messages used to encourage or discourage behaviors can be informative and persuasive, but they can also include fear, humor, irony, imperative, or emotional appeals (Alves and Galan-Ladero 2019: 8), or even storytellings and testimonials. Messages should focus on communicating the benefits of the desirable behavior and how overcoming the barriers (Basil et al. 2019: 33). The language (formal or informal) and the information process route (peripheral or central) used are also essential to reach the target audience.

Therefore, depending on the target audience, it will be necessary to decide the type of language to use (formal or informal), the message (direct or indirect, and what aspects to highlight: the benefits of the behavior sought, the effects of that behavior, the consequences to carry it out/not to carry it out, the problems caused by carrying it/not carrying it out, . . .), the means of communication to be used (television, radio, press—print and online newspapers and magazines, social media, brochures, posters, etc.), as well as who transmits it (people: one or more celebrities, influencers, one or more unknown people, nobody; animals or things. Cartoons can also be another option).

E.g. Some examples of messages related to:

- *Flu: "Flu is here!"*
- *Blood/Organ donation: "Be a donor, be a hero"*
- *Traffic safety: "Hurt your helmet not your head"*
- *Smoking: "How many cigarettes a day does your child smoke?", "Don't kill yourself and us too", "Smoking kills"*
- *Healthy habits: "5 A Day"*
- *HIV/AIDS: "You can get HIV!"*
- *Animals: "Animal abuse is unacceptable"*
- *Consumer rights: "Use your consumer rights"*
- *Water: "Save water, save life", "Every drop counts!", "Water is priceless"*
- *COVID-19 Pandemic: "Stay home. Save lives", "Stay home. Stay safe"*

Besides the four Ps presented in previous paragraphs, some leading scholars and practitioners have proposed other variables for the marketing mix. Although there is not a consensus on this matter, a quality-of-life perspective offers social marketing the theoretical basis for incorporating a "fifth P" to the marketing mix: purpose. "The central concept of the quality-of-life theory for social marketing is optimization of a goal hierarchy" (Sirgy et al. 1985: 222). The beneficiaries of social marketing strategies have superordinate goals or ultimate concerns that maximize long-term life satisfaction (psychical, spiritual, and physical). Incorporating "purpose" in the marketing mix implies recognizing that the product should be designed for helping people to solve a problem, becoming meaningful for the strategy's beneficiaries and stakeholders, as well as for the organization itself. Social marketers should identify, through scientific research and impact evaluation, the means-ends chain to attain those goals. From that perspective, a quality-of-life perspective helps to establish a clear connection between organizational mission and vision and its marketing strategy.

Table 1.5 Steps in the planning process for a successful social marketing program

Steps	Actions
1	**Define the problem, the purpose** (behavior to change), **and the focus** (who the target public is) Marketing research is key in this step
2	**Conduct a situation analysis and summarize it in a tool like SWOT analysis**: Strengths, Weaknesses, Opportunities, & Threats
3	**Select target audiences** (e.g. according to demographic & socioeconomic, psychographic or behavioral criteria) Aspects to consider when selecting a target: who has the greatest need for change, who will be receptive to change, who is reachable, who is affordable, if the group size is sufficient/appropriate, if it fits with the organization, if it will be cost effective to reach **Segmentation** is key, because people have different needs, values, interests, and motivations
4	**Set marketing objectives and goals** (specifying desired behaviors and changes in knowledge, attitudes, and/or beliefs—e.g. reinforcing, inducing, rationalizing, or confronting them) **Objectives** should be clear, realistic, and measurable **Goals** should be specific, measurable, achievable, relevant, and time sensitive
5	**Identify factors influencing behavior adoption** (e.g. the barriers that prevent the audience of adopting the new behavior; the benefits they may realize when adopting the new behavior; the influencers of the desired behavior, who can help the persistence of the current behavior or help to change it; etc.) Barriers, benefits, influencers, facilitators, and "competitors" with your efforts (turning a competitor into a complementor or collaborator)
6	**Craft a positioning statement** (according to the target audience's feelings and primary benefits sought when performing the desired behavior) to appeal the target
7	**Develop marketing mix strategies (the 4 Ps)**: product, price, place, promotion
8	**Outline a plan for monitoring and evaluation** (identifying which processes and outcomes will be measured, what methods will be used to measure them, when the measurements will take place, and the costs involved in carrying out the measurements)
9	**Establish budgets** (total costs of the program: including implementation costs, and control and evaluation costs), **and find funding sources** (to support the costs)
10	**Complete the plan for campaign implementation and management** (conceptualizing the outline of the task division: who will perform every task, how much it will cost, and when they should be carried out, including the partners' roles)

Source: Adapted from Kotler and Lee (2008), Alves and Galan-Ladero (2019), and Basil et al. (2019)

The Social Marketing Program

To create a successful social marketing program, Kotler and Lee (2008) proposed several steps in the planning process (Table 1.5).

Marketing research is essential to effective and successful social marketing, and it should be included in all stages of the social marketing program (Basil et al. 2019: 45)—Table 1.6.

Although social and commercial marketing share many similarities, they differ especially in the way they measure effectiveness. While commercial marketing is

Table 1.6 Marketing research in social marketing

When	Research type
Before beginning the program/intervention	**Formative research (diagnostic research)**: to determine what is known, and what would like to know, about what people do, and why; and what people think about it; and what might motivate people to act differently. *e.g. secondary information and also primary information (qualitative & quantitative research).*
During the program/ intervention	**Process research**: to assess how the program is being developed and implemented, and to detect any mistakes (and solve them before the program is over). *e.g. primary research to examine levels of the current knowledge, understanding, interest, awareness, engagement, etc. that arise from ongoing social marketing efforts to achieve the desirable behavior.*
After the program/ intervention	**Evaluation research:** outcome, output, and impact evaluation. *e.g. primary research to determine what succeeded and what did not, to assess how effective the campaign was (e.g. in terms of the cost efficiency of the effort), to understand people's reactions and subsequent behavior, etc.* This research is key to know what should be repeated, changed or eliminated in future campaigns. And also to justify the need to continue with this intervention, to intensify it, or even eliminate it, before the public authorities or organizations that finance the program.

Source: Adapted from Basil et al. (2019)

focused on economic exchanges, social marketing is focused on ethical interactions: "*... social marketers face a number of unique ethical challenges that go beyond anything faced in commerce*" (Peattie and Peattie 2003: 370). The ethical orientation of communication strategies and their impact on people's quality of life are critical components in social marketing programs (Alves and Galan-Ladero 2019: 8). Therefore, as Levitt pointed out (1960: 56), ethical considerations are not a supplementary but a fundamental issue in a book about social marketing.

Ethical Considerations

The definition of social marketing, or its objectives set (which carry implicit value judgments that may, or may not, be shared by all people), raise ethical questions (Quintanilla et al. 1988: 141). Thus, for example, when it is said that "the objective of social marketing is to achieve the well-being of all the individuals that make up society", it can lead to a debate on what is the way or means by which well-being is reached, or on who has to decide which behaviors are socially desirable and which are not (Quintanilla et al. 1988: 141). That is, criticism for possible manipulation (Basil et al. 2019: 36) of public opinion and paternalism (from the government or the

Table 1.7 Ethical dilemmas in social marketing

Reasons	Explanations
Because of the behavior sought or socially desired	It could be controversial, according to a certain culture or religion, and even contrary to traditional practices strongly rooted in a specific society. Thus, the proposed behavior changes may influence and affect community traditions and also its cultural, spiritual, social, and moral values. *e.g. blood & organ donations, vaccination, family planning and promotion of contraceptives, HIV / AIDS prevention, eradication of child marriage or female genital mutilation, gender violence and honor killing, gun control, etc.*
Because of the design, development, and/or implementation of the social marketing program	The message, language, or images used in the campaign could be politically incorrect: Messages: they could create fear appeals or emotions, anxiety, alarm, or even panic, sense of guilt, etc. *e.g. Stay home!* Language: it should be politically correct. *e.g. Using terms as subnormal, fool, deficient, invalid, etc. to refer to a person with a disability would not be acceptable today.* Images: they could recreate excessively harsh real situations, disturbing some viewers. e.g. *traffic accidents, sequelae of cancer and other illnesses, gender violence, drug consumption, etc.*

Source: Adapted from Alves and Galan-Ladero (2019: 9)

organization that promotes that behavior), or intrusion into the individual freedom of people (Quintanilla et al. 1988: 148), could arise.

Ethical dilemmas can appear in social marketing (Table 1.7), especially for two reasons (Alves and Galan-Ladero 2019: 9): (1) Because of the behavior sought or desired, and (2) Because of the design, development, and/or implementation of the social marketing program.

Additionally, external pressure groups, such as business lobbies, could also interfere (Alves and Galan-Ladero 2019: 9). Thus, for example, implementation of anti-smoking campaigns were initially delayed, despite scientific evidence of the health problems caused by tobacco, due to the importance of the powerful tobacco companies. Or campaigns to reduce the consumption of carbonated beverages or junk food are also scarce or nonexistent, despite the illnesses they cause (e.g. obesity, diabetes, cholesterol, . . .).

Finally, two key aspects should be considered in social marketing strategies (Alves and Galan-Ladero 2019: 9):

- Cultural differences: a successful campaign in a country could have a very different result or impact in another country. The effectiveness of a social marketing program will depend on the correct analysis of each situation and its adaptation to the cultural values of each society.
- Not everything is valid to achieve a desired behavior ("the end does not justify the means" in social marketing).

Being ethics a key aspect in social marketing, the Quality-of-Life paradigm offers a clear path to influence behavior through informed, voluntary, and ethical means; and to help social marketers to understand their target publics and give a positive orientation to their programs. From this perspective, a quality-of-life approach would provide an ethical compass to social marketing.

References

Alves H, Galan-Ladero M (2019) Theoretical background: introduction to social marketing. In: Galan-Ladero M, Alves H (eds) Case studies on social marketing. A global perspective. Springer, Cham

Alves H, Vazquez JL (eds) (2013) Best practices in marketing and their impact on quality of life. Springer. https://www.springer.com/gp/book/9789400758773

Andreasen AR (1994) Social marketing: its definition and domain. J Public Policy Mark 13(1):108–114

Archer M (ed) (2017) Morphogenesis and human flourishing. Springer International Publishing. https://doi.org/10.1007/978-3-319-49469-2

ASHA - American Speech-Language-Hearing Association (2020) Social communication definition. https://www.asha.org/public/speech/development/social-communication/

Basil DZ, Diaz-Meneses G, Basil MD (2019) Social marketing in action. Cases from around the world. Springer, Cham

CDC – Centers for Disease Control and Prevention (2011) What is health marketing? https://www.cdc.gov/healthcommunication/toolstemplates/WhatIsHM.html. Accessed 29 Aug 2020

Commission of the European Communities (2001) Green paper: promoting a European framework for corporate social responsibility. Bruselas, 18.7.2001. COM (2001) 366 final

Constantinides E (2006) The marketing mix revisited: towards the 21st century marketing. J Mark Manag 22(3–4):407–438. https://doi.org/10.1362/026725706776861190

Donovan R, Henley N (2010) Principles and practice of social marketing: an international perspective. Cambridge University Press, Cambridge

French J, Russell-Bennett R (2015) A hierarchical model of social marketing. J Soc Mark 5(2)

Galan-Ladero M (2011) Variables que influyen en la actitud hacia el marketing con causa y determinantes de la satisfacción y la lealtad en la "compra solidaria". Doctoral thesis. University of Extremadura

Galan-Ladero M, Alves H (2019) Case studies on social marketing. A global perspective. Springer, Cham

Galan-Ladero M, Galera-Casquet C (2019) Capítulo 11: Marketing para el cambio social. In: Cerdá LM, Ramírez M (coord) Fundamentos para un nuevo marketing. Sindéresis, Madrid, pp 251–284

Grier S, Bryant CA (2005) Social marketing in public health. Annu Rev Public Health 26:319–339

Guardiola J (2020) Chapter 10. Teaching nonviolent economics as a path for achieving quality of life. In: Tonon G (ed) Teaching quality of life in different domains, Social indicators research series, vol 79. Springer, Switzerland, pp 179–196

Hastings G, Domegan C (2014) Social marketing. From tunes to symphonies. Routledge, London
Kotler P, Lee N (2005) Corporate social responsibility. Wiley, New York
Kotler P, Lee N (2008) Social marketing influencing behaviors for good, 3rd edn. Sage, Thousand Oaks, CA
Kotler P, Zaltman G (1971) Social marketing: an approach to planned social change. J Mark 35:3–12
Kotler P, Armstrong G, Saunders J, Wong V (2000) Introducción al Marketing. 2nd European edn. Prentice-Hall, Madrid
Law Insider (2020) Dictionary. https://www.lawinsider.com
Lee D-J, Sirgy MJ (2004) Quality-of-life (QOL) marketing: proposed antecedents and consequences. J Macromarket. https://doi.org/10.1177/0276146704263922
Mack O, Khare A, Krämer A, Burgartz T (2015) Managing in a VUCA world. Springer. https://doi.org/10.1007/978-3-319-16889-0
Martinez J (2020) Chapter 12. Teaching and learning quality of life in urban studies: a mixed-methods approach with walking interviews. In: Tonon G (ed) Teaching quality of life in different domains, Social indicators research series, vol 79. Springer, Switzerland, pp 209–230
Moliner Tena MA (1998) Marketing Social: La Gestion de las Causas Sociales. ESIC, Madrid
Morgan W (2017) Social marketing definition, by the Boards of the International Social Marketing Association, European Social Marketing Association, and Australian Association of Social Marketing. https://www.i-socialmarketing.org/. Accessed 21 Aug 2020
Newton-Ward CM (2016) Syllabus: social marketing in public health PUBH 731 (Spring). North Carolina University
OECD (2017) How's life? 2017: measuring well-being. OECD Publishing, Paris. https://doi.org/10.1787/how_life-2017-en
O'Shaughnessy N (1996) Social propaganda and social marketing: a critical difference? Eur J Mark 30(10/11):54–67
Oxford Dictionary on Lexico (2020) Oxford English Dictionary. https://www.lexico.com/definition/oxford_english_dictionary
Peattie S, Peattie K (2003) Ready to Fly solo? Reducing social marketing's dependence on commercial marketing theory. Market Theory 3(3):365–385. https://doi.org/10.1177/147059310333006
Penelas-Leguía A, Galera-Casquet C, Galán-Ladero M, Valero-Amaro V (2012) Marketing Solidario. El Marketing en las Organizaciones no Lucrativas. Pirámide, Madrid
Quintanilla I, Berenguer G, Díaz R (1988) Problemas y desafíos del marketing social. Esic Market 61:137–151
RAE - Real Academia Española (2020) Diccionario de la Lengua Española. https://www.rae.es/
Rivera R, Santos D, Brändle G, Cárdaba MÁM (2016) Design effectiveness analysis of a media literacy intervention to reduce violent video games consumption among adolescents: the relevance of lifestyles segmentation. Eval Rev 40(2):142–161. https://doi.org/10.1177/0193841X16666196
Santesmases M (2007) Marketing. Conceptos y Estrategias, 5th edn. Piramide, Madrid
Santesmases M (1999) Marketing. Conceptos y Estrategias, 4th edn. Piramide, Madrid
Sirgy MJ (1996) Strategic marketing planning guided by the quality-of-life (QOL) concept. J Bus Ethics 15(3):241–259. https://doi.org/10.1007/BF00382951
Sirgy MJ, Morris M, Samli AC (1985) The question of value in social marketing: use of a quality-of-life theory to achieve long-term life satisfaction. Am J Econ Sociol 44(2):215–228. https://doi.org/10.1111/j.1536-7150.1985.tb02336.x
Sull DL, Ruelas-Gossi A (2010) Strategic orchestration. Bus Strateg Rev 21(4):58–63. https://doi.org/10.1111/j.1467-8616.2010.00707.x
Tonon G (ed) (2015) Qualitative studies in quality of life: methodology and practice. Springer International Publishing. https://www.springer.com/gp/book/9783319137780
Tonon G (ed) (2016) Indicators of quality of life in Latin America. Springer International Publishing. https://www.springer.com/gp/book/9783319288406

Tonon G (ed) (2020) Teaching quality of life in different domains. Springer International Publishing. https://doi.org/10.1007/978-3-030-21551-4
Varey RJ (2013) Marketing in the flourishing society megatrend. J Macromark 33(4):354–368. https://doi.org/10.1177/0276146713489150
Weinreich NK (2006) Spare change: social marketing vs. "social marketing" Smackdown. 09.06.2006. http://www.social-marketing.com/blog/. Accessed 02/01/2008
Weijers D (2020) Chapter 2. Teaching well-being/quality of life from a philosophical perspective. In: Tonon G (ed) Teaching quality of life in different domains, Social indicators research series, vol 79. Springer, Switzerland, pp 15–42
WHO – World Health Organization (1948) Constitution. https://www.who.int/about/governance/constitution

Chapter 2
Laboratory of Hemoderivative: Commitment to the Quality of Life. Social Marketing Campaign "Donate Plasma, Donate Smiles"

Enrique Bianchi, Mariana Mendoza, Romina Paiaro, Daniela Fontana, and Natacha Beltrán

Abstract The Laboratory of Hemoderivatives (LH) is a public pharmaceutical company of the Universidad Nacional de Córdoba (Argentina), created in 1964 with the purpose of improving the quality of life of people by making medicines derived from human plasma.

Its mission, for five decades, has been based on the implementation of actions framed within the perspectives of Quality of Life marketing (QoL marketing). Its commercial policies distinguish it from other competitors: international quality products under strict compliance with Good Best Manufacturing Practices, low prices, priority supply to the public sector, exchange agreements with blood banks and hemotherapy services guaranteeing national and Latin American supply.

The social marketing campaign "**Donate Plasma, Donate Smiles**" began as a Communicational Campaign for the Voluntary Donation of Plasma with the aim of increasing the availability of plasma and contributing to raising awareness of the importance of voluntary and altruistic donation. In this context, the concept of quality of life was approached from two perspectives: (a) from access to health, starting from having high-quality blood-derived medicines produced in the country, available at much lower cost; (b) from the quality of life focused on the way of life that patients under treatment with these drugs may have.

Over time, it became a comprehensive marketing program, seeking to create and retain communities of regular volunteer donors through relationship marketing.

Keywords Hemoderivative products/blood products · Quality of life · Social marketing · Plasma donation · Social impact

E. Bianchi (✉) · M. Mendoza · R. Paiaro · D. Fontana · N. Beltrán
National University of Cordoba, Córdoba, Argentina
e-mail: enrique.carlos.bianchi@eco.unc.edu.ar; mariana.mendoza@unc.edu.ar; romina.paiaro@unc.edu.ar; daniela.fontana@unc.edu.ar; natacha.beltran@unc.edu.ar

M. M. Galan-Ladero, R. G. Rivera (eds.), *Applied Social Marketing and Quality of Life*, Applying Quality of Life Research,
https://doi.org/10.1007/978-3-030-83286-5_2

Introduction

The **Laboratory of Hemoderivatives (LH)** is an Argentine public pharmaceutical company (non-profit) specialized in the manufacture of medicines derived from human plasma. It produces essential medicines from the liquid part of the blood, composed of proteins of therapeutic interest. It is distinguished from the other existing plasma fractionation plants in the world as it is the only one that belongs to a public university, the Universidad Nacional de Córdoba (UNC), at the service of national and Latin American public health (Laboratorio Hemoderivados 2019).[1]

In the context of the Argentine health system, it is the only laboratory in the country that supplies the national market and distributes its products to neighboring countries with which it has an agreement. Thus, the UNC fulfills, through the LH, its social purpose of being not only the trainer of new generations of professionals and scientists capable of responding to the challenges of society, but also the contributor of the country's development and of the improvement of life quality of its inhabitants.

The social marketing campaign "Donate Plasma, Donate Smiles" is framed within the perspective of Quality of Life marketing (QoL marketing). It states that the role of the organization is "to develop goods, services and to market such products effectively and efficiently to minimize negative side effects for consumers and other audiences, while generating long-term profitability" (Sirgy and Lee 1996, p. 21), to improve the quality of life of people.

The QoL philosophy focuses through the commercialization, consumption or provision of goods and services on: (a) improving the welfare of consumers, (b) reducing side effects on target consumers and (c) on other audiences beyond of the consumer (d) and increasing profitability in the long term. Hence, it is a type of "societal marketing" in which the business mission is defined in terms of social systems (Kelley 1974 cited by Alves and Vázquez 2013), oriented to the consumers' wellbeing and quality of life.

Well-being and quality of life are sometimes understood as synonyms but they actually differ from each other (Tonon 2020, p. 16). Well-being is the good prudential life, in other words, the life that is good for those who live it. Quality of life is the perception that each individual has of his/her position in life, within the cultural context and the value system in which he/she lives, in relation to his/her expectations, interests and achievements (Tonon 2020, p. 2). Quality of life is currently defined as a multidimensional concept that comprises a series of domains that people consider and evaluate differently according to the importance they attach to each domain in their lives. Therefore, this definition incorporates both an objective quantitative approach (what people have and can be observed directly) and a subjective qualitative approach (what people feel and can be observed indirectly) (Tonon 2020).

[1]Lab Institutional video—https://youtu.be/rZo8YvcCtdk).

In this sense, it is the responsibility of marketing to manage the subjective and objective well-being of the patient throughout his/her life cycle. The first refers to the feelings of satisfaction/dissatisfaction that he/she experiences and how this contributes to his/her quality of life. In turn, the objective well-being refers to an evaluation carried out by experts from objective secondary data referring to the benefits received, prices and costs (affordability), availability (accessibility), quality of care, claims and complaints, etc., related to goods and services purchased and/or consumed (Sirgy and Lee 2007, 2008).

Citizens' Health and Access to Hemoderived Medicines

The production of medicines and their accessibility are a crucial aspect for any health system. In this regard, drug policies must guarantee two objectives: availability (present in the market) and affordability (in economic terms) of medicines to the population (WHO 2001, 2004). **The pharmaceutical industry** thus improves the health of the population, in tune with the priority objectives of the World Health Organization (WHO) and the United Nations' Sustainable Development Goal 3 (SDG3). They seek to guarantee a healthy life and promote universal well-being through universal health coverage, in particular the protection against financial risks, access to quality essential health services, and access to safe, effective, affordable and quality medicines and vaccines for all.

Hemoderivative products are used in the treatment of complex diseases that can seriously affect people's health. They are prescribed in patients with blood coagulation defects such as hemophilia, alterations of the immune system, severe burns, some diseases of neurological origin, transplants, and in the prevention of tetanus, among others. In other words, these medicines help improve the quality of life of many people and save the life of many others.

They are high-cost drugs due to their biological origin and the complexity of obtaining their raw materials, as well as their production process. Most countries do not produce them, so they must be imported; this further increases their value. The existence of the HL makes Argentina one of the 50 countries in the world that obtains plasma-derived medicinal products through the fractionation of plasma collected in the country itself, as suggested by the PAHO (2014) (**Annex I**).

The WHA (2012) urges to develop **national transfusion systems** based on unpaid voluntary donors and to work to achieve self-sufficiency in the availability of blood and blood components. Only 62 countries obtain their national blood supplies from unpaid voluntary donations, while 40 countries continue to depend on donors close to patients, and even on paid donors (WHO 2017).

A **regular number of unpaid volunteer donors** ensures a safe and sufficient blood supply. This is the safest group of donors, as they have the lowest prevalence of blood or plasma contagious infections. However, the realities of the countries are different. In the United States, for example, plasma destined for the pharmaceutical industry is obtained from paid donors, in collection centers belonging to companies that produce blood products. In Argentina, on the other hand, both blood for transfusion purposes and plasma destined for the pharmaceutical industry can only be obtained from the voluntary and solidarity donation of individuals and the selling of these strategic resources is prohibited by the National Blood Law No. 22,990. Such law determines that blood and/or plasma donations can only be made in duly authorized public and private blood banks.

A Different Laboratory

The Argentine government, when President Arturo Umberto Illia was in office, promoted the LH in 1964. From its beginning, it was projected an organization with a clear social objective within the industry. As reflected in its **institutional mission**: "We are a non-profitable, public pharmaceutical laboratory, with a strong social commitment and with the pride of belonging to the Universidad Nacional de Córdoba, that seeks to improve the people's quality of life by developing accessible, high-quality, safe and effective products, providing answers to critical demands in national and regional health." The **values** that lead its policies and actions are: commitment to life—quality in products and processes—efficiency in the performance—and transparency in management.

President Illia decreed that this plant belonged to the UNC to protect it from the great economic interests of the time. This decision, years later, prevented the transfer of the LH to international private companies with profit criteria that would have resulted in serious damage to the quality of life of citizens.

Throughout its history, the LH became a key actor in the Argentine health system, by deciding to produce medicines such as edta calcium and hematine (still in development) that other pharmaceutical industries do not produce due to their low profitability (ANLAP 2017).

The LH has diversified its production by incorporating injectable drugs for hospital use (2002) and the processing of bone tissues for therapeutic use in traumatology and dentistry (2003). However, blood products continue to be its main production line, generating more than 90% of its income.

The HL does not use funds from the university budget, since it is economically and financially self-managed. The income obtained from the marketing of its products is reinvested in supplies, equipment and the salaries of its 300 collaborators. It maintains commercial policies that distinguish it from other market actors:

- Low prices: their prices are at least 5% below those of foreign laboratories in the national market.
- Priority supply to the public sector.
- Plasma exchange agreements with blood banks and hemotherapy services in Argentina.

- Supply to the national market in the first instance, and then to the rest of the Latin American countries.
- Excellence and quality of its products.

As a result, the LH has an impact on the substitution of imports of high-therapeutic valued drugs and regulates the prices of the blood product market.

The LH conceives blood products as social goods. Therefore, it offers products of the same quality and effectiveness as foreign competitors do, at more accessible prices, and based on strict compliance with Good Manufacturing Practices of the national health authority and the National Administration of Medicines, Food and Medical Technology (ANMAT). Internationally, processes and products meet the requirements established by organizations like the WHO and the European Pharmacopoeia (EF).

Since 2003, LH implements the Drug Donation Program, by which it provides its products to people without means.

Although it has different marketing promotion strategies from those of the rest of the pharmaceutical industry, the LH leads the national market for Endovenous G Immunoglobulin (IVL) and Human Serum Albumin. (HAS). The same market that it shares with foreign multinational companies such as Grifols (Spain), CSL Bhering (USA), KedrionS.p.A. (Italy), Octapharma (Switzerland), and BPL (United Kingdom).

Distribution is carried out through direct sales to public and private institutions (healthcare insurance, hospitals, and clinics) as well as through distributors covering all the geographical regions of the country.

At the **regional level**, LH exports plasma derivatives to five Latin American countries: Chile, Uruguay, Paraguay, Bolivia and the Dominican Republic. With the first three countries, it does so through the plasma-blood product exchange agreement (**Annex I**).

In 2019, LH distributed 436,808 blood products to treat some 48,688 patients.

A Campaign Focused on Quality of Life

- **The first moments, the first steps**

The Communicational Campaign of Voluntary Donation of Plasma of the LH was proposed, in its beginnings, in 2009: (a) increase the availability of plasma destined for the industry, (b) contribute to the population's awareness about the importance of voluntary donation, altruistic and repeated, of both blood and plasma, and (c) inform the community what plasma donation is for.

Initially, the planning and organization of the campaign was in charge of the Biological Raw Material Collection area of the LH, with the support of the UNC Blood Bank.

The campaign took its first steps with a pilot test period focused specifically on the institution's workers. With them, a series of internal actions were carried out with the aim of informing them about the plasma donation process and raising awareness about the importance of this donation. By the end of 2009, the first collection was completed.

Plasma collections were only done the UNC Blood Bank, located 200 meters from the LH, in the University campus.

In 2010, the campaign was spread in other places outside the LH but within the UNC. The diffusion focused on offering short talks to students from different university careers. Brochures with information on the Plasma Voluntary Donation Campaign and on the development of an own blog were delivered in these interventions.[2]

In the first communications, the concept of **quality of life** was not included, because they were focused on the solidarity of the donor and on the medicines that are made from plasma donations.

Over the years, the LH campaign team then focused on promoting the formation of donor communities in different institutions. The culture of voluntary plasma donation is shared with them and, as a result, they become promoters of the campaign.

Within these communities, mobile plasma collections began to be implemented. This meant that donors no longer had to go exclusively to donate to the UNC Blood Bank, but extractions could rather be made in the places arranged by each donor community. Thus, collection days began to be held at the LH (exclusively for its staff) and in some academic units of the UNC as well as in the Youth community of the Capuchinos Church of Córdoba and in institutions in cities like Villa María (153 km far from Córdoba city).

In 2011, the number of donations reached its highest point, accounting for 1000 donations per year. Yet, it began to decrease during the following 4 years (period 2012–2015). This might be explained by the absence of a campaign positioning strategy in the medium and long term.

- **A leap towards social marketing**

The turning point in the campaign was in 2016. That year, the campaign itself became a transversal objective between the Biological Raw Material Collection Area and the LH Institutional Communication and Marketing Department.

In this way, a new communication and marketing strategy was then planned and managed, which did not abandon the campaign objectives defined in 2009 but strengthened them. It was more focused on (a) informing, sensitizing and raising awareness among the population about plasma voluntary donation, particularly to the university community, and (b) building loyalty to communities and regular voluntary donors through relationship marketing strategies.

The communication strategy fixed its attention on making visible the impact that solidarity donation of plasma has for patients who need blood products. The

[2]Plasma Voluntary Donation Campaign Blog—http://donaplasma.blogspot.com/

messages and actions aimed to show the close connection between the act of donating plasma and the patient's possibility of enjoying a good **quality of life**.

In this context, the concept of **quality of life** was approached communicationally from two perspectives. On the one hand, from patients' access to health assistance since they have available plasma-derived medicines produced in the country and at a much lower cost than those obtained from foreign laboratories. On the other hand, the **quality of life** focused on the lifestyle that patients under treatment with these drugs could have, without which, it would be impossible.

Work was done on a new communication code, which sought to generate more closeness to the campaign through testimonial advertisement which show the effects of the donation. That is, to show in their different communication pieces people who represent the ultimate recipients of the plasma donation. The chosen images were photographs of children and adults enjoying simple moments of life such as a game in a square, a warm grandpa to grandson hug and a birthday celebration.

Phrases such as "Donate smiles", "Donate goal hugs", "Donate opportunities" and "Donate sprints" were included in the communication pieces to transmit a donor that he is donating much more than his plasma (Fig. 2.1).

At this stage, a new visual identity (logo) was also designed for the campaign that would accompany each of the broadcast pieces.

- **Communicational objectives**

In this new stage, the axes of the communication campaign were aimed at informing, sensitizing and raising awareness in the community about plasma donation. Therefore, we sought to provide greater visibility to the subject. The focus was on the university community, in which the LH is immersed, together with the central areas and the different academic units of the UNC.

It was the first time that heavy-traffic areas for students, teachers and administrators were intervened within the university campus with billboards and images of the Donate Plasma campaign (Fig. 2.2), including strategic points such as the Argentina Pavilion, which is both the UNC's central management building and the epicenter of numerous academic and cultural activities.

An informative stand was placed for the first time in the annual university Career Exhibition. This is a four-day event, during which senior high school students come to the University to look for information on different degree career offerings. Each year more than 40,000 adolescents and young people from the entire province of Córdoba and neighboring provinces, future university students and potential new donors, visit this open-door career exhibition.

In addition, informative content in the form of short animated videos on plasma donation was produced. They explained what plasma donation was, what it was for, and what medicines were made from plasma.

Regarding the axis of sensitization and awareness, testimonials of patients, family members, health professionals and loyal donors were filmed. The first three were based on the improvement in patient health as a result of better access to complex and expensive drugs, while the donors' testimonials were focused on the reasons that had led them to become regular donors.

Fig. 2.1 Broadcasting poster of Donate Plasma campaign (2016). Donate Smiles You donate us plasma We distribute and donate medicines Many people can improve their quality of life. Source: The HL (2016)

These contents circulated mainly through the LH's social networks as well as through the WhatsApp application, being the latter the main channel of direct contact of the campaign's health team **with current donor and potential donors**. All of them are available both on the LH YouTube channel[3] and also on social networks (Table 2.1).

The campaign was promoted primarily through Facebook and Instagram. Whereas, the management of stories and interviews in the traditional mass media

[3]The HL YouTube Channel https://www.youtube.com/channel/UCNXeofpyBU3EzVhX-

Fig. 2.2 Some of the eight billboards placed in the University campus. Source: The LH (2020)

has been a complementary dissemination strategy to install plasma donation in society.[4]

Another initiative to increase the visibility of the plasma donation campaign at the national level, was the project to declare May 21th (anniversary date of the LH's founding) as the National Plasma Donor Day. The project was approved and promoted by the Superior Council of the UNC and, in April 2019, it obtained half sanction in the Chamber of Deputies of the Argentine Nation.

[4]"Donate blood, an easy way to become a heroe". News report published in La Voz del Interior newspaper, June 12th 2017. https://www.lavoz.com.ar/salud/donar-sangre-una-forma-sencilla-de-convertirse-en-heroe

"The LH celebrates its 53th anniversary with a Plasma Collection". News report published in La Mañana newspaper, May 24th 2017, and in other local media. https://lmdiario.com.ar/contenido/14625/hemoderivados-celebra-sus-53-anos-con-una-colecta-aniversario-de-plasma

"The Donate Plasma campaign is resumed at the Laboratory of Hemoderivatives". News report published in Radio Mitre Córdoba website as well as in other local media, February 19th 2019. https://radiomitre.cienradios.com/reanudan-la-campana-dona-plasma-laboratorio-hemoderivados/

Table 2.1 Patients, families and health professionals' testimonials

Lucas Balagué A patient with Diagnosis of primary immune deficiencies (DPI)	"I feel refreshed after I get the gamma globulin infusion. For me it is like renewing my strength and wanting to get up to run, to walk, to do some sports, because it is the defense that my body needs." https://youtu.be/h9wFOQsAgUI?list=PLvO6zngQhxYsLlB6BV6NQfQR_eGw8CC1T
Natalia Roig Mother of a patient with DPI	"His treatment changed his life. He was then able to start doing normal activity." soccer . . . he couldn't even play because he was shaking, his breathing was not normal. Now he can play soccer, he can run, he can ride a bike. He sleeps. Before it, he did not sleep non-stop. Today Santiago feels very good, he is another child. He feels good, he lives a normal life. The gamma has really changed it 100%." https://youtu.be/PB4sjxxSzwE
Mauricio Vega, uncle of a patient with Hemofilia	When Benjamin started taking prophylaxis, his life changed radically. We are not all the time at hospital and he can live a fairly. . . normal life." https://youtu.be/17qojZrbRMQ?list=PLvO6zngQhxYsLlB6BV6NQfQR_eGw8CC1T
Alejandro Lozano, pediatrician doctor specialized in Allergy and Immunology	If you ask if it changed their lives . . . this gamma globulin has changed their lives. It has allowed them to live, play, be happy, make others happy. Families who were hopeless at watching their sick children, today they see them grow, become adults. . . it is more than just gamma globulin." https://youtu.be/en49uJUyX80?list=PLvO6zngQhxYsLlB6BV6NQfQR_eGw8CC1T

Source: Elaborated by the authors (2020)

- **Donation logistics**

The communication and marketing strategy was accompanied by changes in the logistics of campaign implementation. Thus, the personnel assigned to its execution increased, as did the number of mobile collections at the Laboratory headquarters and in new communities. Year after year, new donation stands were added to increase the capacity of donor care. In February, some 100 mobile collections were estimated and planned for 2020 (Fig. 2.3).

- **Donor experience**

In 2016, the management of the donor cycle and the experience of the donor became a central axis. In other words, The Blood Donation Center sought hard to make the donation experience as satisfactory and gratifying as possible from the moment donors scheduled an appointment to donate.

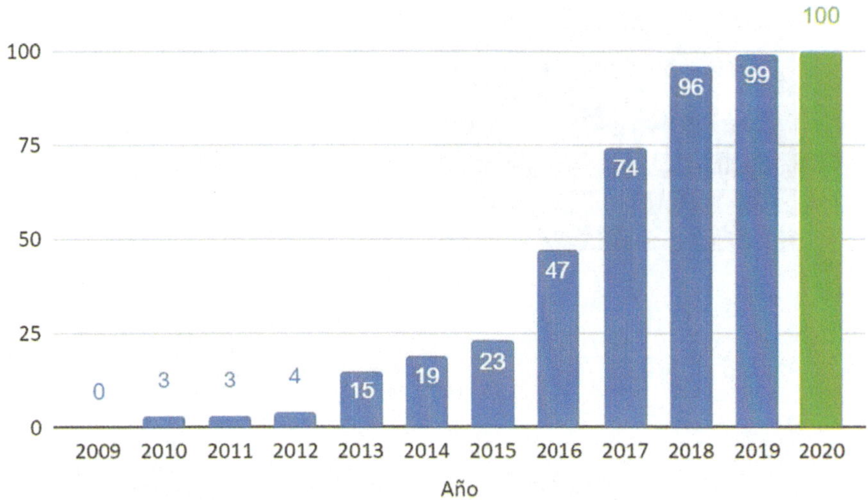

Fig. 2.3 Evolution of mobile collections. Source: The LH (2020)

Fig. 2.4 Mural made by donors and patients (2018). Source: The LH (2020)

The objective was that the donation stage was to be lived as a pleasant moment for those who show solidarity and donate plasma. A third focus on **quality of life** appears here, highlighted in those who choose to donate because in this way they feel that they can help many people, in a win-win relationship (Fig. 2.4). Consequently, the pre and post donation stages received the same significance as the donation itself.

In the pre-donation stage, the emphasis was on providing donors with the most complete information about what donation is like, how donors should prepare themselves for it (food and rest indications), and the clinical reasons why they

Fig. 2.5 Communication piece with the donors (2018). 1. Come to donate. Bring your ID. Do not forget it!, 2. Medical interview. To help others, you have to be healthy, 3. Plasma donation. It's simple. A few minutes of your time helps a lot, 4. Super Breakfast. Don't leave without eating something tasty!, 5. You transformed lives. You changed your life and the lives of many people. Source: The LH (2020)

should postpone their donation. In addition, donors receive reminders of their scheduled appointment (Fig. 2.5).

On the day of the donation, the doctors who make up the campaign's health team are in charge of welcoming the donors, carrying out the required (medical) anamnesis interview and assessing their clinical aptitude to donate. They also monitor the donation development and donor's health during the donation.

The donation room has a lounge in which a table is set with food and drinks up so that donors can have a snack after their donation. Besides, it has a second room where the extraction stands are located. So as to loosen up and relax, donors can watch music videos and TV series. Yet, many of them choose to read or to spend the time in the social networks with their mobile phones.

After their donation, they are invited to have a "superb breakfast" and to take a photograph to be shared on the LH networks. The aim is to show the community that these people choose to be caring and supportive by doing this.

The day after the donation, the campaign doctors contact donors to check how they felt after their donation experience. Also, emails are sent to donors on behalf of a patient, a family member or a health professional[5] to express their gratitude because constant care of plasma donors is a priority for the campaign.

---

[5] Thank you video: https://www.youtube.com/watch?v=MnfiKNEXC3c&list=PLvO6zngQhxYsLlB6BV6NQfQR_eGw8CC1T&index=15

Fig. 2.6 Donors and patients' gathering (2019). Source: The LH (2020)

- **Donor retention and loyalty strategies**

In order to personally identify and maintain a relationship with donors, a gathering was planned between them and the patients, who are the ultimate beneficiaries of the campaign. In it, donors could see not only the dimension but also the impact of their donation. Therefore, the "**Because you make it possible**" Meeting between Donors and Patients was created (Fig. 2.6).

This annual social gathering focuses on recognizing the solidarity of donors as well as showing them how their donation helps improve the quality of life of many people. During them, patients, who need the blood products made from plasma donations, share their life stories. It has already taken place three times.[6]

It is worth mentioning that, unlike other types of donations, in plasma donations the relationship between donor and patient is not immediate, linear and direct (one to one). This is so because many donations of blood and plasma are required to obtain the quantity of raw material necessary to make a batch of any of the blood-derived drugs.

The campaign has the unconditional support of patients' relatives. Some of them are both plasma donors and active promoters of the campaign. The same happens with many of the LH collaborators, who are also regular donors.

- **Campaign results**

The results of the Donate Plasma Campaign have been encouraging. The number of annual donations grew 95% in the last 3 years (Fig. 2.7). That is to say, the number of annual donations increased from 865 registered in 2016 to 1693 in 2019. The number of donations projected for 2020 would be more than 2030.

[6] Summaries of Social gatherings First gathering between donors and patients "Because you make it possible" (summary) https://youtu.be/ExGIwMod8ZI—Third gathering between donors and patients: "There's chemistry and you make it possible" (summary) https://www.facebook.com/unchemoderivados/videos/514506755808790/

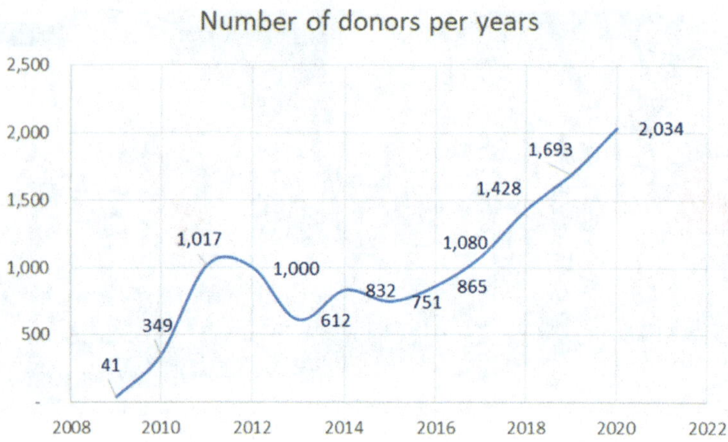

Fig. 2.7 Growth in donor numbers. Source: The LH (2020)

In the future, with the aim of growing and expanding the campaign, there are projects planned to be implemented in 2020, such as:

- Installation of an online appointment scheduling software linked to a communication and loyalty platform since both appointment dates and reminders are nowadays manually handled.
- Incorporation of a conditioned vehicle for mobile collections.
- Celebration of 10th anniversary of the campaign with an event that gives it great visibility among young people (18–30 years old).
- Development of a new communication and marketing campaign, focused mainly on university students.

Discussion Questions

1. LH is defined "as a public non-profit company, with a strong social commitment . . .". Analyze the organization's mission statement and its institutional role in the community based on the definition of Quality of Life (QoL).
2. Regarding the LH's social marketing plan, to what extent is the QoL marketing perspective intuitively present in the organization? Consider the following criteria: (a) market segment (b) development of inclusive and ethical marketing (c) reduction of negative impacts or positive externalities on the community (d) profitability as a long-term goal.
3. With respect to the different plasma donation marketing campaigns developed, what have the objectives been focused on? And, what have the strategies and intentions been used, bearing in mind the donors and the community in general? Consider the following marketing plans: (a) to reinforce ideas, attitudes and behaviours (reinforcement strategy), (b) to induce the performance of a desirable behaviour (induction strategy), (c) to generate a change of attitude (rationalization strategy) and/or (d) to generate a change of attitude and behaviour (confrontation strategy). Back up your answer.

Teaching Notes

1. **The LH is defined "as a public non-profit company, with a strong social commitment ...". Analyze the organization's mission statement and its institutional role in the community based on the definition of Quality of Life (QoL).**
   Quality of life is currently defined as a multidimensional concept that comprises a series of domains that people consider and evaluate differently according to the importance they attach to each domain in their lives. This definition incorporates both an objective quantitative approach (what people have and can be observed directly) and a subjective qualitative approach (what people feel and can be observed indirectly). Quality of life is the perception that each individual has of their position in life, within the cultural context and the value system in which they live, in relation to their expectations, interests and achievements (Tonon 2020).

   Sirgy and Lee (1996, p. 21) point out that "QoL marketing states that the role of the organization is to develop goods and services and market those products effectively and efficiently to minimize negative side effects for consumers and other audiences, while generating long-term profitability." Therefore, the QoL philosophy focuses on: (a) enhancing the well-being of consumers through marketing and/or consumption of goods and services, (b) reducing negative side effects related to marketing and/or consumption of goods and services by target consumers, (c) diminishing negative secondary effects associated with the commercialization and/or consumption of goods and services from consumers other than the target consumers, and (d) improving long-term profitability.

   QoL's marketing approach can be expressed as "the commercial mechanism that plans, sets prices, promotes and distributes cheap consumer goods with the aim of maximizing consumer welfare" (Sirgy 2001, p. 8). Therefore, the concept provides a business philosophy that guides managers in the development and implementation of marketing strategies that act on consumer well-being throughout the consumer/product life cycle: acquisition, preparation, consumption, possession, maintenance and disposal of consumer goods (Sirgy and Lee 2008). In this sense, consumer wellbeing is formed by the feelings of satisfaction and dissatisfaction experienced during the acquisition, preparation, consumption, possession, maintenance and disposal of consumer goods, which leads to the quality of life of the consumer (Sirgy and Lee 2008).

   The LH has, since its founding, a clear awareness of its mission: to be a non-profit public pharmaceutical laboratory, with a strong social commitment and with the pride of belonging to the University. Attention is mainly focused on the search for people's better quality of life, by developing accessible, high-quality, safe and effective products, by providing answers to critical demands in the field of national and Latin American health, and by promoting efficient, transparent and sustainable resources, through a high level of performance and commitment of its staff.

Quality of life is highlighted here as the central purpose of the laboratory, which is very significant, not only in symbolic but also strategic terms. It aims to be an innovative and cutting-edge public organization, which has an efficient management model based on optimization of processes and continuous improvement as well as on the development of high quality products to improve the social impact in the region.

In the context of the health emergency posed by the COVID-19 pandemic, the UNC Laboratory of Hemoderivatives is working on the development of concentrated antibodies to treat severe COVID-19 patients. Such a drug is considered as a highly-effective and biologically-safe therapeutic option. This initiative is supported by the National Ministry of Health. The lab is working together with the National Blood System and other institutions to make progress in the various facets involved in a project of this scale (UNC 2020; La Voz del Interior 2020).

UNC (2020). *Covid-19: Hemoderivados será el único centro del país en producir inmunoglobulinas enriquecidas*, Accessed May 29, 2020, from www.unc.edu.ar/comunicaci%C3%B3n/covid-19-hemoderivados-ser%C3%A1-el-%C3%BAnico-centro-del-pa%C3%ADs-en-producir-inmunoglobulinas

La Voz del Interior (2020) El Laboratorio de Hemoderivados desarrolla un tratamiento para el covid-19, Accessed May 29, 2020, from www.lavoz.com.ar/espacio-de-marca/laboratorio-de-hemoderivados-desarrolla-un-tratamiento-para-covid-19

2. **Regarding the LH's social marketing plan, to what extent is the QoL marketing perspective intuitively present in the organization? Consider the following criteria: (a) market segment (b) development of inclusive and ethical marketing (c) reduction of negative impacts or positive externalities on the community (d) profitability as a long-term goal.**

The LH develops blood products for the entire population without distinction (mass market) and there is no segmentation that excludes any type of patient, clinic or hospital or to which produced blood products are denied.

Therefore, its trade policies are oriented towards high quality and top excellence products, at affordable prices, with a distribution policy across the country and even across borders. Distribution is carried out through direct sales to public and private institutions (healthcare insurance, hospitals, and clinics) as well as through distributors covering all the geographical regions of the country.

At the regional level, the LH exports plasma derivatives to five Latin American countries: Chile, Uruguay, Paraguay, Bolivia and the Dominican Republic. With the first three countries, it does so through the plasma-blood product exchange agreement.

For plasma collection, the LH maintains a Plasma Exchange Program for Blood Products with more than 200 public and private blood banks in Argentina, and with the health portfolios of Chile, Uruguay and Paraguay.

To sum up, the LH maintains commercial policies that distinguish it from other market actors:

- Low prices: their prices are at least 5% below those of foreign laboratories in the national market.
- Priority supply to the public sector.
- Plasma exchange agreements with blood banks and hemotherapy services in Argentina.
- Supply to the national market in the first instance, and then to the rest of the Latin American countries.
- Excellence and quality of its products.

As a non-profit organization, the surpluses (profits) that it obtains from the commercialization of its products are reinvested in supplies, equipment, technology infrastructure and training for the more than 300 employees.

3. **With respect to the different plasma donation marketing campaigns developed, what have the objectives been focused on? And, what have the strategies and intentions been used, bearing in mind the donors and the community in general? Consider the following marketing plans: (a) to reinforce ideas, attitudes and behaviours (reinforcement strategy), (b) to induce the performance of a desirable behaviour (induction strategy), (c) to generate a change of attitude (rationalization strategy) and/or (d) to generate a change of attitude and behaviour (confrontation strategy). Back up your answer.**

   The Communicational Campaign of Voluntary Donation of Plasma of the LH intended in its beginnings to (2009): (a) increase the availability of plasma destined for the industry, (b) contribute to the awareness of the population about the importance of voluntary donation, altruistic and repeated, of both blood and plasma, and (c) inform the community what plasma donation is for. However, our starting point was a scenario of non-negative but indifferent attitudes, with a low level of awareness and emotional involvement and with very low levels of effective behaviours, measured in terms of donors.

   Strategies applied in the process of social change

Stage	Donor situation		Recommended strategy	Actions taken
	Attitude	Behaviour		
Start 2009–2015	Negative/ indifferent	Non-engaged	Confrontation strategy	• Pilot test with LH personnel from the biological raw material collection area • Awareness of LH staff • Collections in one place: LH • Delivery of brochures to students from different careers, especially those related to health • Own blog development • First mobile collections • Creation of first donor communities
2016 onwards	Positive	Non-engaged	Induction strategy	• More mobile collection locations • Greater communication and

(continued)

Stage	Donor situation		Recommended strategy	Actions taken
	Attitude	Behaviour		
				dissemination • More emotional and empathetic communication pieces
	Negative	Engaged	Rationalization strategy	• More collection locations, adapted to donor schedules • Simplification of the donation process • Improved donating experience • Customer experience management: Pre and post donation
	Positive	Engaged	Reinforcement strategy	• Donor communities • Gatherings with donors and patients • Donor cycle management

Source: Own production

Therefore, it was necessary to act on unwanted but socially desirable attitudes and behaviours (not to donate blood and plasma), trying to modify the motivations through different actions (**Confrontation Strategy**). We started with internal marketing in a more permeable and sensitive audience (health-related career students), first mobile collections and the creation of donor communities. The results were positive and limited but then, after the peak of 1000-annual donations, it began to decrease.

In 2016, when there was still much to do and without abandoning these initiatives, the LH met donors who had donated and found it hard to donate again (go through the first donating experience and doubt about becoming a regular donor). Others, who after having lived a dissatisfactory experience, doubted or were reluctant to continue donating. And finally, those who within the framework of donor communities, their experiences and companionship of others were necessary to maintain and retain. By generating a more permanent bond, they could even join the campaign and share their testimonies and experiences.

The campaign's coverage base is open to the entire university community and beyond. Thus, different communication strategies were developed, namely greater broadcast resources, more emotional communication pieces, and greater face-to-face counselling in the stand within the university community (**inductive strategy**). In addition, special emphasis was placed on the perception of a "simpler" process (Welcoming/Arrival, Medical Interview, plasma donation, departure after having breakfast), with more appropriate scheduled appointments and better staff assistance to guarantee a substantial improvement in the donating experience, mainly during the pre and post donation stage (**Rationalization Strategy**). Finally, concrete actions of relationship marketing were implemented to enhance long-term customer retention and customer loyalty and satisfaction through donor community promotion, activities and gatherings between donors and patients (**Strengthening Strategies**).

References

Alves H, Vázquez JL (eds) (2013) Best practices in marketing and their impact on quality of life. Springer

ANLAP (2017). Acuerdo para la provisión pública del inyectable Edta Cálcico. Ministerio de Salud Pública de la Nación, Agencia Nacional de Laboratorio Públicos (ANLAP). https://www.argentina.gob.ar/noticias/acuerdo-para-la-provision-publica-del-inyectable-edta-calcico. Accesed May 12, 2020

Kelley EJ (1974) Integrating social feedback into business decisions: value system conflicts and corporate planning. In: Clewett RL, Olson JC (eds) Social indicators and marketing. American Marketing Association, Chicago, pp 129–145

La Voz del Interior (2020) El Laboratorio de Hemoderivados desarrolla un tratamiento para el covid-19. www.lavoz.com.ar/espaciode-marca/laboratorio-de-hemoderivados-desarrolla-un-tratamiento-para-covid-19. Acceses May 29, 2020

Laboratorio Hemoderivados (2019) Video institucional del Laboratorio. June 4, 2019. https://youtu.be/rZo8YvcCtdk. Accesed May 12, 2020

PAHO (2014) Resolución CD53/6. Plan de acción para el acceso universal a sangre segura. https://www.paho.org/es/documentos/documento-plan-accion-paraacceso-universal-sangre-segura

Sirgy MJ (2001) Handbook of quality-of-life research: an ethical marketing perspective. In: Social indicators research series, vol 8. Kluwer Academic Publishers, Dordrecht

Sirgy MJ, Lee DJ (1996) Setting socially responsible marketing objectives. Eur J Mark 30(5):20–34

Sirgy MJ, Lee DJ (2007) Ethical foundations of well-being marketing. In: Vilcox MW, Mohan TO (eds) Contemporary issues in business ethics. Nova Science Publisher, New York

Sirgy MJ, Lee DJ (2008) Well-being marketing: an ethical business philosophy for consumer goods firms. J Bus Ethics 77(4):377–403

Tonon GH (2020) Teaching quality of life in different domains. In: The importance of teaching quality of life theory and methodology in social sciences programs. Springer, Cham, pp 1–14

UNC (2020) Covid-19: Hemoderivados será el único centro del país en producir inmunoglobulinas enriquecidas. www.unc.edu.ar/comunicaci%C3%B3n/covid-19-hemoderivados-ser%C3%A1-el-%C3%BAnico-centro-del-pa%C3%ADs-en-producir-inmunoglobulinas. Acceses May 29, 2020

WHA (2012) Disponibilidad, seguridad y calidad de los productos sanguíneos. 2012. https://apps.who.int/gb/ebwha/pdf_files/WHA63/A63_R12-sp.pdf?ua=1

WHO (2001) How to develop and implement a national drug policy, 2nd edn. Geneva. https://apps.who.int/iris/bitstream/handle/10665/42423/924154547X.pdf?sequence=1. Accesed May 25, 2020

WHO (2004) Estrategia Farmacéutica de la OMS 2004–2007. Lo esencial son los países. Ginebra: Organización Mundial de la Salud. https://apps.who.int/iris/handle/10665/68724. Accesed May 25, 2020

WHO (2017). Disponibilidad y seguridad de la sangre a nivel mundial. https://www.who.int/es/news-room/fact-sheets/detail/blood-safety-and-availability

Chapter 3
The Importance of Social Marketing in Skin Cancer Prevention: The Case of Portugal

Juliana Correia, Susana C. Silva, and Paulo Duarte

Abstract Sun-tanned skin was once associated with the sun-exposed manual labour of individuals. However, this association has changed dramatically, and tanned skin has become a standard of beauty in Western society. Tanned skin is therefore glorified and sought after, making people feel pressured to conform to standards. Current scientific and medical studies indicate that there is a clear link between sun exposure and skin cancer and consequently with quality of life (QoL). Social marketing effects behaviour change, improving the quality of life of the target group as a result of that change. This case-study is based on social marketing campaigns by the Portuguese Skin Cancer Association warning people about the dangers of excessive sun exposure. Qualitative analysis of the benefits, challenges, and outcomes of the campaigns according to the people involved are presented and discussed.

The results show that despite the campaigns devoted to sun exposure dangers, individuals have psychological resistance to adopting behaviours that have the potential to benefit their health and QoL in the future. To face the challenges of skin cancer prevention, the organisations involved must diversify the location of their campaigns, look for additional support from national and local authorities, and invest in social media marketing strategies.

Keywords Social marketing · Skin cancer prevention · Quality of life (QoL) · Social marketing · Behavioural change

---

J. Correia · S. C. Silva (✉)
Universidade Católica Portuguesa, Católica Porto Business School, Porto, Portugal
e-mail: ssilva@porto.ucp.pt

P. Duarte
University of Beira Interior, Covilhã, Portugal
e-mail: pduarte@ubi.pt

M. M. Galan-Ladero, R. G. Rivera (eds.), *Applied Social Marketing and Quality of Life*, Applying Quality of Life Research,
https://doi.org/10.1007/978-3-030-83286-5_3

Introduction

The incidence of melanoma (the most dangerous skin cancer type) has increased over the years in Portugal. Currently, it is estimated that its incidence is 10 new cases per 100,000 inhabitants, per year, which means 1000 new cases, per year, and it is expected that this number will increase in the coming years (APCC 2019). However, changing sun-related behaviours remains a challenge, especially among adolescents. What makes skin cancer prevention so relevant is the fact that skin cancer is mostly preventable, as long as individuals follow certain behavioural guidelines to reduce the risks of being exposed to the sun (Koch et al. 2016). As ozone levels are reduced, the atmosphere loses its protective filtering function and more solar UV radiation reaches ground level. It is estimated that a 10% decrease in ozone levels will result in an additional 300,000 non-melanoma and 4500 melanoma skin cancer cases (WHO 2020); therefore, prompting prevention is crucial. Social marketing may play a decisive role in helping to prevent this social problem affecting the QoL of thousands of people worldwide.

The ultimate goal of social marketing is to improve the well-being of individuals, by helping them to change their unhealthy behaviours to healthy ones (behaviour change). This behaviour change should be made voluntarily (Silva and Silva 2012). To reach the target audience, social marketers generally use educational campaigns to raise awareness of the topic (Wymer 2011). The Health Belief Model[1] (Rosenstock 1974; Janz and Becker 1984; Stretcher and Rosenstock 1997) assumes that people are more likely to change a health-related behaviour if they feel that a threat to their health can be avoided by changing their behaviour and if they feel that the benefits of their actions exceed the perceived efforts needed. There are two main criticisms of this model: that there is not a clear explanation of the relationships between the model variables and the model does not mention relevant causes of health behaviour change (Brennan et al. 2014).

Social marketing strategies should consider their impact on the targeted population's QoL. Quality of life (QoL) is the perception each person has of his/her place in life, within a cultural context and the system of values he/she complies with, related to expectations, interests, and achievements (Tonon 2015). Understanding the target group's perceptions, opinions, feelings, ideas, and interpretations is essential because it would improve the application of the social marketing model. This is the case with the HBM. This knowledge of QoL can also be used to help to improve the Health Belief Model (HBM) outcomes. The Health Belief Model provides a framework for assessing the factors that best predict behavioural changes.

[1]The Health Belief Model provides a framework for considering behaviours and interventions, as well as, their associated behavioural changes. It considers that there is a better chance that people will change a health-related behaviour if they feel that a threat to their health can be avoided by changing their behaviour; if they feel that the benefit of their action is superior to the perceived barriers; and if they feel that the change can be made successfully. According to the Health Belief Model, the variables that guide health actions are perceived susceptibility, perceived severity, perceived benefits, perceived barriers and cues to action.

According to social marketing models, behavioural change is associated with perceived susceptibility (this refers to subjective assessment of the risk of developing a health problem), perceived severity (referring to the subjective assessment of the severity of a health problem and its potential consequences), perceived benefits (referring to an individual's assessment of the value or efficacy of engaging in a health-promoting behaviour to decrease the risk of disease), perceived barriers (refers to an individual's assessment of the obstacles to behaviour change), cues to action (refers to triggers necessary for prompting engagement in health-promoting behaviours), and self-efficacy (refers to an individual's perception of his or her competence to successfully perform a behaviour). The HBM model and QoL are related: if individuals are prompted to think about the HBM factors, it is believed that the odds of them changing their behaviour in order to improve QoL are higher. When evaluating their QoL, individuals often take into consideration all the factors relevant in forming a judgement of the overall quality of their lives. However, people can also choose aspects of their lives and evaluate them separately. It is important to bear in mind that QoL is influenced by factors like demographics, cultural traits, and psychosocial characteristics of the communities, among others.

The correct understanding of the causes of a social problem can be a crucial success factor in a social marketing campaign. This can be done using the domains of QoL. An example of a successful campaign on these matters is the SunSmart Program in Australia and New Zealand. The goal of the program is to reduce the incidence of preventable skin cancer. It correctly identified a knowledge deficit (individuals were not aware they needed to protect themselves) and an unhealthy attitude (individuals did not care about skin cancer). To solve these two problems, SunSmart has created communication programs to educate and increase awareness (Wymer 2011). However, we have to keep in mind the importance of local culture; because the population is very heterogenous, segmentation is needed to reach priority groups, as it allows tailored messages and materials to be created, with differentiated details (colour scheme, tone of voice, music, and means of diffusion). The methodology for an effective social marketing campaign segmentation should always include audience research (research literature, use of questionnaires, focus groups, interviews) (Gallivan et al. 2007) to understand their preferences and be able to select the right messages and attributes.

Another two key aspects that should be taken into consideration when designing a social marketing campaign aimed at promoting QoL are:

- The perception people have regarding their QoL.
- The level of danger people attribute to the underlying behaviour.
- Cultural differences, especially in an international context, since the success of campaigns will depend on adaptation to cultural settings.
- The ethics of social marketing, which means that the end does not justify the means. Not everything is right and valid just to achieve a certain behaviour goal, and marketers should be aware of the impact their campaign will have on the population (Alves and Galan-Ladero 2019).

Development of the Case

Skin Cancer: Description of the Disease

There are two types of skin cancer: non-melanoma skin cancers and malignant melanoma (Fig. 3.1). The first one includes basal cell carcinoma, which is the most common and least dangerous form of skin cancer and squamous cell carcinoma, which is the second most common form of skin cancer. Although these two forms of skin cancer are seldom fatal, they do require appropriate treatment, such as surgical removal. Malignant melanoma is the most dangerous form of skin cancer. It is less usual than non-melanoma skin cancers; nevertheless, it represents the major cause of death from skin cancer (WHO 2020).

The risk of melanoma increases as people age. According to the World Cancer Research (2019), the average age of people diagnosed is 63 years old. But melanoma is not uncommon even among those younger than 30. Young men aged 15–39 are 55% more likely to die from the disease than women of the same age (World Cancer Research Fund 2019). In fact, it is one of the most common cancers in young adults (especially young women). There is evidence that as children grow older, they tend to adopt riskier behaviours towards the sun (Rodrigues et al. 2014). Since tanned skin is valued among this age group, they tend to feel pressured to increase the amount of time they are exposed to the sun. Moreover, this age group is also influenced by current trends, fashion, and their group of friends (Rodrigues et al. 2014). This explains the fact the most popular sun protection method among adolescents is sunglasses, as they can be considered "trendy" and a fashion accessory.

Social Marketing and Skin Cancer

The Health Belief Model (HBM) has guided multiple social marketing campaigns, namely in the health sector. To better understand how the HBM could be applied to a skin cancer prevention campaign, let us imagine a campaign targeting adolescents. Regarding the first dimension of HBM, **perceived susceptibility**, we can say that

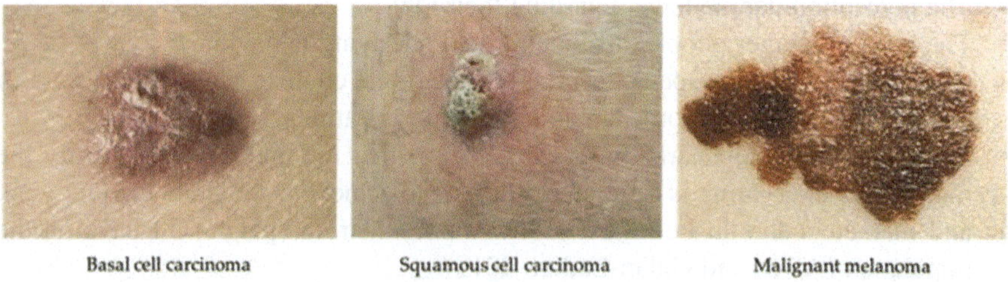

Fig. 3.1 Skin cancer types. Source: APCC (2019)

adolescents who do not think they are at risk of skin cancer are unlikely to change their sun protection behaviours; as for **perceived severity**, we can say that if adolescents do not believe that skin cancer is dangerous, it is unlikely they will change their sun protection behaviours; as for **perceived benefits**, we can consider that adolescents will probably not stop going to the beach during the most dangerous hours if they do not think that doing so will improve their lives in some way; as for **perceived barriers**, we can surmise that if a group of friends always goes to the beach at 1 p.m., it is hard for one member to take the opposite position and go at 5 p. m., for instance; and, finally, as for **Cues to action**, we can consider that adolescents seeing a skin cancer prevention campaign offering hats might eventually be persuaded to wear a hat when going to the beach. The HBM suggests that if these 5 dimensions are completed, there is a higher chance that the target audience will change their behaviour.

The Skin Cancer Portuguese Association (Associação Portuguesa de Cancro Cutâneo—APCC, in Portuguese) has been promoting skin cancer prevention campaigns since 2003 to raise awareness and educate the population about skin cancer. One of the most relevant initiatives of the campaign which has promoted by APPC since 2003 on the crowded beach of “Praia da Falésia” (Vilamoura), in the Portuguese region of Algarve, consists of a full day awareness program, from 8 a.m. to 9 p.m. Over the course of this day, a stand, posters, billboards, promotional and informational material, as well as volunteers, are placed at the main entrance of Praia da Falésia. This is a strategic location for the stand because everyone who enters the beach passes through this entrance (Fig. 3.2).

The volunteers participating in this campaign are pharmaceutical professionals, medical doctors, medical school students, and medical sales representatives. As the implementers, these volunteers conduct surveys on people entering the beach concerning sun-related behaviours, distribute informational flyers, offer gifts, and advise people on skin cancer and sun protection topics (Fig. 3.3). Additionally, during the morning there is also the participation of mass media (TV and radio) to interview participants and to promote the initiative (Fig. 3.4). During the rest of the day, additional activities are undertaken, such as sweepstakes, running activities at the beach, the presence of public figures, such as soap opera actors and producers, and running athletes (Fig. 3.5). All these activities aim to drive more attention and

Fig. 3.2 APCC Campaign in Praia da Falésia, Vilamoura. Source: APCC (2019)

513523_1_En_3_Fig2_Print.tif

Fig. 3.3 Stand with flyers, gifts, and offer personalised advice. Source: APCC (2019)

Fig. 3.4 Media coverage. Source: APCC (2019)

curiosity to the campaign from the target audience. By having public figures present, the target audience tends to feel more interested in finding out more about what was being promoted at the campaign stand.

Methodology

To achieve a broader understanding of the skin cancer prevention campaigns carried out by APCC, interviews were conducted on nine people, from the 12th–14th December 2018, who had been involved in the APCC campaign in Praia da Falésia for one or more years. The objectives of the interviews were as follows:

Fig. 3.5 Campaign activities at the beach and the presence of public figures. Source: APCC (2019)

Table 3.1 Profile of the interviewees

#	Role	Age	Gender	Occupation
1	Implementer	59	Female	General Manager
2	Planner	40	Female	Medical Doctor (Dermatologist)
3	Implementer	40	Male	Office employee
4	Implementer	54	Male	Medical sales representative
5	Planner	57	Male	Medical Doctor (Dermatologist)
6	Planner	47	Male	Medical Doctor (Dermatologist)
7	Audience	23	Male	University student
8	Audience	16	Female	High School student
9	Audience	19	Female	University student

Source: Own elaboration

- Objective 1: Understand the perception of appropriateness to the audience of the campaign activities, therefore contribute to improving QoL.
- Objective 2: Identify the main challenges and difficulties faced by social marketing campaign promoters when addressing issues with an impact on the individuals' QoL.
- Objective 3: Collect recommendations for future campaigns aimed at improving QoL perception related to cancer.

The interviewees were segmented at three different levels, according to the roles they played during the campaign (Table 3.1):

Table 3.2 Summary of the interviews

	Campaign activities	Challenges	Recommendations
Planners and implementers	– Free gifts – Leaflets – Posters – Surveys – Media – Public figures – Personalised advice – Solar clock	– Logistics – Weather conditions – Behaviour change – Adolescents – Myths – Pharmaceutical industry support – Promotion of sweepstakes – Skin screenings – Geographic coverage	– Diversification of campaign places – Additional support by the authorities – Volunteers clothing – VAT reduction on sunscreens – Partnership with other medical specialities – Awareness campaign – Social media
Audience	– Posters – Public figures – Personalised advice – Solar clock	– Survey duration – Social media – Posters format	– Social media – Live videos – Influencers – Workshops

- Planner: people involved in the strategic planning of the campaign
- Implementer: volunteers and non-volunteers who were in the field
- Audience: those people exposed to the campaign

Content analysis was used to analyse the data gathered from the interviews to fulfil the three main objectives proposed. To aid the understanding of the information extracted from the interviews the findings were organised in four tables. The first table (Table 3.2) presents the main topics mentioned by the interviewees. The remaining three tables are devoted to detailing the information on the three main categories of information analysed: (1) campaign activities that made a perceived positive impact on the audience (Table 3.3); (2) challenges (Table 3.4); (3) recommendations for future campaigns (Table 3.5).

Results

The interviews proved to be quite helpful in gaining a better understanding of what were the main challenges over the years, which activities were better received by the audience, and also to give space to suggestions for future campaigns. The interviewees at the planner and implementer level participated in the campaign from its first year (2003). The interviewees at the audience level reported being aware of, and having participated in, the 2016 and 2017 campaigns.

Table 3.3 presents detailed information regarding the campaigns that made a perceived positive impact on the audience, from the perspective of the planners,

Table 3.3 Campaign activities influencing a positive perception on the audience

Planners and implementers
– Gifts: *"The delivery of materials such as hats, activity books, t-shirts, and backpacks was important to attract the attention of the population"*. Catch people's attention, arouse their curiosity, attract more people to answer the survey because they feel their time is being rewarded; gifts (e.g. hats and shirts) appropriate for wearing immediately at the beach
– Leaflets: "E*veryone who stopped by our stand always took at least one leaflet that related more to its profile. They are quite small and compact, really easy to read."* Different topics to different audiences, such as "Sun and Summer", "Sun and Sports" and "Sun and Work"
– Posters: *"The posters are very appealing to arouse curiosity"*. Posters with more visual elements are more appealing; people usually stop by skimming through the information and ask additional questions about it
– Surveys: *"In general, people are polite and receptive to listening to advice, and as such, we feel a certain satisfaction for "teaching" people to change their behavior"*. People are happy to help and to find out more about the cause; some still try to escape because they worry the survey will take too much time
– Media: "*The media are fundamental to amplify the message*". Essential to disseminate the information to a large number of people and captivate the interest of the population to the campaign stand
– Public figures: *"Public figures help a lot in the dissemination/purpose of campaigns"*. Sport athletes (Rosa Mota, Paulo Guerra), TV shows presenters (Jorge Gabriel), soap opera actors and soap opera directors; extremely important to increase the impact of the message and the interest not only of the people at the beach but also of the people at home watching the news reports
– Personalised advice: The opportunity to talk personally to a dermatologist is something that is appreciated because the audience can clarify information or ask for advice; the audience becomes more open to receiving additional information when they have a specialist talking directly to them, giving them personalised advice
– Solar clock: *"People are not indifferent to it, they take a look at the clock and make some kind of comment: '—Look, we're going to the beach at the green hour'"*
Audience
– Posters: *"I think the posters caught my attention as they showed "not-so-pretty" images of skin moles. The fact that there were real images on the posters made me curious to find out what they were and how could I see if I also had moles similar to those"*. People stopped to find out more about the topic of the poster or to take a better look at the pictures, curious about the cause and what was happening
– Public figures: The presence of Rosa Mota (Winner of a marathon gold medal) attracted attention, as people wanted to learn why she was there; public figures make the campaign more "appealing" because they offer a chance for the audience to have a face-to-face conversation
– Personalised advice: *"[Something] I really appreciated on that day was the fact that I actually received advice on something I wasn't sure about: I run and play a lot of tennis outdoors and I wasn't sure if I was wearing the best clothing fabrics or colours. I was able to ask one of the medical doctors that were on the stand that explained to me what the best options for my activity would be"*. Offer solutions to sun-related questions or the concerns of the audience
– Solar clock: *"The solar clock was an interesting addition to the campaign (...) I didn't have to overthink what was the right time to go to the beach, it was right there, like a reminder/alert"*. Easy tool to remind people of the best of the day to go to the beach

Table 3.4 Challenges of the campaign

Planner and Implementer
– Logistics: *"The assembly of the entire stand in order to make it appealing and welcoming"*. Assemble the stand (tables, chairs, posters, mannequins, beach umbrella), in an appealing and not confusing way
– Weather conditions: *"Weather conditions with too much wind or heat influence the number of beach entries/exits"*. Extreme weather conditions (heat, wind) influence the number of people that go to the beach that day, influencing the number of people that answer the survey and are exposed to the campaign materials
– Behaviour change: *"We feel like we are swimming against the tide because we still are very few contributing to the important disclosure of the health risks of excessive exposure to ultraviolet radiation"*. People still find that being tanned is good and beautiful and have difficulty changing schedules and having appropriate sun-related behaviours; a large number of people might be aware of the problem, but they are still unwilling to change their behaviour towards the sun
– Adolescents: *"Find the right way to communicate with adolescents and convince them that it is in their best interest to change their sun protection behaviors has proven to be a very difficult challenge"*. Hardest group to target because they are less willing to be involved in the campaign and to change their behaviours, particularly if that change influences their routines with their friends (e.g. going to the beach at a different time than their friends go is a significant barrier for adolescents)
– Myths: *"Some people still think that the sun at the beach is more dangerous than elsewhere"*. Some people still think that the sun is less dangerous at the park, at the pool, running or working outdoor, so they use less sun protection comparing to when they go to the beach
– Pharmaceutical industry support: There is only support for sunscreen promotion and not for the use of appropriate clothing, hats, or looking for places with shade
– Promotion of sweepstakes: *"When we promote the sweepstake, some people think it is nothing new, it is not very functional and not very practical as the participants need to be at the stand when we announce the winner"*. It doesn't work clearly and functionally, because people might not be at the beach when the winner is announced
– Skin screenings: A false impression among the audience that the campaign is all about skin screenings or free consultations; the space of the stand doesn't offer the appropriate tools and light for the complete observation of patients
– Geographic coverage: Physical limitations as the campaign materials cannot reach people who are only in the swimming pools during summer; to fill this gap, in 2018 APCC chose to take a tour through Portugal with stops at the river and coastal beaches
Audience
– Survey duration: *"At first, I wasn't 100% on board for the interview because I didn't know exactly how long it would take, if it would be 2–3 min or really 20 min long"*. People were not aware of how long it would take to answer it; their first instinct was not to answer and say they were not interested in participating
– Social media: *"I wanted to share some photos I took the campaign on social media and I wanted to tag the association that was promoting, but I didn't find them on social media"*. No social media presence; difficult to keep track of what going on the stand has access to the flyers, posters, and additional advice after the campaign day
– Posters' format: Too much text, sometimes with a font size too small to be seen at a longer distance. With longer texts, people were not willing to spend so much time reading them, they just read the titles and subtitles

Table 3.5 Recommendations for the future

Planner and Implementer
– Diversification of campaign places: *"APCC should maintain the initiatives it has carried out in 2018, that is, take the initiatives to several cities/districts, to river beaches, to the most forgotten regions in Portugal. Much more visibility is achieved and allows you to get to know the whole country and its different needs"*. Raising awareness of sun care in different places (besides the traditional place, that is, the beach) is important to create involvement at a national level for further visibility and amplification of the message
– Additional support by the authorities: With the pressure of the increasing number of skin cancers and the costs associated with it growing exponentially, there will be more of a political and social impact, drawing more attention to skin cancer-related issues
– Volunteers' clothing: All the volunteers, on the day of the campaign, could add to the APCC shirts they usually wear a catchy phrase, a slogan, or something else that creates an identity and makes an impact
– VAT reduction on sunscreens: Promotion of a petition to reduce the VAT on sunscreens, from the normal rate (23%) to the reduced rate (6%); inform the media about it to raise awareness
– Partnership with other medical specialities: Partnerships with other medical specialties, e.g. ophthalmology; by having access to ophthalmology materials, the campaign would have additional relevant content for the audience, raising awareness to the impact of sun exposure to the eyes
– Awareness campaign: "Campaign focus should be more of an awareness campaign about skin cancer early diagnosis using the skin self-exam". Higher focus on raising awareness for early diagnosis, that is self-examination and guidance to family doctors
– Social media: Invest on social media to reach its audience better and provide relevant content for its followers; improve the APCC website to make it more responsive and user-friendly
Audience
– Social media: *"Create social media profiles and share a lot of content about the cause and the campaign, live videos would be great!"* Use of social media to give information on sun protection behaviours and to share content throughout the year, and not only on the campaign day; fundamental networks: Facebook, Instagram, and YouTube
– Live videos: Create engagement and create curiosity about the campaign; a good tool to attract more people to the campaign location and it also helps people that can't be physically present at the location to feel part of the campaign
– Influencers: Invite influencers that match the target audience characteristics to the campaign day and ask them to create posts about sun protection behaviours before/after the campaign
– Workshops: *"I definitely would be interested in attending small workshops (around 15 min) where we could listen to more practical information and ask questions"*. To explain more complex information (e.g. self-examination and the amount of sunscreen to apply), medical doctors could do live demonstrations of these topics addressing the doubts of the audience

implementers, and of the members of the audience. As planners and implementers have almost identical opinions the responses were grouped.

It is interesting to highlight that when evaluating the campaign activities the three groups of interviewees pointed out as extremely positive the use of posters, the presence of public figures, the offer of personalised advice by the volunteers to the audience, and the presence of the solar clock at the entrance to the beach. Table 3.4 details the main challenges faced in the campaign identified by the interviewees.

It is important to notice that the challenges identified by the planners and implementers do not overlap with any of the challenges identified by the audience. The insights on recommendations for the future are described in Table 3.5.

APCC should invest in their social media profiles, using social media power to more efficiently communicate with the target audience since many of them are addicted to its use.

Conclusions

Marketing gives marketers tools to do good for their community and society, providing them with the power to change behaviours for the better. Social marketing offers key tools for designing well-structured and effective campaigns that can influence people's behaviours, helping society to fight the problems imposed by skin cancer on the quality of people's lives. These campaigns are influenced by the concept of QoL of the target audience, that is, the perception of individuals and society concerning their standard of living and wellbeing. If marketers understand the main factors underlying the audience's wellbeing and their characteristics and needs, the campaign will have a higher chance of being successful at changing behaviour.

A strategy that combines listening to the experience of the people involved in previous campaigns, as well as exploring the linkages between the theoretical constructs of the Health Belief Model—namely the perceived susceptibility, perceived severity, perceived benefits, and perceived barriers and the individuals' perception on the importance of adopting a positive response to social marketing campaigns appeals—may help promoters and public health agents to improve QoL. Since cultural factors are absent from the HBM model, different approaches are needed to understand which cultural and societal factors need to be addressed to improve the success of social marketing campaigns aimed at improving QoL.

In the case of APCC, it is advisable to follow a strategic social marketing plan such as the one proposed by Silva and Silva (2012) concerning analysis, planning, implementation, strategy, budget, and control, which the promoter may use also to evaluate the campaign results and to improve the likelihood of success, framed upon a robust theoretical model.

Concerning the offline strategy, it is advisable to use posters which are simple, with a strong visual appeal, a clean look, and easy to understand taglines. It is important that when the target audience passes by, they are curious about the content and see that the content is relevant to them. The use of gifts is recommended as it has proven in the past to elicit a positive reaction from the audience. Gifts must act as cues to action to behaviour change. Offering sunscreen samples could also be a good way to convince people to apply sunscreen even if they did not bring their sunscreen to the beach. Moreover, the use of technology is highly attractive to adolescents and sometimes they just "need to see to believe". By using UV cameras (add a UV photography compatible lenses to a camera) in the campaign, the effect of UV rays is directly visible on the skin and shows that sun protection makes a genuine difference, as you can see at that moment whether you are using the sufficient amount of sunscreen on your face and body.

Additionally, for the online strategy, APCC must invest in social media marketing plan to identify and engage with the target audience by sharing relevant and updated content with followers, on its actions and the risks of ignoring the danger associated with overexposure to the sun. As has been seen in previous campaigns developed by APCC, the presence of public figures is very much appreciated. Bearing this in mind, APCC should find influencers that are close to the target audience and who share its values concerning safe sun-related behaviours.

The use of social marketing to promote healthy behaviours towards the sun is imperative, especially targeting adolescents (at-risk group) who have shown greater resistance to behaviour change so far.

Final Remarks

In 2019, APCC pursued the awareness campaign promoted in 2018. The campaign took place on different beaches, parks, and other relevant locations throughout Portugal. The campaign lasted one day in each location, with the presence of dermatologists and pharmacists. During that day, several materials were available for the audience: the children's book "Brinca e Aprende com o Zé Pintas" ("Play and Learn with Jo Spots", in English), informational flyers, posters. Additionally, there were informational sessions where the audience could discuss relevant topics with the dermatologists, such as "How to perform a skin self-exam". APCC believes this is an effective strategy to reach a wider audience in a personalised format. In the meantime, due to Covid-19, in 2020 APCC had to make some changes to its summer skin cancer prevention campaign. As an example, APCC kept its partnerships with the municipalities by placing outdoors/mupi throughout Portugal to raise awareness of the dangers of overexposure to the sun. The APCC website was also updated with the latest updates on informational flyers, as well as the new edition of the children's book "Brinca e Aprende com o Zé Pintas".

Discussion Questions

1. What do you think is the degree of concern about skin cancer at an international level nowadays?
2. Has any information related to skin cancer been provided in your country? If so, what kind of information has been provided? Where does the information come from (e.g., medical sources, governmental sources, the mass media, others)?

3. What social marketing campaigns related to skin cancer have been promoted in your country? How long did they last or have lasted so far? How do they communicate with the target audience?
4. What kind of strategy would you choose for a social marketing campaign related to skin cancer that targets adolescents?

Teaching Notes

1. **What do you think is the degree of concern about skin cancer at an international level nowadays?**
   The purpose of this question is to analyse whether students are aware of what skin cancer is and how they can prevent it, as well as relevant data such as mortality rates. Moreover, this question aims to understand if students are concerned about skin cancer or if they believe that it is not dangerous; do they believe skin cancer is an international concern or only applies to certain countries? Are they familiar with international initiatives around skin cancer prevention?
2. **Has any information related to skin cancer been provided in your country? If so, what kind of information has been provided? Where does the information come from (e.g., medical sources, governmental sources, the mass media, others)?**
   The idea of this question is to identify the main sources of information about skin cancer. Understand how students did find out about skin cancer, where can they find information about skin cancer statistics regarding their country. It would also be interesting to discuss the different skin cancer prevention awareness campaigns in different countries.
3. **What social marketing campaigns related to skin cancer have been promoted in your country? How long did they last or have lasted so far? How do they communicate with the target audience?**
   The question aims to delve further into the topic of skin cancer social marketing. The idea is to discover if those campaigns are a public or private initiative, if the campaign is focused on offline or online strategy, who the students believe to be the target audience of these campaigns and how do they feel impacted by these campaigns.
4. **What kind of strategy would you choose for a social marketing campaign related to skin cancer that targets adolescents?**
   The idea of this question is to discuss strategies and creative concepts of skin cancer social marketing campaigns that target adolescents. For example, if the students wanted to change adolescents' behaviour towards the sun, i.e. influence them to be outdoors at the sun at appropriate hours, to use sunscreen, hats,... How would they communicate with this audience? Would they give out any free materials to promote a certain behaviour? What would their online and offline strategy include?

References

Alves HM, Galan-Ladero MM (2019) Theoretical background: introduction to social marketing. In: Galan-Ladero MM, Alves HM (eds) Case studies on social marketing. Springer International, pp 1–10. https://doi.org/10.1007/978-3-030-04843-3_1

APCC – Associação Portuguesa de Cancro Cutâneo (2019) Associação Portuguesa de Cancro Cutâneo – APCC. http://www.apcancrocutaneo.pt. Accessed 28 Dec 2019

Brennan L, Binney W, Parker L, Aleti T, Nguyen D (2014) Social marketing and behaviour change: models, theory and applications. Edward Elgar. https://books.google.pt/books?id=uCqlBQAAQBAJ

Gallivan J, Lising M, Ammary NJ, Greenberg R (2007) The National Diabetes Education Program's "control your diabetes. For life." Campaign: design, implementation, and lessons learned. Soc Mark Q 13(4):65–82. https://doi.org/10.1080/15245000701678453

Janz NK, Becker MH (1984) The health belief model: a decade later. Health Educ Q 11(1):1–47. https://doi.org/10.1177/109019818401100101

Koch S, Pettigrew S, Hollier LP, Slevin T, Strickland M, Minto C, Lin C et al (2016) Trends in Australian adolescents' sun-protection behaviors: implications for health campaigns. Aust N Z J Public Health 40(5):468–473. https://doi.org/10.1111/1753-6405.12561

Rodrigues A, Fernandes-Machado S, Neves Alves M, Corrêa MP, Correia O, Césarini P (2014) Sun-protection amongst Portuguese children and adolescents: a cross-sectional study. Psicol Saúde Doença 15(3). https://doi.org/10.15309/14psd150321

Rosenstock IM (1974) Historical origins of the health belief model. Health Educ Monogr 2 (4):328–335. https://doi.org/10.1177/109019817400200403

Silva SC, Silva MF (2012) Failure is a stepping stone for success. Int Rev Public Nonprofit Market 9(2):153–179. https://doi.org/10.1007/s12208-012-0084-2

Stretcher V, Rosenstock IM (1997) The health belief model. In: Glanz K, Lewis FM, Rimer BK (eds) Health behaviour and health education: theory, research and practice. Jossey-Bass, San Francisco

Tonon G (ed) (2015) Qualitative studies in quality of life methodology and practice. Social indicators research series, vol 55. Springer, Heidelberg

World Cancer Research Fund (2019) Skin cancer statistics. https://www.wcrf.org/dietandcancer/cancer-trends/skin-cancer-statistics. Accessed 18 Feb 2019

World Health Organization (2020) Skin cancers. https://www.who.int/uv/faq/skincancer/en/index1.html. Accessed 02-02-2020

Wymer W (2011) Developing more effective social marketing strategies. J Soc Mark 1(1):17–31. https://doi.org/10.1108/20426761111104400

Chapter 4
Quality of Life as an Outcome Disclosure of Positive Appeals in Social Advertisements: The Case of HIV/Aids Prevention Campaigns

Beatriz Casais and João F. Proença

Abstract This chapter illustrates examples of how social advertising campaigns for HIV/AIDS prevention express quality of life as an outcome of behavioural change. The authors take the perspective of the gain-frame appeals in the message to promote quality of life and present examples of positive appealed social advertisements that show how positive appeals are expressed in the narrative and the claims of social ads. The cases analysed were extracted from a database of 375 social advertisements aimed at preventing HIV/AIDS from Germany, France, Italy and Portugal that were broadcast in the first 30 years of the epidemic—from 1981 to 2011. The chapter discusses how quality of life is promoted in these cases of health-related social marketing through the language used. Particularly, the examples express positive appeals according to the theory of social norms. This understanding may help social marketers to take decisions in the future with the knowledge of previous examples of positive appeals in social marketing messages to promote quality of life.

Keywords Positive appeals · Social advertisements · Quality of life (QoL) · Behaviour change · HIV/AIDS prevention

---

B. Casais (✉)
University of Minho, Braga, Portugal
e-mail: bcasais@eeg.uminho.pt

J. F. Proença
University of Porto, Porto, Portugal

University of Lisbon, Lisbon, Portugal
e-mail: jproenca@fep.up.pt

M. M. Galan-Ladero, R. G. Rivera (eds.), *Applied Social Marketing and Quality of Life*, Applying Quality of Life Research,
https://doi.org/10.1007/978-3-030-83286-5_4

Introduction

Social advertisements on television are important tools of social marketing and tend to be designed in reaction to epidemic dynamics (Casais and Proença 2018). Social advertisements are built with appeals for social change, which may be expressed positively or negatively according to the intention of guiding behaviours (Brennan and Binney 2010). Positive appeals aim to show the direct benefits and gains of behaviour change as an incentive for the desired action. Negative appeals describe losses and unintended consequences of certain attitudes and behaviours by creating psychic discomfort.

This distinction follows the assumptions of Prospect Theory (Tversky and Kahneman 1981), which considers the existence of gain-framed and loss-framed messages that affect the risk-seeking and the risk-averse attitudes (Rothman et al. 1993). The loss-frame is related to negative appeals that activate fear and threat through shocking graphic contents (Casais and Proença 2015). The purpose is to create shame and guilt (Brennan and Binney 2010) and fear or compassion (Gomes and Casais 2018) to provoke a behaviour change reaction (Das et al. 2020). The gain-frame is related to positive appeals that incentivise behaviour change and show the quality of life achieved with the desired social behaviours and attitudes (Brennan and Binney 2010). Positive appeals are based on humour, irony, hope, portraying benefits and using celebrities or social models who activate the coping response (Hastings et al. 2004; Lewis et al. 2007). Positive appeals have effectiveness in health behaviours over longer periods of time by increasing perceptions about their benefits for individual quality of life and for a better society (Basu and Wang 2009; Chiang et al. 2018; O'Keefe and Jensen 2008). Positive appeals have the advantage of reducing stigma and discrimination associated with illness or high-risk populations by not showing shocking images. The use of positive appeals in health-related social marketing may reduce traumatic symptoms in people who have already suffered from the diseases in question (Lewis et al. 2007; Slavin et al. 2007).

Positive appeals tend to show that the desired behaviour is the one society as a whole expects as being the general norm of behaviour. This perspective is conceptualised in the social norms' theory that proclaims that behaviours taken by citizens are a consequence of the generalised social norms considered in society (Burchell et al. 2013). With that purpose, social marketing appeals should promote behaviour change as a natural process to the normality expected by society.

The gain and loss frame perspectives have been widely researched in social marketing, particularly in the way social marketing appeals take form and regarding their effectiveness in behaviour change (Hastings et al. 2004). There are inconclusive findings about the most effective appeals in social marketing (Lewis et al. 2007). Researchers have shown that it depends on individual characteristics of the targets and the ability to manage emotional information (Taute et al. 2011). However, the results also depend on the involvement with the cause (Yoon and Tinkham 2013) and the context (Teng et al. 2019). This chapter explores the perspective of gain-frame appeals in social marketing to promote quality of life under the assumptions of social norms' theory as an incentive for behaviour change.

Case Development

HIV/AIDS is a good example to explore how social advertisements present positive appeals to promote quality of life. It represents a global problem for which a wide number of social marketing interventions have been developed by both public services and non-governmental organisations (NGOs). Also, the fact that HIV prevention ads involving the discussion of fracturing issues, as well as stigma and discrimination linked to the disease, may concern social marketers and public policy makers and lead them to avoid targeting strong threat messages to the most at-risk populations and to prefer incentives and not stigmatise positive appeals. That stigma persists nowadays despite science realising that HIV infection is a global epidemic that can be transmitted by basic unprotected behaviours of any human-being (Merson et al. 2008). Nevertheless, people have moved away from prevention programmes because of the lack of conscious self-vulnerability (Gruskin et al. 2007). Fighting HIV/AIDS infection, including fighting against HIV discrimination, is a public policy challenge worldwide and one of the UN's millennium goals.

This chapter shows the case of positive appeals used in the narratives and claims of 375 national HIV prevention advertisements from four European countries broadcast on TV since the diagnosis of the infection in 1981 to the end of 2011. This 30 year period represents the most concerning period of the life cycle of disease in Europe when there was a consistent policy of developing HIV prevention campaigns on television of which 146 were from France (38.9%), 115 from Germany (30.7%), 76 from Portugal (20.3%) and 38 from Italy (10.1%). The selected database of social advertisements has been previously analysed in the perspective of the response to epidemic dynamics and represents a reactive response of social marketers to the evolution of cases in terms of target and messages (Casais and Proença 2018).

This chapter explores the narrative and the claims used in those advertisements and shows the words and expressions used to express incentives for behaviour change. The words and expressions relate to the gain frame of social marketing and the way quality of life is expressed as an outcome of behaviour change. Besides the gain frame, the words and expressions also represent the desired behaviour that should be seen as a social norm and not requiring a behaviour change campaign in the future because it is the behaviour expected and predominant in society and relates to the theory of social norms.

The authors used a content analysis model previously tested to classify positive and negative appeals in social advertisements (Casais and Proença 2015). The authors coded the narratives and claims in 'NVivo' software and conducted a content analysis in line with the categories of the mentioned model: words were coded as positive when related to life, health, smile, love, respect, protect, prevent, treat, good,

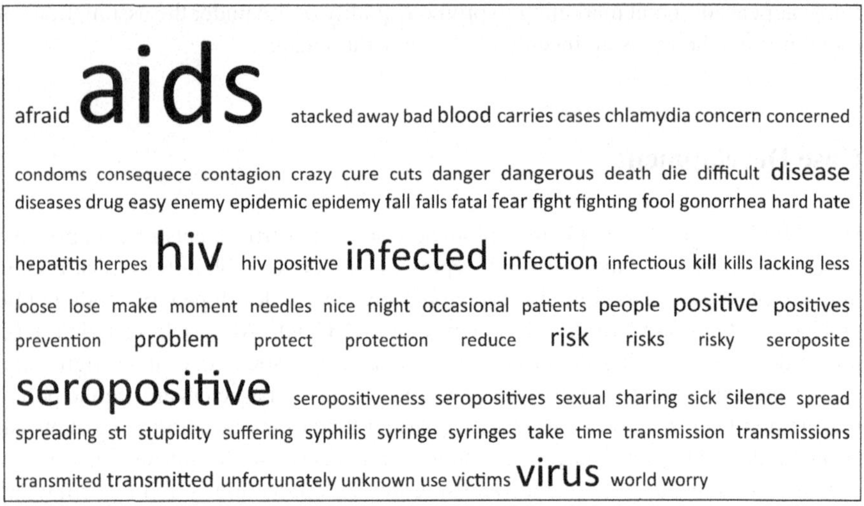

Fig. 4.1 Word cloud of negative words in the narrative of analysed ads. Source: Authors. Nvivo Output

responsibility, copy, save, gains, intended, efficacy; words were coded as negative when related to death, disease, illness, danger, fatality, fear, guilt, shame, risk, losses, bad, consequences, threat, unintended effects.

The authors found that the narrative was negative in 33.9% of the data and the remaining ads expressed positive appeals in the narrative. The coding process was contextually sensitive both in terms of cultural semantics and syntax. For instance, the word "drugs" was sometimes coded as negative when the contextual meaning was connoted with a higher risk of HIV transmission by its use, and sometimes it was coded as positive when concerning AIDS treatment therapies. Another example is the word "positive," which can mean having a positive life or being HIV positive, depending on the context.

Figures 4.1 and 4.2 show the word clouds of negative and positive codes, respectively. Word clouds are outputs of content analysis and represent the prevalence of words in the text. Note that the bigger the font size, the higher the prevalence the word has in the analysed text. Negative words are highly related with names of diseases and disease risks while positive words are related with protection practices. The word clouds help to understand how quality of life is expressed in positive words and show the positive outcomes of taking the intended behaviours. As can be seen, quality of life is shown in the positive appealed word cloud with the assumptions of a normal and happy life and not as an exception for those people who need to take special health concerns. Positive appeals show that everyone should be committed to the cause and the normal and expected behaviour leads to quality of life.

The word cloud of positive narrative shows that positive appeals for social change are associated with quality of life and express feelings of love, happiness, friendship, pleasure, and safe protection. Positive appeals relate to the prevention of the disease,

Fig. 4.2 Word cloud of positive words in the narrative of analysed ads. Source: Authors. Nvivo output

the solidarity towards seropositive people and the treatment, considering that AIDS is a chronic disease with which it is possible to live with a relative quality of life. When comparing positive with negative words, we can see the difference between the gain and the loss frame in social marketing. Positive words express confidence and hope in the future while negative appeals are based on the fear and threat of suffering.

When analysing the slogans and claims of the ads organized in Table 4.1 by country and year, this idea is also perceived. Positive claims express the assumptions of the social norms' theory, which represents the behaviour that should be normal in a society and for that reason implies behaviour change. The condom use as an ordinary behaviour in life and as a meaning of love, security and happiness is highly expressed in the claims and contradicts the traditional campaigns that posited condom use as a mandatory action to prevent the danger of sexual transmitted diseases. Equality, solidarity, and non-discrimination behaviours are also expressed in the narrative and slogans as evidence of the social norms' theory.

Table 4.1 Positive appealed claims used in social ads

Claim	Country	Year
Condoms preserve everything but love	France	1989
Condoms wish you nice holidays	France	1989
Condoms. Nowadays everyone says yes	France	1983
People living with HIV have a life, friends, love, projects like you and me	France	1995
One can love, be loved and be HIV-positive	France	1995
A person living with HIV who is socially integrated is someone who lives better	France	1995
You're lucky you can still decide to avoid AIDS	France	1995
AIDS. Today we can do a lot, but nothing without you	France	1998
Treat seropositives as the boss. Exactly like any other employer	France	2001
And if condom was a product like others? Condoms. Think about it	France	2003
Love is a pleasure to share	France	2006
Explore. Just Protect yourself	France	2010
The future is ours. Act now	France	2010
Don't give Aids a chance	Germany	1987–2011
Out of all gestures of love, a gesture of love	Italy	2009
Seropositives live, love, work and fight everyday just like everyone. And they must be legally protected from abuses and discrimination of social, sanitarian or labour character (Law 135/90)	Italy	2009
Before you become pregnant, consult your doctor. Be the carrier of a healthy child	Portugal	1991
Condoms—you may not die from love of them but use them because love is to be lived	Portugal	1993
There is only one way to know. Take the HIV/AIDS test	Portugal	2005

Source: Authors

Positive claims express incentives to change behaviour and show the promise of a better quality of life with hope, love, happiness, and health. In fact, these assumptions of quality of life and social marketing may be an important technique to promote quality of life in society. One important message connected to quality of life expressed in the claims is the solidarity towards people living with HIV and the need to fight stigma and discrimination. This perspective shows that tolerance and equality in rights are part of a society with quality of life and that social marketing is important to promote those attitudes and behaviours as part of a social norm.

Interestingly, Germany used the same claim for decades. "Don't give Aids a chance" is a strong slogan and shows that prevention leads to quality of live and citizens have the power to prevent the disease by taking preventive behaviours considered the social norm.

Conclusions

This chapter explored the case of HIV prevention messages to show how positive appeals in social marketing may promote quality of life. A selection of social advertisements from four European countries that represent a longitudinal perspective of the first 30 years of the epidemic present an interesting perspective on how social norms are manifested in social marketing messages to promote quality of life.

The analysis conducted shows that positive appeals express quality of life and explore the gains of behaviour change for a better future with love, happiness, health, and solidarity. The case explores the importance of reducing stigma and discrimination connected to the disease as an important step to creating a society with quality of life and values of equality and solidarity. Also, social marketing positive appeals express how preventing HIV/AIDS, wearing condoms or testing are part of the social normality and the expected behaviours in society and which correspond to the assumptions of the theory of social norms.

Following the model used to code the content analysis conducted, the authors suggest that social marketers who look for promoting quality of life through the gain frame perspective in social advertisements may use signs that represent life, health, smile, love, respect, protect, prevent, treat, good, responsibility, copy, save, gains, intended, efficacy. These representations should be shown in scenes figuring a social normality and revealing the expectations of the whole society instead of a difficult change that must be made because of a danger and threat.

Discussion Questions

1. Identify in Table 4.1 the claims representing the theory of social norms.
2. How do you think the claims express quality of life with incentives for behaviour change?
3. Do you think that social marketing using positive appeals to express quality of life are the most or the least prevalent direction used in your country?
4. Do you think that there are differences in the expression of quality of life through social marketing appeals according to the social marketing topic?

Acknowledgement João F. Proença gratefully acknowledges financial support from FCT-Fundação para a Ciência e Tecnologia (Portugal), national funding through research grant UIDB/04521/2020.

Teaching Notes

The case was developed to be discussed in a social marketing course with the main purpose of describing the following topics:

1. Social marketing narrative;
2. Social norms' theory;
3. Positive appeals in social marketing as an element of quality of life.

Students are asked to look at the examples shown to discuss how positive appeals express quality of life and how the narrative implies the theory of social norms. Further, a discussion in class is promoted on cultural differences in the use of positive appeals in social marketing to express quality of life.

Question 1—***Identify in*** Table 4.1 ***the claims representing the theory of social norms.***

Students are called to discuss each claim in Table 4.1 and explain how it promotes an ordinary and expected behaviour considered as a social norm and not an exception only directed to vulnerable populations.

Question 2—***How do you think the claims express quality of life with incentives for behaviour change?***

Expressing the desired behaviours as a social norm and promoting them with words associated to happiness, love, solidarity, friendship and protection, quality of life is highly expressed with positive social marketing appeals.

Question 3—***Do you think that social marketing using with positive appeals to express quality of life are the most or the least prevalent direction used in your country?***

Students are called on to look at the country differences expressed in Table 4.1 and discuss the strategies of social marketing in their own country and whether positive or negative appeals are highly used. Further, students may discuss the consequences of the prevalence of positive and negative appeals in their country in terms of the perception of the outcome of quality of life connected to behaviour change.

Question 4—***Do you think that there are differences in the expression of quality of life through social marketing appeals according to the social marketing topic?***

This case expresses the use of positive appeals to promote quality of life in HIV prevention social marketing campaigns. Students may discuss other topics in which this technique could also be adequate and other social marketing topics that might be more effective with fear and threat appeals.

References

Basu A, Wang J (2009) The role of branding in public health campaigns. J Commun Manag 13 (1):77–91

Brennan L, Binney W (2010) Fear, guilt, and shame appeals in social marketing. J Bus Res 63 (2):140–146

Burchell K, Rettie R, Patel K (2013) Marketing social norms: social marketing and the 'social norm approach'. J Consum Behav 12(1):1–9

Casais B, Proença JF (2015) A model to classify television social advertisements according to their use of positive appeals. In: Banks I, DePelsmacker P, Okazaki S (eds) Advances in advertising research, vol 5. Springer, Wiesbaden

Casais B, Proença JF (2018) Social advertisements for public health and epidemic dynamics: a study based on HIV/AIDS prevention television advertisements in four European countries. J Soc Mark 8(4):397–420

Chiang K-P, Chan A, Milan R (2018) Social marketing and advertising appeals: on perception and intention to purchase condoms among college students. Int J Healthcare Manage 11(2):71–78

Das S, Dutta A, Mudgal A, Datta S (2020) Non-fear-based road safety campaign as a community service: contexts from social media. In: Rautaray SS, Eichler G, Fahrnberger G (eds) Innovations for community services. Springer International, pp 1–17

Gomes RF, Casais B (2018) Feelings generated by threat appeals in social marketing: text and emoji analysis of user reactions to anorexia nervosa campaigns in social media. Int Rev Public Nonprofit Market 15(4):591–607

Gruskin S, Mills EJ, Tarantola D (2007) History, principles, and practice of health and human rights. Lancet 370:449–455

Hastings G, Stead M, Webb J (2004) Fear appeals in social marketing: strategic and ethical reasons for concern. Psychol Mark 21(11):961–986

Lewis IM, Watson B, White KM, Tay R (2007) Promoting public health messages: should we move beyond fear-evoking appeals in road safety? Qual Health Res 17(1):61–74

Merson MH, O'Malley J, Serwadda D, Apisuk C (2008) The history and challenge of HIV prevention. Lancet 372(9637):475–488

O'Keefe DJ, Jensen JD (2008) Do loss-framed persuasive messages engender greater message processing than do gain-framed messages? A meta-analytic review. Commun Stud 59(1):51–67

Rothman AJ, Salovey P, Antone C, Keough K, Martin CD (1993) The influence of message framing on intentions to perform health behaviors. J Exp Soc Psychol 29:408–433

Slavin S, Batrouney C, Murphy D (2007) Fear appeals and treatment side-effects: an effective combination for HIV prevention? AIDS Care 19(1):130–137

Taute HA, McQuitty S, Sautter EP (2011) Emotional information management and responses to emotional appeals. J Advert 40(3):31–44

Teng L, Zhao G, Li F, Liu L, Shen L (2019) Increasing the persuasiveness of anti-drunk driving appeals: the effect of negative and positive message framing. J Bus Res 103(October):240–249

Tversky A, Kahneman D (1981) The framing of decisions and the psychology of choice. Science 211(4481):453–458

Yoon JH, Tinkham SF (2013) Humorous threat persuasion in advertising: the effects of humor, threat intensity, and issue involvement. J Advert 42(1):30–41

Chapter 5
COVID-19 Pandemic and Social Marketing: Enhancing Quality of Life in a Global Health Crisis

M. Mercedes Galan-Ladero, Reynaldo G. Rivera, Enrique Bianchi, Edy Lorena Burbano, Helena Alves, Jose Luis Vazquez-Burguete, and Maria Purificacion Garcia-Miguelez

Abstract In this case, an international group of scholars analyze the role of social marketing in the face of the COVID-19 pandemic: how it was applied, its effectiveness, and its effects on people's quality of life. To this purpose, authors carried out an exploratory analysis in four countries which share cultural commonalities: Argentina, Colombia, Portugal, and Spain, exploring the institutional campaigns implemented especially in the first months of the pandemic. They were then compared, to find similarities and differences between them.

These campaigns were characterized by applying a health belief model mostly based on simple, clear, short, repetitive, homogeneous, consistent messages, focused on informing about COVID-19 symptoms and how to behave to prevent contagion (e.g. hygiene measures to follow). In addition, there was a call to citizens for a joint

M. M. Galan-Ladero (✉)
University of Extremadura, Badajoz, Spain
e-mail: mgalan@unex.es

R. G. Rivera
Austral University, Buenos Aires, Argentina
e-mail: rrivera@austral.edu.ar

E. Bianchi
National University of Cordoba, Cordoba, Argentina
e-mail: enrique.carlos.bianchi@unc.edu.ar

E. L. Burbano
University of San Buenaventura Cali, Cali, Colombia
e-mail: elburban@usbcali.edu.co

H. Alves
University of Beira Interior, Covilhã, Portugal
e-mail: halves@ubi.pt

J. L. Vazquez-Burguete · M. P. Garcia-Miguelez
University of Leon, Leon, Spain
e-mail: jose-luis.vazquez@unileon.es; mpgarm@unileon.es

M. M. Galan-Ladero, R. G. Rivera (eds.), *Applied Social Marketing and Quality of Life*, Applying Quality of Life Research,
https://doi.org/10.1007/978-3-030-83286-5_5

action to avoid community transmission of this disease. Another characteristic was the use of different tones, ranging from imperative to purely informational, and with emotional appeals in some cases. And finally, it is worth noting that these campaigns were cross-media, using all types of available media (legacy and interactive ones), and the collaboration of celebrities and influencers.

Keywords Social marketing campaigns · Public health emergency or international concern (PHEIC) · Pandemic · COVID-19 · SARS-CoV2 · Prevention campaigns · Awareness campaigns · Quality of life (QOL)

Introduction

The disease caused by the SARS-CoV2 virus (COVID-19)[1] became a global disease in early 2020. It was initially thought that, as it had already happened on previous occasions, it was a new epidemic located in China that would remain as a "local" problem (there would only be some imported cases in other countries, which could be quickly controlled). However, the determination of a Public Health Emergency of International Concern (PHEIC) made by the World Health Organization (WHO) in the face of the rapid spread of the virus triggered all the alarms worldwide. Journalism played a key role reporting about the pandemic and its seriousness even before several governments.

The fact that news from China began to leak (related to the situation that was being experienced in that country), as well as the appearance in the international press of images of people who died in the streets of Wuhan (victims of the virus—AFP 2020), or news about the drastic measures taken in some Chinese cities such as walling up the homes of infected people to prevent the spread of the virus (Chaparro 2020), and the rapid construction of new hospitals in the city of Wuhan in record time, increased fear and uncertainty about what was really happening. Simultaneously policy makers were forced to take action in order to protect people's lives, especially in developing countries.

The quick spread of the coronavirus to new geographical areas,[2] its lethality and the serious consequences of the disease in many infected people, the lack of information about the virus,[3] the uncertainty about its different forms of transmission

---

[1] "*Observing best practices, that name was chosen to avoid inaccuracies and stigmatization; therefore, it does not refer to a geographical location, an animal, a person or a group of people*" (WHO 2020).

[2] The cases of contagion were more and more numerous, with an exponential growth. Being a new coronavirus, the population had never been exposed to it, so had no immunity.

[3] Although initially it was thought that the focus was on a seafood and fish market in the city of Wuhan (China), it has subsequently been discarded, although it has been confirmed that the virus spread through that place (RTVE.es 2020). It is believed that it arose from some type of bat, but at the end of 2020 it was not yet known whether it had subsequently mutated into some other animal before passing to humans (RTVE.es 2020).

and the real dimension of the problem (the actual incidence of cases), the lack of international planning and coordination (despite the alerts made by organizations like the World Economic Forum), as well as the lack of availability of valid tests for the diagnosis of the virus, and the fact that there were no vaccines or specific treatments available or preventive therapies to protect the most vulnerable groups (the poor, elderly and people with other pathologies, mainly), caused deep international concern at all levels (health, political, economic, and social ones).

The collapse of health systems in many countries, and particularly the saturation of Intensive Care Units (ICUs) in hospitals, led to having to build field hospitals alongside the reference hospital centers, and even to adapt hotels as hospitals and create temporary health facilities (e.g. in sports centers, fair spaces, etc.)[4] to accommodate the growing number of people who required medical attention. On the other hand, the shortage of medical supplies (e.g. Personal Protective Equipment—PPE: masks, gloves, gowns, ...; alcohol and other disinfectants, etc.) in hospitals in the first months, increased the number of infections among healthcare personnel. The situation was particularly dramatic in Latin America but also in some European countries.

To try to stop, or at least slow down, the spread of the virus, compulsory social isolation and home confinement were reached in practically every country in the world. This lockdown led to the suspension of most of the usual activities: formal education (which switched to online mode), physical presence in the workplace (which switched to teleworking, whenever possible) and commercial activities (non-essential stores and establishments had to close). Major international events were also canceled or delayed: important sporting events were postponed, such as the Tokyo 2020 Olympic Games and various world or continental championships; business events, such as trade shows and conferences; cultural events, such as concerts, shows, etc.; multitudinous fiestas and celebrations, such as the Venice Carnival or the processions of Easter week in Spain; and even face-to-face religious worship activities were prohibited. In addition, tourism was paralyzed with the closure of borders, the cancellation of flights, the closure of museums and monuments, hospitality and nightlife venues, hotels, etc.

At the end of 2020, most of the mass media and online social networks continued to have, as a central argument, the different strategies implemented by governments to control the second wave of the pandemic. Meanwhile, the first vaccines started to appear (approved in less than 12 months with emergency protocols), which began to be distributed especially in developed countries. The COVID-19 pandemic maintained its risk at a global level and virus infections continued to be reported in countries around the world, with second and successive waves of infections, as

[4]E.g. In Madrid (Spain), the IFEMA Exhibition Center was adapted as a hospital for COVID-19 patients in the first wave. Later, in the second wave, on December 1, 2020, the Hospital "Nurse Isabel Zendal" was inaugurated, also in Madrid. The hospital was built in only 100 days to assume the bulk of the care burden of hospitalizations in the ward, keeping all patients infected by COVID-19 that require hospitalization, and thus free up public hospitals, avoiding potential infections from other patients and professionals during hospitalization (Becares, 2020; Roces, 2020).

Table 5.1 Chronology of COVID-19 evolution

Date	Fact
31st December, 2019	WHO first learned of this new virus, following a report of a cluster of cases of "viral pneumonia" in Wuhan (China)
17th January, 2020	WHO warns of the danger of this new virus The Ministries of Foreign Affairs of many countries begin to recommend not traveling to the affected areas of China
30th January, 2020	WHO declares an international health emergency ("Public Health Emergency of International Concern"—PHEIC)
11th February, 2020	WHO announces that the disease caused by the new coronavirus would be called COVID-19
11th March, 2020	WHO considers COVID-19 is a pandemic WHO calls on countries to adopt a pan-governmental and pan social approach (it is not just a public health crisis, it will affect all sectors)
13th March, 2020	Europe becomes the epicenter of the pandemic
11th August, 2020	Russia announces the registration of the first vaccine in the world against COVID-19
16th October, 2020	China begins to administer the Sinovac vaccine against COVID-19
09th November, 2020	Pfizer advertises that its vaccine is 90% effective. A week later, Moderna announces that its vaccine is 94% effective
08th December, 2020	Vaccination of the population starts in the UK The following week, vaccination starts in the USA And, before the end of the year, vaccination begins in Latin America and Europe

well as the appearance of new strains of the virus that were even more contagious (like the one that appeared in the UK, or another in South Africa). Table 5.1 summarizes the most relevant facts about the pandemic in 2020.

Case Development

COVID-19: Description of the Disease

COVID-19 is the disease caused by a new coronavirus called SARS-CoV-2 (*Severe Acute Respiratory Syndrome Coronavirus-2*), which had not been previously identified in humans (ECDC 2020). According to WHO (2020), among those who develop symptoms,[5] most (about 80%) recover from the disease without needing

[5]The most common symptoms of COVID-19 are "*fever, dry cough, and fatigue*"; other less common symptoms are "*loss of taste or smell, nasal congestion, conjunctivitis, sore throat, headache, muscle or joint pain, different types of skin rash, nausea or vomiting, diarrhea, chills or dizziness*"; but symptoms of severe COVID-19 disease include "*shortness of breath, loss of appetite, confusion, persistent pain or pressure in the chest, high temperature (above 38 °C), and/or*

hospital treatment; about 15% become seriously ill and require oxygen; and 5% become critically ill and need intensive care.

People aged 60 years and older, those living in long-term care facilities, and those with underlying medical problems like high blood pressure (hypertension), heart and lung problems (cardiovascular disease, chronic respiratory disease), diabetes, obesity or cancer, and/or with weakened immune systems are at higher risk of developing serious illness (ECDC 2020); however, "*anyone can get sick with COVID-19 and become seriously ill or die at any age*" (WHO 2020). Some people who have had COVID-19, whether they have needed hospitalization or not, continue to experience symptoms, including fatigue, respiratory and neurological symptoms (WHO 2020).

The virus can spread from an infected person's mouth or nose in small liquid particles when they cough, sneeze, speak, sing, or breathe heavily (WHO 2020; ECDC 2020). These liquid particles "*are different sizes, ranging from larger 'respiratory droplets' to smaller 'aerosols'*" (WHO 2020). Aerosol transmission "*can occur in specific settings, particularly in indoor, crowded and inadequately ventilated spaces, where infected person(s) spend long periods of time with others*" (WHO 2020), such as offices, cafeterias and restaurants, gyms, stadiums, pubs and nightclubs, cinemas and theaters, choir practices, places of worship, and public transport.

Other people "*can catch COVID-19 when the virus, in these liquid particles, gets into their mouth, nose or eyes, which is more likely to happen when people are in direct or close contact (less than 1 meter apart) with an infected person*" (WHO 2020). Or people may also become infected by touching contaminated surfaces or objects (such as tables, doorknobs, handrails; pens, computer keyboards, money; touch screens—in ticket vending machines, ATM, etc.—, fingerprint scanners, elevator buttons, grab bars, handles, stop push buttons, etc.) and then touching their eyes, noses, or mouths without having washed their hands first (WHO 2020; ECDC 2020).

The time from exposure to COVID-19 to the moment when symptoms begin is, on average, 5–6 days and can range from 1–14 days (WHO 2020; ECDC 2020). Once the disease is over, "*the virus excretion phase lasts an average of 20 days, in which patients can still spread the virus*" (WHO 2020). Furthermore, "*once exposed to the virus, it is also not known for sure whether individuals develop prolonged immunity or, on the contrary, can be reinfected again*" (WHO 2020).

In summary, the virus spreads primarily through human-to-human transmission, and it can be very dangerous. It can be confused with seasonal influenza, malaria or dengue, and it is easily transmitted: any situation in which people are in close proximity to one another for long periods of time (especially in indoor locations)

---

even neurological complications"—WHO (2020). Complications leading to death may include "*respiratory failure, acute respiratory distress syndrome (ARDS), sepsis and septic shock, thromboembolism, and/or multi-organ failure, including injury of the heart, liver or kidneys*" (WHO 2020).

increases the risk of transmission. Thus, transmission can occur more easily in the "Three C's" (WHO 2020):

- Crowded places with many people nearby;
- Close-contact settings, especially where people speak and have conversations very near each other;
- Confined and enclosed spaces with poor ventilation.

In consequence, poor quality of life conditions are related to a higher degree of being infected by the virus.

Finally, to stay physically safe, some precautions should be taken (WHO 2020), such as social distancing, wearing a mask (especially when distancing cannot be maintained), keeping rooms well ventilated, clean and disinfected, avoiding crowds and close contact, regularly cleaning the hands, and coughing into a bent elbow or tissue. Both isolation and quarantine (14 days) are effective methods of preventing the spread of COVID-19, although more research is needed to determine the psychological and social consequences of those measures, which would affect people's quality of life (Wang et al. 2020).

Consequences of the Public Health Emergency of International Concern (PHEIC)

The consequences of the WHO declaration of a Public Health Emergency of International Concern (PHEIC) by COVID-19 have been very diverse, both in the short and long term. Among the most prominent for their social and media relevance, we can cite some socio-demographic, economic, technological, environmental, political, and legal consequences (Table 5.2).

Measures for the Management of the COVID-19 Pandemic

Despite being scarce, the reports published in 2020 indicate that the health communication and management outcomes of countries depends on: (1) Investment in preventive testing; (2) Contact tracing; (3) Border tight controls and transport limitation; (4) Centralized quarantine strategy; (5) Public communication strategy that generates empathy and trust, through an adequate audience segmentation and message design; (6) Promotion of mask use and social distancing; (7) Financial assistance to people and organizations in difficulty; and (8) Low incidence of housing overcrowding and informality in the labor market (which makes almost impossible practices like home office and social distancing).

Table 5.2 Consequences of the declaration of a pandemic by COVID-19

Consequences	Comments
Socio-demographic	More deaths,[a] especially among the elderly and people with some previous pathologies (particularly in poor and developing countries) Forecasts of negative demographic balances in some countries (more deaths and fewer births[b]) Possible emigration to low-density urban centers or rural areas Increased risk of experiencing mental health and socialization problems Possible decrease in educational attainment and quality
Economic	Significant fall in GDP in virtually all countries Acceleration of digitization, robotization, and the fourth industrial revolution Some sectors were especially affected: Negatively: – Media, cultural industries, and audiovisual productions: the production and distribution of several cultural products were suspended – Tourism[c] (and businesses directly or indirectly related to tourism), both internationally and nationally, by restricting mobility within and outside countries: hotels, restaurants, bars and cafes; monuments, museums, cultural exhibitions, concerts, cinemas, theaters, etc.; means of transport (airlines, bus companies, trains, taxis); tourist guides, travel agencies, souvenir shops, ... – Health systems: they have been overwhelmed, with tensions due to the direct and indirect costs generated – Non-essential shops and establishments: they have been closed for months, or with severe time restrictions – Automotive industry: production was suspended, demand was drastically reduced, and the production chain was disrupted – Education: suspension or reduction of activities, radical transformation that leaves institutions with low adaptability out of the market Positively: – Hospitals: they have been reinforced with more personnel and more resources[d] – Research centers: they have received special funds to investigate COVID-19, and international collaborations have increased – Pharmaceuticals: they have received government and supranational grants to speed up the creation of a vaccine,[e] have developed diagnostic tests to detect the virus, and are looking for specific drugs to treat the disease – Cleaning and disinfection services: in high demand, with specific protocols for COVID-19 – Medical supplies and disinfection companies[f]: they have had to increase their production capacity significantly and urgently – Companies that provided services to adapt the facilities of the different businesses to new regulations and security measures (for example, in restaurants and pubs, in offices[g]) – E-commerce and online business: sales through the Internet have increased, practically in all sectors – Delivery companies and applications: to make it possible to deliver online purchases to buyers' homes – Digital information and entertainment platforms – Banks and financial services entities (VISA, Mastercard, ...): they have seen an increase in the use of debit/credit cards, as well as online banking
Technological	New applications of existing technologies and development of new technologies:

(continued)

Table 5.2 (continued)

Consequences	Comments
	– Tests to detect the disease, new vaccines and medications – Apps to control the contacts and movements of the population – Artificial intelligence: applied to software to anticipate the spread of the virus – Drones to control crowds of people and send samples between hospitals – New digital infrastructures (video chats, video conferences, etc.).
Environmental	Genetic manipulation of the virus (ethical problems) Reduction of investment in climate change prevention Effects of cleaning products on the environment (bleach and other disinfectant products), and the greater personal use of disinfectant sprays and gels, a greater expenditure of water and energy (due to the increase in the number of showers, washing hands, washing clothes more intensively and at high temperatures, cleaning homes and all kinds of establishments—educational centers, offices, shops, etc.)
Political and legal	Management of the epidemic: effect on the reputation of political representatives and institutions[h] Increase in social tensions and the fragility of democratic systems Negative impact on health resources in the most affected countries Higher incidence of domestic gender violence National responses to the virus have revealed significant gaps or deficiencies in many countries (developed or not)[i] Restriction of the citizens' fundamental rights, forcing confinement, the mandatory use of masks, with a curfew, etc. The regulations of many countries and supranational bodies, such as the European Union, have been adapted to the urgency of the moment, in order to accelerate the development, authorization and availability of vaccines, while maintaining the standards of quality, safety and efficacy of vaccines (European Commission 2020)

Source: Own elaboration

[a]By the end of 2020, almost two million people had died from COVID-19 in the world

[b]In countries like Spain, the situation of uncertainty due to the evolution of the pandemic, and economic and job insecurity, suggests a fall in the birth rate

[c]During the Public Health Emergency of International Concern, tourism has experienced a significant decline in all affected countries, due to the general closure of borders, and even restrictions on internal mobility within countries (between regions, and even perimeter closure of municipalities). Large economic losses have been found in those countries heavily dependent on tourism (for example, Spain or Italy).

[d]The demand for medical services has increased (and particularly microbiology, virology and infectology services)

[e]The economic effort made had not been known before. Thus, for example, "*in order to reduce the risks of pharmaceutical companies and accelerate and increase the production of vaccines, the European Commission made advance purchase agreements with each vaccine producer on behalf of the Member States. In exchange for the right to purchase a specified number of doses of vaccines in a specified period and at a specified price, and once their efficacy and safety had been demonstrated, the European Commission financed part of the initial costs incurred by vaccine producers under the Emergency Support Instrument (this financing was seen as a payment on account of the vaccines that the Member States would actually buy). In addition, it provided additional support through loans from the European Investment Bank*" (European Commission 2020)

[f]E.g. Manufacturers of PPE—masks, gloves, gowns, . . .—, hydro-alcoholic gels and disinfectant sprays; respirators for ICUs, thermometers to measure temperature, test tents, disinfection tunnels,

(continued)

Table 5.2 (continued)

disinfectant mats, dispensers of hydro-alcoholic gel; and, since the end of 2020, for mass vaccination, manufacturers of syringes, special refrigerators to keep vaccines at a very low temperature, special transport services—to avoid breaking the cold chain, etc.

[g]They had to create safe areas for receiving products, online shopping collection stations, dividers for greater protection in terraces and lounges of bars and restaurants, as well as in offices, protective screens in windows and customer service areas, etc.

[h]For example, the attitude adopted by political leaders such as Donald Trump in the United States or Jair Bolsonaro in Brazil has been different from the attitude adopted by Angela Merkel in Germany or Jacinda Ardern in New Zealand

[i]E.g. overwhelmed health systems, which had suffered cuts in recent years, and lack of protective equipment and personnel; difficulties to stop the spread of the virus and contain the contagions; lack of coordination at different levels of government (central, regional, and local), saturation and overflow of certain services, lack or limitation of government aid to assist people affected by Temporary Employment Regulation File (TERF) and business closures, as well as the sectors most affected by the measures taken against the pandemic (closure of the hotel industry, tourism stoppage, . . .)

Unfortunately, the pandemic made clear the lack of coordination between countries, regions and cities; as well as the lack of contingency plans for these types of situations.

At the end of the first year of the pandemic, some strategies would be proposed for managing the most urgent problems generated by the COVID-19 (Table 5.3).

Social Marketing in the Face of COVID-19

One of the main measures to face the COVID-19 pandemic has been to raise awareness for the prevention of infections and the appeal to individual and social responsibility to solve the problem. Thus, social marketing campaigns have been decisive.

Considering social marketing from the perspective of quality of life, the COVID-19 pandemic and the policies implemented by governments have led us to ask ourselves what was done and what is still being done, from the point of view of social marketing; what campaigns were developed and which ones are still being developed; which strategies were implemented or which could be implemented in the future.

To that aim, an exploratory study analyzed different campaigns carried out by the WHO and four countries: Argentina, Colombia, Portugal, and Spain. Being part of Iberoamerican region and having important socio—cultural similarities, they represent, from a perspective of quality of life, two different types of societies in terms of political stability, economic development, social welfare, educational attainment and quality, environmental security, urbanization policies, international relevance, and COVID-19 resilience.

Table 5.3 Measures for the management of the COVID-19 pandemic

Term	Management measures
Very short term (very urgent)	To identify the new virus, study its characteristics, and know the real dimension of the problem To stop community transmission To increase private and public international coordination and solidarity To find drugs (already approved to treat other diseases) that improve the COVID-19 treatment and reduce mortality (until obtaining the vaccine) To expand hospital capacity, especially in ICUs, to be able to care for all people sick with COVID-19 who require admission to health centers To obtain medical supplies (PPE: masks, gloves, . . .; respirators, tests, . . .) to face the pandemic To strengthen epidemiological surveillance and create laboratory capacity to detect the virus To formulate recommendations on the clinical care and follow-up of people infected with the virus ("trackers") To define priority research areas on COVID-19 and its possible complications New medical protocols to prevent and cure this disease International collaboration for the generation of knowledge through research and development of new technologies for diagnosis, treatment and prevention To generate and disseminate updated and checked information about the virus
Short term	To attempt to stop, or at least slow down, the spread of the virus To find new specific drugs that improve the COVID-19 treatment (until obtaining a vaccine) To intensify the population's personal and social measures to control contagions[a]: large-scale application of "non-pharmacological" public health measures, such as case detection and isolation, contact tracing and follow-up, and their quarantine, as well as community collaboration To appeal to personal and social responsibility to avoid contagion To try new applications of existing technologies and innovative technological solutions Greater collaboration between different sectors (governments, international organizations, universities, companies, local communities, etc.), to avoid the lack of coordination and fragmentation of the programs of preventive measures and containment of the pandemic, as well as for an adequate management of information Prevention and awareness campaigns, to avoid contagion Democratic and rational borders control
Medium term	Vaccines: development and distribution of effective and safe vaccines against COVID-19, securing general access to them, including poor and excluded people Definition and planning of large-scale vaccination strategies[b] To increase vaccine uptake and preventive social behaviors through effective health communication
Long term	To improve the globalization and economic model, including geographic mobility of the population (e.g. tourism and business) To promote a more just, equitable, and sustainable development To offer long-term government aid to assist those affected by Temporary Employment Regulation File (TERF) and business closures

(continued)

Table 5.3 (continued)

Term	Management measures
	(unemployment benefits, aid for the self-employed, etc.) To dedicate additional financial resources for contingency plans, comprehensive health services, virus surveillance, etc. To build stronger health systems and foster global collaboration to deal with future pandemics

Source: Own elaboration

[a]Recommendations on the measures to take to avoid contagions, use and placement of masks and gloves, washing clothes, safe use of disinfectants, specialized cleaning in centers with a high number of infections, etc.

[b]For example, in the European Union (EU), the following aspects have been taken into account (European Commission 2020):

– Capacity of vaccination services to supply vaccines, including skilled workers and medical and protective equipment;

– Easy access to vaccines for target populations, both in terms of affordability and physical proximity;

– Deployment of vaccines with different characteristics and storage and transport needs, particularly with regard to the cold chain, refrigerated transport and storage capacity;

– Clear communication about the benefits, risks, and importance of COVID-19 vaccines to build public trust

Methodology

We run independent manual internet queries in each country using Google and Google Scholar search engines and two search keywords[6]: *COVID virus campaigns / COVID campaigns*. In order to avoid algorithm limitations, we run separated manual online and offline searches of communications from relevant official sources (e.g. WHO, European Commission, Ministries of Health of affected countries, etc.) and press.

We carried out a content analysis of the secondary information, using an analysis tool focused on the following aspects (based on Galan-Ladero and Galan-Ladero, 2019): main message of the campaign, message tone, objective, graphic design, country, organization/s that promote it, media dissemination and target audience, approaches and strategies.

Social Marketing Strategies at an International Level

During this time, the World Health Organization (WHO) has led the actions to be followed, although the role developed by the European Center for Disease Prevention and Control (ECDC), Pan-American Health Organization (PAHO), The United States Centers for Disease Control and Prevention (CDCs), or Institutions such as Oxford University and Johns Hopkins University, has been also very important. For example:

[6]In three languages: Spanish, Portuguese, and English.

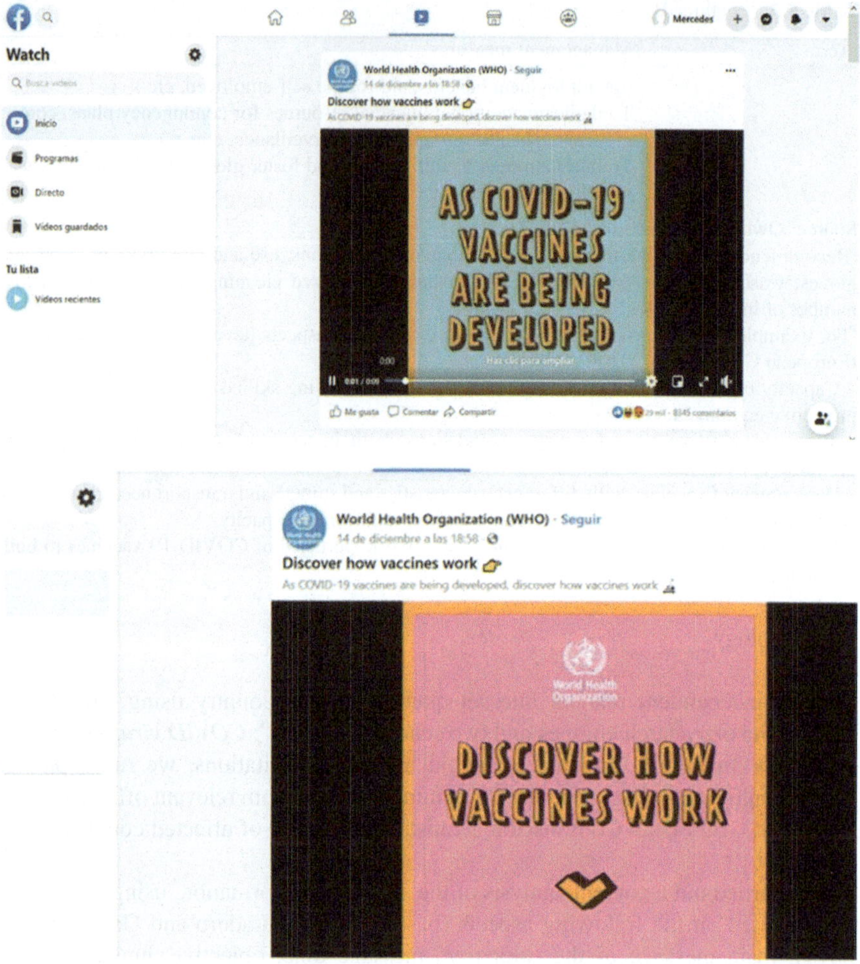

Fig. 5.1 Examples of messages sent to the individuals' profiles on Facebook. Source: Coordinator's own profile on Facebook (2020)

- WHO launched chatbots and services for sending notifications and health alert messages, with instant and accurate information on COVID-19, in several languages and with users around the world (applications in WhatsApp, Rakuten Viber, or Facebook Messenger—see Fig. 5.1).
- It launched the WHO Academy mobile app, designed with the aim of providing information to health workers to help them care for COVID-19 patients and protect themselves. Along with it, the WHO Info application, for the general public.
- WHO launched, in collaboration with FIFA, the awareness campaign "*Spread the word and eliminate the coronavirus*", spearheaded by well-known international footballers, calling on people around the world to protect their health. The

campaign focused on hand washing, the proper way to sneeze, as well as the importance of avoiding touching the face, maintaining the appropriate physical distance, and keeping those who are not feeling well at home (March 23, 2020).
- It updated the recommendations on the use of masks, including a new section with recommendations for decision-makers regarding the use of masks by healthy people in the community (April 6, 2020).
- WHO presented the #WearAMask challenge on social networks, to help spread information on how and when to wear a mask to protect against COVID-19 (August 5, 2020).
- It organized concerts, such as "One World: Together at Home", held in collaboration with Global Citizen on April 18, 2020, a special live global edition to celebrate and support frontline healthcare workers.
- WHO also joined, on World Humanitarian Day (August 19, 2020), with United Nations partners to pay tribute to frontline workers around the world responding to COVID-19 and other health emergencies. These aid workers on the front lines (#RealLivesHeroes) include refugees who are playing essential roles as health workers in the response to the pandemic.
- End of December 2020: messages sent through social networks to reduce the fear of vaccines (informing about them).

Situation in Argentina, Colombia, Portugal, and Spain

Argentina

Reynaldo G. Rivera and Enrique Bianchi

The COVID-19 pandemic spread progressively in Argentina. On March 3, the first case was registered, and only on June 21 there were more than 1000 daily cases. Community transmission was concentrated, at least until July, in the three most important urban conglomerates: the cities of Rosario, Buenos Aires and its metropolitan region, confirming the role of urban concentrations as one of the relevant factors of virus transmission.

Although Argentina occupied one of the first positions in different statistics related to COVID-19 at the end of 2020, unlike most countries in the region and the world, the government opted from the beginning for strict mandatory lockdown, which implied the impossibility of people's mobility, not only between provinces but also between areas of the same city. Public transport was immediately suspended for the population not included in essential sectors (such as health care and security), all citizens had to circulate with an official permit obtained through a website and after a specific mobile application ("*Cuidar*"—"Caring", in English), all international and domestic flights were canceled, and the suspension of all non-essential economic activity was ordered.

All this generated not only a great negative impact on the economy but also high levels of stress and psychological distress in the population. Despite the fact that some international publications applauded the Argentine government's attitude, since October 2020 the management of the Argentine health and social crisis has been classified as one of the worst experiences at a global level.

The Argentine State, both at the national and provincial levels (Argentina is a Federal Republic in which the provincial and municipal authorities retain a great margin of autonomy in terms of public policies), was highly proactive in the function of raising awareness for the prevention of community transmission of the virus:

- In March, a personalized SMS campaign began to prevent Argentines in transit abroad (about 140,000).
- The Ministry of Health made a website with useful information available to the public: (https://bancos.salud.gob.ar/recurso/coronavirus-covid-19-saber-para-prevenir), and disseminated it through its social networks.
- Awareness campaigns aimed at mitigating the impact of Covid-19 and dengue fever were also carried out, especially in the City of Buenos Aires:
  - Territorial tours were conducted with loudspeakers and megaphones.
  - Messages were disseminated through social networks, SMS to geo-located contacts, telephone calls, brochure distribution, WhatsApp messages by the referents of neighborhood cooperatives, and Neighborhood Councils.
  - Community radio stations and religious institutions were used to reach lower-class neighborhoods, articulating in them the action of the State with religious leaders from the neighborhoods.

From the beginning, and on a daily basis, the Ministry of Health of the Nation communicated the number of infected, deaths and policies implemented. The latter followed the WHO recommendations regarding territorial discrimination by phases according to the health situation of the population (see https://www.argentina.gob.ar/coronavirus/aislamiento/fases).

On March 20, all the country's journalistic media, together with numerous institutions from the academic, professional and communication world, joined in a common message under the hashtag: #somosresponsables ("#WeAreResponsible", in English) and the slogan "*Al virus lo frenamos entre todos*" ("We'll stop the virus together", in English). The Association of Argentine Journalistic Entities (ADEPA)'s website presented a summary of the campaign, with images from the main journalistic media in the country (ADEPA, 2020).

All of the above was highly effective until, at least, the month of May 2020, when various specialists (e.g. Rivera and Bianchi 2020) began to warn about the fatigue of the population, the great economic crisis produced by strict and indiscriminate government policies, the absence of audience segmentation in the design and implementation of communication strategies, and the lack of technological innovation that, as in Colombia and Korea, allowed the early and effective identification of positive cases. In June, Argentina was the only Latin American nation mentioned by Time magazine for its effective management. In November, the resilience ranking published by Bloomberg places the country in the second to last position. Added to the aforementioned problems, the growing lack of government transparency in the

Fig. 5.2 #ArgentinaAplaude ("#ArgentinaIsClapping", in English). Translation: Thursday, March 19, 9 p.m. Argentina is clapping. In your house, on your balcony, on your terrace, we applaud our doctors, nurses and health assistants. Support for the fight against coronavirus. Source: Clarin (2020)

management of statistical data, the delay in the purchase and distribution of vaccines, the growth of inflation and political instability, and the reduced impact of economic subsidies aimed at compensating for the general lack of activity. Only in December 2020 some positive indicators of production recovery were achieved in some specific sectors.

The exposed context reveals the extreme difficulty that civil society and the private sector in Argentina had to face at all levels. Despite all the limitations imposed on the country with the longest compulsory social lockdown in history, increased by tax pressure and the lack of investment incentives, most social organizations, non-governmental institutions and businesses made constant efforts to protect people's lives and their quality of life, which in many cases were translated into social marketing strategies.

Thus private initiatives arose, such as "#ArgentinaAplaude" ("#ArgentinaIsClapping", in English)—Fig. 5.2: under this hashtag, many users of WhatsApp and other social networks called on citizens to applaud doctors, nurses, and health assistants, who were fighting Covid-19 on the front line.

The Argentine Football League launched the campaign "*Everyone [is playing] against the same rival*" in March, within the framework of the health emergency due to the coronavirus pandemic that forced the suspension of the tournament. It spread the following messages through its social networks and those of the 24 teams:

Fig. 5.3 #UnaSolaHinchada ("#FootballFansTogether", in English). Translation: #FootballFansTogether. United by solidarity. Source: innovarsustentabilidad.com (2020)

> "*Próxima fecha: todos contra el mismo rival. Este partido lo ganamos juntos. #QuedateEnCasa*" (Translation into English: "Next date: all against the same rival. Together we will win this match" [Only together will we beat this rival]. #StayHome").
>
> "*Hoy, el rival a vencer es el mismo. Al #Coronavirus le ganamos con el compromiso de todos, jugando en equipo y con responsabilidad. #QuedateEnCasa #SAF ⚽#DondeNacenLasEstrellas ★★★ pic.twitter.com/oqrpuVnd2m*" (Translation into English: "Today, the rival to beat is the same. We'll beat the #Coronavirus with the commitment of all, playing as a team responsibly. #StayHome #SAF ⚽ #WhereTheStarsAreBorn ★★★ pic.twitter.com/oqrpuVnd2m").
>
> - Argentine Super League (@superliga) March 19, 2020.
>
> "*Hoy, el rival a vencer es el mismo. Al #Coronavirus le ganamos con el compromiso de todos, jugando en equipo y con responsabilidad*" (Translation into English: "Today, the rival to beat is the same. We'll beat #Coronavirus with the commitment of all, playing as a team, responsibly").

At the same time, the Argentine Football Association, aware of the almost religious importance of football and its myths in the population, mobilized the population to fight against the hunger generated by the crisis in excluded sectors of society (Fig. 5.3).

It also released a short film with images of athletes like Maradona and Messi, while transmitting the following messages:

> Hoy tenemos el partido más difícil de nuestra historia y Argentina te necesita para ganar. Por eso . . . Respetá la distancia, no salgas a cualquier lado que quedás en offside y perjudicás al equipo. No se amontonen todos arriba. Abran la cancha, ventilen cada vez que puedan. Porque aunque parezca que el rival no existe, es peligrosísimo a la hora de atacar. Vamos Argentina, este partido lo ganamos jugando en equipo, porque en este país hay una fuerza que es más fuerte que cualquier pandemia: la de volver a encontrarnos adentro de la cancha o en cualquier otro lugar (Infobae 2020).

Translation into English: Today we have the most difficult game in our history and Argentina needs you to win. Therefore . . . Respect the distance, do not go anywhere that you are offside and you harm the team. Don't all pile up on top. Open the field, ventilate whenever you can. Because even if it seems that the rival does not exist, it is very dangerous when attacking. Come on Argentina, we will win this game playing as a team, because in this country there is a force that is stronger than any pandemic: the hope of meeting again on the field or in any other place.

The social marketing of the private sector was oriented to three main objectives:

- To sensitize the population about the risks of Covid-19 and the strategies for care, accompanying in this way the effort made by public agencies.
- To offer alternatives to maintain closeness and relationships with its customers and users, either for the delivery of products or the remote provision of services.
- To sustain and increase the brand positioning as an ally in improving the people's quality of life (customers, employees, etc.).

Multilatinas such as Mercado Libre, and private universities such as the Austral University (HUA, 2020), contributed to the dissemination of messages from the Ministry of Health. But they also offered useful digital content for families and organized streaming events that allowed not only to accompany people in situations of loneliness and isolation, but also increased training and skills that are especially useful for times of the pandemic and for the "new normal" phase.

In August 2020, the Government launched a campaign of spots with famous personalities about the risk of social gatherings ("*Seguí cuidándote*"—"Follow care", in English). In this sense, companies such as Telefonica incorporated classic prevention messages from the health behavioral model to reinforce the need to stay home as much as possible and use protection devices such as masks and alcohol gel.

Finally, three aspects can be highlighted in the social marketing strategies implemented by both the public and private sectors:

1. Consistent and homogeneous information based on data aimed at preventing community contagion.
2. Messages with a positive and motivating tone, oriented towards a common effort, towards a new normal.
3. Useful content that improves the recipients' quality of life, consistent with the brand and products of the organization.

Colombia

Edy Lorena Burbano

The Colombian Ministry of Health reported the first case of COVID-19 on March 6, 2020. Due to the appearance of new infections, the Government made the decision to implement the first strict and localized quarantine campaign on March 25. This was established in order to contain the spread of the pandemic and to avoid the collapse of the hospital health system in the future, as well as the negative consequences in socioeconomic areas.

The Government set up a two-fold strategy:

- First, the identification and detection of affected areas and people close to a positive diagnosis. The idea was based on establishing daily communication and updated information on the pandemic data. This was launched through the free *CoronApp* application, which facilitated real-time monitoring of the figures collected from the emergency operations center of the National Institute of Health (*Instituto Nacional de Salud*—INS, in Spanish). Thus, a national network was formed to act quickly and provide support in coordination with the authorities throughout the country.
- Secondly, the creation of a close link between the government and the Colombian society. This has been carried out through a daily speech, on national television, and through the Coronavirus Colombia website, in which the president and his ministers presented daily data about the pandemic (confirmed cases, number of deaths, and recovered). This strategy was replicated by other Governments in Latin America (e.g. Argentina).

According to the World Bank report (Banco Mundial, 2020), the Government implemented other early emergency response measures: it declared a state of emergency, closed the country's borders, and imposed a mandatory quarantine. It also announced a sizeable fiscal stimulus package (USD4.2 billion or 1.4% of GDP, with the potential to increase to USD13.6 billion). Colombian Government also provided additional resources to the health system, generated special lines of credit for companies in the sectors most affected by the crisis, made financial transfers to vulnerable groups (e.g. elderly people), and approved subsidies to agriculture, education, and tourism.

On March 27, the social assistance program generated the first strategy focused on benefiting 600 workers who were with suspension of their employment contract or on unpaid leave. Within the same program, the Government launched the following campaigns: "*Colombia está contigo*" ("Colombia is with you", in English) and "*Programación de Alimentación Escolar (PAE) en casa*" ("School Food Programming—SFP—at home", in English). The first one was focused on vulnerable groups, without neglecting the ethnical differences within the country; and the second one was focused on reaching poor households with food. The latter implied a change in regulations and sought that business organizations and society donated to distribute basic products among the most vulnerable population in different regions of the country.

Likewise, at the end of 2020, the line of action framed in strengthening existing programs was still in force: "*Familias en Acción*" ("Families in Action", in English) and "*Adulto Mayor*" ("Senior Citizen", in English); and, on the other hand, "*Jóvenes en Acción*" ("Youth in Action", in English). In both cases, the idea was based on helping financially. In the first campaign, products were delivered to people who have no income or benefits from the Government; in the other campaign, a monetary collaboration was offered. In practice, they were aligned with the prevention and action plan as a COVID-19 mitigation strategy.

From another perspective, companies in Colombia have also been aware of the changes that the pandemic has produced. For this reason, they have joined efforts to support the affected population and, as if that was not enough, they have adapted to the consumers in times of pandemic. Thus, Ahmed et al. (2020) stated that the crisis tests companies from two perspectives: (1) their commitment to society and their employers; and, of course, (2) it generates pressure on the Government to acquire economic aid and financial relief.

Analyzing all the edges of the problem, the Government established, for June 19, July 3 and 19, 2020, *days without VAT*, in order to mitigate the economic impacts. In addition, the union of companies such as the National Association of Colombian Entrepreneurs (ANDI) maintained its action plan aimed at responding as solidarity actors to the crisis through the slogan #UnidosSomosMasPaís ("We're more of a country together", in English).

Its members were invited to help in health, humanitarian and non-food care issues. As a result, the following was achieved: donation of mechanical fans, product delivery, a solidarity bond "*Unidos somos más*" ("Together we're more", in English) was created, and social responsibility plans were launched, focusing on food aid, donations to the health sector, free transportation for health personnel, and creation of solidarity funds.

In sum, several sectors aligned themselves with the different campaigns: "*#QuedateEnCasa*" ("#StayHome", in English), "*#EmpiezaPorTusManos*" ("#StartWithYourHands", in English), "*#LimpiaTusManos*" ("#WashYourHands", in English), and "*El primer control contra el coronavirus es usted*" ("You are the first line of defense against the coronavirus", in English). The government also strengthened the "*Mito-Realidad del Coronavirus*" ("Myth-Reality of the Coronavirus", in English) campaign to socialize and make the population aware of the reality of the virus.

Portugal

Helena Alves

During the first wave of the pandemic caused by COVID-19, Portugal was considered one of the best examples of a country that managed to control the spread of the virus quite well. This news item appeared in much of the European media, such as Forbes on March 19, CNN on March 30, Der Spiegel on April 9, and many others. However, the question often asked is whether Portugal did really control the pandemic more effectively, or if this was merely luck or a miracle, as some classified it (New York Times, April 7).

The first cases in Portugal were registered on March 3, 2020, when four were confirmed, together with 101 suspected cases (European Centre for Disease Prevention and Control, 2020). Worldwide, on that day there were already 90,663 cases and 3043 deaths, with transmission in the community being confirmed in China, Iran, Italy, Japan, Singapore, and South Korea. On March 16, schools, discotheques, restaurants, and border crossings with Spain were closed, and visits to care homes were restricted. On March 22, the State of Emergency was declared.

Fig. 5.4 "We are only one voice: only together will we beat this pandemic". Source: YouTube (2020)

Perhaps contributing to that success was the fact that neighboring countries (Spain, France, and Italy) had seen their national health systems collapse completely, confirming and announcing thousands of deaths. This led to the Portuguese disciplining themselves and adhering to the lockdown rules imposed, as well as following the World Health Organization's recommendations at an early stage. In addition, credit must be given to all political parties in Portugal, especially the opposition party, which gave full support to the Prime Minister from the outset, allowing a rapid and flexible response. As for the measures adopted, it is important to highlight that Portugal gave temporary full rights of citizenship to all immigrants and refugees, ensuring they had complete access to the National Health Service, aiming to control the spread of the disease among these populations.

Added to all this, the way information was conveyed to the people may have been an important contribution, as the four main television channels (RTP, SIC, TVI and CMTV), in collaboration with the Health Authority (DGS), made themselves available to the country under the slogan "*We are only one voice: only together will we beat this pandemic*" (Fig. 5.4). There was responsible transmission of the measures that each Portuguese person should adopt, as well as clarifying doubts that were of great concern to all.

From the beginning, the message conveyed to the Portuguese by the Health Authority was the request for everyone to be an agent of health through the hashtag "#Be an agent of public health: protect yourself and others" (Fig. 5.5). This message, transmitted on all media and social networks, both online and offline, was strengthened by the use of prominent personalities from diverse areas (sport, television, etc. . .), with the focus on giving information, clarifying doubts and advice to follow, in simple language and by well-known television faces (journalists, actors, footballers, football managers, and many more (Fig. 5.6). These messages and videos

Fig. 5.5 Slogan of the campaigns to prevent the spread of COVID-19. Legend: NEW CORONAVIRUS. Be an agent of public health. Protect yourself and others. In case of doubt call SNS24 808 24 24 24. Source: Portuguese Health Authority (2020)

Fig. 5.6 Campaign "*Be an agent of public health*" with well-known personalities. Source: Ministério de Saúde (2020) and DGS (2020)

were also transmitted in the main languages of immigrants in Portugal (Nepalese, Hindi, Creole, Arabic) and in sign language.

The various campaigns launched by the DGS covered topics including general advice, social distancing, hand-washing, cleanliness, sanitization, the correct use of masks (especially after these became obligatory in closed and public spaces), recommendations for different age-groups, mental health issues and recommendations for companies and health professionals. Added to all these campaigns were those launched by various companies and local authorities asking people to stay at home (*#stayathome*).

After lockdown, it was necessary to manage the lifting of restrictions, so that all the work done previously was not lost, as similarly to what happened in other countries, the effects of lockdown were devastating for the whole economy and society. Many lives were saved, but many others were lost, due to a lack of medical care, as health services were focused only on the pandemic. Today, the mistake of turning away many patients from the National Health Service (SNS) is recognized. Some because they were not given priority and others because fear stopped them from seeking help from the SNS. There were also very serious problems in education, due to the lack of access to online teaching for many disadvantaged families, although before the end of lockdown, the Portuguese government was providing classes for primary and secondary years via television-school. This is without mentioning the many jobs lost and the closure of companies, caused by the pandemic and the lockdown. However, many positive things also occurred, such as the emergence of many charitable actions to help those who were isolated, ill or unemployed. This originated many fund-raising campaigns to help these causes.

The post-lockdown campaigns adopted the slogan "*#don't make things easy: we are all agents of public health*", aiming for people to resume a "normal" life in safety. Although directed at the whole population, many focused on young people, as they belonged to the population segments most anxious to go out again, spend time with friends and enjoy themselves as a group. Here too, well-known personalities and influencers were used particularly to appeal to young people to re-invent themselves and find new ways of socializing without putting the safety of everyone at risk (Fig. 5.7).

As mentioned, during the first wave of the pandemic, Portugal stood out as an example of good practices and as one of few countries that controlled the pandemic so that the SNS did not collapse, something that did not happen in the second wave. Unity gave strength, both among politicians and the Portuguese population in a joint effort: "*All together we will manage to beat the pandemic*". However, after the summer and after some encouragement from the government so that the Portuguese would not be afraid to go out, enjoy holidays in Portugal, go to restaurants and cultural events, the situation began to get worse. Perhaps as during the first wave the Portuguese did not feel the same burden of deaths that was felt in many countries, many people began to lose their fear and underestimate the virus, as they had begun to resume their professional activity as normal, and schools were open, among many other aspects. This underestimation will also have involved the government, which dismantled the campaign hospitals that had been set up in the first wave and had not been necessary. Similar to other countries, the effects of a second wave began to be felt, for which the country was not completely prepared. A deadlier wave than the first, something that Portugal had not yet fully experienced.

 # Don't make things easy: ...don't arrange parties or meeting up with a lot of people...

 # Don't make things easy: ...re-invent yourself...

Fig. 5.7 Videos appealing for a responsible post-lockdown. Source: Health Authority (2020)

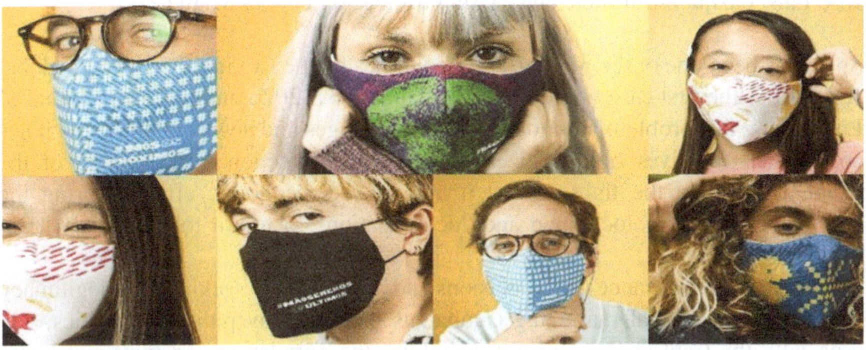

Fig. 5.8 Images from the campaign targeted at young people "*don't drop your mask*". Source: SNS (2020)

In October 2020, the number of cases and deaths started to increase, becoming even worse in November. Predicting a difficult situation, the government implemented restrictions to mobility and socializing, intermittently, to try to control the significant rise in cases. Campaigns were launched aiming to make people aware of the importance of using a mask in all situations of proximity, something already defended by the movement "*mine protects you and yours protects me*", and appealing to young people to use the mask as a form of expression, but also appealing to sustainable behavior involving recycling so that disposable masks did not end up on the ground, under the slogan "*don't drop your mask*" (Fig. 5.8).

The growing number of positive cases and deaths led to predictions of an even worse scenario with the Christmas and New Year celebrations, and so the government brought in more restrictions, above all for the New Year festivities. However, many family get-togethers were forecast, especially with older members. Here, some campaigns emerged with much stronger emotional appeals, making grandchildren and children responsible for the possible death of grandparents, and also of friends. Under the slogan "*Don't let the virus in*" to your body, your home, your family, and "*it's up to each one of us to stop it*", there were pictures of old people or even young ones in intensive care after family reunions to celebrate birthdays or Christmas. Together with these campaigns, others appeared with statements from well-known personalities who had been infected with the virus, calling for social distancing, as they had been lucky, but not everyone would be, and the consequences could be fatal.

In January 2021, despite the start of vaccinations and all the associated enthusiasm, the situation got worse every day and the government declared a new lockdown (exception for schools, public services, health services, and primary and essential goods stores) to delay the spread of the virus which at that moment was already causing some hospitals to reach breaking point.

Spain

Jose Luis Vazquez-Burguete and Maria Purificacion Garcia-Miguelez

Spain has been one of the most affected countries by the Covid-19 crisis on a global scale. After the first case was detected on January 31, 2020 on the Canary Island of La Gomera, this problem has monopolized front pages and news bulletins, and it has conditioned the lives of all citizens, both in the infection or expansion of the pandemic, and in the fight against it and its socioeconomic effects, during the successive phases of lockdown and "de-escalation" to return to normality ("new normal").

The social significance of all decisions and actions led to seeking their legitimacy through intense social marketing campaigns promoted by public authorities, and especially the Central Government, to inform the population and raise awareness about attitudes to adopt and actions to be taken in every moment. Parallel campaigns by the media, companies and NGOs followed suit, replicating content, particularly while government channels acted as a "single source" of information. In this context, the Government assumed the role of the only legitimate source of information from the beginning of the epidemiological crisis, moving from an initial phase of "denial of evidence" to a second phase of "call for unity in the face of a state of national emergency".

Regardless of what could be the specific moment in which the Government was aware of the pandemic and its possible devastating effects (to the point of complaints have been filed in the courts against a possible negligent action), the truth is that the initial content of the messages was aimed at denying the evidence of the crisis not only in China, but also in much closer countries—Italy, in particular—until the celebration of the women's vindication days on March 8. The importance of the COVID-19 infection was minimized, making it similar to that of a flu or other seasonal diseases. Political marketing and its objectives prevailed over other issues, distorting the content of social marketing campaigns. Such "denial of the evidence" would be later replicated in Eastern European countries, or in the American continent—Brazil, in particular—with the same dire consequences.

Furthermore, the effects of the "political conditioning" on the effectiveness of social marketing were aggravated by having resorted to seek the legitimacy of the messages based on the scientific experts chosen to transmit them. Since February, the dissemination of information corresponded almost exclusively to technicians and scientists, being personified in the figure of Dr. Fernando Simon, Director of the Center for the Coordination of Health Alerts and Emergencies of the Ministry of Health since 2012, who had already been spokesman for the special committee on Ebola in Spain in 2014. They wanted to avoid, precisely, the errors of interpretation and communication of that time, while shifting the level of responsibility and criticism before the (at least apparent) neutrality and impartiality of the scientists.

After the exponential expansion of the pandemic from March 8, the appearances of the President of the Government on March 13 and 14 marked "a turning point" in the management and communication of the crisis. On the 14th, the Decree of the State of Alarm was announced due to the extreme seriousness of the situation, followed by the activation of a storytelling and some cognitive frameworks (Lakoff 2007) aimed at minimizing its political impact, "obviating" the question of the scientific experts' credibility, who went from minimizing to magnifying the impact of Covid-19 (or giving it its true dimension). Intense campaigns appealed to shared responsibility with messages such as "*este virus lo paramos unidos*" ("this virus we will stop it together", in English), or "*quédate en casa*" ("stay at home", in English), and their corresponding hashtags, contextualizing the causes of the problem in an European and global framework, and demanding help and solutions also from international scale, which included articles signed by Pedro Sanchez, the President of the Spanish Government, in national newspapers (Rojo and Soler 2020).

Thus, the underlying message of the social marketing campaigns since March 14 was the unity around the President of the Government, who assumed sole command in a situation of war against a common and invisible enemy. This was helped by the incorporation of the Armed Forces members, scientists and some politicians in the successive informative appearances during the lockdown and State of Alarm. Society was very receptive to this message of unity and responsibility, whose greatest exponent was social networks, and initiatives such as the daily applause for health personnel or the famous remake of the song "Resistiré" ("I will resist", in English).

Meanwhile, added issues led to new social marketing campaigns during the lockdown, such as those aimed at promoting healthy eating and exercise (physical health), avoiding or reducing psychological disorders (mental health), or preventing teleworking occupational hazards. Other administrative bodies joined the Government in its effort, as well as the media, companies and other organizations, which became involved with corporate social marketing campaigns, cause-related marketing programs, and other actions of a philanthropic nature, which included donations or the reconversion of productive chains for the manufacture of masks and sanitary gowns, respirators, and other products that were practically impossible to obtain through the usual channels, or, at least, to provide them in the necessary quantity. Slogans spread by entities that habitually carry out their activity abroad, such as "*esta vez ayudamos en casa*" ("this time we help at home", in English), are clearly illustrative of a collective movement that transcended the health field to reach socio-economic issues, helping the most vulnerable groups to survive, or supporting

Fig. 5.9 Examples of messages from Government campaigns against Coronavirus in Spain. Translation: (1) "*#Este virus lo paramos unidos*" ("#This virus we will stop it together", in English). "*Detener el coronavirus es responsabilidad de todos y todas. Si te proteges tú, proteges a los demás*" ("To stop the coronavirus is everyone's responsibility. If you protect yourself, you protect others", in English). (2) "*Un día más, un día menos*" ("One day more, one day less", in English). "*Cada día que pasamos en casa, estamos más cerca de parar al virus. Quédate en casa. Por ti, por todos*" ("Every day we spend at home, we are closer to stopping the virus. Stay at home. For you, for everyone", in English). Source: Ministerio de Sanidad, Consumo y Bienestar Social (2020)

consumption (for example, from national producers or small companies, which began to feel the effects of the incipient economic crisis very soon).

However, the increasingly evident and progressive fatigue of the population as the successive extensions of the State of Alarm occurred without a definitive solution to the pandemic in the short term, made the primary message of "stay home" (used not only in Government campaigns, but also widely replicated by the aforementioned "mirror" campaigns of other administrations, companies and organizations) to progressively loose its initial effectiveness, which led to "reinforcing it" with that of "*un día más, un día menos*" ("one day more, one day less" [of confinement])—Fig. 5.9.

By detailing in the public sphere, and as these extensions of the State of Alarm occurred, the "unique" leading role of the Central Government began to be shared with regional governments, multiplying contradictions and anecdotes in appearances and with respect to information on the phases of "deconfinement" and the way to face "the day after". This evident intention to obtain political revenues (both from the Government and from opposition parties and other groups), together with activity on social networks, would make it impossible to continue with the initial objective of unity of action and content.

The new "plurality" of opinions, even restricted in the press, radio, or TV, found an ideal broadcast channel on social networks. Being debatable the reliability of part of this information, the Government opted for a new call to unity, describing as "fake news" everything that opposed its messages (a similar attitude to that of Donald Trump in the USA), which it did nothing but sow doubts about a possible "control" or "censorship" of the social networks, and increase the questioning of institutional messages.[7]

[7] For example, the newspaper *El Mundo* published on April 22 that a significant percentage of support on social networks for the Central Government campaigns came from false profiles (Ollero, 2020). That media was involved, together with others, in stopping to attend official appearances, claiming that the questions were filtered, then not attending them until that situation was corrected.

Before summer 2020, in the midst of an economic crisis, and taking into account the importance of the tourism sector for the Spanish economy,[8] a deconfinement plan, in successive phases or stages,[9] was approved on May 23. The Government's slogan was also changed: "*Salimos más fuertes*" ("we're coming out stronger", in English). This slogan would accompany different campaigns to support this sector, such as the one carried out on social networks facing abroad from June 2 ("*Never Stop Dreaming*", *#SpainWillWait*), or the national one on all types of media (television, radio, press, social networks . . .) from June 18 ("*descubre lo increíble*", "*lo increíble está más cerca de lo que crees*", "*#DescubreLoIncreible*"—"Discover the incredible", "The incredible is closer than you think", "#DiscoverTheIncredible", in English).

In contrast to the apparent euphoria posed by the "return to normality",[10] the increase in infections in August revealed the anticipation of a "second wave" in the pandemic, which was not expected until late September or early October, and in which a new change of slogan took place[11]: "*España puede*" ("[All together] Spain can [come out of this]", in English). Likewise, a specific campaign was carried out for the youth group, given the relatively high non-compliance with preventive measures by those who believed themselves to be immune in these age ranges—similar to what happened in other countries -, under the hashtag "*#EstoNoEsUnJuego*" ("#ThisIsNotAGame", in English).

Despite the upward trend of the contagion curve, and analogously to the general trend regarding work activity, a face-to-face return to the classrooms at all educational levels was chosen. The regional governments were allowed to adopt and/or specify the guidelines or indications given by the Central Government, depending on the health situation at all times and in each territory, such as during the deconfinement.

The institutional purchases of useless tests and defective masks were also criticized. This provoked a new reaction from the Government, which even went so far as to forbid health personnel from talking about COVID-19 or spreading videos and messages on social networks (where they showed photos with the precarious resources to which they had to go due to the lack of materials and equipment). All this while, now from the highest public authorities, the dissemination of fake news through false profiles was denounced. Even the news about the State security forces and bodies had been asked to carry out reports on hoaxes that could generate disaffection with official campaigns and positions was spread, so giving rise to a new controversy regarding what was identified as attempted control and censorship of the content of social networks.

[8]Until the beginning of the pandemic, Spain ranked the second position as a tourist destination worldwide (UNWTO 2019).

[9]Whose relative complexity also gave rise to debate and conflicting positions, as well as the deconfinement itself: it was late for some people, adequate for others, and hasty for many, who supported that economic motivations should not take precedence over health.

[10]One of whose manifestations was, for example, the low download rate of the "Radar Covid" app, launched by the Ministry of Economic Affairs and Digital Transformation, available since the beginning of August.

[11]The previous one had been the subject of strong criticism: Who had emerged stronger from the confinement?

Fig. 5.10 Examples of messages from government campaigns against Coronavirus in the second wave and at Christmas. Translation: (1) "*#EstoNoEsUnJuego*" ("#ThisIsNotAGame", in English). "*Si no seguimos las recomendaciones sanitarias, ponemos en peligro nuestra vida y la de los demás. Ayúdanos a cumplirlas*" ("If we do not follow the health recommendations, we put our lives and the lives of others at risk. Help us by complying", in English). (2) "Cuidarnos. El mejor regalo de esta Navidad" ("Take care of ourselves: the best gift this Christmas", in English). Source: Ministerio de Sanidad, Consumo y Bienestar Social (2020)

Regardless of the fact that this situation would persist over time and that it would be the subject of debate once again (as up to 17 types of "additional" measures have coexisted with the indications or guidelines given by the Central Government, the European Union, and the international organizations such as the WHO, not always being easy to understand and reconcile), there was an improvement in the numbers of infections and hospitalizations until the end of November, interrupted after a new relaxation of measures in early December. In this context, the political will to not overstress the restrictive measures during the Christmas season was complemented with a new and intense campaign—particularly on social networks—, under the slogan "*Cuidarnos: el mejor regalo de esta Navidad*" ("To take care of ourselves: the best gift for this Christmas", in English), and the hashtag "*#ElMejorRegaloEsCuidarnos*" ("#TheBestGiftIsToTakeCareOfOurselves", in English)—Fig. 5.10.

Once again, this campaign was supported by other "mirror" campaigns by public, private, and nonprofit organizations, highlighting the work of raising students' awareness by the Universities (Fig. 5.11).

The availability of the first vaccines at the end of December also led to a very intense campaign to raise awareness about their benefits, given the high number of people who did not want to get vaccinated, according to surveys. This campaign was eminently informative (in news bulletins, social networks, ...) and it could be considered successful, despite the relative uncertainty regarding effectiveness and/or possible side effects. At this purpose, the opinions and testimonies of health experts were used again (as it had been done previously); and also the example of individuals belonging to the most vulnerable and priority groups in the vaccination calendars, disseminating images of the moments in which they were being vaccinated.

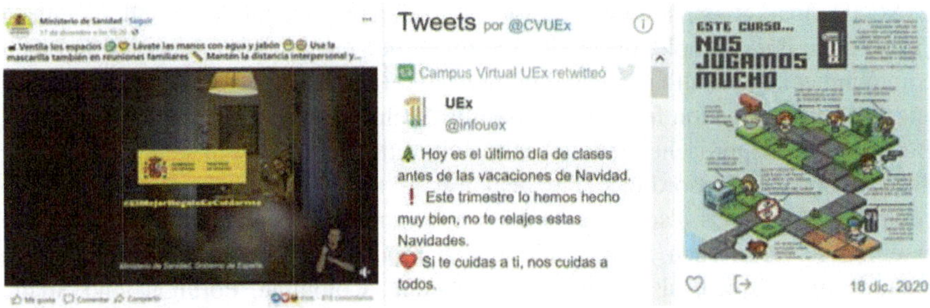

Fig. 5.11 Examples of messages on social networks, by the Government and other entities, to avoid the relaxation of behaviors against the Coronavirus at Christmas 2020. Translation: (1) "*#ElMejorRegaloEsCuidarnos*", by the Spanish Ministry of Health ("#TheBestGiftIsTakeCareOfOurselves", in English). (2) "*Hoy es el último día de clases antes de las vacaciones de Navidad. Este trimestre lo hemos hecho muy bien, no te relajes estas Navidades. Si te cuidas a ti, nos cuidas a todos*", by the University of Extremadura—UEx ("Today is the last day of class before Christmas break. We have done very well this term, don't relax this Christmas. If you take care of yourself, you take care of us all", in English). Source: Ministerio de Sanidad, Consumo y Bienestar Social (2020), and University of Extremadura (2020)

Despite all this, the "third wave" of Covid-19 become a reality in the first days of 2021, giving rise to new campaigns emphasizing the need to respect preventive measures and anticipating the adoption of more restrictive measures (insinuating the possibility of reaching another confinement, as in case of the year before), in line with the actions carried out in other European countries.

In summary, social marketing in Spain during the COVID-19 crisis, whose greatest exponent has been the government campaigns, has been characterized by:

- A number of slogans and hashtags adapted to the circumstances and objectives of each moment, and in conjunction with political marketing and economic motivations (even being subject to them),
- The search for legitimacy in experts and professionals,
- Outsourcing or generalization of responsibilities, and,
- The use of storytelling as a management weapon (as indicated by Rojo & Soler, 2020).

Meanwhile, the crisis was used to consolidate leadership. The effectiveness of this strategy is unknown and it will have its answer in the future.

Main Results In the four countries analyzed, social marketing and health communication campaigns related to COVID-19 have been varied according to their different cultures and local situation. However, some common patterns were also found. In fact, these countries implemented legal, technological, economic and informational complementary approaches to marketing in their policies (Table 5.4).

Social marketing strategies targeted different audiences in all countries (Table 5.5). For example, the WHO informed the general public (citizens and their communities) and health personnel on prevention measures, detection of symptoms, and their differentiation from other diseases (such as influenza, malaria, or dengue). But WHO also approached public health authorities and policy-makers encouraging them to lead and coordinate the response to the pandemic in their respective countries. WHO has also targeted private companies to ensure the continuity of essential services, such as maintaining the food chain, public services, and the manufacture of medical supplies. In Argentina, Colombia, Portugal, and Spain, institutional communication was focused mainly on the general population, but it also existed for the other targets.

In general, social marketing strategies combined reinforcement and induction, but also rationalization and confrontation strategies (Table 5.6).

The messages have been diverse, but they have focused on informing about the virus (what it is, how it is transmitted, what its symptoms are, how it differs from the flu, etc.), calling the citizens for joint action (appealing to unity as a country, to individual and social responsibility), inviting reflection, appealing individuals to carry out certain behaviors, etc. (see Appendix 1).

Strategies can use different tones: affirmative, interrogative and negative; imperative, ironic, humorous, positive (encouragement), explanatory (appealing to each individual, or individual and/or social responsibility), or plead (see Appendix 2). The four countries analyzed have also followed this trend: affirmative ("Colombia is with you", "[All together] Spain can [come out of this]"), interrogative ("Have you already downloaded Radar Covid App?"), and negative slogans ("We won't stop. We are always on", "This is not a game"); imperative tone ("Stay at home"), ironic—play on words ("wear mask or wear mask" [comparing two images: a young person wearing a mask, and a young person with an oxygen mask in the ICU]), positive ("Together we'll win this game", "The virus we will stop it together"), guilty ("Unprotected family meeting = burying your grandmother"), or pleading tone ("Help us to stop the virus").

The reiteration and repetition of homogeneous consistent messages have been used to offer information frequently (daily) and thus reduce uncertainty, stress, anguish, or even fear. The campaign messages have changed as the pandemic has evolved, to avoid that the continuous repetition of the same message could tire and, therefore, lose effectiveness over time.[12] Thus, it has gone from launching messages of tranquility in the first months of 2020 (January-early March), to overexposure

[12] However, there were contradictory messages (e.g. about the usage of masks): given the shortage of masks (and the threat of supplies for health personnel), government authorities initially downplayed their use (and even advised against it), despite its effectiveness in preventing infections. Later, when they could already guarantee supplies, they imposed them on a mandatory basis (for example, in Spain).

Politicians such as Donald Trump (in the USA) and Jair Bolsonaro (in Brazil) also created confusion, because they despised the use of masks and quarantine, contrary to what had been advised.

Table 5.4 Complementary approaches to social marketing

Approach	Policies and measures applied
Legal	Specific laws and mandatory regulations For example, declaration of a state of alarm, home confinement, curfews, imposition of restrictive timetables, prohibition to leave the municipality, to travel to certain countries, closure of borders; mandatory use of masks in public spaces, etc. Mandatory training in the workplace with recommendations to follow (e.g. how to use masks, how to greet each other, how to wash hands, how to keep the social distance, etc.)
Technological	Increased precision of medical diagnostic tests for the detection of the virus in clinical laboratories Acceleration of research to obtain vaccines and specific drugs New medical techniques and treatments were developed and tested Development of telecommunications and digital infrastructures Usage of big data, artificial intelligence, robotics, etc. to anticipate the evolution of the pandemic[a]
Economic	Central banks released massive liquidity into the markets and Governments launched several subsidies and financial assistance programs Provision of free (or low-cost) disinfection services in public spaces, nursing homes, schools, etc. Price controls to avoid speculation (e.g. masks) Provision of masks to people without resources and vulnerable groups Development of contingency plans; investments in research and capacity building of clinical laboratories; increase of epidemiological surveillance Financial aid to the people and companies affected. Significant amounts have also been earmarked to develop the various campaigns and disseminate it in the various media
Informative	A priority space has been dedicated to COVID-19 on the official websites of the Governments and Ministries of Health, the news and daily information about the pandemic have been generalized in all the available media, and official information from the different Ministries involved was aimed at the affected population and other essential groups For prevention, public health messages have been disseminated; and also to change people's attitude (active participation in the prevention of infections). In addition, information on prevention measures, symptoms, differentiation from other diseases (such as the flu) has been provided On the other hand, an attempt has been made to offer real-time information to healthcare personnel, as well as new action protocols

Source: Own elaboration

[a]For example:

Use of drones to avoid crowds of people in city centers

Analysis of social networks to check the perception of the population about the problem of COVID-19 and avoid "fake news"

Use of Big Data analysis techniques to make predictions about the spread of infections

Proposal of mathematical prediction models: they allow to improve long-term control actions, by studying possible scenarios and determining the impact of the virus according to conditions, areas, and lifestyles of the inhabitants, based on different variables

Mobile applications to monitor population movements, or meet people who have been close to someone positive for COVID-19

Possibility of obtaining epidemiological information in real time

Table 5.5 Main targets in social marketing strategies

Target	Measures and actions
Health personnel	Recommendations on clinical care and follow-up of people infected by COVID-19 Active training to learn about the new action protocols to prevent contagions and treat the disease, and to know the information (especially from the WHO and the national epidemiological surveillance networks) Provision of updated information on COVID-19 to all medical personnel, especially microbiologists, virologists, and epidemiologists, in addition to family or primary care doctors, as well as emergency services
Citizens	Awareness-raising campaigns to: Intensify personal hygiene and prevention measures, both at home and at work, in common spaces and public places, in commercial establishments, or on public transport Protect themselves and avoid being infected or infecting other people (always wearing a mask, keeping a safe distance, frequent hand washing/disinfection, ventilated spaces, avoiding closed spaces, and promoting outdoor activities and in open spaces, etc.) Safe use of disinfectants (to avoid allergies and skin damage) Identify the symptoms of the disease (distinguish it from others with similar symptoms, such as seasonal flu, malaria or dengue)
Health and Public Authorities	To fulfill their obligation, as public representatives, to organize and protect public health through preventive measures of the necessary benefits and services Advice on pandemic control Advice on the safe use of masks and disinfectants, and thorough cleaning and ventilation of buildings, to avoid sources of contagion in public spaces in cities Promotion of greater collaboration between different sectors (governments, experts, international organizations, Universities, companies, etc.) to avoid lack of coordination and fragmentation of preventive measures programs Guidance for border closure To manage aid for the prevention and treatment of people, companies, and sectors affected Recommendations to promote telework programs Guidance to spread public health messages and limit community transmission of the virus

Source: Own elaboration

(March–April) and preparing the de-escalation to reach the new normal (in Europe from late April–June, later in Latin America)—Rocamora (2020); to promote tourism on holidays, to remember the threat of a second wave, and to avoid infections at Christmas.

In general, the messages have been simple, straightforward (avoiding the use of technicalities), clear, and brief (e.g. "Stay home"), to reach the entire population or particularly three specific groups (health workers, youth, and policy makers), but without using other segmentation techniques (e.g. those based on psychographics). In many cases, messages were accompanied by images and explanatory drawings (with colors, to facilitate the different behaviors: as a traffic light, from red to green),

Table 5.6 Social marketing strategies

Strategies	Features
Reinforcement	It oriented towards people who have a positive attitude towards prevention and carry out the recommended behavior *E.g. Remembering the need to use the mask at all times, informing about the main prevention measures to take to avoid contagions, as well as the symptoms that the disease presents (to identify it as soon as possible, not self-medicate and go to the doctor; and to isolate oneself and not infect other people)*
Induction	It aims at people who have a positive attitude towards prevention and the recommendations of health authorities, but do not carry them out, for various reasons (due to forgetfulness, not being part of their daily routine; ignorance, etc.) *E.g. Remembering the hygiene measures to follow (hand washing) and the need to maintain social distance, ventilate closed spaces, as well as the use of a mask* *For example, putting signs at the entrance of buildings, dispensers of hydro-alcoholic gel, disinfectant carpets, ...*
Rationalization	It focused on people who have a negative attitude, although they finally carry out the desired behavior (for example, to avoid being fined) *E.g. Awareness campaigns so that people know why certain behaviors are recommended or even forced (such as staying at home, wearing a mask, not traveling, etc.), continuously reporting the situation, offering celebrities' testimonials, etc.*
Confrontation	It aims at people who have a negative attitude towards prevention and, in addition, do not carry out the recommended behaviors (e.g. not wearing a mask, going to areas with crowds of people where safety measures in terms of distance and protection are not kept—illegal parties, trips, etc.). They are called "deniers" *In this case, the strategy followed has been awareness campaigns (explaining why we have to wear a mask, why we have to keep a safe distance, why we have to wash our hands frequently, ...), complemented by financial sanctions (fines: for not respecting confinement, for not wearing a mask, etc.) and even prison sentences (for repeat offenders)*[a]. *In some cases, they have even had to visit hospital ICUs to be aware of the serious effects of COVID-19*

Source: Own Elaboration

[a]In countries like Bolivia, police disguised as coronavirus have walked the streets and harassed pedestrians to raise awareness and inform citizens that they do not go out to the street

But the most controversial measures denounced by human rights organizations have taken place in Africa, where police violence has been generalized to contain the pandemic. In countries like Kenya or South Africa, the police have used excessive force and even killed for not respecting the curfew. And in the Philippines, the president himself has ordered the police to shoot anyone who violates the quarantine

However, these types of extreme measures have not been applied in any of the four countries analyzed in this chapter

to indicate the hygiene measures to follow (how to wash hands, how to put on a mask and gloves, how to sneeze into the elbow, how to avoid touching eyes, nose and mouth; how to exercise at home, etc.). The colors of national flags have also been used to illustrate the messages of the institutional campaigns of many governments. They tried to reach all social levels and ages (children included) with little or even none adaptation to specific subcultures or lifestyles.

The story of unity and pride of the country to emerge from the pandemic has been widespread. In the specific case of the European countries analyzed, it has been common, since the European Commission wanted to give a common European response, showing European solidarity ("#StrongerTogether"). The warmongering narrative has been added in many countries: appeals to war, use of a warlike language, supported by the image of the representatives of the Army and Security Bodies. In other countries, like Argentina, the sports language was preferred. Stronger emotional appeals were used in Portugal, a country where mask recycling was also promoted.

Analyzed campaigns used all types of available media and tools to spread the message:

- Traditional media: radio, television, press, billboards, posters, brochures, public address system, public appearances and service announcements, press conferences, etc.
- Interactive media: websites, YouTube, online social networks (e.g. Facebook, Twitter, Instagram), mobile applications, SMS, banners.

But personalized information[13] has also been used, and even guerrilla actions in the street.

Signs have also been used to remind people of the need to maintain a safe distance. For example, markings on the ground in establishments where queues form, such as supermarkets, banks, customer service offices, etc.; signs with arrows to circulate in only one direction; etc.

The use of influencers and celebrities should also be highlighted: famous people (athletes, actors, singers, etc.) encouraged followers to follow hygiene and prevention measures.

In summary, prevention campaigns have been characterized by:

- Being mainly institutional. They were developed by the governments of the affected countries, and replicated or adapted by non-profit organizations (associations and NGOs), international organizations (led by WHO), and also numerous businesses.
- The main purpose was to raise awareness for the prevention of infections and the appeal to individual and social responsibility to collaborate in the problem solution.
- Having a multimedia design, based on simple, repetitive, homogeneous and consistent messages; using tones ranging from imperative to purely informational; including emotional appeals, but segmented by a few demographic characteristics.

[13] In Spain, the police have informed people who were on the street, or who were trying to leave the municipality . . . Also, in the second wave, groups of young people have approached other young people who were in the street to sensitize them to the need to wear a mask. The army has also collaborated in cleaning and disinfecting residences for the elderly, as well as in tracing the contacts of people who have tested positive for PCR.

– Legitimacy of the messages has been given by scientific experts and professionals. The collaboration of all kinds of celebrities and influencers (personalities, but also members of neighborhood associations, religious institutions, and NGOs) has also been relevant.

However, some criticisms arise. Although still scarce, studies (Kim and Kreps 2020; Lee 2020) on the communication strategies implemented by governments to manage the pandemic highlight, in some cases: (1) Confusion and lack of trust on governments, which increased population's vulnerability; (2) Regulatory inconsistency between countries and regions; (3) Contradictory example of political leaders, who increased the polarization and politicization of public discourse; (4) Dissemination of fake news and lack of cooperation and coordination between political forces, regional governments and State offices; (5) Lack of segmentation strategies; (6) Lack of efficient government-citizen dialogue channels; (7) Information overload; (8) Public communication systems and strategies unprepared for twenty-first century communication; (9) In some countries, low level of cooperation with the private sector and messages that clashed with cultural and linguistic diversity.

Effects of COVID-19 Pandemic on Quality of Life (QOL)

The COVID-19 pandemic has impacted on all dimensions of the people's quality of life, worldwide:

– *Happiness*: many people have suffered because of lockdown, restrictions on mobility, or suspension of basic freedoms and rights. Recent studies highlight the possible negative future effects of those policies.
– *Health and personal security*: they have been threatened, due to the risk of becoming infected and ill (and even dying). Prevalence of mental health problems generated by lockdown and other policies will increase in the near future.
– *Work and employment*: many people have lost their jobs, either temporarily or permanently. And those that have been able to maintain them, have had to adapt to the new situation (teleworking, avoiding face-to-face contact, etc.), and uncertainty and job instability have increased.
– *Family*: many families have had to be separated, or have not been able to visit or come together for family celebrations (weddings, birthdays, Christmas and New Year's meals, etc.), to avoid endangering the most vulnerable members. And displays of affection (kisses, hugs, etc.) have been discouraged. Also the impossibility of accompanying sick relatives in hospitals, or even going to funerals.
– *Friends and co-workers*: restrictions on group meetings reduced the possibilities for interpersonal relationships. Video calls replaced face-to-face contacts.
– *Housing and urban settings*: many houses and cities were unprepared for lockdown and restrictions.
– *Education*: limitations to physical assistance to educational centers forced institutions to adopt online teaching with none or limited training and resources. Some

children had few lessons online without the proper conditions for their age and capabilities.
- *Transportation*: avoiding public transportation due to its high risk of contagion limited people's mobility.
- *Religion and Traditions*: people could not practice their religions or rites; traditional events and gatherings were cancelled.
- *Lifestyles and Values*: further studies should analyze the change in the people's scale of values and lifestyles in the "new normal" and after long periods of isolation and stress.
- *Economic and political stability* was threatened (drop in GDP, growth in public debt, etc.).
- *Well-being*: alterations in people's living conditions under stress and without proper management would lead to a generalized loss of well-being.
- *Stress and fear of being with other people, entering closed places, living in isolation and uncertainty about the future.*

Social marketing has been key during this pandemic for the adoption of certain socially desirable behaviors (to adopt measures to prevent and avoid contagions: to wear masks, to maintain social distance, frequent hand washing, etc.). It has also helped to sensitize, aware, and educate the population about this disease and the problems it generates. And it has contributed to reducing that stress, that fear, and increasing individual and societal resilience and well-being.

Conclusions

In the case of COVID-19, social marketing campaigns have played a fundamental role.

They have been varied, offering differences according to the countries' situations but also some similarities. They have been characterized by having an attractive design, with drawings and little text, to reach large audiences. Using multimedia formats, the COVID-19 pandemic motivated the first global cross-media and massive social marketing effort. However, coordination and a perspective of quality of life lacked. In fact, the messages have focused on awareness-raising, preventing contagions, and calling for unity, for joint, social and responsible action of the citizens to stop the spread of the virus. Different tones have been used: from the imperative to the simply informative, also using fear and social alarm, and emotional appeals.

The main criticisms of the strategies have focused on the lack of coordination and publics' segmentation, information overload and some contradictions that emerged in the messages.

At the end of 2020, the pandemic maintained its risk at a global level, with the appearance of new, more contagious strains of the virus, and the threat of a third wave of infections in January 2021.

Discussion Questions

1. What do you think the concern about COVID-19 is currently and internationally?
2. Was any information provided on COVID-19 in your country? What type? What were the sources (e.g. health authorities, the government, the media, ...)?
3. What social marketing campaigns related to COVID-19 were carried out in your country? During how much time? Are there currently any in force? What impact did they have on the quality of life of the population?
4. Assess the main consequences (demographic, economic, social, environmental, cultural, technological, political—legal, ...) of COVID-19 since the international health emergency was declared in early 2020. What have been its effects on the people's quality of life?
5. Would a perspective of quality of life increase the impact of social marketing campaigns in the countries analyzed?

Appendix 1: Some Examples of Messages

Message aim	Examples
To report the virus	**Argentina**: "*Nuevo Coronavirus Covid-19. Saber para prevenir*" ["New Coronavirus Covid-19. To know is to prevent"] **Colombia**: "*Mito—Realidad del Coronavirus*" ["Myth-Reality of the Coronavirus"]
Call for joint action (unity, responsibility, country)	**Argentina**: citizens as a soccer team "*Al virus lo frenamos entre todos. Viralicemos la responsabilidad*" ["We'll stop the virus together. Let's Viralize Responsibility"], "*#SomosResponsables*" ["#WeAreResponsible"], "*Todos ante el mismo rival. Este partido lo ganamos juntos*" [Only together will we beat this rival], "*Al coronavirus le ganamos con el compromiso de todos, jugando en equipo y con responsabilidad*" ["We'll beat the coronavirus with the commitment of all, playing as a team responsibly"], "*#UnaSolaHinchada*" ["#FootballFansTogether"], "*#ArgentinaAplaude*" ["ArgentinaIsClapping"]. **Colombia**: also as a soccer team. "*El futuro es de todos*" ["The future belongs to everyone"], "*#UnidosSomosMasPais*" [We are more of a country together], "*Colombia está contigo*" ["Colombia is with you"], "*Colombia sigue adelante*" ["Colombia is going ahead"], "*Ganar entre todos este partido. #TiempoExtraEnCasa*" ["Winning this game together. #ExtraTimeAtHome"]. **Portugal**: always "on" (internet). "*Nao paramos. Estamos ON*" ["We won't stop. We are always on"], "Continuamos ON" ["We're still on"].

(continued)

Message aim	Examples
	Spain: unity, responsibility, effort. "*Este virus lo paramos unidos*" ["This virus we will stop it together"], "*Salimos más Fuertes* ["We're coming out stronger"]. *Gracias a la responsabilidad y al esfuerzo de todos, hemos llegado hasta aquí. Esa es nuestra fuerza*" [Thanks to everyone's responsibility and effort, we have come this far. That is our strength"], "*España puede*" [(All together) Spain can (come out of this)].
Thought/Reflexion	**Spain**: "*Esto no es un juego*" ["This is not a game"] "*Este curso nos jugamos mucho*" ["In this academic year, there is a lot at stake] (University of Extremadura—Spain)
Behaviors	**Argentina, Colombia, Portugal, Spain and many others:** "*#QuédateEnCasa*" ["#StayAtHome"] **Argentina**: "*Argentina Aplaude*" ["Argentina is clapping"] **Colombia**: "*Limpia tus manos*" ["Wash your hands"] **Portugal**: "*Alerta Cibersegurança COVID-19. Durante o isolamento, proteja-se*" ["COVID-19 Cyber Security Alert. During lockdown, protect yourself"] "*Proteja-se a si e as outros*" ["Protect yourself and others"] **Spain**: "*¡Lávate las manos!*" ["Wash your hands!"]
To appeal to each individual or to individual responsibility	**Argentina, Colombia, Portugal, Spain**: "*#YoMeQuedoEnCasa*" ["I'm staying at home"]. **Colombia**: "*El primer control contra el Coronavirus es usted*" ["You are the first line of defense against the Coronavirus"]. "*Prevenir el Coronavirus #EmpiezaPorTusManos*" ["Preventing Coronavirus #StartsWithYourHands"]. **Portugal**: "*Cabe a cada um de nós fazê-lo parar*" ["It's up to each one of us to stop it"]. "*Nao deixes o virus entrar*" ["Don't let the virus in"]. "*#MascaraParaTodos. A minha protege-te. A tua protege-me*" ["*#Mask for everyone. Mine protects you. Yours protects me*"]. **Spain** "*Este virus lo paramos unidos*" ["This virus we will stop it together"] "Lo paramos si ayudas y haces caso a nuestros profesionales" ["We'll stop it if you help by listening to our professionals"] "Cumple las recomendaciones" ["Follow the recommendations"]

Source: Adapted from the official messages of the countries mentioned

Appendix 2: Examples of Different Tones Used in the Campaigns

Tone	Examples
Affirmative	**Argentina**: "Nuevo Coronavirus Covid-19. Saber para prevenir" ["New Coronavirus Covid-19. To know is to prevent"] "#SomosResponsables" ["#WeAreResponsible"] "Argentina Aplaude" ["Argentina is clapping"] **Colombia**: "Colombia está contigo" ["Colombia is with you"] **Portugal**: "Continuamos ON" ["We're still ON"] **Spain:** "España puede" [(All together) "Spain can" (come out of this)]
Interrogative	**Spain**: "¿Te has descargado ya Radar Covid?" ["Have you downloaded Covid Radar yet?" "¿Cómo debo lavarme las manos?" ["How should I wash my hands?"]
Negative	**Portugal**: "Não *paramos. Estamos ON*" ["We don't stop. We're still ON"]. "Não *deixes o vírus entrar*" ["Don't let the virus in"]. *"Don't drop your mask".* *"Don't make things easy: we are all agents of public health".* **Spain**: "*Esto no es un juego*" ["This is not a game"]. "*Never Stop Dreaming. #SpainWillWait*".
Imperative	**Almost all countries**: "Stay (at) Home". **Argentina**: "*Seguí cuidándote*" ["Follow care"]. **Colombia**: "*Limpia tus manos*" ["Wash your hands"]. **Portugal**: "*Durante o isolamento, proteja-se*!" ["During lockdown, protect yourself!"] "*Proteja-se a si e as outros*" ["Protect yourself and others"] "Seja um agente de Saúde Pública. Proteja-se a si e aos outros" ["Be an agent of public health. Protect yourself & others"]. **Spain**: "¡*Lávate las manos*!" ["Wash your hands!"] [Radar Covid] "*Frena la cadena de contagios*" ["Stop the chain of infections"], "*Protégete y protege a los tuyos*" ["Protect yourself and your loved ones"],

(continued)

Tone	Examples
	"*Cumple las recomendaciones*" ["Follow the recommendations"], "*Descubre lo increíble*" ["Discover the incredible"]
Ironic (play on words)	**Portugal**: *"A decisão é tua. Usar mascara ou usar máscara"* [comparing two images: the first one, a young person wearing a mask; and the second one, a young person with an oxygen mask in ICU].
Positive/encouragement	**Argentina**: "*Al virus lo frenamos entre todos*" ["We'll stop the virus together"] "*Todos ante el mismo rival. Este partido lo ganamos juntos*" [Only together will we beat this rival] "#UnaSolaHinchada" ["#FootballFansTogether"] **Colombia**: "*#UnidosSomosMasPais*" ["#WeAreMoreOfACountryTogether"] "Ganar entre todos este partido. #TiempoExtraEnCasa" ["Winning this game together. #ExtraTimeAtHome"] **Portugal**: "Somos todos uma só voz" ["We are only one voice: only together will we beat this pandemic"] **Spain**: Este virus lo paramos entre todos" [""This Virus We Will Stop It Together"], "Salimos más fuertes" ["We're coming out stronger"], "Cuidarnos. El mejor regalo de esta Navidad" ["Take care of ourselves. The best gift this Christmas"]
Explanatory, appealing to each individual or to individual responsibility	**Portugal**: "*Cabe a cada um de nós fazê-lo parar*" ["It's up to each one of us to stop it"]. **Spain**: "*#YoMeQuedoEnCasa*" ["I stay at home"]. "*Lo paramos si ayudas y haces caso a nuestros profesionales*" ["We'll stop it if you help by listening to our professionals"].
Guilt	**Spain**: *"Saltarse la cuarentena = intubar a tu mejor amigo"* ["Break quarantine = intubate your best friend"]. *"Reunión familiar sin protección = enterrar a tu abuela"* ["Unprotected family meeting = burying your grandmother"].
Plead	**Spain**: "*Ayúdanos a frenar el coronavirus. Protege a los más vulnerables*" ["Help us to stop the coronavirus. Protect the most vulnerable"]. "*Ayúdanos a cumplir las recomendaciones sanitarias*" ["Help us to comply with health recommendations"].

Source: Adapted from official messages found on Google (2020)

Teaching Notes

1. **What do you think the concern about COVID-19 is currently and internationally?**
When students work on this case, surely the situation related to the COVID-19 pandemic will be different from that reflected in this case (which is limited to the first year of the COVID-19 pandemic, 2020).
The idea is that students assess the international situation of the pandemic at that moment and, as far as possible, compare it with the situation in 2020.
2. **Was any information provided on COVID-19 in your country? What type? What were the sources (e.g. health authorities, the government, the media, ...)?**
These questions focus on analyzing how information on COVID-19 was provided in the students' countries.
Following the structure of the chapter, readers/students are also asked to analyze what type of information was provided in their respective countries, and what the main source was (e.g. the Government, health authorities, the media, etc.).
If the students come from different countries, comparisons could be made (e.g. see if the information provided was similar in all of them or, on the contrary, there were significant differences).
3. **What social marketing campaigns related to COVID-19 were carried out in your country? During how much time? Are there currently any in force? What impact did they have on the quality of life of the population?**
The idea behind these questions is for students to remember and/or look for information about the main social marketing campaigns that were developed in their respective countries, or that could even continue to be developed (everything will depend on the evolution of the pandemic in the coming years).
By carrying out this analysis, students will also be able to draw on their own experiences to assess the impact that these campaigns have had (or continue to have, if applicable) on the quality of life of the population in their country, region and/or city.
They will be able to compare their results with those reflected in the chapter (i.e. see if there are similarities or differences). Or, if the students in the class come from different countries, they can also compare them and discuss which they think were the best/worst social marketing campaigns, or which ones had more/less impact on the people's quality of life.
4. **Assess the main consequences (demographic, economic, social, environmental, cultural, technological, political—legal, ...) of COVID-19 since the international health emergency was declared in early 2020. What have been its effects on the people's quality of life?**
When the students work on this case, they will have a more complete perspective of the situation, because more time will have passed and they will not have to focus only on 2020. They could discover new consequences and effects

that have not been considered in the case study, depending on the evolution of the COVID-19 pandemic in the coming years.

5. **Would a quality of life perspective increase the impact of social marketing campaigns in the countries analyzed?**

   This question focuses on the students thinking and expressing their opinions about the impact of social marketing campaigns since a quality of life perspective.

   An alternative activity could be to divide the class into two groups. One in favor that a quality of life perspective increases the impact of social marketing campaigns, and another against this ("quality of life perspective does not increase the impact of social marketing campaigns"). Each group should defend its position with well justified arguments (preferably based on real examples from their respective countries), to discuss this topic properly.

References

ADEPA (2020) Los medios y la sociedad civil de Argentina se unen frente al coronavirus. 20/03/2020. https://adepa.org.ar/somosresponsables/

AFP (2020) Un hombre yace muerto en la calle en Wuhan, foco de la epidemia de coronavirus en China. El Mundo, 31/01/2020. https://www.elmundo.es/ciencia-y-salud/salud/2020/01/31/5e3415b321efa02b0a8b4591.html

Ahmed O, Brockmeier D, Lee K, Chapman WC, Doyle MB (2020) Donación de órganos durante la pandemia de Covid-19. Rev Estadounidense Trasplantes 0:1–2

Banco Mundial (2020) Colombia: panorama general. https://www.bancomundial.org/es/country/colombia/overview

Becares R (2020) Así es por dentro el Hospital Isabel Zendal: más de mil camas, última tecnología y aire renovado 14 veces a la hora. El Mundo, 1st December. https://www.elmundo.es/madrid/2020/12/01/5fc53eb7fc6c8391388b4661.html

Chaparro C (2020) Tapiar casas para encerrar a las familias en cuarentena por coronavirus y evitar que escapen: está ocurriendo en China. Yahoo Noticias, 27/02/2020. https://es.noticias.yahoo.com

Clarin (2020) Argentina aplaude: convocan hoy a apoyar a los profesionales de salud que trabajan contra el coronavirus. Flyer from Twitter. Clarin, 19th March. https://www.clarin.com/sociedad/argentina-aplaude-convocan-hoy-apoyar-profesionales-salud-trabajan-coronavirus_0_Jd-ZHsIle.html

European Centre for Disease Prevention and Control (2020) COVID-19 pandemic. https://www.ecdc.europa.eu/en

European Commission (2020) Coronavirus vaccines strategy. https://ec.europa.eu/info/live-work-travel-eu/coronavirus-response/public-health/coronavirus-vaccines-strategy_en. Accessed 19 Dec 2020

Galan-Ladero MA, Galan-Ladero MM (2019) The importance of social marketing in global health emergencies. The case of Zika virus infection. In: Galán-Ladero M, Alves H (eds) Case studies on social marketing. A global perspective. Springer, Cham

Google (2020) Official Website. https://www.google.com

HUA (2020) Hospital Universitario Austral - Hospital Solidario Covid. https://www.hospitalaustral.edu.ar/hospital-solidario-covid/

INFOBAE (2020) El emotivo video de AFA para concientizar sobre el aislamiento obligatorio: "Nadie sale campeón solo". 29th March. https://www.infobae.com/deportes-2/2020/03/29/el-emotivo-video-de-afa-para-concientizar-sobre-el-aislamiento-obligatorio-nadie-sale-campeon-solo/

Kim KD, Kreps GL (2020) An analysis of government communication in the United States during the COVID-19 pandemic: recommendations for effective government health risk. World Med Health Policy 12(4):398–412

Lakoff G (2007) No pienses en un elefante. Complutense, Madrid

Lee NR (2020) Reducing the spread of COVID-19: a social marketing perspective. Soc Mark Q 26 (3):259–265

Ollero DJ (2020) Facebook borra las cuentas falsas que elogiaban al Gobierno pero no desvela su autoría. El Mundo, 22/04/2020. https://www.elmundo.es/tecnologia/2020/04/22/5ea0459bfc6c83ed398b45c5.html

Rivera R, Bianchi EC (2020) Qué cuarentena es la mejor para la Argentina. Perfil, 28th May. https://www.perfil.com/noticias/coronavirus/opinion-reynaldo-rivera-enrique-carlos-bianchique-cuarentena-es-mejor-argentina-pandemia-coronavirus.phtml

Rocamora J (2020) Comunicación institucional durante la crisis del coronavirus: cómo la han gestionado empresas y políticos. Marketing 4 Ecommerce. https://marketing4ecommerce.net/

Roces P (2020) Isabel Díaz Ayuso inaugura el hospital de Madrid para pandemias Isabel Zendal: "Es un centro abierto a todas la comunidades de España". El Mundo, 1st December. https://www.elmundo.es/madrid/2020/12/01/5fc6270dfdddff50bf8b45fc.html

Rojo JM, Soler A (2020) Comunicación política en tiempos de alarma. El caso español. Más poder local 41:36–38

RTVE.es (2020) ¿Qué se sabe del Coronavirus? https://www.rtve.es

University of Extremadura (2020) Official Website. Virtual Campus. https://campusvirtual.unex.es/portal/

UNWTO (2019) Panorama del turismo internacional. https://www.e-unwto.org/doi/pdf/10.18111/9789284421237

Wang C, Pan R, Wan X, Tan Y, Xu L, Ho CS et al (2020) Immediate psychological responses and associated factors during the initial stage of the 2019 coronavirus disease (COVID-19) epidemic among the general population in China. Int J Environ Res Public Health 17:1729. https://doi.org/10.3390/ijerph17051729

World Health Organization (2020) Official website. https://www.who.int/home

Chapter 6
From "Stoptober" in the UK to "Mois Sans Tabac" in France: How to Import and Evaluate a Complex and Large-Scale Social Marketing Campaign

Romain Guignard, Auriane Djian, Anne Pasquereau, Aurélie Blanc, Karine Gallopel-Morvan, Olivier Smadja, Justine Avenel-Roux, Félicie David, Jennifer Davies, Guillemette Quatremére, Pierre Arwidson, and Viêt Nguyen-Thanh

Abstract Beyond health improvement, quitting smoking also affects the quality of smokers' lives by actually improving mental health and wellbeing: it can improve mood and help relieve stress, anxiety and depression. In order to increase the health (and thus the quality of life) of French people, *Santé publique France*, the French National Public Health Agency, launched for the first time in 2016 "Mois sans tabac", a social marketing campaign inspired by Public Health England's "Stoptober". "Mois sans tabac" is an ongoing intervention based on the PRIME theory of motivation and on the social contagion theory. It sets smokers the challenge of being smoke-free for the month of November. This campaign uses social marketing principles (the 5Ps, branding, mass-media campaign, cessation help services, etc.) and targets smokers but also their loved ones, with a view to encouraging the latter to support smokers in their attempts to quit their habit. This campaign was strongly rooted in collaboration between *Santé publique France* and various public and private partners who can influence smokers' behaviours (health professionals and facilities, NGOs, companies, etc.), in particular by implementing

R. Guignard · A. Djian · A. Pasquereau · A. Blanc · O. Smadja · J. Avenel-Roux · F. David · J. Davies · G. Quatremére · P. Arwidson · V. Nguyen-Thanh
Santé Publique France, Saint-Maurice, France
e-mail: Romain.GUIGNARD@santepubliquefrance.fr; Anne.PASQUEREAU@santepubliquefrance.fr; olivier.smadja@santepubliquefrance.fr; Justine.Avenel-Roux@santepubliquefrance.fr; Felicie.DAVID@santepubliquefrance.fr; Jennifer.DAVIES@santepubliquefrance.fr; Guillemette.QUATREMERE@santepubliquefrance.fr; Pierre.ARWIDSON@santepubliquefrance.fr; Viet.NGUYEN-THANH@santepubliquefrance.fr

K. Gallopel-Morvan (✉)
EHESP School of Public Health, Rennes, France
e-mail: Karine.Gallopel-Morvan@ehesp.fr

M. M. Galan-Ladero, R. G. Rivera (eds.), *Applied Social Marketing and Quality of Life*, Applying Quality of Life Research,
https://doi.org/10.1007/978-3-030-83286-5_6

actions at the local level which focus on awareness and provide help for smoking cessation.

This chapter has two aims: (1) to describe theoretical and social marketing principles of "Mois sans tabac" implemented in France in 2016 (and later); (2) to present how this complex and large-scale social marketing campaign was evaluated.

Keywords Social marketing · Smoking cessation · Adaptation · Evaluation

Introduction

In 2016, Santé publique France (the French National Public Health Agency) launched for the first time "Mois sans tabac", an intervention inspired by the ongoing Public Health England's "Stoptober" campaign. "Stoptober" has proven to be a great success, generating 350,000 additional attempts to quit among smokers in its first edition in 2012 (Brown et al. 2014), and has been implemented in the whole United Kingdom. "Mois sans tabac" was the first large-scale French anti-tobacco campaign based on social marketing principles. As it was a success, it was launched again in 2017, 2018, 2019, 2020 and still exists in 2021.

Both programs are based on the challenge of being smoke-free for 1 month (in October in the UK and in November in France), positive messaging, and include social marketing tools (the 5Ps, traditional and digital media, a website, cessation help services, etc.) and a call for support from smoker's relatives and friends, the building of partnerships and local dissemination.

This campaign was launched in a French context where smoking prevalence was particularly high, and where large inequalities existed between people with different socioeconomic statuses. Smoking prevalence in 2016 was 34.5% in people aged 15–75 (28.7% were daily smokers) (Pasquereau et al. 2017), contrasting with approximately 25% in Germany and Spain and 15.5% in England (World Health Organization 2017). In addition, in 2016, 50% of unemployed adults were smokers in France compared with 31% of employed adults. In 2015, over 75,000 deaths were attributed to tobacco consumption in this country (Bonaldi et al. 2019).

The aim of the "Mois sans tabac" campaign was to help the 60% of French daily smokers who want to quit (Guignard et al. 2015). Quitting smoking has several advantages: it reduces disease risk, death due to smoking and widely, it increases the quality of life (Piper et al. 2012). The latter includes psychological benefits (quitting tobacco decreases depression, anxiety, and stress and improves positive mood compared with continuing to smoke; Taylor et al. 2014), economical benefits (according to the World Health Organisation, smoking burdens the global economy with an estimated US$1.4 trillion in healthcare costs and lost productivity each year[1]) and ecological ones (tobacco smoking leads to the emission of 2,600,000 tonnes of carbon dioxide and about 5,200,000 tonnes of methane[2]).

The aim of this chapter is to describe a real social marketing campaign, "Mois sans tabac", implemented in France in order to increase quitting smoking and thus the quality of life (Gallopel-Morvan et al., 2017). The first purpose of this case study is to describe theoretical and social marketing principles of this campaign (the PRIME theory of motivation, the social contagion theory, the 5Ps). This section will also show how Santé publique France has adapted the British "Stoptober" campaign by favouring a regional smoking prevention network and by building an innovative partnership strategy to reach smokers. The second aim of this chapter is to describe how this complex and large-scale social marketing campaign has been evaluated. Literature in social marketing has highlighted that several kinds of evaluation are usually necessary (Doner 2003; Hastings and Domegan 2017; Lee and Kotler 2019). This chapter will highlight which methods, sources and indicators have been used for evaluating "Mois sans tabac".

Theoretical Frameworks and Social Marketing Principles of the "Mois sans tabac" and Adaptation of the Campaign to a French Context

Theoretical Frameworks and Social Marketing Principles

Objective The main aims of this campaign were (1) to encourage smokers to quit smoking for the whole month of November, (2) to encourage non-smokers and partners of the campaign to support them, and (3) to encourage smokers to use available smoking cessation services during their quit attempt. By doing this, the campaign sets out a SMART goal (*Specific, Measurable, Assignable, Realistic, Time-related*) (Doran 1981), which constitutes an intermediate objective that facilitates the achievement of the desired behaviour.

Target and Segmentation "Mois sans tabac" mainly targets smokers aged 20–49 years old, the age group with the highest smoking prevalence in France (Pasquereau et al. 2017).

Theoretical framework Like the "Stoptober" campaign, the initial design of "Mois sans tabac" was based on the PRIME theory of motivation (Plans, Responses, Impulses, Motives, and Evaluations) (West and Brown 2013). According to this theory, "*behaviour is determined on a moment-to-moment basis by a wide variety of motivational inputs, from impulses and inhibitory forces, through desires, drives,*

[1] https://www.who.int/tobacco/economics/background/en/

[2] http://www.ash.org.uk/files/documents/ASH_127.pdf; London: Action on Smoking and Health; 2015.

and emotional states, to evaluations and plans. As a result the motivational system is inherently unstable and requires constant balancing input to maintain a constant pattern of behaviour. Apparently small external triggers can affect a sudden transition in the system [. . .]. Thus, interventions to affect change are more likely to be successful if they target the whole motivational system, rather than just some elements of it [. . .]." (Brown et al. 2014). Therefore, campaigns like "Stoptober" or "Mois sans tabac" are designed to multiply incentives to quit smoking, by using as many channels as possible (media, local awareness actions, tools to help smokers quit, etc.). "Mois sans tabac" and "Stoptober" also integrated the social contagion theory, a process by which individuals influence each other to adopt a new behaviour (Einstein and Epstein 1980; Bilgicer et al., 2015). It is dependent on consumer characteristics, and the persons interacting with and living near to consumers, the former being the population most likely to influence the latter (Langley et al. 2012). This theory has been used in commercial marketing (Plé and Demangeot 2019) but rarely in social marketing. However, it is relevant in the context of smoking: research has shown that smokers are 67% more likely to quit when their spouse stops smoking, 36% more likely when a close friend quits, and 34% more likely when someone they work with quits (Christakis and Fowler 2008).

Brand For the first time in France, a specific national anti-smoking brand was created for the campaign's launch in 2016: "Mois sans tabac", which means "Me/Month without tobacco", and is a play on the French words "*mois*" (month) and "*moi*" (me). The brand relies on three principal levers: (1) a literature-proven rational promise that after 30 days without tobacco the smoker is five times more likely to quit permanently (West and Stapleton 2008); (2) an emotional promise that the quit attempt will be easier and even enjoyable if it is attempted together with others; (3) a positive and encouraging tone built around the symbol V for victory, a warm yellow and red logo design (see Fig. 6.1).

Product The product of "Mois sans tabac" consists in setting smokers a challenge: they are encouraged to quit smoking for the whole of November. To achieve this, they can benefit from different cessation services: the help of health professionals, the "Tabac Info Service" quitline (3989), and a variety of free resources (a quit kit, "Tabac Info Service" mobile app, flyers, etc.). The "Tabac Info Service" quitline

Fig. 6.1 The brand, logo and slogan for "Mois sans tabac". Source: Santé Publique France (2016)

existed before the 2016 launch of the campaign, while the mobile app and the quit kit were specifically created for it. People motivated to quit or to help smokers were invited to register on a specific website (https://mois-sans-tabac.tabac-info-service.fr/) or via the "Tabac Info Service" quitline, which provided personalised help from an expert. The quit kit was developed in partnership with the French NGO Ligue contre le cancer (League against cancer) and contained a preparation brochure, a 30-day calendar with day-to-day advice, a leaflet with breathing exercises, a badge, a sticker with nutritional recommendations to avoid weight gain and a cardboard wheel to estimate the savings made every day without tobacco. It was pretested in 2015, before the first edition of the campaign, with four focus groups, each comprising eight to ten smokers, followed by individual telephone interviews 4 weeks later.

Price A key point of the campaign was to make the cost of quitting as low as possible. Therefore smokers were not charged for cessation services, apart from the "Tabac Info Service" quitline, where calls are charged at a standard rate.

Place and partners *Santé publique France* created a network of partners to increase both the visibility of the campaign and access to smoking cessation services placed in proximity to smokers' living and working environments.

As usual when anti-tobacco campaigns are launched, health professionals of all kinds—doctors (general practitioners: GPs, and specialists), nurses, pharmacists, dentists, midwives—were involved in the campaign because of their ability to engage in constructive discussion about tobacco cessation with their patients. Involving health professionals is imperative as attempts to quit are more successful when smokers are supported by health professionals and use nicotine replacement treatments. For the launch of "Mois sans tabac", Santé publique France met with health professional organisations (orders, colleges, unions, scientific organisations) to invite them to join the campaign. Health practitioners could order posters or flyers that echoed campaign messages (for example "*Here, we support all smokers who decide to quit*") as well as more general leaflets ("*Quitting smoking, need help?*", "*Why quit smoking?*" and "*Tobacco-free pregnancy*").

For the first time, Santé publique France built a network of public and private partners in order to boost the profile and impact of the campaign. Public partners included *L'Assurance Maladie* (a public body in charge of reimbursing health costs and involved in prevention and health education actions), *Pôle Emploi* (the public service dedicated to helping people return to employment, the objective here being to increase campaign visibility among unemployed people), and *Le Conseil national de l'Ordre des Pharmaciens (*the National Council of the Order of Pharmacists). Regional health agencies were invited to steer the campaign at a regional level. Project leaders (also named "ambassadors") were recruited to help the regional health agencies disseminate the campaign by promoting it to regional stakeholders (healthcare facilities, health professionals, media, associations, local authorities, private companies, etc.), by setting up methodological advice services, and by reporting awareness and smoking cessation help actions implemented locally. The value of support from families, friends, colleagues and non-smokers in helping smokers quit was also emphasized in the campaign (this message was displayed in mass media). Campaign partners' principal activities were to increase public awareness of the campaign, organize cessation follow-up sessions, and set up relevant actions to encourage employees or clients to quit smoking. They could order physical (posters, flyers, quit-kits, windbreakers), and digital (email signatures, logos, graphical charts) tools on the website http://partenaires-mois-sans-tabac.tabac-info-service.fr/.

Promotion (media campaign) The campaign slogan was "*En novembre, on arrête ensemble*" ("In November, we're quitting together"). Its budget aimed at obtaining a 530 Gross Rating Point (GRP) for TV spots (a 689 GRP including online videos), 680 GRP for radio spots and 1195 GRP for street posters. A total of 103.9 million web banners were also displayed.

For the first edition in 2016, the campaign included three stages: the first took place in September and consisted in informing health professionals (GPs, specialists, pharmacists, midwives) about the launch of the campaign through a combination of mass mailing, advertising in professional press and websites, and the development of a dedicated website (pro.tabac-info-service.fr). The second stage occurred between 10 and 31 October 2016 and comprised a mass-media campaign using both traditional and digital media in order to encourage widespread participation. The target groups for traditional media were 25–49 years old, and 20–49 years old for digital media. Communication messages were created for TV, radio, the internet, social networks and street posters. A roadshow also promoted the campaign in eight French cities. Moreover, the theme of the campaign (including its brand) and some of its tools (posters, cessation tools) appeared in a popular French television sitcom ('*Plus Belle la Vie*'). The third stage was the implementation of the challenge itself in November 2016.

Adaptation of the "Stoptober" Campaign to the French Context

Before implementing the "Mois sans tabac" campaign, Santé publique France had to analyse the British and French' specific national contexts and resulting similarities and differences regarding the French campaign development compared to "Stoptober" intervention.[3] A contextual analysis was performed regarding smoking prevalence, health services and culture. In addition, a meeting was organised between Public Health England and Santé publique France to share details about the UK experience.

The two campaigns had common elements (presented in the Table 6.1) but also differences to fit with countries' context and environment.

[3] A more complete description of how the Mois sans tabac campaign was adapted from Stoptober is detailed elsewhere (Djian et al. 2019).

Table 6.1 Similar and different elements of the French and British campaigns

<table>
<tr><th>Social marketing elements</th><th>The United Kingdom</th><th>France</th></tr>
<tr><td rowspan="2">Tobacco context in 2016</td><td>Smoking prevalence in the UK was 15.8%</td><td>Smoking prevalence in France was 34.5%</td></tr>
<tr><td colspan="2">Smoking prevalence was about twice as high in France as in the United Kingdom, leading to a lower degree of denormalisation of smoking</td></tr>
<tr><td rowspan="2">Objective</td><td colspan="2">For both campaigns: to encourage smokers to quit smoking for a whole month and to use collective leverage to help them quit</td></tr>
<tr><td>The quitting month was October</td><td>The quitting month was shifted to November to avoid competing with another French public health campaign, "Octobre rose", which encourages breast cancer screening</td></tr>
<tr><td>Theoretical framework</td><td colspan="2">Both campaigns were based on the PRIME theory of motivation and on the social contagion theory</td></tr>
<tr><td>Target and segmentation</td><td colspan="2">Both campaigns mainly target smokers aged 20–49 years old who are motivated to quit</td></tr>
<tr><td rowspan="2">Products</td><td>Different cessation support tools (website, app, quit kit, quitline, etc.)</td><td>Previous French cessation supports were used for the campaign, a new mobile phone app was created, and the quit kit of the UK was adapted to France</td></tr>
<tr><td colspan="2">Both campaigns provide a wide range of cessation support tools: text supports, a mobile phone application, a quitline, websites, social networks and a quit kit to guide smokers</td></tr>
<tr><td rowspan="2">Prices</td><td>Smoking cessation resources are practically free of charge throughout the UK network</td><td>In 2016, nicotine replacement therapies were only partly reimbursed through a national system, with a maximum reimbursement of 150 euros per year per smoker until 2018</td></tr>
<tr><td colspan="2">Apart from nicotine replacement therapies, all resources were free of charge</td></tr>
<tr><td>Availability and partnership</td><td>There was high quality assistance provided by "Stop Smoking Services" located near smokers' residences. These structures are present all over the country, with a focus on more deprived areas.
All healthcare practitioners in the UK can benefit from basic training on tobacco cessation (GPs, pharmacists, nurses, psychologists, social workers, etc.)</td><td>Santé publique France had to adjust the British model by favouring a regional smoking prevention network and by building an innovative partnership strategy to reach the target. Cessation support services were mainly provided by GPs and hospital-based cessation services, and smoking cessation consultations were only provided by tobacco specialists (health professionals with a diploma in tobacco addiction)</td></tr>
<tr><td rowspan="2">Promotion</td><td>Brand name, logo, slogan, mass media and digital media</td><td>The campaign, including the brand name, its logo and its slogan, was created to fit in with the French culture and language. Mass media and digital media were mobilised</td></tr>
<tr><td colspan="2">Both campaigns deliver the same positive tone through popular and cheerful messages and through mass and digital media</td></tr>
</table>

Evaluation of "Mois sans tabac": Various Methods, Indicators, Sources and Results

The overall aim of the "Mois sans tabac" campaign is to increase the number of attempts to quit among smokers in France, with a view to decreasing national smoking prevalence. Fundamental to its design is the engagement not only of smokers, but also of non-smokers and various public and private partners. Therefore, to evaluate "Mois sans tabac", a global process evaluation of campaign was performed, using several indicators. More specifically, various quantitative and qualitative self-report methods together with observational measures were used.

Impact of the Campaign on the Main Target: Smokers

We evaluated the impact of the campaign on smokers using different sets of indicators: use of cessation services (the "product" of the campaign), perception of the campaign, and behavioural impact (attempts to quit, evolution of smoking prevalence).

The use of cessation services was evaluated with registrations on the campaign's dedicated page in the "Tabac info service" website and the use of help services: visitors to the website, calls to the quit helpline, phone-based app and quit kit. Perception of the campaign was measured with a qualitative post-test (six focus groups) carried out in December 2016 on 32 smokers who wished to quit and who had heard about "Mois sans tabac". Focus groups comprised smokers who made a quit attempt during the campaign and smokers who did not. The objectives were to get their opinion on the campaign, to identify levers and barriers to participation and to attempts to quit and to obtain feedback about communication tools. Two quantitative surveys were conducted to measure (1) monthly quit attempt rates among smokers in the last quarter of 2016 (compared with previous months in 2016 and with 2015); (2) number of attempts to quit attributable to "Mois sans tabac" in the last quarter of 2016; and (3) evolution of smoking prevalence in France between 2016 and 2017. The first survey was a monthly quota-based study of attempts to quit, conducted by phone each month on a sample of 2000 people aged between 15 and 85 years old, including approximately 500 smokers. The second survey was the 'Health Barometer', a large annual random phone survey of health behaviours and perceptions of people living in France: 15,216 people aged 15–75 were interviewed between January and August 2016, and 25,319 people aged 18–75 were interviewed in 2017 (same period) (participation rate: around 50%). Among other questions, people were asked in these two surveys their smoking status and, for smokers, if they tried quitting smoking in the last year/month.

Compared with the U.K.'s "Stoptober" campaign, which led to approximately 3% of smokers registering in 2012 (275,000 smokers registered online as participants in this challenge) (Fenton 2016), 1.3% (i.e., 180,113 smokers) of France's estimated

14 million daily smokers registered in the first edition of "Mois sans tabac". Beyond registrations, 66,613 accounts were created using the phone app, and the number of calls to the quit helpline was 15,618. For the later, it was over twice the number for the same months in 2015 (6956). The number of unique visitors to the www.tabac-info-service.fr website was 1.58 million in October and November 2016, over three times higher than in 2015 for the same period (0.51 million). "Mois sans tabac" was therefore associated with a substantial increase in calls to the quit helpline and unique visitors to the website.

The qualitative post-test underlined that communication tools, including social networks, were quite well received. It is in line with literature that revealed that interactions on social networks are effective at engaging consumers and may be of value in the smoking cessation context (Naslund et al. 2017; Schivinski et al. 2016). However, smokers reported a lack of guidance and visibility during the month of November on social networks, such as Facebook, and in face-to-face encounters in their living and working environments.

The monthly survey of attempts to quit showed that in October 2016, 11.4% of smokers attempted to quit. Only 7% attempted to quit in November, and 11.9% in December. These results were surprising as the highest smoking cessation rates corresponded to October and December 2016, whereas November was the month designated for the challenge. This may be due to some smokers attempting to quit without waiting for 1 November, resulting in an earlier than expected increase in quit attempt rates, and no increase at the expected time. Indeed, while some smokers plan their attempts to quit, some quit spontaneously (West and Sohal 2006). The quit attempt rates in October and December 2016 were the highest for 2016 (7.7% to 10.8% between January and September) but they were not significantly different from those observed during the same quarter in 2015.

The Health Barometer survey showed that 15.9% of daily smokers had made an attempt to quit in the last quarter of 2016, and 18.4% of them reported it was directly related to "Mois sans tabac" (Guignard et al. 2018a, b). This represents about 380,000 attempts to quit due to "Mois sans tabac" in 2016, which was a little bit higher than the 350,000 attempts to quit observed in the UK in 2012 (Brown et al. 2014). Between 2016 and 2017, the daily smoking prevalence dropped from 29.4% to 26.9% among 18–75 year olds living in France (Pasquereau et al. 2018). This decrease was certainly partly a result of the first edition of "Mois sans tabac", and partly a result of important related public policies such as the implementation of plain packaging for cigarettes in January 2017 and an increase in healthcare system reimbursements for nicotine replacement therapies in November 2016.

Engagement, Involvement and Attitude of Partners

Objective indicators were used to measure participation: number of partners, number of events organised, number of ordered posters, flyers, etc. Data on actions at a local level were collected using the database OSCARS (Observation and Cartographic

Reporting of Regional Health Actions, http://www.oscarsante.org/). It records and maps events in details (localization, actors, intervention content, objectives and supports used for each action, target audience).

Because general practitioners (GPs) are key opinion leaders to motivate patients to quit smoking, a qualitative post-test using individual interviewing was conducted among 24 GPs from January to February 2017. Its objectives were to obtain feedback about "Mois sans tabac" (knowledge of the campaign, level of support for the intervention, perceived credibility of the campaign message) and to assess if the intervention had an impact on GPs' practices and on their patients' requests in terms of tobacco use and motivation to quit.

Results of this part of the evaluation highlighted a considerable participation nationwide: 7350 health professionals ordered campaign-related tools, 17,000 posters had been displayed in pharmacies (which played a major role by distributing smoking cessation kits), and approximately 365,000 quit kits were delivered. All distribution channels combined, more than 635,000 quit kits were dispensed, 50,000 posters and 800,000 leaflets. A total of 3206 regional partners registered on the website dedicated to partners, and 100 national public and private sector partners were selected for collaboration by Santé publique France. Fourteen 'ambassadors' from 14 regions (out of a total of 18 regions in France including five overseas departments) participated in the campaign and deployed it at a local level. A total of 1980 related actions were reported on the OSCARS database during the 2016 edition of "Mois sans tabac". The great majority of these actions aimed at communicating the campaign to the general public and informing them about the risks of smoking and the benefits of quitting. Numerous local actors (health facilities, associations, etc.) also organized consultations dedicated to smoking cessation, as well as collective workshops to help smokers with issues such as stress and weight gain.

With regard to GPs, few of them were aware of "Mois sans tabac". However, a majority of interviewed doctors perceived the campaign positively. As a consequence, efforts are still needed to involve GPs more in tobacco cessation, especially as they represent the point of access for smokers in the French healthcare system.

Evaluation of Exposure to and Perception of the Campaign of the Whole Population

In order to test the social contagion process of "Mois sans tabac", a quantitative post-test was carried out on a quota-based sample of the French population aged 15 years and over (2017 individuals, including 811 smokers). Although smokers were the main target of the campaign, non-smokers were also encouraged to support their relatives or friends trying to quit, and therefore constituted a secondary target. All individuals were interviewed face-to-face at home. The sample was selected such that the quota variables reflected the sociodemographic structure of the French population. The aim of this survey, which took place in November 2016, was to evaluate the campaign’s recruitment phase, especially in terms of spontaneous recall of the campaign, how well it was known, recognition of its main tools, and perception of its impact on behavioural changes (Guignard et al. 2018a, b).

Results indicated that campaign visibility was high: 35% of those interviewed were able to spontaneously describe the content of the campaign (40% of smokers and 31% of non-smokers), without any significant difference according to socioeconomic status. This represented the highest level of unassisted recall for any anti-tobacco campaign in France since 2004. When the “Mois sans tabac” name and logo were specified, 74% of people interviewed reported hearing about the campaign or seeing the logo (79% in smokers and 70% in non-smokers). Manual workers more frequently reported hearing about the campaign only through health professionals, on an information stand or at an event that took place near their home or at their workplace, or by word of mouth (vs. through the media) (7% vs. 4% in the rest of the sample). When respondents were shown the campaign’s various elements, global recognition of the communication actions was 62% (66% in smokers and 60% in non-smokers). A large majority (93%) found “Mois sans tabac” to be clear and understandable (91% of smokers and 95% of non-smokers), and 84% considered it useful (82% of smokers and 86% of non-smokers). In addition, smokers found the campaign to be particularly good at motivating them to think about their tobacco consumption (55%) or to quit (38%). The motivational impact was particularly strong among 25–34 year olds (66% and 51% for the two dimensions, respectively), among smokers who heard about the campaign through local awareness actions (85% and 54%, respectively) and among those who heard about it from a health professional (75% and 59%, respectively). No differences were found between smokers with low and high socioeconomic statuses. These levels were among the highest observed for all smoking cessation campaigns implemented by Santé publique France since 2004. Among non-smokers, 72% reported the campaign encouraged them to support a loved one who would try to quit smoking, and overall 27% had talked about the campaign with someone they knew (30% among smokers and 24% among non-smokers).

Conclusions

The two aims of this chapter were: (1) to detail the implementation and the adaptation of the “Mois sans Tabac” intervention inspired by the British “Stoptober” campaign and (2) to describe how this complex and large-scale social marketing campaign has been evaluated. This example may be useful for other countries that wish to develop a similar program based on the same positive messaging at local and national levels and that aims to increase quitting smoking rates and thus the quality of smokers’ lives.

With “Mois sans Tabac”, it was the first time that a French anti-tobacco campaign had been based on social marketing principles. Numerous other anti-smoking campaigns were previously implemented in this country from the 1970s onwards, but all were built on social advertising principles and looked like traditional mass-media campaigns targeting smokers and public health actors. "Mois sans tabac" was also the first campaign in France that aimed at reaching not only smokers but also national and regional actors, partners (public and private) and health professionals.

As "Mois sans Tabac" was large, innovative and multimodal, evaluating how the various stakeholders and targets mobilized was a key element of the campaign based on the social contagion theory. Different indicators were collected through various methods and samples: qualitative and quantitative research based on self-reports, and observational data. These different indicators showed that "Mois sans Tabac" had high visibility among the general French population and that its impact on behavioural change intentions on smokers was stronger than previous anti-tobacco campaigns implemented since 2004. "Mois sans tabac" also generated great interest from local stakeholders who implemented many related actions. In 2016, efforts were still needed to support smokers in their tobacco cessation and to involve health professionals and GPs more. The evaluation of "Mois sans tabac" 2016 was very useful for improving the next editions of the campaign, which was renamed #MoisSansTabac.

Discussion Questions

1. Imagine you decide to implement a campaign such as 'Stoptober' and 'Mois sans tabac' in your country or in a regional area. How could you adapt it to the context, the culture, etc. of your country/the regional area?
2. Beyond the PRIME theory of motivation and the social contagion theory, what are other relevant theoretical models that could be mobilised for the 'Mois sans tabac' campaign?
3. The campaign strongly relies on the brand "Mois sans tabac". Because of time and budget constraints, it was not possible to evaluate brand equity and brand loyalty. How could you evaluate them (which questions, which targets, which methods)?
4. Which indicators and methods could be used to evaluate if the 'Mois sans tabac' campaign reached journalists at a local and national levels?

Teaching Notes

1. Imagine you decide to implement a campaign such as 'Stoptober' and 'Mois sans tabac' in your country or in a regional area. How could you adapt it to the context, the culture, etc. of your country/the regional area?
   It is suggested to use Table 6.1 *to answer this question. The first column is kept similar, and the second one is replaced by specificities and the context of another country (instead of France). Based on this table, the 5Ps that could be relevant and adapted to the context, the culture and the situation of your country can be described and designed.*

2. Beyond the PRIME theory of motivation and the social contagion theory, what are other relevant theoretical models that could be mobilised for the 'Mois sans tabac' campaign?

   *'Mois sans tabac' can be analysed with the theory of reasoned action (*Fishbein and Ajzen 1975*) and the theory of panned behaviour (*Taylor et al. 2006*). They describe factors that influence behaviours:*

   - *change behavioural beliefs: The 'Mois sans tabac' campaign gives information on advantages, barriers and benefits of quitting smoking. This information can influence beliefs that can influence behaviours;*
   - *change behavioural attitude: the positive tone of 'Mois sans tabac' may have an impact on the attitude of smokers towards smoking quitting and decrease negative reactions (e.g. rejects, denials) when they face anti tobacco campaigns;*
   - *change subjective norms: because the 'Mois sans tabac' campaign is based on the social contagion theory, it may positively influence beliefs of quitting smoking (quitting may be perceived trendier);*
   - *change perceived behavioural control: the reassuring tone of the 'Mois sans tabac' campaign and the different cessation support tools offered to smokers (website, app, quit kit, quitline, etc.) may increase confidence in their ability to quit smoking;*
   - *change behavioural intentions: by influencing beliefs, social norms and perceived behavioural control, the 'Mois sans tabac' campaign may change intentions to quit smoking.*

3. The campaign strongly relies on the brand "Mois sans tabac". Because of time and budget constraints, it was not possible to evaluate brand equity and brand loyalty. How could you evaluate them (which questions, which targets, which methods)?

   *Creating a social marketing brand is recommended (*Keller 1998*). Different indicators are used to measure brand equity and loyalty: trust, satisfaction, attitude toward the brand, brand relationship, attachment, perceived value of the brand, etc. (*Rundle-Thiele and Mackay 2001*).*

   Brand equity can be measured with questionnaires, on all the targets of the campaign: smokers who are motivated to quit, non smokers, health professionals in general (general practitioners, tobacco specialists, pharmacists, midwives NGOs, nurses, dentists), public and private partners of the campaign (regional health agencies, media, local authorities, private companies, etc.).
4. Which indicators and methods could be used to evaluate if the 'Mois sans tabac' campaign reached journalists at a local and national levels?

   Different measurements can be used to assess the success of press coverage: the number and the content of the articles on the 'Moi(s) sans tabac' campaign that were published (positive, negative, neutral), their visibility, the amount of reads, the website traffic, social sharing of articles that deal with the campaign, etc.

References

Bilgicer T, Jedidi K, Lehmann DR, Neslin SA (2015) Social contagion and customer adoption of new sales channels. J Retail 91(2):254–271
Bonaldi C, Boussac M, Nguyen-Thanh V (2019) Estimation of deaths attributable to tobacco smoking, in France from 2000 to 2015. Bull Epidémiol Hebd (15):278–284. http://beh.santepubliquefrance.fr/beh/2019/15/2019_14_2.html
Brown J, Kotz D, Michie S, Stapleton J, Walmsley M, West R (2014) How effective and cost-effective was the national mass media smoking cessation campaign 'Stoptober'? Drug Alcohol Depend 135:52–58
Christakis NA, Fowler JH (2008) The collective dynamics of smoking in a large social network. N Engl J Med 21:2249–2258
Djian A, Guignard R, Gallopel-Morvan K, Smadja O, Davies J, Blanc A, Mercier A, Walmsley M, Nguyen-Thanh V (2019) From "Stoptober" to "Mois Sans Tabac": how to import a social marketing campaign. J Soc Mark 9(4):345–356
Doner L (2003) Approaches to evaluating social marketing programs. Soc Mark Q 9(3):18–26
Doran GT (1981) There's a S.M.A.R.T. way to write management's goals and objectives. Manage Rev 70:35–36
Einstein S, Epstein A (1980) Cigarette smoking contagion. Int J Addict 15(1):107–114
Fenton K (2016) Stoptober: supporting smoking cessation in England, Bull Epidémiol Hebd 30–31:496–498
Fishbein M, Ajzen I (1975) Belief, attitude, intention and behaviour: an introduction to theory and research. Addison-Wesley, Reading, MA
Gallopel-Morvan K, Smadja O, Mercier A, Safta E, Davies J, Guignard R, Arwidson P, Nguyen-Thanh V (2017) 'Mois sans tabac': the first collective challenge for smoking cessation launched by Santé publique France. In: Hastings G, Domegan C (eds) Social marketing: rebels with a cause, 3rd edn. Routledge Taylor & Francis Group, Oxford, pp 444–452
Guignard R, Beck F, Richard J-B, Lermenier A, Wilquin J-L, Nguyen-Thanh V (2015) La consommation de tabac en France en 2014: caractéristiques et évolutions récentes, Inpes, Saint-Denis
Guignard R, Andler R, Pasquereau A, Smadja O, Wilquin JL, Gall B et al (2018a) Contributions and limits of post-tests to assess media campaigns: the example of Mois sans tabac. Bull Epidémiol Hebd (14–15):304–309. http://invs.santepubliquefrance.fr/beh/2018/14-15/2018_14-15_7.html
Guignard R, Richard JB, Pasquereau A, Andler R, Arwidson P, Smadja O, le groupe Baromètre santé et al (2018b) Quit attempts in the last quarter of 2016 and relation with Mois sans tabac: first results from the 2017 Health Barometer. Bull Epidémiol Hebd (14–15):298–303. http://invs.santepubliquefrance.fr/beh/2018/14-15/2018_14-15_6.htm
Hastings G, Domegan C (2017) Social marketing: rebels with a cause, 3rd edn. Routledge Taylor & Francis Group, Oxford
Keller LK (1998) Branding perspectives on social marketing. In: Alba JW, Hutchison JW (eds) Advances in consumer research, pp 299–302
Langley DJ, Bijmolt THA, Ortt JR, Pals N (2012) Determinants of social contagion during new product adoption. J Prod Innov Manag 29(4):623–638
Lee NR, Kotler P (2019) Social marketing: behavior change for social good. Sage
Naslund JA, Kim SJ, Aschbrenner KA, McCulloch LJ, Brunette MF, Dallery J, Bartels SJ, Marsch LA (2017) Systematic review of social media interventions for smoking cessation. Addict Behav 73(Suppl C):81–93
Pasquereau A, Gautier A, Andler R, Guignard R, Richard J-B, Nguyen-Thanh V, Health Barometer Group (2017) Tobacco and e-cigarette in France: levels of consumption according to the preliminary resultants from the 2016 health barometer. Bull Épidémiol Hebd 12:214–222
Pasquereau A, Andler A, Guignard G, Richard JB, Arwidson P, Nguyen-Thanh V, le groupe Baromètre santé (2018) Tobacco consumption in France: preliminary results from the 2017

Health Barometer. Bull Epidémiol Hebd (14–15):265–273. http://invs.santepubliquefrance.fr/beh/2018/14-15/2018_14-15_1.html

Piper ME, Kenford S, Fiore MC, Baker TB (2012) Smoking cessation and quality of life: changes in life satisfaction over 3 years following a quit attempt. Ann Behav Med 43(2):262–270

Plé L, Demangeot C (2019) Social contagion of online and offline deviant behaviors and its value outcomes: the case of tourism ecosystems. J Bus Res. https://doi.org/10.1016/j.jbusres.2019.06.002

Rundle-Thiele S, Mackay MM (2001) Assessing the performance of brand loyalty measures. J Serv Mark 15(7):529–546

Schivinski B, Christodoulides G, Dabrowski D (2016) Measuring consumers' engagement with brand-related social-media content: development and validation of a scale that identifies levels of social-media engagement with brands. J Advert Res 56(1):64–80

Taylor D, Bury M, Campling N, Carter S, Garfield S, Newbould J, Rennie T, et al (2006) A review of the use of the health belief model (HBM), the theory of reasoned action (TRA), the theory of planned behaviour (TPB) and the trans-theoretical model (TTM) to study and predict health related behaviour change. National Institute for clinical excellence, December, London

Taylor G, McNeill A, Girling A, Farley A, Lindson-Hawley N, Aveyard P (2014) Change in mental health after smoking cessation: systematic review and meta-analysis. BMJ 348:g1151

West R, Brown J (2013) Theory of addiction, 2nd edn. Wiley Blackwell, Oxford

West R, Sohal T (2006) "Catastrophic" pathways to smoking cessation: findings from national survey. BMJ 332(7539):458–460

West R, Stapleton J (2008) Clinical and public health significance of treatments to aid smoking cessation. Eur Respir Rev 17(110):199–204

World Health Organization (2017) WHO report on the global tobacco epidemic, 2017: monitoring tobacco use and prevention policies. WHO, Geneva

Chapter 7
Promoting Quality of Life Through a Social Marketing Campaign for Road Safety

João Fins, Beatriz Casais, Filipe Melão, and Susete Pires

Abstract Drivers' distraction on the road due to use of mobile devices has been pointed out as one of the main causes of road accidents. The motorway concessionaire *Ascendi*, in Portugal, as part of its corporate social responsibility program, in partnership with the National Road Safety Authority, and the Police Forces—Republican National Guard (GNR) and Public Security Police (PSP)—, launched a social marketing campaign with the purpose of preventing road accidents, showing the dangers caused by driver's distraction with mobile devices and promoting road safety as an element of quality of life. The innovative aspect of this campaign is the involvement of children aged from 7 to 10 years old, not as final target, but as ambassadors of safety and influencers of adults. Under the claim "Junior Patrol", children take the role of safety agents, conveying the message to adults that they should avoid texting or reading messages in mobile devices, while driving. The campaign was designed to encourage desired behaviours as part of social norms, leading to quality of life. This chapter presents the campaign, exploring below the line communication tactics and digital media.

Keywords Road safety · Social marketing · Social norms theory · Positive appeals · Quality of life (QoL)

J. Fins · F. Melão · S. Pires
Ascendi, IPAM, Lisbon, Portugal
e-mail: fmelao@ascendi.pt; spires@ascendi.pt

B. Casais (✉)
University of Minho, Braga, Portugal
e-mail: bcasais@eeg.uminho.pt

M. M. Galan-Ladero, R. G. Rivera (eds.), *Applied Social Marketing and Quality of Life*, Applying Quality of Life Research,
https://doi.org/10.1007/978-3-030-83286-5_7

Introduction

Road accidents are one of the main causes of death worldwide and the proportion of accidents caused by drivers' distractions by mobile devices is significant (Zatezalo et al. 2018). In Portugal, this phenomenon is also true and, in 2018, the distraction of drivers was the second biggest cause of accidents (32%), only surpassed by excessive speed (35%) (APCAP 2019). A study by ESRA (2017) states that 46% of Portuguese drivers assumed in 2015, having used mobile phone while they were driving at least once, in the last 12 months.

The communication of a social marketing campaign is crucial to its effectiveness and can be transmitted through positive or negative appeals (Noble et al. 2014; Lennon et al. 2010), representing a gain and a loss frame, respectively. Positive appeals show the gains of behaviour change for quality of life and are effective in persuading behaviour change, based on the acknowledgment of the benefit for the person's quality of life. Negative appeals show the loss in quality of life of a certain undesirable behaviour and are effective in terms of demonstrating dangerous social consequences (Teng et al. 2018).

The vast majority of road safety campaigns are based on fear appeals (Lewis et al. 2019). This type of communication stresses on the negative consequences and dangers of accidents (Ngondo and Klyueva 2019) and raises awareness of the dangers of mobile phone use while driving (Buccoliero et al. 2016).

However, a research in Australia showed that positive appeals using humour might promote responsible behaviours, contradicting previous authors, who had demonstrated the effectiveness of negative appeals, with fear and threat items in road safety campaigns (Lewis et al. 2007). The efficacy effect, the cost of change and quality of life gained may be important positive appeals to be used (Brennan and Binney 2010). Gender and age can also be important factors in a different response to positive and negative appeals (Noble et al. 2014). Researchers have shown that male drivers take more risks and young drivers are less influenced by fear appeals (Lennon et al. 2010; Lewis et al. 2007; Tay and Ozanne 2002).

Public figures are important opinion leaders and influencers of social marketing (Luca and Suggs 2010), but children can have a relevant power over their parents in some cultures (Godhani et al. 2012). Working with young generations in social marketing allows to influence social perceptions of what is correct and incorrect in road safety behaviours (Rosenbloom et al. 2009), which is in line with the assumptions of social norms theory (Burchell et al. 2013). This theory regards the postulations of what are the values considered in the norms of a certain society, and what citizens consider to be right and wrong behaviours. Social norms diverge along the years and across societies. Social marketing works with social norms, trying to change undesirable norms so that behaviour change may happen.

Considering that road accident rate is an important indicator of quality of life (Petrov 2016), as well as road safety perception (Ngondo and Klyueva 2019), and positive social marketing appeals may promote the change of social norms mainly in young people, during the construction of their citizenship (Tonon 2012), this chapter explores the case of a social responsibility campaign promoted by a motorway concessionaire in Portugal, in partnership with national safety authorities, in order to promote road safety as part of quality of life, through children ambassadorship.

Case Development

The Campaign

Ascendi is a Portuguese motorway concessionaire. Under its commitment with social responsibility, the company developed a social marketing campaign, in partnership with the National Road Safety Authority (ANSR) and the Police Forces—Republican National Guard (GNR) and Public Security Police (PSP)—, in order to raise awareness for the need of driving safe, without reading or texting in digital devices while driving. The campaign targeted children aged from 7 to 10 years old with the purpose of raising consciousness to road safety as a social norm of future drivers, but at the same time, to turn children into social influencers of adults, namely their parents.

The campaign called "Junior Patrol" was based on a theatre performance that took place in local communities with the collaboration of municipalities schools, ANSR (National Road Safety Authority), GNR (Republican National Guard) and PSP (Public Security Police), and more than just showing the dangers or risks of digital distraction while driving, the campaign invested on making children the patrols of community security as influencers of adults by showing the benefits of road safety for quality of life. Figure 7.1 shows several scenes of the play.

Approaching the communities adjacent to *Ascendi's motorways network*, the company created a play that teaches in a simple, direct and fun way the substantial gain in quality of life when adopting safe driving behaviours.

The play starts with a loss frame perspective, showing consequences of wrong behaviours on driving activity with negative appeals. In order to increase the veracity, credibility and impact on children, real Police agents from GNR and PSP, Ascendi employees, as well as the actors interacted with the children during the play. There were also games and songs alluding to safety, mascots of GNR and PSP connecting with the children in the periods before and after de play. The main figure of the play was a dog that was run over by a person distracted by the cell phone while driving. This incident arises sadness and compassion for the dog and shows the dangers and risks of undesired behaviour.

After negative appeals, children are encouraged to act as promoters of safety, in line with the assumptions of the gain frame through the use of positive appeals in social marketing campaign. At the end of the performance, each of the 5000 participating children was recruited as an agent of Junior Patrol. Each child received from a real agent, a badge and a manual of a good junior patrol agent. As a complement, a contest was established with the hashtag *#ConcursoPatrulhaJunior*,

Fig. 7.1 Scenes of the Junior Patrol Performance. Source: Ascendi (2019)

encouraging children to participate with a drawing/work under the road prevention theme. In the end, 12 winners were awarded for best drawings.

Communication in Digital Media

In order to impact not only the local community and children, but Portuguese society in general, the campaign was also carried out in the digital environment. Thus, several images and videos were collected in each performance and shared on social networks and institutional websites of partners. In addition, two commercial videos were broadcast in social media, with positive appeals encouraging children to be active agents of road safety and influencers of adults.

The first video was represented by a female child who was in the car with her father, driving to school. The child gets out of the vehicle when the father starts looking at his cell phone. The child, noticing his father's incorrect behaviour, discourages him from looking at the mobile phone when driving. When the child talks to the father, the graphic element of Junior Patrol appears, thus fostering the idea that each child is an agent of authority who is always attentive to less correct behaviours of adults (see Fig. 7.2). The response of those who viewed the video was positive, with only positive comments about it. In short, in all published digital channels, including Facebook and Instagram, 44,500 views were recorded.

The second institutional video was represented by a male child and the same father as in the first video. The road prevention message is passed through a scenario

Fig. 7.2 Advertisement of junior patrol campaign. Source: Youtube Channel Ascendi (2019)

Table 7.1 Social media reach

	1st advertisement		2nd advertisement		
Entities	Instagram	Facebook	Instagram	Facebook	Total
PSP	13.7 K	9.8 K		13.5 K	37 K
GNR	9.1 K	11.3 K	5.9 K	18.5 K	44.8 K
ANSR		0.6 K		1 K	1.6 K
Total	22.8 K	21.7 K	5.9 K	33 K	83.4 K
Total	44.5 K		38.9 K		

Source: Own Elaboration, based on social media analysis of partners' followers

that appeals to positive feelings—the father and the child are driving in a car, both happy. This involvement ends when the father receives a message and takes the cell phone. The child becomes a Junior Patrol agent and scolds the adult. The response of those who viewed the video on social networks was also positive, with only positive comments. In short, there were 38,900 views in all published digital channels. Both videos have 35 s in order to be a quick and impactful message, and to make their publication on the social network Instagram viable—it only accepts videos up to 60 s. Table 7.1 shows the social media reach of 83,400 followers.

Also, an aftermovie production was developed, assembling a best-off of the entire campaign and a video promoting the referred contest. These publications were implemented in the digital channels (Facebook and Instagram) of both *Ascendi* (Website, Linked In and Youtube) and the institutional partners: PSP (Website, Facebook and Instagram), GNR (Website, Facebook and Instagram), ANSR (Website, Facebook and Instagram) and local authorities involved (Website and Facebook), which together assemble more than one million followers. The after movie was a sum of the best moments of the plays and was released by PSP, GNR and ANSR on the social network Facebook. As a negative point, it stands out the fact that its publication on the social network Instagram was not feasible because it had more than 60 s and the video was released at Christmas time, where the entities were with a large flow of publications, which consequently resulted in a reduced reach of this communication piece—9500 views.

In order to reach digitally local communities, several videos were created to be broadcast on the channels of the local authorities involved in the project. There was a video by location with the session best moments to be published. The emotion of the actors and children (never showing their faces) was reflected. At the end of each video, there was the testimony of a senior official from the municipality in question—president, vice president or councillor. The person was asked to convey the importance of this type of initiatives to the municipality and finishes with a road prevention message focused on the campaign theme. Finally, testimonies were obtained from the children, asking them to transmit what they had learned on that day.

The total reach of contents in Facebook municipalities was 8.5 K. One of the less satisfactory points was the non-publication of this graphic piece, by some of the municipalities involved, which caused a potential loss of reach of the road prevention message.

A survey conducted 3 months later with 691 childrens' parents evidence that 71.1% were aware of the campaign, and 91.85% received information about the campaign through children, who discussed at home the theatre play content and the importance of road safety. Parents also state that children took the mission of patrolling parents' behaviours on road safety, contributing for a better quality of life, considering the sense of security in family.

Conclusions

The described road safety campaign involved 5000 participating children, recruited as junior patrol agents, with the attribution of a badge and a Good Agent's Manual, in order to alert adults about their behaviours as drivers, specifically the dangers of using digital devices while driving. Ten local communities were impacted.

This campaign is an evidence of the use of the gain frame approach in road safety social marketing campaign in complement to negative appeals traditionally used in the loss approach.

The campaign's feedback was extremely positive for children, institutional partners and local communities, considering the involvement gathered, the impact on children's learning process and the trust given to them, to be agents of road safety in their family environment. Furthermore, the publicity gathered on digital media and the feedback given by children after the event, were quite positive and also, the participation on the contest organized. Due to this success, it was decided that "JUNIOR PATROL" campaign will be repeated every year, with appropriate improvements and formats.

However, the influence of children as patrols of adults might have different results in different countries or cultures, according to the acceptance of children as agents of social marketing for adults' behavior change. This topic might be discussed under the lens of cultural theories.

Discussion Questions

1. How do you describe the use of positive and negative appeals in this case?
2. Do you think the campaign promotes behaviour change under the assumptions of social norms theory?
3. Do you consider that the communication techniques used are appropriate to target children?
4. What are the communication arguments that turn children into social marketing influencers? What other possible actions might be conducted to become children patrols of road safety?

5. How do you think the effects of this campaign in quality of life might be evaluated?
6. Any similar campaign was conducted in your country? If yes, what were the results? If no, do you think a similar campaign would be successful in your culture?

Acknowledgement The authors acknowledge all the professionals involved in the social marketing campaign design, implementation and evaluation, particularly the National Authority for Road Safety, GNR and PSP.

Teaching Notes

The case was developed to be discussed in a social marketing course with the main purpose of describing the following topics:

1. Segmentation in social marketing;
2. Social norms theory;
3. Positive appeals in social marketing
4. Road Safety as an element of quality of life.

In this sense, though the case does not use exclusively positive appeals, but also fear appeals and the dangers and risks of digital distraction on drivers' behaviours, it is proposed a discussion about how this case may influence behaviours of future generations, adopting safety driving behaviours as the social norm. Further, the case also explores the role of children as influencers of adults' behaviours. Influence marketing can be discussed in classroom, and the particular effect of children, as adults' social conduct advisors. Finally, it is also encouraged the discussion of how road safety perception may influence quality of life perception.

Question 1: How do you describe the use of positive and negative appeals in this case?

The case presents both loss and gain frame. First, the negative consequences of an undesirable behaviour are shown, provoking sadness and compassion for the hurt dog. Then, the gain frame is explored encouraging children to promote safety with the empowerment of being a patrol agent with the purpose of influencing adults.

Question 2: Do you think the campaign promotes behaviour change under the assumptions of social norms theory?

The campaign targeted children promoting road safety as a social norm, instead of speed and mobile use. Targeting the next generation of drivers is a way of changing social norms in a long term, since norms may change across generations.

Question 3: Do you consider that the communication techniques used are appropriate to target children?

The theatre performance is adequate to children, as well as the drawing contest and the audio-visual campaigns in social media. An important asset to target this segment is the link with the patrol agent and the empowerment to share the message of road safety.

Question 4: What are the communication arguments that turn children into social marketing influencers? What other possible actions might be conducted to become children patrols of road safety?

Children become influencers of adults, while patrols of road safety, advising parents of accident dangers, as well as of the quality of life gain from driving slowly, without mobile phone. It is proposed that students may present other activities to become children influencers of adults.

Question 5: How do you think the effects of this campaign in quality of life might be evaluated?

Considering the attributes of quality of life, the sense of security in society may be measured, the accident rates and the levels of stress and anxiety.

Question 6: Any similar campaign was conducted in your country? If yes, what were the results? If no, do you think a similar campaign would be successful in your culture?

Students are requested to discuss whether the children influence would be accepted by adults and reflect on the possible application of such a campaign. The cultural differences may be a point of discussion for reflection on the effectiveness of this strategy.

References

APCAP (2019) 2018 Anuário Estatístico Segurança Rodoviária. Associação Portuguesa das sociedades concessionárias de auto-estradas ou pontes com portagens, Lisboa

Ascendi (2019) Patrulha Júnior. www.ascendi.pt/patrulhajunior

Brennan L, Binney W (2010) Fear, guilt, and shame appeals in social marketing. J Bus Res 63(2):140–146

Buccoliero L, Bellio E, Mazzola M, Solinas E (2016) The role of social marketing communications on influencing "text and driving" behaviors: theory and evidence from an international sample. GSTF J Bus Rev 4(3):1–8

Burchell K, Rettie R, Patel K (2013) Marketing social norms: social marketing and the 'social norm approach'. J Consum Behav 12(1):1–9

ESRA (2017) European Survey of Road Users' Safety Attitudes – Portugal 2015 Distração Comportamentos Auto-declarados, Atitudes e Perceção de Risco, Prevenção Rodoviária Portuguesa

Godhani D, Khant D, Jadeja A (2012) Marketer's miracle tool: pester power. Pac Bus Rev Int 5(5):72–84

Lennon R, Rentfro R, O'Leary B (2010) Social marketing and distracted driving behaviors among young adults: the effectiveness of fear appeals. Acad Market Stud J 14(2):95–113

Lewis I, Watson B, Tay R, White KM (2007) The role of fear appeals in improving driver safety: a review of effectiveness of fear-arousing (threat) appeals in road safety adverstising. Int J Behav Consult 3(2):203–222

Lewis I, Forward S, Elliott B, Kaye SA, Fleiter JJ, Watson B (2019) Designing and evaluating road safety advertising campaigns. In: Traffic safety culture: definition, foundation, and application. Emerald Publishing, pp 297–319

Luca NR, Suggs LS (2010) Strategies for the social marketing mix: a systematic review. Soc Mark Q 16(4):122–149

Ngondo PS, Klyueva A (2019) Fear appeals in road safety advertising: an analysis of a controversial social marketing campaign in Russia. Russ J Commun 11(2):167–183

Noble G, Pomering A, Johnson LW (2014) Gender and message appeal: their influence in a pro-environmental social advertising context. J Soc Mark 4(1):4–21

Petrov AI (2016) Road traffic accident rate as an indicator of the quality of life. Economic and social changes: facts, trends, forecast 3:154–172

Rosenbloom T, Sapir-Lavid Y, Hadari-Carmi O (2009) Social norms of accompanied young children and observed crossing behaviors. J Saf Res 40(1):33–39

Tay RS, Ozanne L (2002) Who are we scaring with high fear road safety adverstising campaigns. Asia Pac J Transp 4(Summer):1–12

Teng L, Zhao G, Wu Y, Fu H (2018) Positive versus negative messaging in discouraging drunken driving. J Advert Res 52(2):185–195

Tonon G (2012) Young people's quality of life and construction of citizenship. Springer Science & Business Media

Zatezalo N, Erdogan M, Green RS (2018) Road traffic injuries and fatalities among drivers distracted by mobile devices. J Emerg Trauma Shock 11(3):175

Chapter 8
Micro Documentary "Prevention on the Web" for School Children in the City of El Alto (Bolivia)—A Proposal for Its Improvement

Bryan Fabriscio Peñaranda-Casablanca

Abstract The reality of children in their use of the Internet does not differ, in general terms, from one country to another, except in relation to countries with high rates of extreme poverty. The phenomena that occur from contents that broadcast "influencers" in social media have a global reach.

In this paper we will analyze facts around a case with serious repercussions in May 2017 in several countries, the game called "The Blue Whale", which caused physical and psychological damage in children. This phenomenon came to Bolivia through social media and, in view of the consequences, preventive measures were adopted in the framework of the social marketing for the quality of life.

In the city of El Alto, the Secretary of Citizen Security of the Municipal Government of El Alto developed an initiative in response to this phenomenon, which resulted in the production of a micro documentary.

This chapter includes a proposal for the improvement of this initiative, based on the consideration that when facing social phenomena that negatively affect the well-being of the community, scientific data and information are required to contribute to this purpose.

Keywords Social marketing · Quality of life · "The Blue Whale" challenge · Social media · Microdocumentary

Introduction

The globalization of digital technologies is a fact that is present in all Latin American countries, and brought with it a revolution in telecommunications and forms of socialization of the different societies in the region. Social media represent with

---

B. F. Peñaranda-Casablanca (✉)
Latin American Social Interaction Observer "LASIO", La Paz, Bolivia

M. M. Galan-Ladero, R. G. Rivera (eds.), *Applied Social Marketing and Quality of Life*, Applying Quality of Life Research,
https://doi.org/10.1007/978-3-030-83286-5_8

particular importance a major space in this phenomenon of globalization, because they allow a massive, efficient and immediate socialization and communication through the Internet connection.

There are many benefits of the use of social media, both in educational and work environments as well as in the purely social and entertainment ones. Although they also bring with them risks for the different users, from whom it is considered necessary to distinguish those with a higher level of biological and psychological maturity and who are less affected by such risks than others more vulnerable among which are children.

Making a generic list of risks that bring the use of the Internet and social media for children under 18 years, we can mention: "cyberbullying",[1] sending and receiving inappropriate content for minors being on the one hand the sexual content that could be related to "sexting", exchange of photos, videos, audios, among others, and on the other hand, violent content that brings bloody events, physical and verbal assaults and deaths (Pacheco and Melhuish 2020), in addition to the consumption of substances unsuitable for minors and illegal. There are also risks related to human trafficking and smuggling, extortion (image trafficking), fraud, adults who capture and harass minors (Grooming), among other online risks that can cause serious psychological damage, even violating the sexual and physical integrity of minors.

Scientific studies conducted in different Latin American countries (Garaigordobil et al. 2019, 2020) showed that cyberbullying[2] of adolescents is related to psychopathological symptoms, adaptive and predictive variables. The findings surprise showing the psychopathological symptoms in both victims and aggressors, among which are: "depression, somatization, obsession-compulsion, interpersonal sensitivity, anxiety, hostility, paranoid ideation and psychoticism, among others".

It is clear that online risks for children and adolescents are in addition to those experienced in offline contexts. However, the risk behaviors are interconnected: Dearden et al. (2007) maintain that adolescent students from private schools in La Paz—Bolivia who consume tobacco had also consumed alcohol in excess, participated in some street fights and other risk behaviors. Consequently, online risky consumption styles can increase cases of trafficking and smuggling or manipulation that damages the psychological integrity of minors with extortion and pressure to commit physical harm as in the case discussed in this chapter.

In this context, the Bolivian government, through the Secretary of Citizen Security of the Municipal Government of El Alto (hereinafter: "GAMEA", spanish

[1]Garaigordobil, M., Mollo-Torrico, J. P., & Larrain, E. (2019). Prevalence of Bullying and Cyberbullying in Latin America: a review. Revista Iberoamericana De Psicología, 11(3), 1–18. https://doi.org/10.33881/2027-1786.rip.11301

[2]"Cyberbullying poses a threat to mental health and psychological well-being during childhood, adolescence and youth. Victims of cyberbullying suffer feelings of insecurity, loneliness, sadness, unhappiness, helplessness, anxiety, irritability, depression, suicidal ideation (some, in fact, commit suicide), post-traumatic stress, fear, low self-esteem, anger and frustration, somatization, sleep disorders, eating disorders, phobias, academic performance problems, etc." (Garaigordobil et al. 2020, p. 1).

name), carries out urban projects that seek to prevent and act against social phenomena that negatively affect the citizens of El Alto. Some of these projects have to do with street harassment, trafficking and smuggling, consumption of alcoholic beverages by young people and online risk prevention, such as the one that is studied in this chapter.

Social Marketing for Children's Quality of Life

Online risk prevention for children can be designed, implemented and evaluated through the "use of marketing principles and techniques to influence a target audience" (Kotler and Lee 2008, p. 115).

In 2017 GAMEA developed a social marketing project for quality of life seeking to address reports of physical and psychological harm produced by a viral online challenge called "the Blue Whale Game" that would have negatively affected health, privacy, security and emotional well-being, which according to Cummins and Cahill (2000, p. 188) are components of Quality of Life (QoL).

A project that seeks to design a social marketing campaign for the quality of life that prevents the risks present in the use of internet and social media in childhood in Bolivia would allow a scientifically structured approach to each of the variables and actors involved, and that directly and indirectly influence the "problematic situation". Social marketing for the quality of life would provide its theoretical and strategic framework.

At the same time, according to Casas (2006), studies on quality of life should incorporate the public's perspective by addressing "their perceptions, evaluations and aspirations" (Casas 2006, p. 33), in addition to their social representations. In the case of children and adolescents, it is generally assumed that their parents are the ones who can provide such perspectives on their quality of life, and on many occasions, under this idea, studies are published in which these children and adolescents were not asked about anything, therefore, those who investigate quality of life would not be having a complete vision of these needs, satisfactions, aspirations, perceptions and evaluations.

Considering that social marketing strategies aimed at improving the quality of life of children must necessarily be participatory, we will analyze the Bolivian experience from the perspective of quality of life, to assess the possibilities of improvement that will be key to future similar implementations.

Prevention on the Web, Project from GAMEA in 2017

"The Blue Whale" game started in Russia in November 2015. The first media reports of self-harm and apparent death were related to the case of a girl named Palenkova. The authorities found this game (and its apparent author), which consisted of

50 challenges that violated the psychological and physical integrity of those who played. The challenges were presented by levels: from watching horror movies to cutting your skin and carving a picture of a whale on your arm, walking on the edge of a cliff or hanging yourself.

Polizzi (2017) states that the game became viral 2 years later. And that experts argue that the data on deaths was uncertain and intended to alarm parents in addition to providing gutter press content to gain audience. Even so, the induced behaviors affect children and their parents, and excessive alarms require attention.

No deaths were reported in Bolivia as a result of this challenge, although it was presumed that the death of two young people in the department of Santa Cruz, aged 15 and 16, may have been a result of this macabre game. The Children's Ombudsman also reported that six to seven students were receiving psychological support. Adolescents from La Paz and Cochabamba, Opinión (2017), stated that there were many cases, including one 14-year-old boy in La Paz who was on the verge of losing his life from taking several drugs (the case was classified as a suicide attempt).

The GAMEA started its online prevention project in the city of El Alto due to the alarm raised and reports received by the police related to this game, one of which was at risk of death. Jhenny Luz Portugal (psychologist member of the team that developed the initiative) reported on January 8, 2020 that in response to reports from two girls, aged 12 and 14, with signs of self-harm, the response of GAMEA was immediate, designing and implementing the project in 2 days: "it was necessary to act as soon as possible".

The project consisted of the production and dissemination of a micro-documentary called "Prevention on the Web", prepared by a GAMEA's team that was made up of two psychologists, a doctor, three social communicators and some computer engineers. This micro-documentary addresses, among others, these issues by providing basic explanations (Prevention on the Web 2017) for the general public. Some of them are transcribed in Table 8.1. Some online risks, micro documentary "Prevention on the web".

The theoretical approach in the micro-documentary is interesting. In the part corresponding to types of violence in social media, several risks are identified, but without a complete approach at the time of defining them.

The EU Kids Online Project categorized the main digital risks according to children roles (Table 8.2):

The classification carried out by EU Kids Online allows us to observe that the GAMEA project was designed with a perspective of the child as a receiver, focusing on aggressive content, but without addressing fundamental issues such as values and commercial violence.

The GAMEA micro-documentary was aimed at providing digital education to both parents and young people using social media, but did not pay much attention to digital education in childhood. Portugal (2020) considers the game of "the blue whale" as a cyberbullying act, as it is an aggression. The media also spread it this

Table 8.1 Some online risks, micro documentary "Prevention on the web"

Phubbing	"It comes from the words phone and snubbing. It is the act of ignoring people who are present by paying more attention to the cell phone, tablet or laptop"
Fakers	"They are false profiles that act in a malicious way with everything that is published in social media, they are generally linked to human trafficking and smuggling, seek to relate to users, attract their attention so they easily fall into their networks"
The Blue Whale	"The game called the blue whale, where people who participate get to self-inflicted injuries of various kinds, such as cuts or mark some symbol on both arms and legs with different objects such as pens or cutters and in some cases come to attempt against their own life"
Cyberbullying	"It is violence through social media, it can be insults, humiliating, denigrating and devaluing images or videos against another person either because of their origin or belief"
Grooming	"It is the violence that occurs by an undercover adult with a false identity to establish a relationship of trust with a child or adolescent; its purpose is sexual harassment through blackmail and threats"
Sexting	"Refers to the dissemination of erotic messages or photographs through social media"
Image treat	"It consists of the obtaining, use and sale of photographs without the consent of the user of the networks for pornographic or extortion purposes; likewise, the misuse of social media can make children and adolescents easy prey to some crimes such as human trafficking and smuggling"

Source: Own elaboration based on the Micro documentary "Prevention on the web" from GAMEA (2017)

Table 8.2 Relationship between risks and harm according to children roles

Role of the child	Content, child as receiver (of mass productions) Violent/bloody content	Communication, child participant (adult-initiated activity)	Behavior, child as actor (perpetrator/victim)
Aggressive	Violent/bloody content	Harassment, stalking	Bullying, hostile activity between peers
Sexual	Pornographic content	"Grooming", sexual abuse by contact with strangers	Sexual harassment, "sexting"
Values	Racist/hateful content	Ideological persuasion	Potentially harmful user-generated content
Commercial	Integrated marketing	Misuse of personal data	Games of chance and others

Source: Own elaboration based on Livingstone (2012)

way,[3] because of the psychopathological effects it produces could also be considered as such, although it is debatable.

[3] Arteaga (2017). "Página siete" newspaper.

It is understandable that part of this project has sought media literacy aimed at parents, as recommended by Polizzi (2017), since there was anxiety in parents. But the fact that there were no previous statistical studies related to the topic to work with the schools of El Alto was a mistake by the mayor's office of El Alto. It is understandable that the GAMEA did not receive funding to carry out a larger project, since according to Portugal (2020) having funding would have made it possible to extend it to all of the city's educational units. Although it was reported in the media that the micro-documentary would reach all 14 districts, this was not actually the case.

In the case studied, there was no methodology for measuring results and evaluating impact. They trusted that the dissemination would be carried out among the school children's parents' meetings, a social group that Portugal (2020) recognized as the maximum authority on these issues for the city of El Alto. The awareness would be fulfilled. Not only was the documentary not distributed effectively in each of the educational units of the 14 districts, but they did not operationalize study variables to obtain dimensions and indicators that would measure the impact generated by the project. Perhaps this was due to the objective of "prevention with citizen participation".

For these reasons, we will propose a theoretical model that, based on European research, can be applied in future social marketing projects for the digital quality of life of Bolivian children.

Evaluation of the Model Applied by GAMEA: A Proposal Based on the EU Kids Online Model

The EU Kids Online project and its application over 14 years, since 2006, with the support of a thematic network of multidisciplinary researchers in 21 European countries, was taken as a background. In the theoretical design of this project carried out by Smahel et al. (2020), demographic and psychological elements that influence children when using the Internet and social media are evident. The activities they carry out have risk factors and these can cause harm or indifference. At the same time there is mediation from a social sphere that includes this individual sphere of the child, which is influenced by their peers, school and parents. The unit of analysis of this social sphere is the child.

Finally, there is a larger sphere that encompasses this social sphere and the individual sphere, which is influenced by socioeconomic stratification, the normative framework, the technological infrastructure, the educational system, and cultural values, where the unit of analysis is the State.

The EU Kids Online team built its model following the implementation of surveys for children aged 9 to 16 in the respective educational units in European countries with the help of educators and the approval of principals and parents. The sample taken by this project is categorized as children because there are no exact

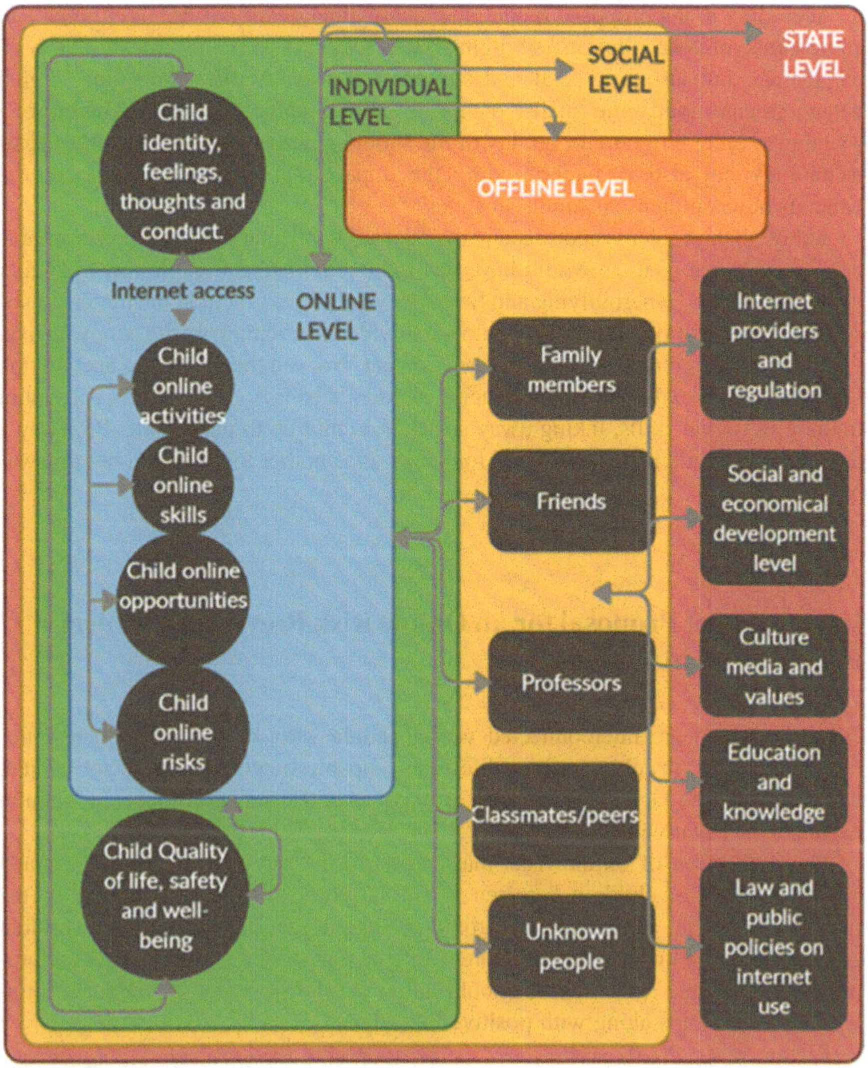

Fig. 8.1 Theoretical model based on EU KIDS ONLINE. Source: Own elaboration based on Livingstone 2020

ages to define when childhood ends. Thus, "a child is defined as any human being under the age of eighteen years" (United Nations, Treaty Series, vol. 1577, p. 2).

In addition to the surveys, they conducted focus groups with teachers, parents, and children, surveying parents as well. For the Bolivian case we built a theoretical model from the EU Kids Online project presented in Fig. 8.1:

Unlike Livingstone's proposal, the GAMEA project does not have a theoretical model like the one presented in Fig. 8.1.

According to the proposed model, the identity and quality of life of children and adolescents influence their use of digital resources. This use is modified by individual factors, but also by social and structural factors. At the same time, digital behaviors can modify the quality of life of children and adolescents. Therefore, a social marketing program for quality of life should guide them not only in the use of technology but also in understanding the impact that their social and cultural contexts have on their consumption styles.

Although the contents addressed in the micro-documentary identified very important issues, some of them would have had to be redefined and explained in greater depth, especially Cyberbullying and Sexting, which do not include the dimension of sexual harassment or extortion with image or video trafficking, or the annoyance on the part of children receiving unsolicited content. Nor did they take into account the importance of social levels in influencing children's behavior, nor did they invest in training in digital skills, taking away spaces for children to participate. Probably a documentary could have been made for adults and another for children, but this was not the case.

Improvement Proposal for an Online Risk Prevention Project for Children in Bolivia

"In effect, there are interconnected young people who, enjoying adequate intra-family relations, develop positive lifestyles, capable of generating social capital, while others, who lack the possibility of dialogue and parental guidance, remain in exclusion or negative consumption of ICTs" (Rivera 2017, p. 83).

The prevention of online risks that can harm the physical, psychological and sexual integrity of children between 9 and 16 years old through the use of the Internet and social media implies providing digital education to parents, children and educators, promoting the creation of Internet and social network spaces appropriate for children. Such spaces should allow the development of adequate intra-family relationships along with positive lifestyles.

Rivera et al. (2020) states that "the development of social marketing models based on theory and scientific evidence facilitates the choice and design of effective strategies and campaigns [. . .] in which, in addition, effects contrary to those sought or boomerang effect on the target audience are avoided" (Rivera et al. 2020, p. 4). Therefore, this proposal is fully inserted in the elaboration of a social marketing project for the quality of life so that as a result it is evident to "interconnected children who, enjoying adequate intra-family relationships, develop positive lifestyles, capable of generating social capital" (Rivera 2017, p. 83).

However, the question arises: ¿How to make children and society change ideas, beliefs, attitudes, values, practices and behaviors (Andreasen 1994), in a way that not only encourages the change of the individual voluntary behavior, but also modifies the environments and social structures that allow such changes? (Alves and Galan-Ladero 2019).

We first understand the need to design and apply a project that, through a competitive theoretical representation in which several authors' definitions of online child risks can be appreciated, from which study variables can be operationalized and measurement indicators obtained.

Through the design of research instruments, whether they are focal groups, surveys or interviews, quantitative and qualitative information is obtained from children between 9 and 16 years old, information about the risks that are mostly present, the damages caused, and the actions taken in response to these phenomena.

Through the design of research instruments, whether they are focal groups, surveys or interviews, quantitative and qualitative information is obtained from children between 9 and 16 years old, information about the risks that are mostly present, the damages caused, the actions taken in response to these phenomena.

Subsequently, the perception of QoL by children, educators and parents should be obtained and a social marketing campaign for the quality of life should be undertaken to address these realities by changing behaviors in the different social environments and based on the value that the different actors perceive and aspire to as quality of life. Bolivia needs this type of initiative, not only for prevention, but also for action, joint action with government authorities, school children, parents and children (both aggressors and victims) and more so, taking into account that information regarding these issues is very scarce.

Conclusions

The use of the internet and social media by children carries both risks and benefits. Risks vary from annoyance to severe physical and psychological harm (case of the blue whale). The GAMEA microdocumentary in 2017 was a rapid and acceptable response to the phenomenon of such play, but it did not present previous studies nor measure the impact generated, so it is believed that there are still fundamental areas to work on.

Having studied the micro-documentary (the core of this project), it is possible to see a logic that moves away from prohibitions on the use of electronic devices. The solution is not for parents to prohibit the use of the internet and social media by their children, but to be aware of the risks present in such use, to educate about such risks and to seek ways to obtain the greatest benefits, avoiding hypertrophy in this activity.

In view of the insufficiency of the GAMEA prevention project, there is still a need to carry out more studies and research regarding risks and damage in the use of the internet and social media by children, in order to progress through research projects that will allow us to influence society in order to face dangers for vulnerable publics.

Discussion Questions

1. How necessary is it to be able to prevent only children from the risks in the use of the Internet and social media versus being able to intervene by facilitating the modification of their raw realities?
2. How can a Social Marketing for Quality of Life project address these types of problems?
3. What kind of care should parents have when regulating their children's use of the internet and social media in relation to risks and damage in order to contribute to the change of these realities?
4. What is the role of educators in the prevention and action against risks and damage from the use of the Internet in schools?
5. What is the role of public authorities in contributing to the creation of safe and appropriate spaces for children?

Teaching Notes

1. **How necessary is it to be able to prevent only children from the risks in the use of the Internet and social media versus being able to intervene by facilitating the modification of their raw realities?**
   Without a doubt, prevention is important, but Social Marketing for Quality of Life projects allow for the modification of thoughts and actions of the collective imagination in search of the common good and contributing to the quality of life of people, therefore, one of these projects would result in an objective and positive interference.
2. **How can a Social Marketing for Quality of Life project address these types of problems?**
   For games like the Blue Whale that are harmful and require that they be addressed from government, family, educational and social environments of children. Therefore, the project should identify the social and political environments and structures that facilitate generating changes and acting on them; the use of ICT would be of great benefit.
3. **What kind of care should parents have when regulating the use of the internet and social media of their children in relation to the risks and damage to contribute to changing these realities?**
   The use of internet and social media by children has risks and benefits, parents should not prohibit them but inform themselves and their children, monitoring their activities and using parental control passwords could contribute to the creation of appropriate use spaces that do not take priority away from their children's offline activities.
4. **What is the role of educators in the prevention and action against risks and damage from Internet use in schools?**
   There is a need for digital literacy for parents and educators that allows for the differentiation between information and misinformation (which is often alarmist).

Educators should specifically identify perpetrators and victims through testing and psychological support, educating about the benefits, risks and harm to their students online.

5. **What is the role of public authorities in contributing to the creation of safe and appropriate spaces for children?**

   Public authorities should be able to develop and finance projects related to citizen security (for example, GAMEA), legislate and regulate online spaces, seeking to guarantee the privacy and digital well-being of users.

References

Alves HM, Galan-Ladero MM (2019) Theoretical background: introduction to social marketing. In: Case studies on social marketing. Springer, Cham, pp 1–10. https://doi.org/10.1007/978-3-030-04843-3_17

Andreasen AR (1994) Social marketing: its definition and domain. J Public Policy Mark 13(1):108–114. https://doi.org/10.1177/074391569401300109

Arteaga W (2017) In El Alto they are distributing videos to prevent cyberbullying the microdocumentary will reach the educational units of the 14 districts of El Alto. The potential victims are teenagers. Page Seven. https://www.paginasiete.bo/sociedad/2017/5/6/alto-distribuyen-videos-para-prevenir-cyberbullying-136730.html

Casas F (2006) Childhood and social representations. Polit Soc 43(1):27–42. https://pdfs.semanticscholar.org/92b4/18e92ca051dbf79370d24ae2e866acaae2c1.pdf

Cummins RA, Cahill J (2000) Advances in the understanding of subjective quality of life. Psychosoc Interv 9(2):185–198. https://journals.copmadrid.org/pi/archivos/63246.pdf

Dearden KA et al (2007) Adolescents in trouble: cigarette use and risk behavior among students in private secondary schools in La Paz. https://www.scielosp.org/article/rpsp/2007.v22n3/160-168/

Garaigordobil M, Mollo-Torrico JP, Larrain E (2019) Prevalence of bullying and cyberbullying in Latin America: a review. Rev Iberoamericana Psicol 11(3):1–18. https://doi.org/10.33881/2027-1786.rip.11301

Garaigordobil M, Mollo-Torrico JP, Machimbarrena JM, Páez D (2020) Cyberaggression in Bolivian adolescents: connection with psychopathological symptoms, adaptive and predictive variables. Int J Environ Res Public Health 17(3):1022. https://www.mdpi.com/1660-4601/17/3/1022

Kotler P, Lee N (2008) Corporate social responsibility: doing what's best for your company and your cause. Wiley. https://archive.org/stream/KotlerLeeCorporateSocialResponsibility/Kotler+%26+Lee+-+Corporate+Social+Responsibility_djvu.txt

Livingstone S (2012) Understanding the relationship between risk and harm: theory, evidence and policy on children's use of the Internet, LSE. http://www.lse.ac.uk/media

Opinion (2017) First case of the game of the Blue Whale in the Llajta mobilizes the Police. https://www.opinion.com.bo/articulo/cochabamba/%EF%BB%BFprimer-caso-juego-ballena-azul-llajta-moviliza-polic-iacute/20170505000100577890.amp.html

Pacheco E, Melhuish N (2020) New Zealand children's experiences of online risk and their perceptions of harm. Evidence from Ngā taiohi matihiko or Aotearoa-New Zealand kids online. Evidence from Ngā Taiohi Matihiko O Aotearoa-New Zealand kids Online (9 February 2020). http://globalkidsonline.net/wp-content/uploads/2020/02/Ng%C4%81taiohimatihikooAotearoaNZchildrensexperiencesofonlinerisksandharm.pdf

Polizzi G (2017) The paradox of the blue whale game, digital literacy and false news. Parenting for a Digital Future. https://blogs.lse.ac.uk/parenting4digitalfuture/2017/05/25/the-blue-whale-game-paradox-digital-literacy-and-fake-news/?from_serp=1

Prevention on the Web (2017) El Alto. Secretary of Citizen Security of the Municipal Autonomous Government of El Alto GAMEA, La Paz

Rivera R (2017) Translife: Jóvenes y Estilos de Vida de la Sociedad Red. ISBN-13: 978-1521593042

Rivera R, Sanchez MC, de Vicente MDD (2020) Social marketing and interpersonal violence. An application model for the development of prevention programs. Quaderns de Polítiques Familiars 5. Recovered from: http://www.quadernsdepolitiquesfamiliars.org/uploads/articulos/45/pdf/05_UIC_QPF_REV05_MarketingSocialViolenciaInterpersonal_REYNALDO_RIVERA.pdf

Smahel D, MacHackova H, Mascheroni G, Dedkova L, Staksrud E, Olafsson K, Hasebrink U et al (2020) EU kids online 2020: survey results from 19 countries. Recovered from: http://www.lse.ac.uk/media-and-communications/assets/documents/research/eu-kids-online/reports/EU-Kids-Online-2020-10Feb2020.pdf

UN: General Assembly, Convention on the Rights of the Child, 20 November 1989, United Nations, Treaty Series, vol 1577, p 3. https://www.refworld.org.es/docid/50ac92492.html. Accessed 22 Mar 2020. https://www.un.org/es/events/childrenday/pdf/derechos.pdf

Chapter 9
Social Marketing, Quality of Life, Well-Being, and Violence Against Women: Analysis of the Hashtag #MeToo

Araceli Galiano-Coronil and Manuela Ortega-Gil

Abstract This case shows how social networks and, specifically, Twitter can be used as social marketing tools to improve women's quality of life and well-being. It has focused on gender violence and sexual abuse, one of the factors that measure Women, Peace, and Security Index (WPS). Violence against women and sexual abuse are discussed in this case through the hashtag #MeToo. This hashtag represents the MeToo movement, a social movement that played a crucial role in the online mobilization by utilizing messages and appealing hashtags during the social movement. The methodology is based on data mining techniques and, the virality (number of tweets shared and published) of the messages with the mentioned hashtag is analyzed. The results show that countries with higher values in the WPS index are not those where the messages have been most shared. Also, there are differences between countries according to message content, posts shared, and emotional tone.

In conclusion, it has been shown that Twitter is useful as a social marketing tool to combat gender violence and increase the women's quality of life, because of the high impact that these issues have achieved on social networks. It has led to more awareness in society to this social problem. Also, it favors the deployment of public powers to tackle it.

Keywords Quality of life · Social marketing · Well-being · Violence against women · Twitter

A. Galiano-Coronil (✉) · M. Ortega-Gil
University of Cadiz, Cádiz, Spain
e-mail: araceli.galiano@gm.uca.es; manuela.ortega@uca.es

M. M. Galan-Ladero, R. G. Rivera (eds.), *Applied Social Marketing and Quality of Life*, Applying Quality of Life Research,
https://doi.org/10.1007/978-3-030-83286-5_9

Introduction

Violence against women is a significant public health problem and a violation of women's human rights. WHO has published that about 1 in 3 (35%) of women worldwide have experienced physical and sexual intimate partner violence or non-partner sexual violence in their lifetime (WHO 2017). Also, women around the world are disproportionately impacted by gender-based violence in the workplace. Millions of female workers are forced to work in an intimidating, hostile, or humiliating environment. Also, women are asked for sexual favors, exposed to inappropriate jokes, insinuations, comments, and unwanted physical contact. More than half (52%) of women, and nearly two-thirds (63%) of women aged 18–24 years old, said they had experienced sexual harassment at work, according to new research from the Trade Union Center (TUC) in collaboration with the Everyday Sexism Project published, one of the most extensive pieces of research on sexual harassment at work in Europe (TUC 2016).

This problem is part of the well-being of women, according to the Georgetown Institute for Women, Peace, and Security (GIWPS 2020). This Institute has studied these factors that influence women's well-being for years and has created an indicator called Women, Peace, and Security (WPS). According to WPS researchers, the world is safer, more peaceful, and more prosperous when women are given full and equal rights and opportunities than men. Besides, the WPS includes indicators of inclusion in women, justice, and security as essential factors in their well-being. Many researchers, including Tonon (2014) and Sirgy (2002), have used well-being and quality of life as multidimensional concepts. In this way, the study of quality of life refers to the material environment (social well-being) and the psychosocial environment (psychological well-being). It also implies citizens' participation in evaluating what affects them, becoming a concept with political significance, contributing to the study of people's well-being. In this sense, the theoretical proposal for quality of life raises a social and political reality based on respect for human rights and trying to ensure that the vision of the protagonists is taken into account when making public policy decisions (Tonon 2007). Social networks are particularly relevant to listen to the protagonists of gender violence and other users since they constitute a means of communication within reach of citizens. Besides, they also function as social marketing tools because their interactive and participatory nature encourages conversations on various topics and allows for the creation of user communities (Burkhardt 2009). In this sense, Hestres (2014) commented that organizations should focus on understanding social media use. In the end, organizations must work to determine how to transform their supporters into vocal promoters of their causes (Bernhardt et al. 2012). The same research lines are the studies of Dooley et al. (2012) and Kotler (2011), who showed that social marketing could go beyond creating awareness and changing behaviors. Some authors consider that using these media favors citizens' participation and mobilizes individuals who otherwise remain inactive (Bonilla and Rosa 2015). Correctly, Twitter (with 330 million users in 2019 in the world, according to Statista (2019)) has been configured as a resource for citizens to debate socio-political issues (Penney and Dadas 2014; Yu 2016).

For this reason, it has been considered interesting to study the Me Too movement on Twitter using the hashtag #MeToo. This hashtag has been chosen because it represents an international movement against sexual assault and harassment that emerged in 2017. A study in Canada confirmed that the #MeToo movement had a significant effect since more than a 50% of women left anonymity and reported that they had experienced unwanted sexual pressure at work, and one in every ten women said that sexual harassment is 'fairly common' in their workplace (Anderson 2017). Also, there is evidence that these social movements have increased the awareness and sensitivity of young people to this problem, making them more likely to report cases of violence than older people (Godley 2018).

Case Study Development

Violence Against Women Campaigns on Social Media: #MeToo Case Study

Gender-based violence constitutes one of the most critical public health problems actually, and it is also one of the most widespread and frequent human rights abuses in our country and the world. In 2019, 36,745 women registered as victims of gender violence and domestic violence in Spain (INE 2020). Due to these concerns, in recent years, several campaigns have been developed. Some examples focus on campaigns for increasing awareness and knowledge about violence against women. An example of it is the campaign "Australia Says No" (2004–2005) or others that primarily target adult men who are already engaging in violence against women such as The Non-Violence Alliance in the United States (2002) that focuses on work with men who engage in family violence, specializing in increasing awareness of the effects of their behavior on children (Donovan and Vlais 2005). Some campaigns allude to fear of consequences such as the "Zero tolerance" campaign in Spain (2008) (Sierra et al. 2019).

On Twitter, we can find several violence against women campaigns that have been analyzed, such as those carried out with the following hashtags: "The Best Men Can Be" by Gillette (Xu and Zhou 2020) and #ShineTheLight (London Abused Women's Centre 2020). Gillette's campaign claimed to tackle issues related to toxic masculinity and promote a healthier role model for younger generations. The #ShineTheLight campaign aims to end male violence against women. Other campaigns on violence against women are those related to feminist movements. In this sense, the rise of feminist activism in social networks is noteworthy, which has led to a series of studies on the use of hashtags such as #iamafeminist (Jimsook 2017) and #BringBackOurGirls (Córdoba 2017) to foster conversations about movements regarding women safety. Another initiative to highlight on Twitter is the #MeToo case. This movement has launched a women's protest against sexual harassment and violence in different places and languages. Below a study about the #MeToo on Twitter is presented.

In this study, hashtag #MeToo is analyzed on Twitter because it is a powerful outlet for sharing messages and information. Twitter is expressly devoted to disseminating information, in that users subscribe to the broadcasts of others and then turn around and produce their broadcast, making it a prime platform for exploring viral content (Bakshy et al. 2011). This social networking can change attitudes and behaviors, channeling ideas and information, and facilitate the balance between reason and emotions (Papacharissi 2015; Rúas-Araújo et al. 2016).

The hashtag #MeToo was coined by Tarana Burker and gained importance in 2017 when allegations of abuse surfaced against American executive and film producer Harvey Weinstein (El País 2020). The repercussion was such that the hashtag was used around 500,000 times, it had approximately eight million mentions on Facebook, and According to the Pew Research Center, this hashtag has been used on Twitter more than 19 million times in 2017 (France 2017; Peiron 2018). The hashtag has trended in at least 85 nations, including India, Pakistan, and the United Kingdom (Strum 2017). The term was even translated in several countries around the world (#YoTambién in Spain, #NiUNaMenos in Argentina, #BalanceTonPorc in France, #IAmNotAfraidToSpeak in Rusia and Ucrania, and #QuellaVoltaChe in Italy), which contributed to increasing its virality considerably. The popularity of #MeToo grew when celebrities like Lady Gaga, Reese Whiterspoon, Martha Stewart, Gwyneth Patrol, and Angelina Jolie, among many others, began using it. The fact that public and admired characters took the step caused a chain reaction in women around the world who had suffered similar situations. Actresses, singers, and models in the industry also took advantage of the movement to reveal traumatic experiences in their lives related to cases of sexual abuse, and to denounce the violence against women in the industry itself (Petit 2017).

Case Study Methodology

For the development of this case, data mining techniques have been used. Initially, 46,937 Twitter messages containing #MeToo have been collected during the first 5 days of 2020, and they have been analyzed with the Nvivo 12 plus program). This process is summarized in the phases specified in Fig. 9.1. Once the data are prepared are analyzed. A descriptive analysis and a content analysis will be carried out with a dual approach, both quantitative and qualitative. The quantitative approach aims to measure the data and to establish the frequency of the appearance of the elements considered as information units (Landry 1998). In this sense, this analysis allows obtaining information such as virality, measured by the number of times a tweet is shared, activity measured by the number of messages issued, and the reach of users (number of followers) (Bruns and Stieglitz 2013). In this sense, text mining is used for text summarization, keyword analysis, and word frequency analysis.

Fig. 9.1 Procedure to determine relevant knowledge from social media. Source. Own elaboration

Sentiment analysis has also been carried out to understand the emotional connotation of the messages according to the origin of the users Nvivo 12 identify expressions of sentiment in the content using the Auto Code Wizard. The process uses a scoring system. Each word containing sentiment has a pre-defined score. Each sentiment node represents a range on a sentiment scale, positive, negative, neutral, and mixed. After sentiments have been identified, we have made a coding matrix to know about the sentiments from each selected country.

Results

First, the results of the descriptive analysis are shown. In total 46,937 publications were collected (31,926 retweets and 15,011 tweets). The average number of retweets per message is 879.19, which indicates the high "Me Too" movement's virality. Analyzing in more detail the data, Figs. 9.2 and 9.3 show the most published hashtags and mentions.

The most published hashtag is #HarveyWeinstein, and in second place #Weinstein, both refer to the former Hollywood producer who has been convicted of rape and sex crime (BBC 2020). The third is #TimesUp, an anti-harassment movement founded on January 1, 2018, by Hollywood celebrities in response to the Weinstein effect, the feminist movement, and #MeToo (TimesUp 2020). The most published mentions are shown in Fig. 9.3 below.

Concerning the mentions, the most published is @VanityFair, an American magazine of culture, fashion, and politics. In second place is Sonam Kapoor, an Indian actress famous in the Bollywood film scene. During the #MeToo movement in Bollywood, actress Sonam Kapoor was one of the few people to condemn sexual harassment in the workplace and encourage various victims inside and outside the

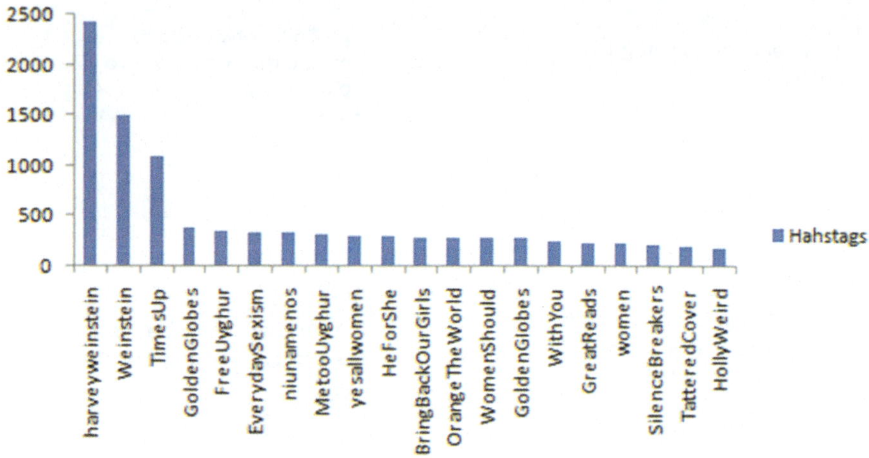

Fig. 9.2 Published hashtags in messages that contain #MeToo. Source. Own elaboration

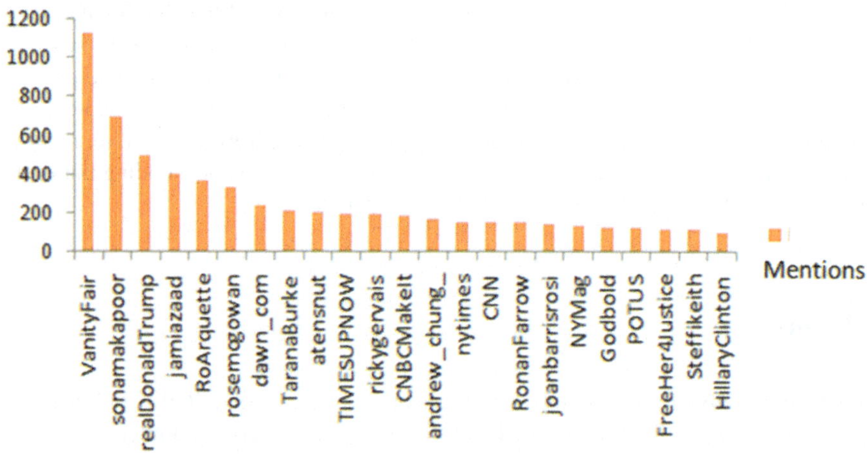

Fig. 9.3 Most published mentions in messages that contain #MeToo. Source. Own elaboration

film industry to speak out and bring the harassers justice. @RealDonaldTrump, a Twitter user of the President of the United States, has also been mentioned on numerous occasions.

It should be noted that the most published hashtags and mentions correspond to users from the USA, which is logical since it was the country of origin of the "Me Too" movement. This country is ranked number 19 in the report on the global indicator Women, Peace, and Security (WPS), a study that offers one of the most comprehensive measures of women worldwide's well-being. A selection of the countries considered in the WPS indicator that has published more English messages has been made. The information obtained is summarized in Table 9.1.

Table 9.1 English-speaking messages from countries in the WPS indicator

País	Retweets	Tweets	Total mensajes	Ranking en WPS
USA	1871	921	2792	19
India	993	338	1331	133
Canada	647	233	880	11
UK	194	111	305	7
Australia	109	95	204	6
Germany	151	67	218	17
Ireland	53	54	107	16
Total	4018	1819	5837	

Source. Own elaboration

As it is shown in Table 9.1, the most significant number of messages and shares come from users in the USA and India. This fact stands out because the USA is among the 20 countries with the highest well-being for women and, India is ranked 133rd out of 168 countries. The cause may be the film industry, present in both countries (Hollywood and Bollywood) since the movement arose from the denunciation of the American film producer Weinstein. In India, the publications on social networks of one of the most famous Bollywood actresses in favor of women victims of harassment had great media repercussions. Another fact to emphasize is that although the movement is against crimes and sexual harassment, there are messages that seem to talk about the opposite; that is, it questions the harassment. It is an example of one of these messages, the one most retweeted of the sample (from @RealCandaceO retrieved from Twitter):

> Reading Matt Lauer's accuser's story & it's EVERYTHING I hate about the #metoo movement. She admits she consensually went to his hotel room but was "too drunk to consent." She also admits she had multiple consensual sexual relations with him after her alleged rape. PERISCOPE SOON.

This message highlights the opposite of what the Me Too movement represents since it criticizes this phenomenon by commenting that their relationships were consensual.

With regards to users Fig. 9.4 has been created, which shows the users that have published more tweets (the most active users, blue line), and the ones with the highest number of followers (users more readily available, red line).

The user with the most reach is @htTweets, with a total of 7,040,700 followers. It corresponds to *Hindustan Times*, an Indian newspaper published in English. In second place is 'USATODAY' with about half the followers than '@hTweets'; 3,946,749. It is the largest national newspaper in the United States and the second-largest in the English-speaking world. In terms of activity, the most notable is the user @PulpNews, with 3,321,129 tweets published. This user has been moveto@OddCrimes. The website, OddCrimes.com, is the newest version of PulpNews.com, which collects and stores information on the latest crime news. It should be noted that the user with the most activity is not the one with the most

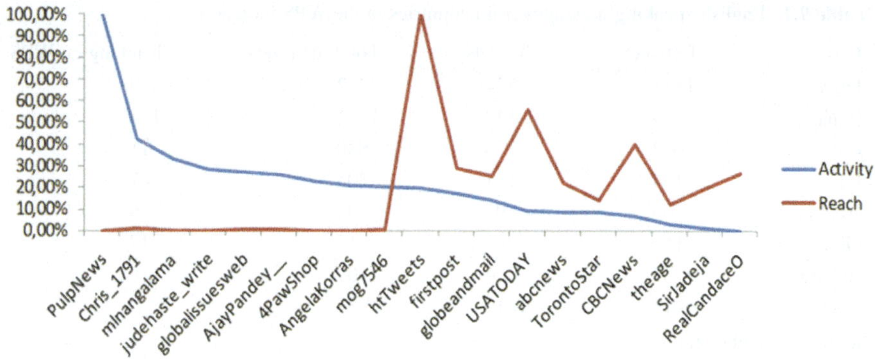

Fig. 9.4 Users with more activity and reach. Source. Own elaboration

reach, and vice versa, the one with the most number of followers, is not the most active. It may be an indication that publications' content quality is paramount.

On Fig. 9.5 we can see the most recurrent terms have been identified by country.

Concerning the word clouds in general, the most published are *women* and *Weinstein*. However, differences are depending on the country from which the posts have been published. In Australia, the messages that mention abuse in the workplace are the most common. There are words related to the cinema in India, but the main focus is not on Weinstein but 'Sonamakapoor' although the reason is not sexual abuse itself, as seen in the following tweet retweeted from @jitengajaria, the most retweeted message from India.

> Dear @sonamakapoor, since you talk of DNA, you father used to dance at underworld parties for money. Your family used to sit with Dawood to watch matches even after 1993 blasts. World knows how your aunt died in Dubai. Want more DNA tests? Some #MeToo stories? https://t.co/f1QMgRTO10.

In Germany, the themes are centered on Weinstein's trial in The Netherlands, also on Weinstein, but focusing on police aspects of sexual abuse. In the UK, there is talk of other hashtags related to sexual crimes such as #BOYCOTTCYPRUS, a label created to raise awareness of the shameful treatment of a 19-year-old British rape victim by the Cypriot police and judiciary. In the USA and Canada, the issues are more focused on Weinstein's case, and in Ireland, they talk about abuse by groups of young men.

Figure 9.6 shows that users from the USA, Canada, and Ireland have published the most negative messages, and users from Australia have published the most positive messages.

The following are several examples of messages (Table 9.2), both negative and positive, posted by users in different countries.

In summary, the results show: Firstly, several hashtags and mentions appear in the messages together with #Metoo; secondly, the country where this movement has had the most repercussion is the USA, since it is where the actresses have spoken out against the abuses suffered by the film producer Weinstein; thirdly, this movement

Fig. 9.5 Most published words with the hashtag #MeToo. Source. Own elaboration

has spread throughout the world; the fourth is that the judgment about sexual abuse has been the most recurring theme in the analyzed tweets; and finally, the sentiment analysis shows that most publications have a negative connotation, especially in the USA and Canada. In Australia, there are more messages with a positive tone, referring to the victims' courage.

Conclusions

The spread of sexual abuse and violence against women through social networks, such as Twitter, has had implications from the point of view of social marketing since the repercussion of #MeToo on this social media has led to a more conscious society about this social problem. Also, it has favored the mobilization of public authorities to eradicate it. In this sense, it is interesting to comment that most

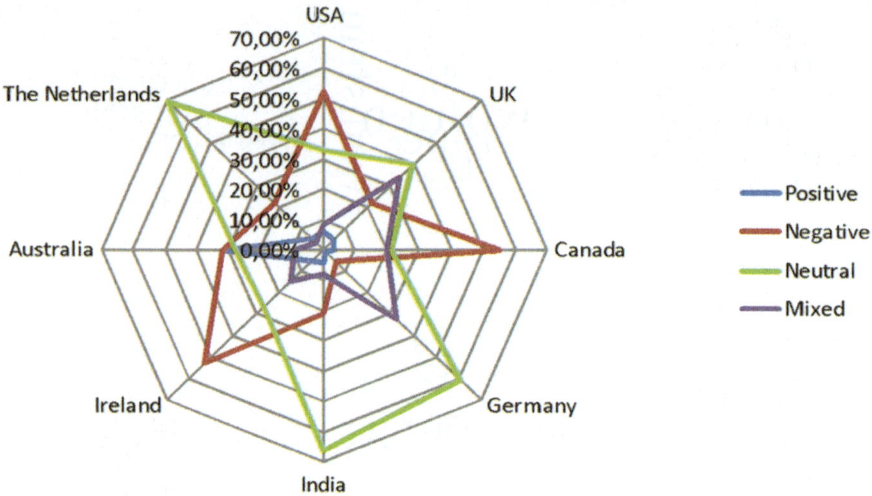

Fig. 9.6 Emotional connotation of messages by country. Source. Own elaboration

Table 9.2 Examples of messages with different emotional connotations by country

Sentiment	Tweet	Country
Negative	Abusing more than 80 women takes its toll on your legs and hips(?), I guess. https://t.co/WZGyG54xpD #MeToo #HarveyWeinstein #LockThemAllUp	USA
	Just a reminder that #Weinstein stands accused of rape. It's an ugly word, 'rape', for an ugly crime. When reports say he faces accusations of "non-consensual sex", that minimizes it	Canada
	Call rape what it is. #MeToo#Enough	
	ReSisters joining a protest today at the Cypriot Embassy at 12pm against the brutal treatment of the young woman raped by 12 men Convicted of false reporting, detained in #Cyprus & faces a jail sentence	
	This image tells her story	
	@DominicRaab	
	#BoycottCyprus #MeToo	
	#IBelieveHer https://t.co/42uQOXP6mt	Ireland
Positive	The reformation is in progress!	Australia
	Well done, Ladies	
	Ladies thankyou for finding the courage to step forward #MeToo https://t.co/1Oe4fRnPAe	

Source. Own elaboration

messages have an informative purpose, they give information on the issue, hence their neutral tone. It can be explained because the users that have published the most are newspapers internationally recognized. However, many publications with a negative tone speak of the mistreatment suffered by women who have reported their cases. Besides, it should be noted that the emotional connotation depends on the country where the message comes from. Australian users are the ones who have posted the most positive messages, appreciating the courage of women who have reported their cases of abuse. Although, it is interesting to comment that despite the support obtained by these women, there are still people who question the abuse's veracity. It is precisely one of the most viral messages.

Another point to comment is that the messages do not directly call for action (that is, they are not behavioral messages), but they have achieved a great reaction from the public, which has increased the problem's visibility. Consequently, there are two important aspects to highlight from the perspective of social marketing. On the one hand, women's behavior has changed because they are less afraid, so they feel less alone and are more likely to report abuse cases. On the other hand, public powers have been mobilized to toughen laws against gender violence.

It should be noted that users made their contribution as speakers and social promoters of the cause, which would otherwise have gone unnoticed. These users participated in social causes in a timely, direct, and independent way, thanks to the networks' possibilities. The effectiveness of these small but essential Twitter participants lies in being an engine of opinion and visibility, generating transnational sensitivity and solidarity. Another aspect that has increased visibility has been the publication of specific hashtags and mentions, such as #HarveyWeinstein, which refers to indicted American film producer. Regarding the mentions, the most published ones are related to important mass media or people involved in politics.

Concerning the most recurring themes, it should be noted that differences depend on the user's origin country. There are countries whose messages focus on Weinstein and the trial; others talk about political aspects related to gender-based violence against women, and several ones about different kind of abuses that have occurred, especially those carried out by young men who attack in groups.

Other aspects to highlight are: On one hand, the position of the countries in the WPS index (that measures women's quality of life) has not been relevant in this study to determine the messages' virality published with #MeToo. Examples of this are the USA and India users since they are the ones who have shared and published more tweets with #MeToo. However, the USA occupies one of the first positions in the index, and India one of the last. On the other hand, the methodology used, based on data mining, has served to study the virality of the messages, identify the most recurrent themes, the emotional connotation, and which countries from the WPS index have shared and published the most number of messages with #MeToo. However, it is necessary to highlight that the short period time is a limitation of the study.

In conclusion, this case has shown how the use of Twitter as a social marketing tool can improve women's quality of life since society is more aware of mistreatment and sexual abuse, and the public powers have mobilized to seek solutions.

Discussion Questions

1. Do you think that gender violence campaigns can influence people's behavior? Justify your answer from the perspective of Social Marketing.

2. Do you think Twitter could be an effective social marketing tool?
3. Do you think it is necessary to create specific indicators for the analysis of women's well-being and quality of life? Justify your answer

Teaching Notes

Answer to Question 1. Do you think that gender violence campaigns can influence people's behavior? Justify your answer from the perspective of Social Marketing.

Currently, gender violence has boomed worldwide. According to UN data, 35% of women worldwide have suffered physical and sexual violence by partners or someone else at some point in their lives. Women who have suffered physical or sexual violence from a partner have higher rates of depression and a greater chance of having an abortion. Especially striking is the number of women murdered by gender-based violence worldwide: the total number is 87,000 dead women, of which 58% (about 50,000) were murdered by their partners or family members (UNODC 2019).

One of the most common problems regarding acts of gender violence is that they remain invisible, and women do not usually request help from the relevant authorities. We are dealing with a type of "invisible" violence that can be understood as any behavior, physical or verbal, active or passive, that threatens the emotional integrity of the victim, in a continuous and systematic process in order to produce intimidation, devaluation, feelings of guilt or suffering (León 2012). In this context, social marketing can enhance visibility since gender-based violence campaigns can encourage women to talk about the abuse they have suffered. If they do it on social networks, these women's voices can become the voice of a community. This community claim can contribute to make laws harder or to improve preventive measures and care for victims. Besides, movements like #MeToo have had a significant impact on social networks, arise interpersonally in community networks, and do not take long to impact society's culture (Aguado-Peláez 2019).

Three examples of campaigns that have had a high social impact are specified in Table 9.3.

Answer to Question 2. Do you think Twitter could be an effective social marketing tool?

This question can be answered by considering two aspects. Firstly, Twitter's importance as a communication channel in social marketing, where discourses on social causes encourage citizens to participate, and secondly, putting some examples of social movements that have had an impact on Twitter through their hashtags.

Regarding the relationship between social marketing and social networks, it is necessary to comment that organizations should focus on understanding social networks' use. It will provide the opportunity to offer exciting content to the public, which will lead to greater dissemination and visibility of the information. In this

Table 9.3 Examples of gender-violence campaigns on social media

Campaign/years	Description	Objective	Link
The UN women-run "JOIN by 2030" campaign (2016 and 2019)	In 2019, during the 16 Days of Activism Against Gender Violence, from November 25 to December 10, the slogan was "Paint the world in orange: Generation Equality condemns rape." With the theme Join the initiative! The campaign encouraged to share photos, messages and videos showing how to participate in the campaign on Facebook, Instagram and Twitter using the hashtags #PintaElMundoDeNaranja and #GeneraciónIgualdad. It is also highlighted the 2016 campaign, in which buildings around the world were illuminated in orange to raise funds. For 16 days, emblematic buildings such as the City Hall in New York, the city of Venice and the Blue Mosque in Istanbul were illuminated. Events were held around the world and in New York the event was hosted by United Nations Goodwill Ambassador Actress Nicole Kidman. The money raised was used to put a close to violence against women and girls	To prevent and eliminate violence against women and girls around the world	https://www.unwomen.org/es/what-we-do/ending-violence-against-women/take-action
The campaign "best advertisement in history" (2017)	Sun communications in collaboration with the company Jui beautiful hair from Bangladesh launched an ad to raise awareness about gender violence through a moving story that is going around the world. This campaign was carried out to raise awareness about the problem of gender violence in	To raise awareness about the problem of gender violence in Bangladesh	https://www.adsoftheworld.com/media/film/jui_haircut

(continued)

Table 9.3 (continued)

Campaign/years	Description	Objective	Link
	Bangladesh, where 72% of women have suffered some type of violence. The short film, which has more than half a million views, shows a woman cutting her hair, symbolizing that no one else will be able to pull it. The campaign has transcended borders and has been described as the "best advertisement in history" against male violence		
The campaign "dear daddy" (2015)	Norwegian short film made by the association care Norway against gender violence in 2015. Within our "super dad" campaign we have done adaptation and voice-over on Serbian of "dear daddy" video, a very strong and emotional short film, developed by CARE Norway, that sends a strong message about the problem of violence against women and the need for prevention from an early age. This tells the perspective of a girl who narrates the difficulties she will face during her life as a girl. The campaign is receiving great support from men, and the video has almost four million views on YouTube	To raise awareness that men must be a positive role model and renounce active violence	https://youngmeninitiative.net/en/2016/12/17/dear-daddy-2/

Source. Own elaboration

way, organizations will be able to work on determining how to transform their supporters into vocal promoters of their causes (Bernhardt et al. 2012).

In this sense, Twitter is a participatory and collaborative online media that enables users to contribute information about a topic. The development of microblogs like Twitter reflects the human desire to share and consume information and knowledge. In the case of tweets, these can be understood as micro discourses that can support collective mobilization processes (Gualda et al. 2015). It may be since activists can initiate speeches that are not usually carried out in other media (Penney and Dadas 2014). On the other hand, hashtags are often used to create spaces where users talk about specific topics, such as racial justice, gender equality, or health-related issues (Kuo 2018). These hashtag communities have tremendous power to shape conversations and mobilize users. Furthermore, they do not require users to follow each other, separating hashtag-based communities from follower networks (Bruns and Burgess 2011).

Answer to Question 3. Do you think it is necessary to create specific indicators for the analysis of women's well-being and quality of life? Justify your answer.

Well-being and quality of life are multidimensional concepts that include those factors that affect the material, social and psychological state of positively or negatively (Tonon 2015). Therefore the quality of life will depend on the coverage of the needs and problems of citizens. Gender-based violence and sexual abuse are problems that affect the well-being of women and that are not included in the general indicators on the quality of life and well-being. These differences have led to the creation of the Women, Peace, and Security (WPS) indicator, which includes the singularities of gender in well-being. The results of this work have shown that countries that rank first in the WPS index are not the ones that have published the most messages with the hashtag #MeToo. Since fewer abuses and gender violence, women in these countries do not feel threatened and are countries with less inequality.

References

Aguado-Peláez D (2019) Violaciones en serie: Dominaciones y resistencias tras las agresiones sexuales de ficción en la era del #MeToo. Feminismo/s 33:91. https://doi.org/10.14198/fem.2019.33.04

Anderson B (2017) Sexual harassment of women is widespread in Canada. Aba-cus Data. Retrieved February 22, 2018, from http://abacusdata.ca/sexual-harassment-of-women-is-wide-spread-in-canada/

Bakshy E, Hofman JM, Mason WA, Watts DJ (2011) Everyone's an influencer: quantifying influence on twitter. In: Proceedings of the fourth ACM international conference on Web search and data mining, February 2011

BBC News (2020) Harvey Weinstein: how a Hollywood giant faced his reckoning. Retrieved from https://www.bbc.com/news/world-us-canada-51451977

Bernhardt J, Mays D, Hall A (2012) Social marketing at the right place and right time with new media. J Soc Mark 2(2):130–137

Bonilla Y, Rosa J (2015) #Ferguson: digital protest, hashtag ethnography, and the racial politics of social media in the United States #Ferguson. Am Ethnol 42(1):4–17. https://doi.org/10.1111/amet.12112

Bruns A, Burgess J (2011) The use of twitter hashtags in the formation of ad hoc publics. August proceedings of the 6th European consortium for political research (ECPR) general conference 2011. Retrieved from https://eprints.qut.edu.au/46515/1/The_Use_of_Twitter_Hashtags_in_the_Formation_of_Ad_Hoc_Publics_(final).pdf

Bruns A, Stieglitz S (2013) Towards more systematic twitter analysis: metrics for tweeting activities. Int J Soc Res Methodol 16(2):91–108. https://doi.org/10.1080/13645579.2012.756095

Burkhardt P (2009) Social software trends in business: introduction. In: Tiako P (ed) Software applications: concepts, methodologies, tools, and applications. Information Science Reference, Hershey, PA, pp 3180–3195. https://doi.org/10.4018/978-1-60566-060-8.ch184

Córdoba (2017) El slacktivismo como recurso de movilización en redes sociales: el caso de #BringBackOurGirls. Comunicación y Sociedad 30:239–263

Donovan R, Vlais R (2005) VicHealth review of communication components of social marketing/public education campaigns focusing on violence against women. Victorian Health Promotion Foundation, Melbourne

Dooley, J., Jones, S. e Iverson, D. (2012). Web 2.0: an assessment of social marketing principles. J Soc Mark, 2(3), 207–221

El País (2020) Cronología de un movimiento global, January 5. Retrieved from https://elpais.com/especiales/movimiento-metoo/cronologia/

France L (2017) #MeToo: social media flooded with personal stories of assault. CNN, October 16. Retrieved from https://edition.cnn.com/2017/10/15/entertainment/me-too-twitter-alyssa-milano/index.html

Georgetown Institute for Women, Peace, and Security Contact GIWPS (2020) Women, Peace, and Security Index (WPS). Retrieved from https://giwps.georgetown.edu/the-index/

Godley J (2018) Everyday discrimination in Canada: prevalence and patterns. Can J Sociol 43 (2):111–142. https://doi.org/10.29173/cjs29346

Gualda E, Borrero J, Cañada J (2015) La 'Spanish Revolution' en Twitter (2): Redes de hashtags y actores individuales y colectivos respecto a los desahucios en España. Redes. Revista Hispana para el Análisis de Redes Sociales 26(1):1–22

Hestres L (2014) Preaching to the choir: internet-mediated advocacy, issue public mobilization, and climate change. New Media Soc 16(2):323–339

INE (2020). Estadística de Violencia Doméstica y Violencia de Género (EVDVG) Año 2019. https://www.ine.es/prensa/evdvg_2019.pdf

Jimsook K (2017) #iamafeminist as the "mother tag": feminist identification and activism against misogyny on twitter in South Korea. Fem Media Stud 17(5):804–820. https://doi.org/10.1080/14680777.2017.1283343

Kotler P (2011) Reinventing marketing to manage the environmental imperative. J Mark 75:132–135

Kuo R (2018) Racial justice activist hashtags: Counter publics and discourse circulation. New Media Soc 20(2):495–514. https://doi.org/10.1177/1461444816663485

Landry R (1998) L'analyse de contenu, Recherche sociale. De la problemátique à la collecte des données. In: Gauthier B (ed) Sillery, Presses de l'Université du Québec, pp 329–356

León G (2012) Empleo del marketing...¿ La solución? Pangea: revista de la Red Académica Iberoamericana de Comunicación 3(1):51–63

London Abused Women's Centre (2020) #ShineTheLight Shine the Light on Women Abuse Campaign – 2019. Take action! Retrieved from https://www.lawc.on.ca/shine2019

Papacharissi Z (2015) Affective public: sentiment, technology, and politics. Oxford University Press. ISBN: 9780199999743

Peiron F (2018) Diecinueve millones de #MeToo. El País, October 21. Retrieved from https://www.lavanguardia.com/vida/20181021/452453646870/metoo-aniversario-acoso-sexual-criticas-casos.html

Penney J, Dadas C (2014) Tweeting in the service of protest: digital composition and circulation in the occupy wall street movement. New Media Soc 16(1):74–90. https://doi.org/10.1177/1461444813479593

Petit S (2017) #MeToo: sexual harassment and assault movement tweeted over 500,000 times as celebs share stories. People, October 16. Retrieved from https://people.com/movies/me-too-alyssa-milano-heads-twitter-campaign-against-sexual-harassment-assault/

Rúas-Araújo J, Puentes-Rivera I, Míguez-González MI (2016) Capacidad predictiva de Twitter, impacto electoral y actividad en las elecciones al Parlamento de Galicia: un análisis con la herramienta LIWC. Observatorio (OBS*) 10(2)

Sierra G, Jurado J, Rincón D, Tamayo G (2019) Campañas de prevención de violencia de géneroen Colombia y España. Un análisisdesde la Psicología Social y la Publicidad Social. Fondo Editorial, Universidad de Manizales, Colombia

Sirgy M (2002) *The psychology of quality of life*. Retrieved from https://www.springer.com/gp/book/9789401599047

Statista (2019) Ranking de las principales redes sociales a nivel mundial según el número de usuarios activos en abril de 2019. Retrieved from https://es.statista.com/estadisticas/600712/ranking-mundial-de-redes-sociales-por-numero-de-usuarios/

Strum L (2017) Twitter chat: what #MeToo says about sexual abuse in society. PBS News Hour Archived from the original on October 26, 2017. Retrieved October 25, 2017

TimesUp web (2020). Retrieved from https://timesupnow.org/about/

Tonon G (2007) La propuesta teórica de la calidad de vida. HOLOGRAMÁTICA – Facultad de Ciencias Sociales – UNLZ – Año IV, Número 7, V1 (2007), pp 15–21

Tonon G (2015). Relevance of the use of qualitative methods in the study of quality of life. In: Qualitative studies in quality of life, pp 3–21. Retrieved from https://www.springer.com/gp/book/9783319137780

Tonon G, Aragón S, Rodríguez L (2014) Investigar la calidad de vida de las y los jóvenes en Argentina: El Programa de InvestigaciónenCalidad de vida de la Facultad de Ciencias Sociales de la Universidad Nacional de Lomas de Zamora. Argentina. Anales de la Universidad Metropolitana 14(1):15–29

TUC Changing the world of work of good (2016) Nearly two in three young women have experienced sexual harassment at work, TUC survey reveals. Retrieved from https://www.tuc.org.uk/news/nearly-two-three-young-women-have-experienced-sexual-harassment-work-tuc-survey-reveals

UNODC (2019) Global study on homicide. United Nations office on drugs and crimes. Retrieved from https://www.unodc.org/unodc/en/data-and-analysis/global-study-on-homicide.html

World Health Organization (2017) Violence against women, November 27. https://www.who.int/news-room/fact-sheets/detail/violence-against-women

Xu S, Zhou A (2020) Hashtag homophily in twitter network: examining a controversial cause-related marketing campaign. Comput Hum Behav 102:87–96

Yu RP (2016) The relationship between passive and active non-political social media use and political expression on Facebook and twitter. Comput Hum Behav 58:413–420. https://doi.org/10.1016/j.chb.2016.01.019

Part II
Safe and Healthy Lifestyles

Chapter 10
"For a Million Steps": The Use of Social Marketing and Wearable Devices in the Promotion of Physical Exercise to Achieve Quality of Life

Ana Isabel Polo-Peña, Dolores María Frías-Jamilena, and Francisco Peco-Torres

Abstract Consumer quality of life and well-being are critical objectives of advanced societies. Nowadays, some of the most important problems in these societies are the lack of physical exercise and the sedentary lifestyle, which must be addressed in order to promote the well-being of the population and face the current obesity pandemic. Social marketing and the development of technology offer opportunities to companies and public institutions for the development of new products and their commercialization, which helps to improve the quality of life and well-being of the population.

The development of wearable and smart devices provides new ways of practicing physical exercise and controlling our physical condition and health, responding to the consumer's need for well-being. The initiative "For a million steps" ("Por un millón de pasos", in Spanish) started by public institutions in Andalusia (Spain) allows to take advantage of the possibilities that social marketing and wearable devices offer. It is a program that manages to promote the acquisition of physical exercise habits with the support of wearable devices. This case study describes the objectives and keys of the social marketing program that have achieved a greater quality of life and well-being in the participants through the initiation and/or maintenance of physical exercise.

Keywords Quality of life · Well-being · Social marketing · Wearable · Physical exercise

---

A. I. Polo-Peña (✉) · D. M. Frías-Jamilena · F. Peco-Torres
University of Granada, Granada, Spain
e-mail: apolo@ugr.es; dfrias@ugr.es; fpeco@ugr.es

M. M. Galan-Ladero, R. G. Rivera (eds.), *Applied Social Marketing and Quality of Life*, Applying Quality of Life Research,
https://doi.org/10.1007/978-3-030-83286-5_10

Introduction

Consumer quality of life and well-being are critical objectives for advanced societies (Tonon 2020, pp. 1–7). Quality of life is currently defined as "a multidimensional concept comprising a number of domains that people consider and evaluate differently according to the importance they attach to each domain in their lives" (Tonon 2020, p. 1). This definition incorporates both a quantitative-objective approach (what people have and can be observed directly) and a qualitative-subjective approach (what people feel and can be observed indirectly). Subsequently, Dasgupta and Weale (1992) claimed that quality of life not only included the constituents of well-being but also its determinants. In this regard, Diener (2006, p. 154) noted that the early studies on quality of life related it to objective conditions in people's lives, and hence a distinction was drawn with the concept of well-being.

One of the situations with the greatest impact on quality of life and well-being for advanced societies is the lack of physical exercise and the diseases associated with the development of a sedentary lifestyle. Specifically, it could be said that Spain is one of the countries that experiences this situation. Sedentary lifestyle and its associated diseases are one of the problems for Spanish society in the social and health field (Ministry of Health, Consumption and Social Welfare 2017). This situation is mainly due to the lack of physical exercise, the high-calorie diets, as well as the so-called passive leisure according to Sánchez et al. (2015); all of that linked to the consumption of products harmful to health. These habits are related to heart and cerebrovascular diseases, which are one of the main causes of mortality in developed countries. In fact, these diseases have led to some 60,000 deaths in Spain during 2018, according to data from the Spanish National Statistics Institute (SNI 2019).

Furthermore, as Gayman et al. (2017) state, developed countries are facing an unprecedented demographic change due to the aging of the population as a consequence of the increase in life expectancy and the decrease in birth rates. This implies that the population must get into sports habits that help them to achieve an active aging less linked to diseases. Statistics predict that the number of adults aged 60 and over in developed countries will increase from 901 million (in 2019) to 2.1 billion by 2050 (United Nations 2019). Myers et al. (2019) point out that the number of obese people in 1975 was 650 million and it has tripled at present. For this reason, the WHO recommends that individuals eat less quantity of low-quality food (such as processed foods, junk food, etc.) and that they do physical and sports activities more regularly (WHO 2019). Consequently, physical activity is an area of interest for researchers and professionals in the field of health, together with public actors responsible for the health and quality of life and well-being of society.

In this situation, physical activity is recommended as a key factor to achieve a more functional lifestyle associated with a better cognitive and physiological functioning, lower risks of having chronic diseases, higher quality of life and a better health and psychological well-being (Taylor et al. 2004). Some studies have shown that regular physical exercise is important for improving health and well-being; in addition, it produces benefits not only physical, but also at a therapeutic and preventive levels. Furthermore, Medina (1994) indicates that physical exercise can serve as an instrument to transmit culture and to reflect the basic values of people's environment, as a product at a social level. Physical exercise becomes an element of socialization, that is, it allows people to create powerful links between them, whether through membership in groups, clubs or teams.

Myers et al. (2019) suggest that the insufficient physical activity among the adult population is a global pandemic and that in order to solve it, the implementation of various strategies is required at different levels within society, such as information, the development of policies to increase physical activity among the population, and to build a suitable environment for such policies. This situation leads to the need to identify certain mechanisms that allow population to get into more active lifestyle habits, in which they incorporate physical exercise, and that improve their quality of life achieving well-being.

Literature provides examples of studies that show how the use of social marketing influences different aspects of consumer well-being, such as the quality of life and consumer behavior (Loo et al. 2016), or the consumption of products and the evaluation of the quality of life (Sirgy and Lee 2008). Hence, companies and public institutions plan to take advantage of the opportunity offered by social marketing to achieve consumer well-being, directing their actions towards the development of products and programs aimed at fostering physical exercise among the population.

This chapter includes a case study based on an initiative of a public institution which seeks to motivate adults in the practice of physical exercise to improve their quality of life and well-being through social marketing and the opportunities provided by technological developments, such as the so-called wearable devices. To do this, we indicate: (1) How social marketing can contribute to the motivation for the practice of activities that improve quality of life and the achievement of well-being; and (2) how advances in technology, such as wearable devices, favor the development of products that motivate consumers to do activities that improve their quality of life and the achievement of well-being.

Wearable Devices to Support Physical Exercise

Wearable or smart devices have been brought into our day to day life allowing new ways to do physical exercise and controlling our physical condition and health (Kim et al. 2019). These are small electronic devices that are attached to the human body, clothing or personal accessories, such as bracelets, watches or glasses that have the ability to interact with the Internet and other smart devices (Shantz and Veillete 2014).

Significant advantages of these wearable devices are the possibility of obtaining feedback on physical activity in real time, and that they are designed to be small, light and to allow movements of any kind while participating in a sports activity (Bailey 2017). The data related to physical activity captured by the wearable device allows users to check their levels of physical activity and make decisions that help them to improve how they do physical exercise, their eating habits and their quality of sleep, which are the three key elements that contribute to a healthy lifestyle and well-being (Rause 2016).

The above aspects are based on the fact that it is a product whose users recognize its potential to improve their way of doing physical exercise, to achieve greater control of their performance and to monitor the activity carried out as well as other vital signs. This results in possibilities of interaction between the device and the users that will allow them to know their activity level more objectively.

Originally, high-level or elite athletes were the main users of wearable devices oriented to physical exercise, and their primary use was to improve performance and avoid injuries. However, in recent years, wearable devices have become a product that is widely adopted by society as a tool that facilitates the acquisition of physical exercise habits related to user well-being (Moore 2016). In fact, according to a report by the German Statistics Company (Statista 2020), it is estimated that the global market for this type of item will go from $16 billion in revenue (in 2016) to $73.27 billion by 2022.

More and more companies offer this type of products because of the possibilities of evolution of these devices, so the purchase decision becomes more complicated for the consumer. That is why there are numerous comparative studies published in specialized forums and websites, as well as in the media (for example, "El País Escaparate", 2019), whose objective is to offer information to consumers about the characteristics that each brand offers and help them to choose the one that best suits their needs.

However, despite the fact that wearable devices facilitate physical exercise among the population, it is possible to identify the groups that do less physical activity, such as older people (European Commission 2018), given that as age increases, less physical exercise is done. Hence the need to carry out actions aimed at those groups that show greater resistance to form these active habits. Payne and Isaacs (2017) observed that a key variable for the acquisition and maintenance of physical exercise habits is that they remain fun and motivating. So, if we want certain groups of the population to become more active, they should begin to get physical exercise through activities that they consider motivating and fun.

Specifically, it is proposed to analyze how a public institution uses social marketing to achieve quality of life and well-being through the "For a million steps" ("Por un millón de pasos", in Spanish) program. This program is designed to promote the adoption of physical exercise among the adult population, relying on the potential offered by wearable devices.

Case Development

"For a Million Steps": Physical Exercise with the Support of Wearable Devices

The "For a million steps" program is an initiative implemented at a regional level by the Health and Family Department of the Ministry of Health and Families of the Government of Andalusia, Spain since 2013 (Fig. 10.1). For its implementation, the collaboration and participation of different associations, groups or organizations that operate at the local level and that promote the participation of the local population of each municipality is required. The main objective of the project is to promote physical activity and/or reinforce its maintenance for those who already carry it out, given that the main activity of the initiative consists of taking long group walks so that, altogether, a total of at least one million steps are reached each month. The set of program objectives are shown in Table 10.1. With the implementation of the program, the adoption of healthy habits is favored, as the length of each achievement is extended by at least one month.

The design of challenges limited in time and with a specific objective results in a strategy that enhances the engagement for the participants. It is attempted to do exercise for a reasonable period of time to incorporate this habit to people who do not have it and to encourage those who already do physical activity.

The implementation of the program is based on the benefits provided by wearable devices. They allow the quantification of the steps achieved by the group. Participation in the challenge is not expensive for the participants since it only requires the possession of wearable devices and, if necessary, the body responsible for the program itself provides two wearable devices to each group. Wearable devices record the steps taken by the wearer and finally by the group. It is also possible to set the device so that it quantifies the steps of who is carrying it and of other

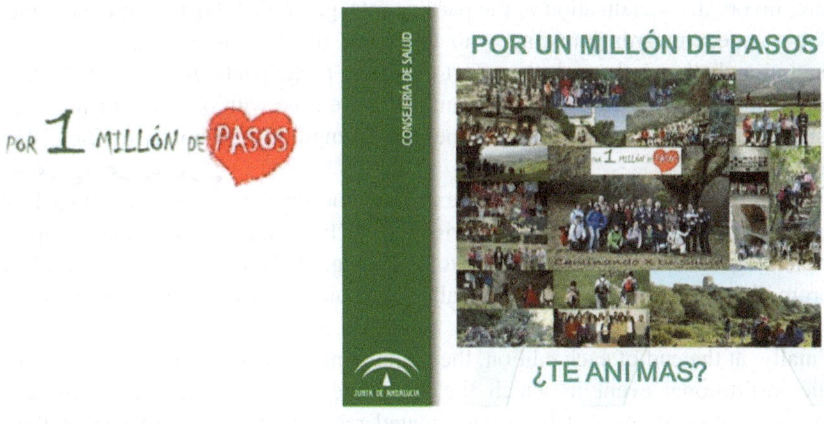

Fig. 10.1 Web presentation of the program "For a million steps". Source: Ministry of Health and Families of the Government of Andalusia, Spain (2020)

Table 10.1 Objectives of the program "For a million steps"

1. To promote physical activity through a cooperative proposal
2. To boost interpersonal and self-support actions among the participants through a group proposal
3. To revitalize associative life by promoting a common task, understanding that an association without challenges or tasks is headed towards its extinction due to boredom or confrontations
4. To promote the role of participants as "active in health" and models of healthy behaviors through the practice undertaken
5. To establish alliances with other administrations through convergence with their Plans and Strategic Lines, based on an attractive project, easy to develop and facilitator of the leading role of citizens
6. To generate pacts in convergence with local governments
7. To favor a transversal intervention strategy with comprehensive plans and other services and projects of the Department of Health of the Andalusian Government (treatment for diabetes, heart disease, mental health. . .)
8. To promote the dissemination of the activity through the communication generated by its recipients: blogs, websites...
9. To generate newsworthy acts of favorable impact for the promotion of physical activity and health

Source: Ministry of Health and Families of the Government of Andalusia, Spain (2020)

companions who do not have one of these devices (once descriptive data of the participants' physical conditions have been registered). In addition, the program requires the creation of the figure of "treasurer of the steps", who will be a member of the group that will be responsible for keeping the records of the activity carried out by the participants. This quantification of the steps of the group provides a great motivating effect for the participants.

It is an integrating program for the participants since all participants' contributions are valuable and useful to achieve the challenge that the group takes on each month. It can be considered that this program, in addition to promoting active leisure, favors the socialization of the participants, given that the goal of the activity is not oriented towards knowing who takes the most steps, but rather towards achieving a challenge through the effort of all the participants. In addition, participating in the challenge allows participants to share time with others, which can be considered as quality active leisure time that strengthens the bonds of friendship between them.

In addition, this activity can be contextualized according to the needs of each of the groups to which the program is oriented, such as, for example, the group of "people diagnosed with epilepsy" or "women" (Fig. 10.2). It might also be solidary by promoting the achievement of the challenge through donations to different causes and/or groups.

Finally, at the end of each edition, the attainment of each group is evaluated in a public institutional event in which the challenges achieved are celebrated, and people and associations that have participated receive certificates of personalized recognition (Fig. 10.3).

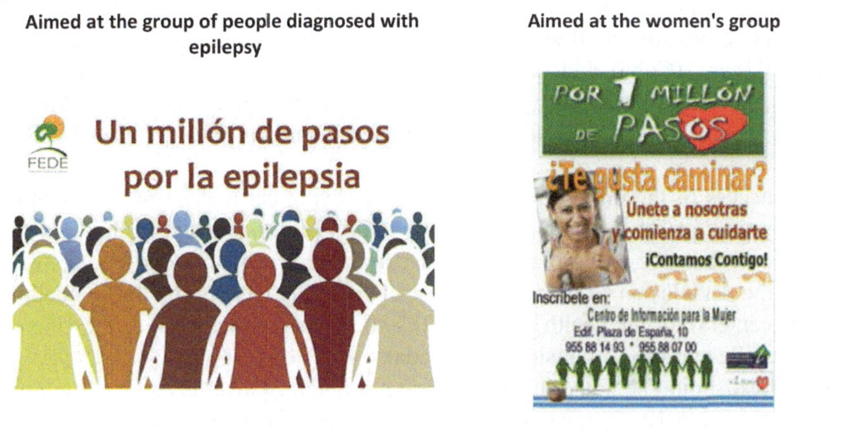

Fig. 10.2 Examples of groups to which the program can be applied. Source: Constantina Town Hall (2019) and the Spanish Federation of Epilepsy (2019)

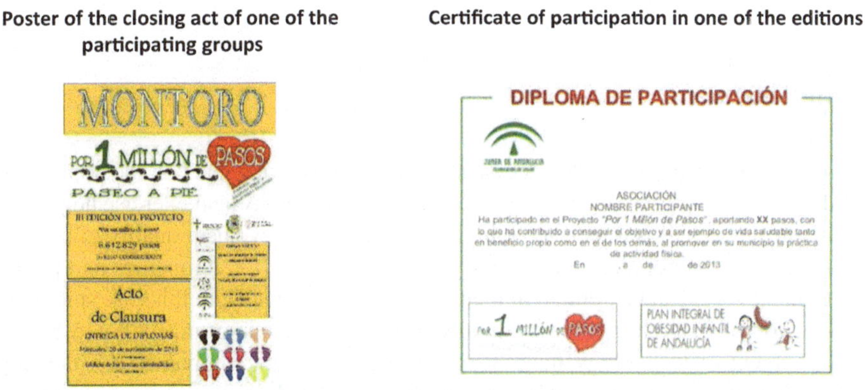

Fig. 10.3 Examples of the posters used to publicize the closing ceremony and to show the group's attainment, along with the personalized certificate that is delivered to the participants. Source: Ministry of Health and Families of the Government of Andalusia, Spain (2013) and Montoro Town Hall (2019)

The fact that the program favors the fun and motivation of the participants has led this program to go through its twelfth edition since its launch in 2008, with the participation of more than 2000 people in each of the editions. The initiative is very successful, so every year participants who start doing active physical exercise through walking are incorporated to it, and other participants have become loyal to it while maintaining the practice of active leisure.

In the attempt to make former participants join the program, they have created the so-called "Imaginary Trips". It is about going on imaginary group trips in which you get to the chosen destination through the number of steps that separate you from the place of origin. In previous editions, links have been established, for example, with Argentinian cities such as Buenos Aires, Mendoza, Rosario, Tucumán, La Plata, as well as Havana (Cuba) and Santander (Colombia). From these Latin American localities, dynamics have been generated to return these "imaginary trips" through steps, as well as to disseminate and exchange the initiatives undertaken by both parties.

The success of the program has led to it also being carried out in coordination with programs of other Andalusian Public Administrations such as those of the comprehensive active aging plan (by the Department of Equality and Social Well-being of the Andalusian Government); those of computer literacy (by the Guadalinfo network centers); or the health campuses (by some universities such as the University of Seville and the University of Granada).

Finally, it should be noted that the project has obtained awards and recognitions, such as: NAOS 2010 (Spanish Ministry of Health and Consumption), Accesit Plan for Physical Activity and Balanced Diet 2010 (Government of Andalusia, Spain), Award of the Argentine Committee for Education for Health in Population 2010 (Argentina).

Conclusions

"For a million steps" is a relevant case study with a positive impact on the population of developed countries since it promotes the adoption of physical exercise helped by wearable devices. It is important to highlight that the achievement quality of life and well-being in the population provides great opportunities for companies and public institutions for the development of their activities. Specifically, in this case study, the orientation of marketing towards quality of life and the opportunity offered by the development of technology have been considered so that companies can develop products that allow them to achieve greater results (such as wearable products that reach a high market demand) and, at the same time, serve the consumer's quality of life and well-being, since these products facilitate physical exercise and make it more efficient. On the other hand, it is an example of an initiative carried out by a public institution that manages to promote the acquisition of physical exercise habits that will have an impact on the greater quality of life and well-being of the population.

Some of the keys to the success of the "For a million steps":

- **The design of an attractive project for the participating people**. It is an activity that is in harmony with the system of values and behavior of the recipients; and is designed from a challenge rather than from the recommendation or the prescription.
- **Responsibility of achievement**. The responsibility to succeed in the activity is left to the self-management of each group. The group is arranged to go out by deciding when and where to do it, providing information on the steps taken by each participant to overcome the assumed proposal by them.

- **Multidimensional intervention**. The implementation of this program has positive implications for the participants' physical activity, as well as their mental and relational health.
- **Accessible to the participation of different types of groups**. The challenge can be adapted and assumed by groups for various purposes: the elderly, women, schools, associations of chronic non-communicable diseases, groups of disabled people, etc.
- **Revitalization of associative and intergenerational life**. The project implies relationships between local residents of different ages. The cooperative nature of the proposal recognizes the contributions (whether many or few) of all participants.
- **Individual and leadership recognition to each participant**. Individual effort, commitment to the group and leadership to achieve the group challenge of each participant are recognized. This recognition is a motivating element because it is made public in a public event, with a certificate that ranks each participant according to their commitment to the activity and through the dissemination in local and regional public media.
- **Low economic cost**. The cost is reduced to the possession of a wearable device for each participant. If in any case this is not available, the responsible entity would provide up to two devices to each of the groups.
- **Transversality**. It is a project that can be adapted to be applied in coordination with multiple plans and programs to achieve more objectives in addition to the acquisition of physical exercise habits.
- **Social visibility**. Thanks to the favorable news generated in the media about this program, visibility is given to health promotion practices through physical exercise.

In general, this case study highlights, on the one hand, the suitability of marketing orientation to quality of life in the actions of companies and public institutions and, on the other, the possibilities offered by technology to develop devices that motivate consumers to do physical exercise.

Discussion Questions

Questions Regarding the Social Marketing Towards Quality of Life

1. Do you consider that technological innovations provide opportunities for companies and/or institutions to adopt an orientation towards social marketing quality of life and well-being?

Questions Regarding the Case Study "For a Million Steps"

2. Do you think that the objectives of the "For a million steps" program are important?
3. Which do you think have been the success factors of the "For a million steps" program?
4. What new proposals would you make so that the "For a million steps" program brings new things to participants of previous editions? What other objectives would you add to the program?

Additional Questions

5. Create and design a program proposal from marketing orientation in general, and from social marketing towards quality of life in particular, towards quality of life to respond to a situation that you want to improve in your environment.
6. Prepare the necessary materials to communicate your proposal to a company and/or public institution (as appropriate) and, as far as possible, try to make an appointment with those responsible for the company and/or public institution to explain your draft.

Teaching Notes

Questions Regarding Social Marketing Towards Quality of Life

1. **Do you consider that technological innovations provide opportunities for companies and/or institutions to adopt an orientation towards social marketing quality of life?**

Taking up the case study "For a million steps", students can identify and propose other possibilities to use new technologies in order to promote the adoption of an orientation of social marketing towards quality of life.

Technological innovations applied in other areas and how they help to achieve a higher quality of life among consumers and/or society can be considered. For example: (a) innovations aimed at monitoring health (with technological devices that control blood sugar levels and help people with diabetes to live better), (b) the technological devices that help elderly and dependent people (with alarm systems tailored to their needs), (c) applications that can contribute to making learning new languages and/or subjects more enjoyable and fun than in the past (such as applications that allow to take advantage of gamification and digital media to develop educational programs), and (d) technological advances that help make a home more comfortable and ecological (such as systems that adjust lighting based on existing solar lighting), among others.

Questions Regarding the Case Study "For a Million Steps"

2. **Do you think that the objectives of the "For a million steps" program are important?**

In this question, students can link the implementation of this program with current data on health and well-being problems associated with sedentary lifestyle among the population of developed countries.

3. **Which do you think have been the success factors of the "For a million steps" program?**

After reading the case, students can identify important keys such as the involvement of the participants in a common project, the development of friendship during their participation in the project, social recognition achieved for each of the participants, the possibilities of customizing the program according to the needs of the group, and many other possibilities.

4. **What new proposals would you make so that the "For a million steps" program brings new things to participants of previous editions? What other objectives would you add to the program?**

The answer to this question may be open to ideas raised by students.

Suggestions that can be taken into account: participation of other groups of the population, adoption of goals associated with the achievement of social challenges, addition of new routes based on nature or culture, theming each of the editions, linking the development of the walks with the benefits of a healthy diet, etc.

Additional Questions

5. **Create and design a program proposal from marketing orientation in general, and from social marketing towards quality of life in particular, to respond to a situation that you want to improve in your environment.**

These questions can be answered by those students who identify an opportunity for improvement in their environment based on the principles of social marketing towards quality of life; and by those who consider that it would be feasible to achieve an improvement in that environment thanks to one of their proposed actions or programs.

6. **Prepare the necessary materials to communicate your proposal to a company and/or public institution (as appropriate) and, as far as possible, try to make an appointment with those responsible for the company and/or public institution to explain your draft.**

At this stage, the teacher could tutor the students to prepare quality presentation materials or proposals, in addition to giving guidelines to manage to make an appointment with a company and/or institution so that they can present a proposal and do an appropriate presentation.

This can be a motivating opportunity for personal growth for the student and for the improvement of the environment.

Additional Reference Material

Chapter 7 "Developing Quality-of-Life Pedagogy in Marketing Courses: A Structured Approach" from the book Tonon (2020).

References

Bailey D (2017) Wearable technology is leading a sports, and healthcare, revolution. Available at https://sponsored.bostonglobe.com/future-forward/wearable-technology-sports-and-healthcare-revolution/. Accessed 18 Mar 2020

Constantina Town Hall (Ayuntamiento de Constantina, in Spanish) (2019) El viernes 25 comenzamos nuestro "Por un millón de pasos": únete a nosotras para lograr el reto. Available at http://www.constantina.es/opencms/opencms/constantina/actualidad/noticias/igualdad/noticia_0019.html#.XnJsWKhKi1s. Accessed 18 Mar 2020

Dasgupta P, Weale M (1992) On measuring quality of life. World Dev 20(1):119–131

Diener E (2006) Guidelines for national indicators of subjective well-being and ill-being. ARQOL 1(2):151–157

El País Escaparate (2019) Pantalla a color y monitor de natación: así es la pulsera de actividad más vendida en Amazon. Available at https://elpais.com/elpais/2019/10/29/escaparate/1572368548_075240.html. Accessed 18 Mar 2020

European Commission (2018) Sport and physical activity. Available at http://ec.europa.eu/commfrontoffice/publicopinion/index.cfm/survey/getsurveydetail/instruments/special/surveyky/2164. Accessed 18 Mar 2020

Gayman AM, Fraser-Thomas J, Baker J (2017) Relational developmental systems metatheory: a conceptual framework to understand and promote older adults' involvement in sport. Eur Rev Aging Phys Act 14(1):12

Kim T, Chiu W, Chow MKF (2019) Sport technology consumers: segmenting users of sports wearable devices based on technology readiness. Sport Bus Manag 9(2):134–145

Loo J, Shi Y, Pu X, Loo JMY (2016) Gambling, drinking and quality of life: evidence from Macao and Australia. J Gambl Stud 32(2):391–407

Medina X (1994) El deporte como factor en la construcción sociocultural de la identidad. VV.AA, Ciencias Sociales Y Deporte, Investigación Social Y Deporte, AEISAD 1, Pamplona

Ministry of Health and Families of the Government of Andalusia (2013) Por un millón de pasos. Information obtained from the Portal of the Junta de Andalucía. Available at: https://www.juntadeandalucia.es/organismos/saludyfamilias/areas/salud-vida/paginas/proyectos-pafae.html. Accessed 18 Mar 2020

Ministry of Health and Families of the Government of Andalusia, Spain (2020). Information obtained from the Portal Web of the Junta de Andalucía. Available at: https://www.juntadeandalucia.es/organismos/saludyfamilias/areas/salud-vida/paginas/proyectos-pafae.html.

Ministry of Health, Consumption and Social Welfare (2017) Encuesta Nacional de Salud. España 2017. Available at: https://www.mscbs.gob.es/estadEstudios/estadisticas/encuestaNacional/encuestaNac2017/ENSE2017_notatecnica.pdf. Accessed 18 Mar 2020

Montoro Town Hall, Ayuntamiento de Montoro (in Spanish) (2019) Acto de clausura "Por un millón de pasos" en Montoro. Available at https://www.montoro.es/agenda/acto-clausura-por-un-millon-de-pasos. Accessed 18 Mar 2020

Moore S (2016) Gartner survey shows wearable devices need to be more useful. Available at https://www.gartner.com/en/newsroom/press-releases/2016-12-07-gartner-survey-shows-wearable-devices-need-to-be-more-useful. Accessed 18 Mar 2020

Myers ND, Prilleltensky I, Lee S, Dietz S, Prilleltensky O, McMahon A, Brincks AM (2019) Effectiveness of the fun for wellness online behavioral intervention to promote welfare and physical activity: protocol for a randomized controlled trial. BMC Public Health 19(1):737

Payne VG, Isaacs LD (2017) Human motor development: a lifespan approach. Routledge, London

Rause SA (2016) Wearable technology: improving exercise habits and experiences in adults (Tesis doctoral). University of Pennsylvania, Indiana

Sánchez DM, García RS, Rodríguez MM, Sanz NP (2015) ¿Qué significa ser activo en una sociedad sedentaria? paradojas de los estilos de vida y el ocio en la juventud española/what does it mean to be active in a sedentary society? paradoxes on lifestyle and leisure of Spanish youth. Empiria 30:77–108

Shantz JAS, Veillette CJ (2014) The application of wearable technology in surgery: ensuring the positive impact of the wearable revolution on surgical patients. Front Surg 1:39

Sirgy MJ, Lee DJ (2008) Welfare marketing: an ethical business philosophy for consumer goods firms. J Bus Ethics 77(4):377–403

SNI, Statistics National Institute (2019) Las 15 causas más frecuentes en España. Available at: https://www.ine.es/dyngs/INEbase/es/operacion.htm?c=Estadistica_C&cid=1254736176780&menu=ultiDatos&idp=1254735573175. Accessed 18 Mar 2020

Spanish Federation of Epilepsy, Federación Española de Epilepsia (in Spanish) (2019) La FEDE organiza para 2019 la campaña «Un millón de pasos por la epilepsia». Available at http://www.fedeepilepsia.org/la-fede-organiza-2019-la-campana-millon-pasos-la-epilepsia/. Accessed 18 Mar 2020

Statista.com (2020) Wearable device revenue worldwide 2016–2022. Available at https://www.statista.com/statistics/610447/wearable-device-revenue-worldwide/. Accessed 18 Mar 2020

Taylor A, Cable N, Faulkner G, Hillsdon M, Narici M, Van Der Bij A (2004) Physical activity and older adults: a review of health benefits and the effectiveness of interventions. J Sports Sci 22(8):703–725

Tonon GH (2020) Teaching quality of life in different domains. Springer, Cham

United Nations (2019) Population profiles. Available at: https://population.un.org/wpp/Graphs/Probabilistic/POP/60plus/900. Accessed 18 Mar 2020

WHO, World Health Organization (2019) Obesity and overweight. Available at: https://www.who.int/en/news-room/fact-sheets/detail/obesity-and-overweight. Accessed 18 Mar 2020

Ministry of Health and Families, The Government of Malta … [illegible]

[illegible]

Chapter 11
The Behobia: San Sebastian Race—Promoting Sport, Health and the Quality of Community Life

Iñaki Garcia-Arrizabalaga, Juan Jose Gibaja-Martins, and Alazne Mujika-Alberdi

Abstract Fortuna Sports Club (FSC) is a fourth-sector organisation located in San Sebastián (Basque Country, Spain). It organizes the race between Behobia and San Sebastián. The promotion of healthy lifestyles among the participants is one of the main concerns of the organisers. This social marketing aim seems to have been met. To prepare for the race, participants alter aspects of their lifestyle linked to health. In terms of the traditional perspective of Quality of Life (QOL), FSC increases runner's well-being. FSC is also concerned about other social marketing goals related to social changes. The "50/50/25 Programme", that aims to achieve parity between female and male participants in the race, or the work carried out to make it easier for people with physical disabilities to take part in the race are aspects that stand out in a fun run, organised by a non-profit sports club, that considers sport to be a tool that can also be used to improve the health and quality of life of its fellow citizens. Indeed, the social marketing perspective is in the DNA of the FSC and QOL marketing philosophy is fully included in it: customer well-being is complemented preserving society's well-being.

Keywords Sport · Health · Gender parity · People with disabilities · Social marketing · Quality of Life · Well-being

Introduction

Health is one of the basic aspects that determine people's quality of life. And it does so in two ways: not only in itself in an absolute sense, but also because of its subsequent impact in other aspects of the quality of life. This is how the Organisation for Economic Co-operation and Development seems to understand it when it states

I. Garcia-Arrizabalaga (✉) · J. J. Gibaja-Martins · A. Mujika-Alberdi
University of Deusto, Donostia/San Sebastian, Spain
e-mail: igarri@deusto.es; jjgibaja@deusto.es; alazne.mujika@deusto.es

M. M. Galan-Ladero, R. G. Rivera (eds.), *Applied Social Marketing and Quality of Life*, Applying Quality of Life Research,
https://doi.org/10.1007/978-3-030-83286-5_11

that "People's health is one of the most valued aspects of people's life. Surveys in many countries consistently found that people put health status, together with jobs, at the top of what affects their living conditions. People's health status matters in itself, but also for achieving other dimensions of well-being, such as having good jobs and adequate income, being able to participate as full citizens in community life, to socialise with others, to attend school and adult education" (OECD 2011).

According to the World Health Organisation (WHO), a sedentary lifestyle is the fourth leading risk factor in mortality worldwide and is responsible for between 21% and 25% of cases of breast and colon cancer, 27% of cases of diabetes and is linked to 30% of cases of ischemic heart disease. Physical activity is a key aspect in preventing cardiovascular diseases or endocrine disorders (WHO 2020).

Furthermore, there exists no doubt about the transformative power of sport. Sport is an intrinsically participative and inclusive endeavour which enables the acquisition of skills such as discipline, trust or leadership, and teaches basic principles such as tolerance, cooperation and respect. However, sport is also about individual and community health, voluntary work, education, social integration and economic development.

The following lines describe the various issues related to the most important event that Fortune Sports Club (FSC) annually organizes: the Behobia-San Sebastián race. The data on the social impact on the health of those taking part, the social inclusion of the disabled, the challenge of gender equality, and the commitment to environmental sustainability give us a better idea of the case that will be analysed in the following section. Surprinsingly, FSC has never used the term social marketing in its programs and activities. However, the way they encourage participants' behavior to create both individual and social changes is a clear signal of the use of it. Really, the social marketing perspective is in the DNA of the organization. It was founded with the aim of promoting sport, and it understood this in its broadest sense, not just as an activity to be enjoyed but also as one for self-improvement and social integration as well. Recently, Fernando Ibarreta, member of the Fortuna management team, states: "Fortuna Sports Club's mission has not changed since its foundation, what has changed is its vision".

The Behobia: San Sebastian Race

The Fortuna Sports Club (FSC) was founded on the 24th of April 1911 in the city of San Sebastián (Basque Country, Spain). It is, therefore, a 100-year-old organisation that currently has a thousand members. Its longevity is an unusual feature in sporting associations or clubs that aim to promote grassroots sport. At the present time FSC

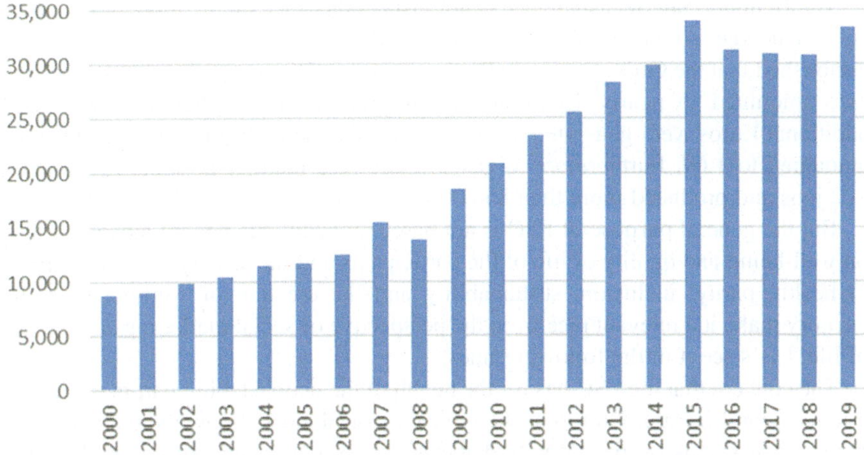

Fig. 11.1 Registered runners in the race. Source: Adapted from Fortuna Sports Club (2019)

can be considered to be a non-profit organisation that forms part of what is called the fourth sector.[1]

Without a shadow of a doubt, the activity that FSC is best-known for is the organization of the Behobia-San Sebastián race, a 20-km footrace between Behobia (on the border between France and Spain) and San Sebastián, which is held each year on the second Sunday in November. This race is deeply rooted in Spain among amateur runners.

Figure 11.1 shows the total number of registered runners in the years that the race has been held this century. In 2000 there were only 8801 runners. Ten years later, in 2010, they were 20,809. Finally, in 2019, a total of 33,379 runners registered to complete the race.

[1]The emergence of the concept of "The Fourth Sector" has made it possible to go beyond the "For-profit/Non-profit" debate and has highlighted the importance of the reality of "For-benefit organisations". According to Fourth Sector Network (2009), organisations form vital elements in any society and are the result of what individuals have gradually designed over time. They are also a mirror of the moment in which they are created, as they reflect the norms, values, priorities and context in which they are created. However, it is also true that organisations evolve in accordance with the needs that emerge in society. As a result, organisations classified as forming part of the primary sector, that is, the private sector, have begun to take significant steps along the continuum regarding the maximisation of benefits, from focusing on maximising economic-financial benefits to maximising social benefits. In the same vein, public sector and non-profit organisations are gradually shifting on the continuum with regard to obtaining financial income from charity or subsidies towards obtaining income by exchanging market value. These trends have been characterised as movements of organisations that converge towards a new playing field and emerging movements that create new hybrid organisations that transcend the traditional classification into private, public or non-profit sectors. This results in fourth-sector organisations that are basically characterised by having a social commitment inherent to their very essence and by certain business methods that lead them to develop gainful activities that are in keeping with their more social aims.

The Behobia-San Sebastián race is not just another race on the more or less local sports calendar. An economic impact study of the race for the city of San Sebastián established that the Gross Domestic Product generated by organising and staging the race amounted to nearly 15 million euros. That is, for each euro spent, 0.69 additional Euros were generated, or in other words, the multiplier effect of the race amounted to 1.69. Furthermore, organising the race made it possible to maintain 122 jobs and produced more than 850,000 euros in tax revenues (DBS 2014).

But the general purpose of FSC is not based on economic benefit alone, but also on well-being and quality of life of the participants and the society. Its commitment to health, parity, inclusion, sustainability and the creation of well-being in the territory make it a relevant race from the perspective of social marketing and quality of life. Let's see it in the following lines.

The concern that the FSC has for the health of the people taking part in the race is a fundamental feature. On top of the typical medical aid stations, there are also the blood-sugar stands for people with diabetes. Up to four stands are set up along the route where anyone with diabetes will be able to measure their glucose levels and specialised personnel will provide glycaemic control supplements if these were necessary. Another outstanding new feature is the "smart" bib initiative. A QR code on the front of the bib is linked to the runner's standard identification on the back which the runner will be able to activate to access an app to provide their personal details in an emergency. If necessary, the medical services will be able to rapidly access important details regarding the runner to ensure more effective intervention. On the web page the runners also have a stroke signs and symptoms questionnaire designed by the Behobia-San Sebastián Medical Advisory Committee. This committee designed a tool with the aim of establishing a fast and simple frontline prevention measure to detect which athletes are at risk of suffering a heart attack or sudden death during exercise. According to the organisers, in 2019 approximately 75% of the participants complete the self-assessment questionnaire.

The Behobia-San Sebastián Race and Improvements in Healthy Lifestyles and the Quality of Life of the Runners

In order to continue deepening a message based on health, healthy lifestyles and well-being in its communication strategy started in 2016, FSC conducted an ad hoc study on the impact that the race had on runners who they decided to participate. The research carried out by the Club, together with the University of Deusto and the University Hospital of San Sebastián (Mujika et al. 2015, 2018), studied, among other things, the following aspects.[2]

Changes in perception:

[2]See the complete study in Mujika-Alberdi, A.; García-Arrizabalaga, I. and Gibaja-Martíns, J.J. (2018); "Impact of the Behobia-San Sebastián Race on Promoting Healthy Lifestyles"; *Apunts.*

Fig. 11.2 Changes in health and weight perception as a result of training for the race. Source: Adapted from Mujika et al. (2015)

- General perception regarding improvements in health.
- Satisfaction with body weight.

Changes in behaviour:

- Improvement in eating habits
- Reduction in smoking.
- Reduction in alcohol consumption.
- Increase in daily sleeping hours.

Concerning changes in perception, when runners were asked about the improvement they perceived in their health due to the training to take part in the race, Fig. 11.2 shows that almost 50% of them claim that it has improved quite a lot or very much (46% of women and 48% of men).

In Gipuzkoa, the geographical area that the race is organised in, the average Body Mass Index is 26. If from 25 upwards it can be said that an individual is overweight, then we can consider that "Gipuzkoa is overweight". On the other hand, the Body Mass Index of the runners in the race is within the range considered to be normal (between 18.5 and 25), with an average of 23.57. In order to get an idea of these amounts, bear in mind that, for example, in the study carried out by Raebel et al. (2004) it was estimated that for each unit increase in the population's Body Mass Index, the health costs for a country increased by 2.3%.

Runners were also asked whether they were more or less pleased with their weight due to the training to take part in the race. In this case, as also indicated in Fig. 11.2, almost 40% stated that they were rather or much more pleased (38% of women and 40% of men).

Educación Física y Deportes; 131, 34–48. Retrieved from https://doi.org/10.5672/apunts.2014-0983.es

Fig. 11.3 Behavioral changes as a result of training for the race. Source: Adapted from Mujika et al. (2015)

Concerning changes in behaviour, Fig. 11.3 shows that training to take part in the race had had a positive influence on:

- Increasing the number of hours that the runners slept each day. 58% of women and 53% of men have changed their behaviour in this sense.
- Reducing the alcohol consumption of the runners. 60% of women and 55% of men did it.
- Reducing in smoking. Hardly 5% of runners confessed that they were regular smokers (more than 5 cigarettes a day) and another 5.4% defined themselves as occasional smokers. In any case, 53% of smoker women and 37% of smoker men had cut down on smoking since they had been training to run the race.
- Improving in eating habits. 91% of women and 89% of men said that the challenge of training to run the Behobia-San Sebastián had had a significant influence on improving their diet.

As it goes into this last question in detail, to observe which foods they had increased and reduced their consumption of, Table 11.1 shows how almost 25% of runners said that they had increased their consumption of fruit and slightly more than 16% said that they had increased how often they ate vegetables. On the other hand, a considerable percentage of runners (between 18 and 23%) said that they had reduced how often they consumed sweets, sugar-sweetened soft drinks, fast food and appetisers or salty snacks.

The study carried out in 2014 demonstrates a positive relationship between runners participating in the Behobia-San Sebastian and the adoption of healthy lifestyles. To replicate the research could be an excellent initiative to observe the evolution of the results.

Table 11.1 Since you have been training to take part in the Behobia-San Sebastián, how often do you eat the following foods?

Food	I have increased the frequency of my weekly consumption	I have reduced the frequency of my weekly consumption
Fresh fruit	24.9%	–
Natural fruit or vegetable juice	13.3%	–
Vegetables	16.5%	–
Cold meats	–	18.3%
Sweets and biscuits	–	20.3%
Sugar-sweetened soft drinks	–	20.3%
Fast food (pizzas, hamburgers, sandwiches)	–	22.3%
Appetisers or salty snacks	–	22.8%

Source: Mujika et al. (2015)

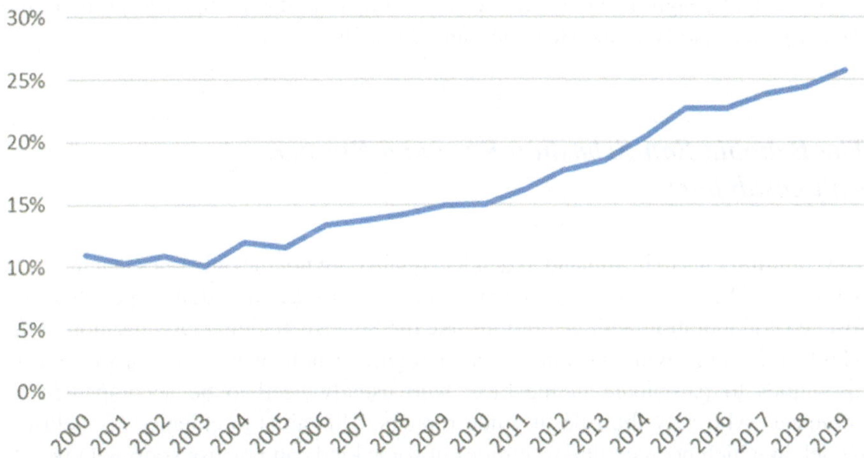

Fig. 11.4 Women participation in the race. Source: Adapted from Fortuna Sports Club (2019)

The Behobia-San Sebastián Race and the Gender Gap

For the Fortuna Sports Club, runners' health is accompanied by another commitment, which is parity in participation between male and female runners. Figure 11.4 shows the percentage of women over the total number of registered runners in the years that the race has been held this century. It has to be pointed out that the percentage of women has consistently increased over the last years: 11.01% in 2000, 14.97% in 2010 and, finally, 25.78 in 2019.

Gender equality is a strategic commitment that the organisation has made for the next few years. In 2018 the organisation launched an initiative to achieve parity between men and women, the 50/50/25 programme, that is, 50% women, 50% men, by 2025. This is a programme that launches strategies based on equality that, above and beyond the figure of 50/50, aims to carry out measures to raise awareness that encourage the social change needed to ensure that this goal can become a reality. The organization has begun a strategic reflection process and they are working on various matters linked to sport and gender.

Within this framework, the organisation has included female pacesetters or hares,[3] a responsibility that a dozen women have taken on who together with another 17 men are responsible for setting different paces for the race. And although there is still a long way to go to achieve parity as far as participation is concerned, the number of women signing up for the Behobia-San Sebastián is constantly increasing as can be seen in Fig. 11.4.

As part of this same course of action, in the 54th edition, in 2018, of the race, Kathrine Switzer, a symbol of the struggle for equality for women in sport, was invited by Deusto University to take part in various events. Switzer was the first woman to run a marathon as a numbered entrant. She did so in the Boston Marathon in 1967 at a time when this distance was run exclusively by men. Her presence in San Sebastián had a significant social and media impact, which helped to promote the idea of gender parity in the Behobia-San Sebastián.

The Behobia-San Sebastián Race and Runners with Disabilities

The commitments to health and to gender equality are not the only ones that the Club has made. The inclusion of disabled runners is another important aspect that has fostered collaboration with institutions like the Spanish National Organisation of the Blind or Kemen, with the aim of encouraging people with physical or sensory disabilities to participate in the race, who usually need to be accompanied by volunteers who play the role of guide runners. This aims to enhance an inclusive model, in which people with disabilities of some kind can practise sport with people without disabilities.

Table 11.2 shows how the number of disabled people who have signed up for the race has evolved.

The spirit of solidarity that characterises the race should also be pointed out. In the latest Behobia-San Sebastián race the runners who so desired had the option of choosing from among a total of 17 different charity projects. Participants can register by purchasing a Charity Bib which consists of paying a supplement of seven euros when they buy the bib and allocating this money to one of the selected social projects. The organisation donates an extra Euro for each runner registered through

[3] "Hares" have the role of setting a fixed pace during part of, or throughout the entire race, so that any participants who so desire can follow them and be helped to achieve a finishing time.

Table 11.2 People with disabilities that have taken part in the Behobia-San Sebastián race

	Wheelchair	Handbike	Visual impairment	Walking impairment	Brain damage	Roller-skaters with impairment	Deaf people	Total
2006	18	2	10	5	3	0	–	38
2007	16	2	14	2	2	0	–	36
2008	15	5	14	3	4	0	–	41
2009	27	3	36	13	2	0	–	81
2010	12	6	27	2	0	0	–	47
2011	9	8	29	0	0	0	–	46
2012	7	16	19	0	0	0	–	42
2013	4	16	20	0	0	0	–	40
2014	4	17	16	2	2	2	–	43
2015	3	20	11	0	1	2	–	37
2016	11	27	17	6	1	1	–	63
2017	10	34	23	6	1	1	–	75
2018	11	37	32	5	1	1	–	87
2019	9	29	26	4	0	1	10	79

Source: Fortuna Sports Club (2019)

the Charity Bib programme. The projects in 2019 include international ones like UNHCR, Vicente Ferrer or the Red Cross and others that are based locally.

The Behobia-San Sebastián Race and Environmental Sustainability

The organisation also continues to show a serious commitment to environmental sustainability. Since 2002, in collaboration with different local public service, the waste produced at the refreshment stands is separated at source to be selectively collected and then recycled. In 2009 the organisation opted to change the refreshments system by switching from plastic bottles to paper cups, which significantly reduced the volume of plastic waste that is produced. In the same year, in collaboration with local public services, they began to collect the abandoned clothes that runners use on the starting line to keep warm. Later on, in 2014 and 2015, the Club carried out an environmental diagnosis of the race in order to find out what the impact of this was, and consequently, to work on reducing it. As a result of this work a report was published that is available on the race's web page. Later on, in 2016 the organisation took another step forward on becoming the first open-air sports event in the region to receive the *Erronka Garbia* certificate issued by IHOBE, which is the Public Company attached to the Basque Government Department for the Environment, Territorial Planning and Housing which supports the Basque Government in developing its environmental policy and in spreading the culture of environmental sustainability in the Basque Autonomous Community. The Environmental Impact Statement for the event is also available on its web page.

Conclusions

Let's identify good practices of social marketing and QOL that could be useful and inspiring for other organisations.

Improving people's well-being and quality of life is not just an issue that concerns governments or public or private social welfare or protection institutions. The Fortuna Sports Club is a good example of this. In terms of the traditional perspective of Quality of Life (QOL), FSC increases runner's well-being promoting the participation in a race. Indeed, QOL marketing philosophy is fully included in FSC: customer well-being is complemented preserving society's well-being. Its commitment to health, parity, inclusion, sustainability and the creation of well-being in the territory make it a relevant race from the perspective of social marketing and quality of life.

FSC's flagship event, the annual organisation of the Behobia-San Sebastián race, is much more than a race. It is a tool, in its own way within the scope of its possibilities, which helps to improve the quality of life of the people who take part in it. As Mujika et al. (2018) state, "the race has become an important event in the personal calendar of amateur runners, and a driving force for sustainable change in the increasingly healthier lifestyles of thousands of runners, as well as being a good investment in public health for Gipuzkoa".

But these things do not just happen by chance. If the Fortuna Sports Club is concerned with encouraging healthy lifestyles among runners, if it works to reduce the gender gap and to raise social awareness about this problem, if it is committed to the integration of people with physical disabilities in sport, if it raises awareness in society about the importance of environmental sustainability, it is because it was founded with the goal of promoting sport, that it understands in its broadest sense, not only as an activity for personal enjoyment but also as one for self-improvement as well as for social integration and for improving people's quality of life. Fortuna Sports Club's use of sport both to enhance individual well-being and to promote social change in innovative ways are at the heart of what social marketing is.

Kotler and Armstrong (2008) add a player in business-market relations, society, so that they state that the marketing strategy must take customers' wishes, business profitability and social wellbeing into account. As a result, this approach goes beyond the focus on the runner. The services provided for runners before, during and after the race are numerous, appropriate and generous. The standardised practice of measuring runners' satisfaction enables the organisation to continually assess all these services and adapt them to meet any new needs and demands that runners may have. The continuous incorporation of technological and digital advances could be seen as part of this context of continuous adaptation and anticipation. The commercial profitability of the project is also confirmed in the economic impact. And finally, the social impact that it causes remains to be observed. The economic impact study carried out by Deusto Business School (2014) shows that, apart from the economic impact of the race, the event also leaves a significant mark in the area in the form of direct expenditure, tax revenue and the jobs that it creates. All this can be considered in terms of the social wellbeing that is created in the area. There is no doubt that the race also encourages healthy lifestyles. This is made quite clear in the health impact study (Mujika et al. 2018). We observe how taking part in the race influences changes in the runners' lifestyles in matters linked to practicing sport, nutrition, smoking and alcohol consumption. The participation of the disabled (Fortuna Sports Club 2019), the 50/50/25 gender equality programme[4] or the commitment to the environment can also be considered to be inputs that contribute to social wellbeing.

Indeed, FSC was founded with the aim of promoting sport, and it understood this in its broadest sense, not just as an activity to be enjoyed but also as one for self-improvement and social integration as well. Together with its multi-sport nature, grass-roots and amateur sport have been its leitmotiv right from the start. "Fortuna Sports Club's mission has not changed since its foundation, what has changed is its vision", states Fernando Ibarreta. The vision is set out in the following terms: "To be

[4] https://bss505025.behobia-sansebastian.com/es/que-es

recognised by society in Guipuzcoa as the benchmark club in promoting grass-roots federated sport and leisure as a basic factor in individual development regardless of age and gender, through: 1) its sections, the management of facilities, the organisation of events and the development of collaborative projects with organisations and entities; 2) the launching of new lines of services that focus on meeting the aims of the Club; and 3) the workers, partners, volunteers and users as the cornerstone of the Club". Really, the social marketing perspective is in the DNA of the organization.

So those public authorities who have the responsibility for promoting citizens' quality of life should not only remember, but should also support these kinds of organisations that can help to achieve this aim, through their respective spheres of activity. Actually, a fourth-sector sport organization can design and implement QOL social marketing adopting specific marketing mix decision: designing an inclusive race and facilitating minor segments to participate in it, and communicating educational and persuasive messages based in the individual and community well-being.

Discussion Questions

1. The OECD has a Project called the "Better Life Initiative". You can visit it at http://www.oecd.org/statistics/better-life-initiative.htm. You will see that the general framework established by the OECD to measure people's well-being, progress and quality of life has 11 basic dimensions (http://www.oecd.org/statistics/measuring-well-being-and-progress.htm).
   Which of these is this case related to?
2. Is Fortuna a club that is doing social marketing or cause-related marketing? What are their differences? Could you give an example of each?
3. What do you think about the 50/50/25 initiative that the Fortuna Sports Club has launched? Do you think that it is realistic? Do you think that a sports club should be involved in promoting initiatives like this? Why?
4. Bearing in mind the 11 dimensions reviewed in the first point, what other initiatives can you think of that a non-profit organisation like the Fortuna Sports Club could develop to improve the quality of life of runners or of society in general?

Teaching Notes

1. The OECD has a project called the "Better Life Initiative". You can visit it at http://www.oecd.org/statistics/better-life-initiative.htm. You will see that the general framework established by the OECD to measure people's well-being, progress and quality of life has 11 basic dimensions (http://www.oecd.org/statistics/measuring-well-being-and-progress.htm)
   Which of them is this case related to? (Fig. 11.5)

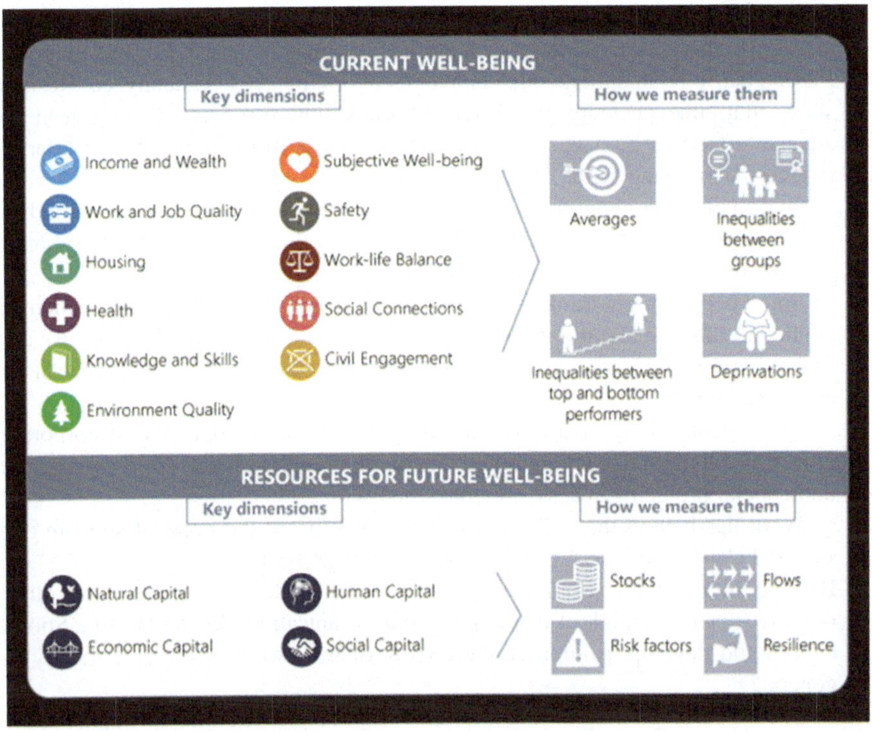

Fig. 11.5 OECD well-being framework. Source: OECD (2020)

Of the 11 dimensions of the quality of life, we think that Fortuna Sports Club is working, through the Behobia-San Sebastián race, on the following:

- Health (more physical activity by runners, improvement in self-rated health status, lower consumption of cigarettes and alcohol, healthier eating habits...).
- Environmental Quality (Sustainability certification for the race, raising awareness among the runners and the population about the environmental impact of the race...).
- Civil engagement (support for humanitarian causes, integration of groups with physical disabilities in the race, commitment to the cause to reduce the gender gap...).

2. Why is Fortuna a club that does social marketing and not cause-related marketing? What are their differences? Could you give an example of each?

   We encourage to read the article "A Study on the Effect of Cause-Related Marketing on the Attitude Towards the Brand: The Case of *Pepsi* in Spain" (https://www.tandfonline.com/doi/abs/10.1300/J054v11n01_08). Cause-Related Marketing is an effective tool for differentiating brands and for obtaining emotional positioning among consumers. However, an utilitarian use of this tool might be counteractive. The referenced research aims to better understand the effect of cause-related marketing on attitude towards the brand. For this purpose, *Pepsi's* cause-related marketing campaigns in Spain have been analyzed. Results show that, unexpectedly, cause-related marketing campaigns might lead to adverse effects as a result of the mercantilist abuse of the concept of solidarity (Garcia-Arrizabalaga et al. 2003).

3. What do you think about the 50/50/25 initiative that the Fortuna Sports Club has launched? Do you think that it is realistic? Do you think that a sports club should be involved in promoting initiatives like this? Why?

   Some people might think that "the business of business is business", which, if applied to this case, would mean that a sports organisation should be exclusively devoted to being more efficient in organising the sports events that it is concerned with.

   Other people may also think that a sports organisation is also a corporate citizen and that, like any committed citizen, it should be involved in solving the main social problems that we are concerned with.

   What lies behind this reflection process is: What is the point of sport in our society? Can we help to transform society through sport?

4. Bearing in mind the 11 dimensions reviewed in the first point, what other initiatives can you think of that a non-profit organisation like the Fortuna Sports Club could develop to improve the quality of life of runners and of society in general?

   The aspects regarding raising awareness about the environmental impact of the race and support for solidarity projects can definitely be improved.

   It seems to be difficult for the race to be able to act in areas such as "Income and Wealth", "Work and Job Quality", "Housing", "Knowledge and Skills", "Safety" or "Work-life balance".

   However, there are areas such as the sphere of "Social Connections" in which it would be possible to imagine, for example, setting up networks or groups of runners who share their experiences (training, comments, concerns, ambitions...).

   Another idea that could be launched is a Behobia-San Sebastián "Third Age" race. In actual fact, versions of the Behobia-San Sebastián for children and for adolescents are held on the days before the main race.

References

DBS – Deusto Business School (2014) Estudio del impacto económico de la Behobia-San Sebastián 2013 en el territorio histórico de Gipuzkoa. Retrieved from https://www.behobia-sansebastian.com/images/000_docs/estudio_impacto_economico_bss_2013.pdf

Fortuna Sports Club (2019) Dossier de prensa Behobia-San Sebastián. Retrieved from https://www.behobia-sansebastian.com/images/BSS_2019_Dossier.pdf

Fourth Sector Network (2009) The emerging fourth sector. Retrieved from http://www.fourthsector.net/learn/fourth-sector

García-Arrizabalaga I, Gibaja-Martíns JJ, Mujika-Alberdi A (2003) A study on the effect of cause-related marketing on the attitude towards the brand: the case of *Pepsi* in Spain. J Nonprofit Public Sect Mark 11(1):111–135

Kotler P, Armstrong G (2008) Principios de Marketing. 12/e. Pearson Educación

Mujika-Alberdi A, García-Arrizabalaga I, Gibaja-Martíns JJ (2015) Un estudio descriptivo sobre la incidencia de la Behobia-San Sebastián en la adopción y fomento de estilos de vida saludable. Universidad de Deusto, San Sebastián

Mujika-Alberdi A, García-Arrizabalaga I, Gibaja-Martíns JJ (2018) Impact of the Behobia-San Sebastián race on promoting healthy lifestyles. Apunts Educ Fís Deporte 131:34–48

OECD – Organisation for Economic Co-operation and Development (2011) Compendium of OECD well-being indicators. Retrieved from http://www.oecd.org/sdd/47918063.pdf

OECD – Organisation for Economic Co-operation and Development (2020) Measuring well-being and progress: well-being research. Retrieved from http://www.oecd.org/statistics/measuring-well-being-and-progress.htm

Raebel MA, Malone DC, Conner DA, Xu S, Porter JA, Lanty FA (2004) Health services use and health care costs of obese and nonobese individuals. Arch Intern Med 164(19):2135–2140

WHO – World Health Organization (2020) Global strategy on diet, physical activity and health. Retrieved from https://www.who.int/dietphysicalactivity/pa/en/

Chapter 12
An Original Social Marketing Campaign to "Try Vegan": Effectiveness and Impact on Quality of Life

Estela M. Díaz, Nora Lado, and David F. Martín-García

Abstract The present case study focuses on the analysis of the social marketing strategies adopted by Veganuary, a non-profit organization that encourages people worldwide to try vegan diet for January and beyond, through a 31-day pledge. Veganuary is probably one of the most significant vegan campaigns in the world, having enlisted more than 1,400,000 people to date. The main objective of this case will be to analyze the impact of the Veganuary transmedia campaign on their main target publics' well-being. In this study, we are especially interested in examining the cognitive, affective, and behavioral impacts of the campaign on people who took the Veganuary's pledge and the other involved actors. Further than focusing solely on the overall final Quality of Life promoted by the vegan lifestyle, this original form of positive, incremental, and supportive social marketing, seems to build its success on the direct benefits offered in terms of wellbeing: an easy, fun (and reversible) transition towards a self-transcendent lifestyle.

Keywords Quality of life · Social marketing · Veganism · Veganuary · Social media

The original version of this chapter was revised. A correction to this chapter can be found at https://doi.org/10.1007/978-3-030-83286-5_27

E. M. Díaz (✉)
ICADE, Faculty of Economics and Business Administration, Department of Management, Madrid, Spain
e-mail: emdiaz@icade.comillas.edu

N. Lado
University Carlos III, Madrid, Spain
e-mail: nora@eco.uc3m.es

D. F. Martín-García
ICADE, Faculty of Economics and Business Administration, Department of Marketing, Madrid, Spain
e-mail: dfmartin@icade.comillas.edu

M. M. Galan-Ladero, R. G. Rivera (eds.), *Applied Social Marketing and Quality of Life*, Applying Quality of Life Research,
https://doi.org/10.1007/978-3-030-83286-5_12

Introduction

Veganism is a philosophy of life that defy the dominant ontological and ethical anthropocentrism (Dzwonkowska 2018) that attributes moral standing only to humans, and posits that nonhuman animals are mere objects to be owned, consumed, and discarded by humans (McGrath 2000). The Vegan Society (2020) defines veganism as "a way of living which seeks to exclude, as far as is possible and practicable, all forms of exploitation of, and cruelty to, animals for food, clothing or any other purpose." Veganism, then, is not merely a diet but a sociopolitical movement that excludes, for moral reasons, speciesist practices that entails the use of animals (Díaz 2017a, b). As a political form of consumerism, the practice of veganism in the market results in the consumption of all kinds of goods and services that do not involve the exploitation of animals (Díaz 2017b). More importantly, veganism is considered to contribute to overall Quality of Life (QoL, hereafter) (Agarwal et al. 2015; Melina et al. 2016). However, veganism continues being a novelty in most countries and some voices are still skeptical about this claim; the analysis of this case intends to shed a light on this controversy.

Obviously, veganism first contributes to non-human beings QoL, since the production and consumption of animals is responsible for a lot of suffering (and, ultimately, the death) of millions of animals every year. But a vegan economic regime would also have positive consequences on people, communities, and—terrestrial and aquatic—ecosystems. Regarding the ecosystems, the wastes of animal agriculture are concentrated in some areas where they cannot be absorbed by the soil, and then end up contaminating the soil and the water (Foodprint.org, n.d.). Likewise, livestock farms also pollute the air we breathe, generating 75% of total agricultural emissions and 18% of greenhouse gases globally, thus surpassing the transport sector (FAO 2006). Animal products also have a higher average water and energy footprint for calories, protein, fat, and product weight than plant products.[1] The environmental issues necessarily imply human health issues: meat is the food with the highest concentration of chemical substances, and over 65% of new human diseases are estimated to be of animal origin. Veganism has also been shown to be effective both in preventing and treating certain serious diseases, such as ischemic heart disease, hypertension, type 2 diabetes, obesity, and some types of cancer (Melina et al. 2016). Moreover, new research paths are being explored regarding the social and psychological potential benefits of veganism. Traditional eating habits have an important cost in terms of social justice, because of its impact on the distribution of the planet's resources. For instance, more than one third of the cereals produced each year worldwide is intended for the feeding of animals to be consumed by the "developed" world.

[1]For instance, to produce 200 g of flour, 550 l of water are needed, compared to the same quantity of cattle that requires 25,000 l of water (Mekonnen and Hoekstra 2010), an amount equivalent to the water consumed by a person in showers during a year. Likewise, an average of 3.3 calories of fossil fuel is required to produce one calorie of vegetable protein, while that amount rises to 28 calories when it comes to producing one calorie of animal protein (Pimentel and Pimentel 2003).

Yet, the transition to veganism is, for most people, neither straightforward nor easy. We are not dealing with a one-sided and static phenomenon. Veganism multifaceted and in constant evolution, adopted through different processes, affected by numerous factors, and inspired by multiple motivations. Our eating habits are deeply shaped by our value system and rooted in our transgenerational heritage (Nestle 2013). And their frames of references are supported by several incumbent and influential economic players and different power structures (e.g. chemical, pharmaceutical, and livestock industries), that work under the logic of producing more, in less time, and cheaper (Robbins 2012). Yet, most citizen-consumers are trapped in cognitive, emotional, and ethical dilemmas, as the famous "meat paradox" expresses: a dissonance people experience when they are aware that their behavior is not aligned with their beliefs and attitudes (Bastian and Loughnan 2017). Then, this promising but radically disruptive stance of veganism (Díaz 2017b) is necessarily bewildering and implies an uncomfortable lifestyle transition, which tackles the issue of how to bridge the gap between advanced veganism and the open-minded "omnivore" targeted by the Vegan movements' social marketing.

The present case study focuses on the strategy adopted by Veganuary, a non-profit organization that encourages people worldwide to try vegan for January and beyond, through a 31-day pledge. Its campaign is probably one of the most significant vegan world campaigns to date. Our main objective will be to analyze the impact of the Veganuary campaign on their target publics' QoL along their process of enlistment and their consecutive engagement. We approach here QoL as a consumers' well-being (Alves and Vazquez 2013) insisting on subjective rather than objective QoL criteria (Martinez et al 2021; Voukelatou et al 2021). In this study, we propose to examine the cognitive, affective, and behavioral impact of the campaign on people who took the Veganuary's pledge, in order to assess simultaneously the efficiency of the campaign and stakeholders' subjective wellbeing along the experience of trying veganism. Some conceptual tools on how to model and measure the process of value creation and the efficiency in a social marketing context should be a useful preliminary step to such a purpose.

Social Marketing

When dealing with services, ideas, or any intangible value, a new conceptualization of value and wellbeing production has become a reference (Vargo and Lusch 2004, 2008) which insists on the processes of exchange of intangible resources and co-creation between different involved actors. This paradigm has been considered relevant in social marketing and cause-related marketing contexts (Alves and Galan 2019). In such a paradigm, the actors form a network of multilateral exchanges of services, generating value and, hopefully, wellbeing for all (Vargo and Lusch 2008). According to this analytical approach, the first recommended step is to identify, adopting a pragmatic and inclusive approach, the list of relevant actors, or stakeholders, directly or indirectly involved in the exchanges. The actors' roles are dynamic and adaptive to different environments and different marketing fields. In a classic marketing context, the main usual actors are "customers" and "service providers", and, at the same time, they are resource integrators and beneficiaries of the exchange (Vargo and Lusch 2004). In a social marketing context, stakeholders' configurations and roles can be more original and singular that the classical approach (e.g. service providers, donors, volunteers, employees, direct beneficiaries, the society) and enriched by positive sustainability improvements, wellbeing progress, or any other positive externality (Galan-Ladero et al. 2013).

Once the actors are identified, the second step is to introduce the concept of exchange, which it must be redefined for the inclusion of all kinds of exchanges, tangibles and intangibles. The whole service exchanges are composed for all the fluxes of information, benefits, skill developments, rewards, feelings, and resources devoted (e.g., time, resources, effort, compromise). Each stakeholder receives benefits or gratifications, and on the other hand s/he brings or offers something (e.g. time, resources, effort, compromise). For the engagement of all the stakeholders, co-creation is key. When a service is co-creating the mutual benefits are incremented and the consequent better understanding among the actors allows to design better services and to encourage the self-esteem of all the involved parts.

In social marketing, the effectiveness is also crucial. For that reason, before the implementation of any social marketing campaign, the objectives must be clear and so the corresponding evaluation system. For this purpose, the classic model of the three levels of effects of marketing communication campaigns are a good starting point. As Vakratsas and Ambler (1999) expose, there are three levels: (1) cognitive, including knowledge and perceptions; (2) affective, which refers to feelings, emotions, preferences, and intentions; and (3) behavioral, covering actions or reactions that are more observable. These levels are also cited as learn-feel-do dimensions of market response in the persuasive hierarchy model. The Foote, Cone and Belding grid (FCB, hereafter), proposed by Richard Vaughn (Ratchford and Vaughn 1989), is an extension of the hierarchy model to different types of purchase decisions. The grid suggests that the learn-feel-do hierarchy varies depending on whether the buying decision is: (1) high vs. low in involvement; and (2) thinking vs. feeling in information processing. Then, the first axis of the FCB grid focuses on the high versus low- level of involvement in the buying decision process. The level of involvement is driven by the interest or motivational intensity, but it also depends strongly on the degree of perceived risk of loss by the potential client facing the decision to buy a product or service. This risk is broadly conceived and includes all possible kinds of losses or risks (e.g. physical, social, psychological, financial). The second axis takes into account the apprehension or approach to information processing by estimating whether or not the purchase decision involves rather emotional aspects (prioritizing feelings, preferences, or values) or is mostly an intellectual decision (prioritizing information, rational aspects, or functional considerations).

The FCB grid can be successfully applied to social marketing context (Peronard and Flemming 2011; see Table 12.1). The methodological recommendations remain the same: choosing a different set of measures for each of the three levels (cognitive, affective, behavioral) for a deep understanding and monitoring of key success factors. For instance, to monitor the Learn level measures like awareness mentions, perceptions, and associations are relevant; for the Feel level, we propose measures

Table 12.1 FCB Grid

	Think	Feel
High involvement	Informative strategy (Learn-feel-do)	Affective strategy (Feel-learn-do)
Low involvement	Habitual strategy (Do-learn-feel)	Satisfaction strategy (Do-feel-learn)

Source: Peronard and Flemming (2011, p. 693)

about preferences, likes, intention to buy, and positive sentiments; and the Do level can be measured by market share, sharing content, engagement, subscribing, or recommendations.

In this paper, we propose to build possible KPIs for Veganuary's campaign effectiveness as well as the characterization and measure of the wellbeing generated for the targets of this campaign. Specifically, we review and analyze the digital marketing operations of Veganuary (brand contents and actions) and their digital echo on their own interfaces and on external social networks with the engagement of several actors, in particular their targets (user generated contents and initiatives).

Case Study: Veganuary

Veganuary was originally born in the UK as a charity project and months later it became a non-profit organization. The campaign was launched by Matthew Glover and Jane Land in late 2013 with the aim of inspiring people to become vegan, an easy lifestyle to adopt that would help them better their life. As Matthew himself expressed "I had been vegan for 3 years and feel fantastic. It has had a huge impact on my life as it has with all of the Veganuary team and we all want to show people how easy, fun and healthy it can be to be vegan—as well as better for the animals" (Fresh Plaza 2014). According to their website Veganuary's vision is to build a vegan world: "A world without animal farms and slaughterhouses. A world where food production does not decimate forests, pollute rivers and oceans, exacerbate climate change, and drive wild animal populations to extinction". They understand veganism as a philosophy of life rooted in anti-speciesism, a discrimination that they perceived connected with other social and moral problems.[2] However, the main focus of their work is on food; in this sense, their mission is to promote "a vegan diet", "compassionate food choices" or "plant-based diet",[3] as a "way of protecting the environment, preventing animal suffering and improving the health of millions of people." This vision and mission are expressed into four specific aims: (1) increasing participation/inspire and support people to try vegan; (2) drive corporate change/ outreach; (3) raising awareness; and (4) creating/growing the global movement.

[2] We can see this connection in a tweet posted on 22 December 2015 "#Racism #Sexism #Homophobia #Speciesism Make the connection #TryVeganThisJanuary: http://Veganuary.com/register-1"

[3] These three terms are used in their website as interchangeable.

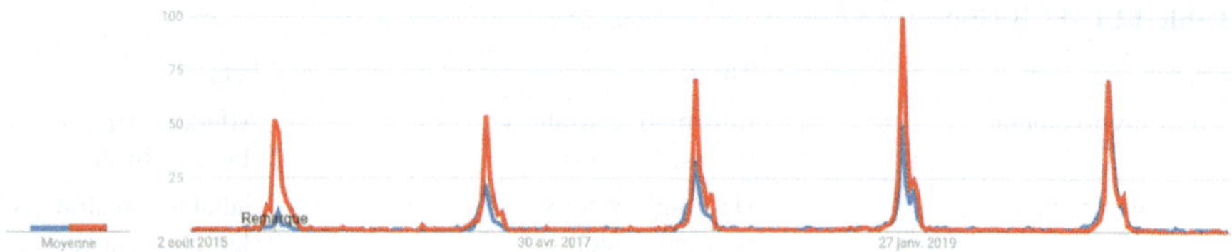

Fig. 12.1 Seasonality of the global interest for "Veganuary" and "Dry January" (Data for all countries, last 5 years). Source: Google Trends (2020)

The (in)direct beneficiaries of their campaigns are, therefore, the animals, the planet, and mankind as a whole; however, the targets of their actions are individuals and companies. The individuals are people who take a pledge of trying to follow a vegan diet for 31 days, affectionately called "veganuarians" by Veganuary's fans and followers. Once people have signed up the pledge, they receive the kit, which consists of daily emails containing recipes and meal plans, together with offers and news, as well as some nutritional information about vegan diet and the impact that diets have on humans, animals, and the environment. Importantly, anyone (independently of their diet or their reasons to engage) can subscribe to the campaign. However, the daily content that the person will receive would differ accordingly to their "current diet" declared when joined the campaign: omnivore or semi-vegetarian; vegetarian or vegan.[4] According to a survey recently conducted by the organization (Veganuary 2020), the main reasons for joining the campaign are mainly three: animals, environment, and health.

In 7 years, since it was launched, Veganuary has gotten to be present in 192 countries around the world and has obtained an exponential growth of participation, with almost 600,000 participants in the last year and more than 1,400,000 people in total. Additionally, more than 600 brands, restaurants, and supermarkets sponsored the campaign, and launched more than 1200 new vegan products and menus in the UK market alone.

Yet, even though the campaign is maintained along the year and the pledge can be taken any time, the moment of most interest in the campaign continues being the end of December and, more significantly, the beginning of January. Thus, the pledge conforms with the temporality of New Year resolutions, like some other post-festive-season radical decisions taken to redeem one's excesses (see Fig. 12.1).In spite of its seasonality, and the risk of cyclical and very temporary interest, we wonder if Veganuary could correlate with a boosted conjunctural or structural interest for more general subjects like "veganism", "plant-based diet", "cruelty free [production]". In this sense, although this correlation it had not been clear in the past, with their 2019/2020 transmedia campaign we observe a significant positive relation in

[4]These categories can be different depending on the country. For example, in Spain the selection is "Omnivore, Semi-Vegetarian, Vegetarian and Vegan", whereas in UK is "Omnivore, Pescatarian, Vegetarian and Vegan."

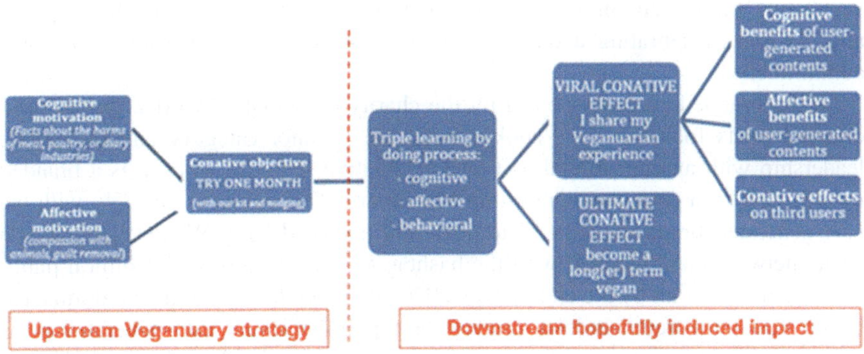

Fig. 12.2 Modelling the process of impact of Veganuary social marketing. Source: Own elaboration

Google trends between "Veganuary" & "Veganism", and "Veganuary" & "Plant-based diet" in UK, a leader country for Veganuary.

Regarding Veganuary's social marketing strategy, the core goal is mainly behavioral: trying the vegan diet for 31 days (and then learn and feel by doing), as well as by sharing and recommending that experience in social media. Yet, they have regular micro-campaigns that focus on cognitive and emotional dimensions to support the process upstream and downstream (see Fig. 12.2). For instance, when they focus on reframing the perception of animals as sentient beings, on enhancing the awareness about harms of meat productions, or on improving the attitudes towards veganism/vegan practices. In traditional media, they launched a TV campaign in UK and USA, that have generated some controversy.[5]

Veganuary Identity Versus User-Generated Content

If we take the example of Instagram, Veganuarys' posts are very alike the brand personality: friendly, educational, positive, encouraging, and very scarcely shocking, which is worth noting in the larger context of the Vegan movement, where harsh denunciations, provocative, and visual reveals of human cruelty with animals have been historically commonplace. You can build a comprehensive typology Veganuary's brand contents by sampling randomly and analyzing the posts in the charity's Instagram account @Weareveganuary. Focusing on the first semester of 2020, we identified the four main categories of posts: (1) Adorable animal begging for a switch of mindset towards them; (2) A "5-reasons" educational series; (3) Images with a slogan promoting the health or environmental benefits of

[5]See these Veganuary's campaigns in YouTube (2019): https://www.youtube.com/watch?time_continue=2&v=4uredLzJa6k&feature=emb_logo

veganism, often echoing a scientific contribution explicated in the caption; and (4) Posts celebrating a famous individual/brand putting forward their vegan commitment.

In the branded contents posted by the charity on social networks, the foodies-oriented posts focusing on a cooked meal are a minor category and they share leadership with an educational text or a celebrative sentence when it is a branded meal issued by a company supporting Veganuary. This contrasts strongly with the user-generated brand contents. The posts not authored by @Weareveganuary on social networks and indexed with the hashtag #veganuary (up to 1.1 billion publications on Instagram by the end of June 2020) are much less text rich and dominated by the foodporn trend. Indeed, among the top-100 relevant user-generated posts indexed with #veganuary on July 1st 2020, we calculated only 3% use solely text, whereas 85% are strictly text-less sensual images of cooked meal; 7% are posts focused on food but with some text or human included; 3% on animals alone; 1% on animal + human; 1% human alone. The captions regularly include some emotions, in general echoing the pleasure or pride of gaining culinary expertise or being successful at following the diet; but mostly, they share some practical tips or the full recipe of the meal.

In other social networks having more affinity with oral or textual narratives (e.g. Blogs and YouTube) the contributions generated by micro-influencers (between 1000 and 100,000 followers) stand out; as newcomer veganuarians, they share their Veganuary month experience[6] or, as more advanced vegans, they encourage to take the pledge. In both cases they reinforce the ethical and affective standpoint of the brand.[7] The next quote, a transcript of some expert of the experience report of Zanna van Dijk (81.7k subscribers) in a YouTube video titled "Veganuary | My Imperfect Vegan Journey" (posted on 3rd January 2019, 13.6k views, 786 likes, 11 dislikes), illustrates the typical soft proselytism, promoting an incremental and self-compassionate progress towards veganism:

> We have to be forgiven for not being perfect, because as soon as you start learning about trying to be more sustainable or trying to be more ethical, you soon realize there's like a thousand ways that you need to change, and some ways that need to be better and you can't do them all at once. And you just have to not just yourself so harshly that's why I'm telling myself like: "Don't be so hard on yourself, Zanna! You're doing your best." So yes, I'm doing my best, and hopefully you guys have found my vegan journey interesting and insightful, and that you appreciate my honesty when it comes to I, and maybe you relate to part of it (. . .). Please try Veganuary, you never know, it might change your life like eating a plant-based diet has changed mine. I feel amazing eating with a purpose which is beyond myself. In the past I used to only eat for my own health, for my own physical, my own aesthetic goals, or how-I-feel goals. But now I eat for the animals, I eat for the planet, I eat for so many reasons that aren't just me. And it feels amazing, and it feels very empowering.

In this narrative, we can also observe the reinforcement of the value of "self-transcendence", especially relevant for millennials (Nikolinakou and Phua 2020),

[6] One example: https://www.youtube.com/watch?v=aNu3qhoipOk

[7] One example: https://www.youtube.com/watch?v=Iv5B2_G3Zzc

referred to broad-mindedness, social justice, fairness, and openness to change, as well as the welfare of one's immediate group (benevolence), and the protection of the environment and animals (universalism). These forms of sharing ethical emotions contribute to a process of co-creation of subjective QoL in the discursive processes of experience sharing online. In fact, a recent spot for television has raised some controversy (Women's Health 2019)[8] for appealing to emotions in a very explicit form.

It is important to note that Veganuary also suffers resistance. Some associations and macro-influencers have not explicitly supported Veganuary from the very beginning, others ignored it, and others expressed distance with the Veganuary "soft" approach of how to promote veganism. Specifically, Veganuary focuses on veganism as a diet and, still worse, as a temporary trial, raises the question of the paradoxical clearing conscience effect. The next quote, posted by a vegan activist in his Facebook page, shows this concern: "Would you consider meaningful trying not to be fascist for 30 days", comparing the process with a typical promotion of "30-day free trial of Netflix" or whatever. However, it is plausible to think that Veganuary could be providing a cognitive, affective, and behavioral coping strategy for some vegan-to-be or even a relief from guilt generated by other organizations and vegans with more confrontational strategies.

Stronger forms of resistance appear when we scrap the social networks using the #veganuary key word. In this case, we found, for example, the alternative branded movement "World Carnivore Month", a platform that exhibits an obvious oppositional loyalty to the Veganuary movement by celebrating carnivore animals under the emblem of a lion. Furthermore, by adopting the typical neo-conservative, reactionary rhetoric, they mimic themselves as a minority resisting the tyranny of promoters of unnatural principles. These forms of reactions, even if it is gaining momentum, proportionally with the buzz of Veganuary have a limited scope. Moreover, these forms of resistances could be, paradoxically, regarded as a qualitative KPI for Veganuary high potential in conquering vegan market shares and, at the same time, in questioning the complex of exceptionality of radicals, as well as the feeling of unquestionable majority of the diehard's carnivores.

Conclusions

In terms of their value proposition, Veganuary offers a new business model (Osterwalder and Pigneur 2010) in promoting veganism based on newness (call to try something exciting and different to what is mainstream), accessibility and convenience (the vegan diet is painted as easy and fun, and supported by a kit and an online community). The efficacy of the campaign is as such a KPI for the progression of overall QoL as far as veganism contributes to animal, planet, and

[8] https://www.youtube.com/watch?v=4uredLzJa6k

human welfare. But in addition to this, it appears that this original form of social marketing in the landscape of the whole Vegan movement, promotes the collective co-creation of wellbeing for a community of newcomers encouraged and nudged by the NGO, some influencers, some (more or less opportunist) commercial brands, and by the online community of veganuarians themselves in their possible journey towards veganism.

For each dimension of the objectives (cognitive, affective, behavioral) we have analyzed some of corresponding key performance indicators. For cognitive: popularity of Veganuary, knowledge about the animal condition and the vegan lifestyle, and other related issues., etc. For affective: emotions provoked, preferences engagement. Finally, for conative: all the actions performed by the different targets of the campaign.

Discussion Questions

1. What is your opinion about the relationship between veganism and Quality of Life?
2. Who are the main actors you can identify in the Veganuary campaign?
3. What are the exchanges fluxes among them in term of benefits and challenges in the Veganuary case?
4. Discuss if it is pertinent to incorporate the learn-feel-do approach to the analysis of this case. Which is the style and strategy (cf. FCB grid) followed in the TV spot campaign?[9]
5. Discuss about the most appropriate measurements for each level.
6. Evaluate the Veganuary effectiveness according to the available data.

Teaching Notes

1. **What is your opinion about the relationship between veganism and quality of life?**

   This question invites to reflect and debate on the following topics:

   (a) *Human actions:* the impacts of students' frames of references and behavior (especially those related to consumption) on themselves, others sentient beings (humans and no humans), and the environment;

   (b) *Veganism as a form of ethical lifestyle:* the concept of veganism and its differentiation/relationship with other forms of ethical consumption (such as vegan diet, plant-based diets, vegetarianism, flexitarianism, freeganism, pescatarianism, reductionism, fair trade or organic consumption).

[9] https://www.youtube.com/watch?v=4uredLzJa6k

(c) *QoL:* the different meanings, aspects, and approaches to quality of life.
(d) *Veganism and QoL:* the influence of veganism (and other forms of ethical consumption) in improving the quality of life of humans and no humans. In this sense, it would be interesting that students investigate and think over the role that animals play in society, as well as reflect on the (des)advantages and implications of adopting a vegan lifestyle. The following table can serve as a guide these activities:

Beneficiaries	Benefits/implications/topics
Humans	• Physical (e.g. reduction of risk of cardiovascular diseases, obesity, cancer, antibiotic resistance) • Psychological (e.g. elimination of cognitive dissonance, reduction of stress) • Economical (e.g. current dependence of the economic system on the use of animals, innovations, degrowth) • Sociological (e.g. distribution of natural resources, reduction of poverty, creation of a more egalitarian society) • Philosophical (e.g. thinking about the meaning of life, the role of the human being on the planet, and our responsibility and connection with other living beings, relations amongst discriminations)
Animals	• Physical (e.g., the five animal freedom, differences between animal wellbeing and animal rights/liberation, preservation of wildlife) • Philosophical (e.g. thinking about the meaning of life, the role of the animals on the planet, speciesism, differences between species, animals' right to live and have a 'good life')
Environment	• Natural resources (e.g. land, water, soil, energy) • Pollution (e.g. fossil fuel usage, CO_2, methane, contaminants, antibiotics) • Waste (e.g. water, soil)

2. **Who are the main actors you can identify in the Veganuary campaign?**
For a deeper knowledge, in addition to the information provide in the case, the students can explore Veganuary web page https://uk.veganuary.com/ for UK, or select the corresponding web page for the different involved countries. The main actors are:

(a) *Service provider:* NGO Veganuary
(b) *Sponsors:* Participating companies, more than 600 companies participated, launching more than 1200 new vegan products and menus in Veganuary 2020 (see website)
(c) *Volunteers and workers*: Veganuary staff
(d) *Direct beneficiaries:* the participants. In particular, the target audience is made up of segments of potential participants who fundamentally accept the challenge motivated by the three main themes (animals, environment, and health).
(e) *Donors*
(f) *Society*: given the positive impact of veganism on humans, animals, and environment.

3. **What are the exchanges fluxes among them in term of benefits and challenges in the Veganuary case?**

As a suggestion of points to be considered:

Actors	Benefits	Challenges
Veganuary volunteers and staff	• Positive effect on self-satisfaction and self-*esteem* for developing actions coherent with them personal values • Share of their style of life values and opinions. Interactions and social integration with other people sharing similar values	• Time and other resources dedication • Mental efforts
Sponsors firms	• Firm image improvements among the interested audience • Product promotion. Customers relationships. New products ideas	• Time and resources dedication • Image engagement with possible no positive perception of some of their consumers
Participants	• Positive effect on self-satisfaction and self-*esteem* for developing actions coherent with them personal values • Share of their style of life values and opinions. Interactions and social integration with other people sharing similar values • According to the survey results, they perceive positive impact on their overall health, energy levels, mood and skin appearance • Learning about veganism • Enrichment in their education about an ethical lifestyle/diet and its consequences • Incorporation of new foods and learn about how to cook new recipes	• Efforts in eliminating the consumption of some liked food • Efforts in terms of changing lifestyle/diet and consumption habits • Efforts in terms of adopting/following the vegan lifestyle/diet and relate with non-vegan friends, family members, and coworkers • Efforts in terms of adopting/following the vegan lifestyle/diet while participating in social event or eating out
Donors	• Positive effect on self-satisfaction for contributing to spread on the society their opinions and values.	• Financial and time contributions.
Society	• Awareness of population about the diet importance on health, animals, and environment • Emergence of innovations and new business models	• Possible negative impact in some industries • Negative reactions from some sectors of the society

4. **Discuss if it is pertinent to incorporate the learn-feel-do approach to the analysis of this case**

The FCB matrix is pertinent as a tool for analyzing the hierarchical structure of the dimensions. This have implications for the communication campaigns.

Applying the FCB matrix to our case and regarding the axis about high or low involvement, in general, we could consider that consumers' decisions about food (and diets) is strongly based on their past experiences. In this sense, we can identify a routine or impulsive buying decisions (low involvement, intellectual apprehension) and, therefore, we could understand that, in this case, the HABITUAL STRATEGY is the adequate. If low involvement and emotional apprehension are considered, the preferences are prominent and the affective response should be the more relevant; then, SATISFACTION STRATEGY would be the appropriate. However, in the Veganuary case, the campaign is based on the stimulation of a HIGH LEVEL OF INVOLVEMENT, driven by the great motivational intensity towards learning veganism and the great interest on information about potential risks associated with choosing some (non-vegan) food options.

With respect of the distinction between thinking vs. feeling, in information processing we can discuss two positions:

(a) If the affective (FEEL) information processing mode is predominant; the AFFECTIVE STRATEGY would be the adequate. In the case of Veganuary, this strategy can be found, for instance, on the information aimed at improving empathy towards animals.
(b) If the intellectual (THINK) information processing mode is predominant; the INFORMATIVE STRATEGY would be the adequate. In the case of Veganuary, this strategy can be found, for instance, on the data and facts about the positive consequences on humans, animals, and environment of adopting/following a vegan lifestyle/diet.

5. **Discuss about the most appropriate measurements for each level.**

The FCB matrix is pertinent as a tool for analyzing the hierarchical structure of the dimensions. This have implications for the communication campaigns. One possible scheme could be:

Dimension	Concepts	KPI's online
Learn (cognitive)	• Awareness • Perceptions • Associations	• Mentions • Online searches • Visits to the Web Page • Topic and content analysis of user generated content or eWOM • ....
Feel (affective)	• Preference • Evaluation • Engagement	• Sentiment analysis in social media comments • Likes • NGO generated content shared (retweets, shares) • ....
Do (behavioral)	• Try or test • Adoption	• Number of participants • Fulfillment of the pledge • Recommendations of the participants • ....

6. **Evaluate the Veganuary effectiveness according to the available data.**

We expect at least some qualitative and quantitative KPIs for each objective, taken from Veganuary's published data and surveys, or from web analytics provided by social networks.

COGNITIVE objectives:

(a) popularity of Veganuary: volumes of mentions and searches online
(b) knowledge about the animal condition and the vegan lifestyle: success of informative posts of Veganuary, or correlated interest for generic 'vegan issues' (ex. how far is "suffering free" being searched in main browsers during the campaign...
(c) content analysis of the veganuarians' post would help identify more qualitative indicators of which type of knowledge they produce and share: typically, about cooking and recipes

AFFECTIVE objectives

(a) success of emotional posts of Veganuary, about animals for instance: number of likes, shares, retweets...
(b) content analysis of the veganuarians' posts help identify more qualitative indicators of which type of emotion are being promoted and shared by the community: proud, the typical pleasures of the alternative hedonist (...)

BEHAVIORAL objectives:

(a) "try vegan one month": number of subscribers.
(b) Promote the experience in one's network: engagement on social network sharing one's month experience as a vegan

References

Agarwal U, Mishra S, Xu J, Levin S, Gonzales J, Barnard ND (2015) A multicenter randomized controlled trial of a nutrition intervention program in a multiethnic adult population in the corporate setting reduces depression and anxiety and improves quality of life: the GEICO study. Am J Health Promot 29(4):245–254

Alves HM, Galan-Ladero MM (2019) Theoretical background: introduction to social marketing. In: Galan-Ladero M, Alves H (eds) Case studies on social marketing. Management for Professionals. Springer, Cham

Alves H, Vázquez JL (eds) (2013) Best practices in marketing and their impact on quality of life. Springer, New York

Bastian B, Loughnan S (2017) Resolving the meat-paradox: a motivational account of morally troublesome behavior and its maintenance. Personal Soc Psychol Rev 21(3):278–299

Díaz EM (2017a) El veganismo como consumo ético y transformador. Un análisis predictivo de la intención de adoptar el veganismo ético. Doctoral dissertation, Universidad Pontificia Comillas

Díaz EM (2017b) The second-curve model: a promising framework for ethical consumption? Veganism as a case study. In: Bala C, Müller K (eds) The vulnerable consumer: the social policy dimension of consumer policy. Consumer Center NRW, Düsseldorf

Dzwonkowska D (2018) Is environmental virtue ethics anthropocentric? J Agric Environ Ethics 31 (6):723–738

FAO (2006) Livestock long shadow. Environment issues and options. Retrieved from www.fao.org/docrep/010/a0701e/a0701e00.HTM

Foodprint.org (n.d.) How industrial agriculture affects our water. Water pollution from industrial agriculture, including CAFOs, causes public health problems and huge environmental impacts. Retrieved from www.foodprint.org/issues/how-industrial-agriculture-affects-our-water/

Fresh Plaza (2014) 3,000 people going vegan for January. UK: New 'Veganuary' charity project. Retrieved from www.freshplaza.com/article/2116995/uk-new-veganuary-charity-project/

Galan-Ladero M, Galera-Casquet C, Valero-Amaro V, Barroso-Mendez MJ (2013) Sustainable, socially responsible business: the cause-related marketing case. A review of the conceptual framework. J Secur Sustain Issues 2:35–46

Google Trends (2020) Retrieved from https://trends.google.co.uk/trends/explore?q=Veganuary, Dry%20january&date=2013-11-15%202021-03-15#TIMESERIES

Martinez J, Mikkelsen CA, Phillips R (eds) (2021) Handbook of quality of life and sustainability. Springer, Switzerland

McGrath E (2000) The politics of veganism. Soc Altern 19(4):50–59

Mekonnen MM, Hoekstra AY (2010) The green, blue and grey water footprint of farm animals and animal products. Hydrol Earth Syst Sci 15(5):1577–1600

Melina V, Craig W, Levin S (2016) Position of the academy of nutrition and dietetics: vegetarian diets. J Acad Nutr Diet 116(12):1970–1980

Nestle M (2013) Food politics: how the food industry influences nutrition and health, vol 3. Univ of California Press, Berkeley, CA

Nikolinakou A, Phua J (2020) Do human values matter for promoting brands on social media? How social media users' values influence valuable brand-related activities such as sharing, content creation, and reviews. J Consum Res 19:13–23

Osterwalder A, Pigneur Y (2010) Business model generation: a handbook for visionaries, game-changers, and challengers, vol 1. John Wiley & Sons, New Jersey

Peronard J-P, Flemming I (2011) User motivation for broadband: a rural Danish study. Telecommun Policy 35(8):691–701

Pimentel D, Pimentel M (2003) Sustainability of meat-based and plant-based diets and the environment. Am J Clin Nutr 78(3):660–663

Ratchford BT, Vaughn R (1989) On the relationship between motives and purchase decisions: some empirical approaches. In: NA - advances in consumer research volume 16, eds. Association for Consumer Research, pp 293–299

Robbins J (2012) Diet for a New America 25th anniversary edition: how your food choices affect your health, your happiness, and the future of life on earth. HJ Kramer, Novato, CA

The Vegan Society (2020). https://www.vegansociety.com

Vakratsas D, Ambler T (1999) How advertising works: what do we really know? J Mark 63:26–43

Vargo SL, Lusch RF (2004) Evolving to a new dominant logic for marketing. J Mark 68(1):1–17

Vargo SL, Lusch RF (2008) From goods to service(s): divergences and convergences of logics. Ind Mark Manag 37(3):254–259

Veganuary (2019) Veganuary TV-Spot: Instinct. Retrieved from www.youtube.com/watch?time_continue=2&v=4uredLzJa6k&feature=emb_logo

Veganuary (2020) Official survey results. Retrieved from www.veganuary.com/wp-content/uploads/2020/03/Survey-results-2020-abridged.pdf

Voukelatou V, Gabrielli L, Miliou I, Cresci S, Sharma R, Tesconi M, Pappalardo L (2021) Measuring objective and subjective well-being: dimensions and data sources. International Journal of Data Science and Analytics 11(4):279–309

Women's Health (2019) New veganuary TV commercial encourages people to go vegan for the month of January. Retrieved from https://www.womenshealthmag.com/food/a30368711/veganuary-challenge-advert/

Chapter 13
The Impact of Sustainable Food Systems on Quality of Life: Innovating Hospital Food for Health, Healing and Well-Being of People and Planet

Marta Rey-Garcia

Abstract The way food is produced, sourced and consumed influences multiple dimensions of quality of life (QOL). Governance of institutional food supply chains (those serving hospitals, campuses or schools) not only impacts material welfare and perceptions of wellness of internal stakeholders, but also interrelates with external organizations, communities, and the environment. Changing their governance through integration of sustainability values—re-localization, justice, environmental integrity and more equitable economic development—allows for more nutritious, safe and just food, that positively impacts QOL of stakeholders through their health, livelihoods and cultural values.

This case deals with Nourish, an innovative social marketing initiative for making food systems sustainable in Canadian health institutions. Nourish aims at developing a national community of practice that empowers leadership across sectors to create a future where food is valued as fundamental for health and healing. Interventions encompass market, psychosocial and policy aspects: (1) *Demand*: empowering a cohort of innovators who make purchase decisions in hospitals; (2) *Supply*: promoting relationships with diverse producers of sustainable, local and traditional food; (3) *Policy*: fostering policy support for food for health; and (4) *Social ideas and behaviors*: fostering a narrative that values the interconnections between food, health, healing and well-being of people and planet.

Keywords Quality of life (QOL) · Social marketing · Food and nutrition for health · Sustainable Development Goals (SDG), secure and just food systems · Governance of institutional food supply chains

---

M. Rey-Garcia (✉)
School of Economics and Business, University of A Coruña, A Coruña, Spain
e-mail: marta.reyg@udc.es

M. M. Galan-Ladero, R. G. Rivera (eds.), *Applied Social Marketing and Quality of Life*, Applying Quality of Life Research,
https://doi.org/10.1007/978-3-030-83286-5_13

Introduction

Quality of life (QOL) concepts provide a unique lens to disentangle the impact of social marketing interventions around systemic problems and complex challenges that are aimed to "enhance customer well-being but also preserving other stakeholders' and society's well-being" (Alves and Vazquez 2013: 4). A QOL approach to social marketing encompasses market, psychosocial, community, and sociopolitical aspects (Tonon 2015).

Food consumption and nutrition have been included not only among basic human needs as part of objective measurements of welfare—starting with United Nations' definition of levels of living (UN 1961)—, but also among the determinants of the different subjective dimensions of QOL, thus influencing individual perceptions of material well-being, health, productivity, security, community or emotional well-being (Cummins 2000).

In order to understand the multilevel influence of food and nutrition on health-related QOL, first the meaning of sustainable food, food security and food justice/sovereignty should be ascertained. Building on the key idea of sustainability as triple bottom line performance (Elkington 2004), Sustain, the U.K. alliance for better food and farming, has defined sustainable food in terms of the following three dimensions (Sustain 2020):

1. Economic impact: sustainable food contributes to thriving local economies and sustainable livelihoods, both domestically and in the countries of origin of imports;
2. Environmental impact: sustainable food protects biodiversity and the welfare of farmed and wild species, avoids damage to or waste of natural resources, and helps fight climate change; and
3. Social impact: sustainable food provides social benefits, such as good-quality, safe and healthy food, and food education opportunities.

Therefore, a sustainable food system entails that both the production and consumption of safe, nutritious food (harvesting, processing, and distributing and intake; including fishing and other wild food harvest) must maintain and enhance the quality of land, air and water for future generations; and provide for adequate livelihoods of people working in it (Food Secure Canada 2020a).

Regarding food security, it exists "when all people, at all times, have physical and economic access to sufficient, safe and nutritious food that meets their dietary needs and food preferences for an active and healthy life" (FAO 1996). As regard to the interrelated concepts of food justice and food sovereignty-, they are defined as "the right of peoples to healthy and culturally appropriate food produced through ecologically sound and sustainable methods, and their right to define their own food and agriculture systems" (La Vía Campesina 2020). According to the grassroots alliance that is leading innovation for a "healthy, just, and ecological" food system in Canada, "food justice requires sustainable livelihoods, … sustainable livelihoods require respect and care for the natural world, and ... all of these demand a democratic voice for the people involved" (Food Secure Canada 2011).

Thus food security and justice not only impact social welfare and individual perceptions of wellness, but also interrelate with communities, institutions and social justice. Food insecurity is intertwined with inequality, physical and mental disease, loneliness, community fragmentation and stigmas associated to situations of need and social exclusion. By contrast, food justice/sovereignty is connected to civic engagement, social innovation, community empowerment and policy engagement focused on the promotion and recovery of sustainable livelihood options through re-localization (local food production and consumption) (Community Food Centres Canada 2019; Food Secure Canada 2011, 2020b).

This case deals with the first phase of development (2015–2019) of an innovative social marketing initiative focusing on achieving healthy, safe and just food in Canadian health care institutions by making their food systems more sustainable (J.W. McConnell Foundation 2020). The mission of this initiative, launched by the J.W. McConnell Foundation under the name of Nourish, consists of creating a future "where food is valued as fundamental for health and healing" (Hsu et al. 2019: 7). Making food systems sustainable, in its turn, calls for changes in their governance, i.e. "the rules and formal and informal processes through which public and private actors articulate their positions and interests for decision-making and implementation" (FAO 2017: 3). Surprisingly enough, while changes in the governance of food systems are typical social innovations, the effects of this type of innovation on QOL and sustainability are rather understudied (Edwards-Schachter et al. 2012).

Development of the Case

The Problem: Changing the Governance of Food Systems in Health Institutions

Over the past several decades, ageing populations, budgetary constraints, and increase in diet-related chronic diseases such as cardiovascular or diabetes have led to reform and restructuring of health care systems, including food services. On the one hand, health institutions are under pressure to become more efficient. On the other hand, hospitals are also compelled to improve service delivery and patient outcomes. Additionally, their food services are subject to compliance with increased legislation regarding food security and traceability around the world, and to the pressure of growing food movements in developed countries such as the US, the UK or Canada (FAO 2017; Murphy 2017).

In this context, the governance of food systems in health institutions has become under the spotlight. The conventional hospital food supply chains that prevail "are deeply rooted in industrial and commercial norms, in other words, price competition, economic efficiency, and forces of standardization through adherence to technical and quality standards" (Klein 2015: 365). By contrast, the emerging values-based supply chains are striving for alternative food systems that integrate conventional supply chain norms of efficiency, standardization, and affordability with sustainability values such as mutually beneficial relationships between supply chain members, environmental stewardship, and social equity (Klein 2015).

Regardless of procurement regime, institutional food systems are highly complex, as they not only impact multiple stakeholders, both internal and external, but also involve multiple decision-makers within institutions in the process of sourcing (Reynolds and Hunter 2017):

- Dietitians create and approve the menus, which food volumes and budgets are forecasted from.
- Procurement staff negotiates contracts with food suppliers (e.g. broadline, regional or specialty distributors or GPO -Group Purchasing Organizations).
- Food and nutrition managers undertake inventory, ordering and budgeting.
- Upper management reports on food service expenses and forecasts budgets available for the coming year.

Available evidence shows a large room for improvement in the actual sustainability of institutional food systems, from both a conceptual and an operational perspective. From a conceptual perspective, most hospitals, long-term care facilities, schools and campuses simply view food as an amenity to be sourced at the lowest cost. In considering that food is not an institutional priority—at least relative to their core health or educational services-, and in undervaluing the impacts of sustainable food on the QOL of relevant stakeholders, these organizations underrate their own potential to strategically leverage their purchasing power in order to become anchor institutions that generate health and wealth in their communities (Reynolds and Hunter 2017).

From an operational perspective, upstream most hospital food is sourced from global, conventional agrifood supply chains that are GPO-governed with a focus on efficiency and standardization. In the U.S. 80–90% of a hospital's foodservice procurement comes through GPO channels (Klein 2015). Figure 13.1 synthesizes the model and the two main types of purchasing pathway prevalent in Canadian health and educational institutions, be they public—compliant with public procurement policies and regulations—, or private—with simpler, unregulated purchasing processes (Reynolds and Hunter 2017):

- *Contracted food service operations*: many institutions contract a food service management company (FSMC) to manage their food services, typically including food purchasing. These contracts tend to be either a "profit and loss" (where the FSMC absorbs any profits/losses) or "management fee" (where the FSMC is paid a fee by the institution, along with a percentage of revenue). FSMC consolidate supply chain volumes from all their clients and negotiate volume discounts with preferred suppliers outside the purview of public procurement policy.
- *Self-operated food services*: public hospitals (public procurement) source most of their food through requests for proposals (RFP) or invitations requiring bidders to

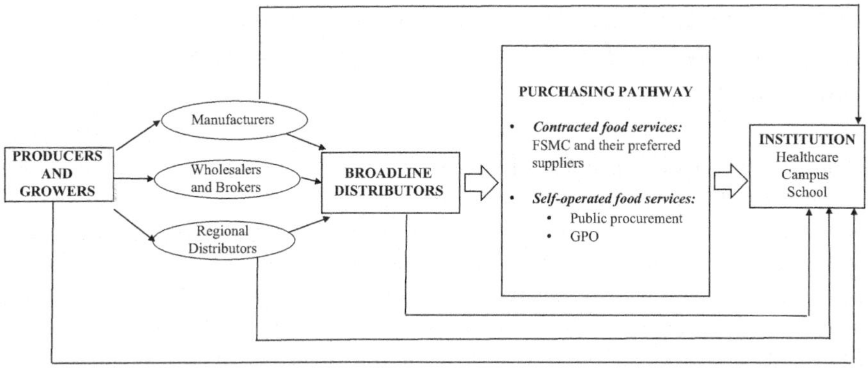

Fig. 13.1 Generic outline of an institutional food supply chain: actors and purchasing pathways. Source: adapted from Reynolds and Hunter (2017: 5) and Klein (2015: 638)

supply a large range of products, ultimately leading to large "bundled" contracts with broadline distributors. Furthermore, many self-operated health care facilities are members of GPOs, which negotiate most of the food contracts for aggregated purchasing volumes of members.

Downstream, low nutritional intakes, wastage and insecurity emerge as the main risks of conventional supply chains (Barton et al. 2000). Preparation and delivery of hospital food mostly relies on processed ingredients and meals. While processed food is used as a means to reduce labor costs, it also lowers control over the presence of antibiotics or genetically modified organisms, or ingredients such as sugar, fat and salt (Food Secure Canada 2020a; Reynolds and Hunter 2017). Regarding waste, estimates for Canada and UK suggest 30–60% of patient food in hospitals is thrown away, resulting in lower than recommended energy and protein intake among patients, financial losses for hospitals, and more waste in landfills (with the accompanying methane emissions) (Murphy 2017; Sonnino and McWilliam 2011). Regarding the risks of food insecurity that are derived from climate change or pandemics like COVID-19, they increase in the absence of the interlinked co-benefits of local food webs. Sustainable public procurement by institutions such as schools and hospitals may play a key role in offsetting those risks by fostering local buying of healthy food (Food Secure Canada 2020b).

At the end of the day, and regardless of purchasing regime, local producers -typically smaller and more specialized than broadline distributors and GPO—face a set of systemic barriers to sell to institutional purchasers. Barriers include undervaluation of the impact of food on QOL, food service models and menus that are reliant on processed ingredients, bundled contracts, limited or non-existent cooking facilities in institutions that prevent cooking from scratch, fixed food budgets, reliance of procurement staff on one-stop shopping, difficulties in identifying the sources of local food, and requirements for sales volumes, discounts and compliance with food safety traceability (Reynolds and Hunter 2017).

The Intervention: The Nourish Program for Making the Impact of Sustainable Food on Health and Healing Understood and Valued

Nourish is an ongoing, pan-Canadian initiative which mission consists of building a future where the impact of food on health is understood and valued. The strategy of Nourish was launched in the fall of 2015 in the background of the portfolio of initiatives led by the J.W. McConnell Family Foundation on "Sustainable Food Systems" during previous years. Early cross-sector partners included relevant actors in the health system and food movement such as HealthCareCAN, Food Secure Canada, Canadian Coalition for Green Health Care, and Health Care Without Harm. In particular, Nourish built upon the lessons learned by the Foundation, Food Secure Canada and other stakeholders in the institutional food system through eight Institutional Food Fund projects (funded by the Foundation with grants totaling $450,000 over 2014–2016) that tried to shift institutional food systems towards greater sustainability (Reynolds and Hunter 2017).

In order to achieve its mission, Nourish aims at removing the first aforementioned barrier against local producers by changing the idea about the impact of hospital food on QOL. More specifically, its goal consists of fostering sustainability values and behaviors among three different targets:

1. Key decision makers in hospitals who participate in institutional food supply chains (dietitians, food procurement staff, etc.).
2. Other relevant stakeholders in health institutions (patients, medical staff, researchers, formal and informal carers, etc.).
3. Key stakeholders in the surrounding communities (food producers and distributors, civil society leaders, media, etc.).

The backbone of the early phase of Nourish' interventions focused on the first target through implementation of the Innovator program (2016–2019). The goal of this program is to support the development of a community of practice among key decision makers in hospital food supply chains. Recruitment began in June 2016 and a national cohort of 26 "Innovators" was selected for their leadership, commitment and vision in elevating the role of food in healthcare and community wellbeing. While their institutions contributed $3000–5000 as a participation fee and the support of a senior leader who sponsored their application to the 2-year program; two full scholarships were provided by Nourish. "Innovators" convened over videoconference for the first time in December 2016 and came together as a community of practice for 2 years, culminating in the "Food for Health Symposium" in May 2019. During that period, "Innovators" worked collaboratively on the challenges and opportunities of leveraging health care institutions to be anchors of QOL, within and beyond their walls, through peer learning, practice and project design. Projects (individual or collaborative) supported by the leadership program included developing new menus that feature more sustainable, nourishing foods that promote healing and comfort; shifting purchasing towards more local sustainable food sourcing; engaging patients, families, and staff in decision-making and food education; developing institutional policies that support a culture of food for health; and addressing social determinants of health (Hsu et al. 2019; Murphy 2017).

If extant literature has highlighted the crucial role of cross-sector resources and systems of relationships in fostering social innovation in social care (Rey-Garcia et al. 2019), this case additionally underlines the relevance of institutional intrapreneurship as a lever for innovating institutional supply chains. However, implementation of sustainable food systems "is not just a matter of broadening and deepening the values and criteria utilized in the food tendering and procurement processes, ... It is also a matter of creating training and feedback mechanisms that mobilize all actors in the food chain and begin to create a shared vision for sustainable development" (Sonnino and McWilliam 2011: 829). This more integrated political approach encompasses the second and third targets of Nourish (other relevant stakeholders in health institutions and in their surrounding communities) and is reflected by the theory of change underlying Nourish design and implementation, as graphically synthesized in Fig. 13.2.

Along the lines of its theory of change, Nourish' interventions encompass three dimensions: market (food production, distribution and consumption), psychosocial (changing social ideas and behaviors relative to the connection between food and health), and policy (inciting policy change that enacts new values and relationships around sustainable food for health). Across those dimensions, four social marketing levers are used to feed a virtuous circle towards more sustainable food value chains in health care (Hsu et al. 2019; Nourish 2020):

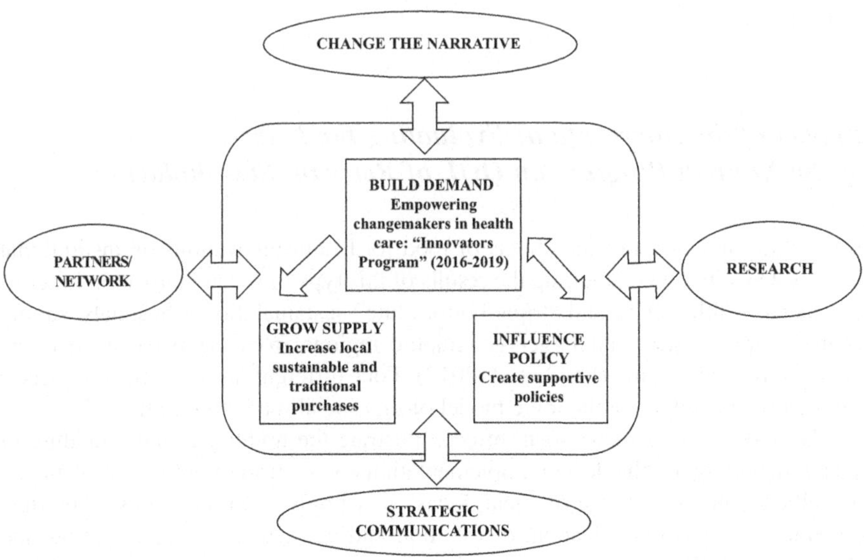

Fig. 13.2 Theory of change of Nourish (2015–2019). Source: adapted from Hsu et al. (2019: 7)

1. *Building demand of sustainable hospital food:* as already mentioned, the focus of Nourish during its first phase has been on the Innovator Program to support the leadership and ideas of decision makers about sustainable food procurement, menus, and programming in healthcare organizations, so that they become empowered as change-makers from within the hospital food system.
2. *Growing supply of sustainable hospital food*: through this changed demand, Nourish expects to increase local, sustainable and traditional food purchases, based on new relationships with a broader array of suppliers.
3. *Influencing policies regarding food for health*: Nourish commissioned Food Secure Canada to conduct a pan-Canadian policy scan and published an inventory of existing health, agriculture and procurement policies that guide food in health care settings in order to identify gaps and opportunities for policy innovation in food for health (Reynolds 2018). The ultimate aim is to create a policy environment that is supportive of food for health.
4. *Changing the narrative*: the first three levers for change are encompassed by overarching change in the dominant narrative towards valuing the interconnections between food, health, society and the planet. This fourth lever is activated through convening, building networks and cross-sector partnerships, composing strategic communications, and conducting research. Examples of interventions include working with articles co-written or written by physicians and dietitians to target high profile stakeholders such as CEOs and doctors; disseminating through networks examples about the value "Innovators'" projects unlocked in their organizations; joint participation with partners in events, conferences, webinars, and presentations; and the collaborative creation of new content, tools, and opportunities to further the development of a national conversation with health care stakeholders around the potential of rethinking food in health care.

Impact of the Intervention: Evaluating the Effects of the Nourish Program on QOL of Relevant Stakeholders

Developing indicators of the effects of food for health innovations on institutional food systems involves capturing the results of this type of social innovation in terms of "social health", QOL and "triple bottom line" sustainability in hospitals, supply chains, communities, and larger geographic regions from the perspective of an "innovation ecosystem" (Land et al. 2012). Four different layers or tiers of effects can be ascertained along the logic model of this social marketing initiative.

The first two tiers of Nourish' effects illustrate the traditional understanding of social marketing as "the design, implementation and control of programs calculated to influence the acceptance of social ideas" that imply "considerations of product planning, price, communication, distribution and marketing research" (Kotler and Zaltman 1971: 5).

The first tier of effects relates to Nourish' outcomes on its intermediate targets, i.e. decision-makers participating in the institutional food chain, and captures the novel focus of social marketing on "ideas" as the product (Galan-Ladero and Alves 2019). Nourish "Innovators" are eager to accept, co-produce and promote new ideas about the relationship between food, health and QOL; and to implement them through their food sourcing, purchase, preparation and delivery decisions, from either the demand or the supply side. Indicators of the impact of the social marketing intervention on the QOL of "Innovators" include their sense of project achievement and overall empowerment, their satisfaction with the new cross-sector partnerships and networks that emerge from the program, and their perceived policy influence.

The second tier of Nourish' effects refers to the implications of the marketing mix decisions "Innovators" adopt under the guidance of sustainability values (Sirgy 1996, 2001), in this case in regard to placement, product and pricing. Their behaviors transform the governance of institutional food supply chains (Reynolds and Hunter 2017):

- In terms of distribution, the main effect consists of leveraging institutional purchasing power to increase sustainable sourcing and production.
- In terms of product, the consequence is to enhance the nutritional, sensory and cultural qualities of food offerings by increasing local, fresh whole and seasonal ingredients and traditional, cooked-from-scratch, and culturally appropriate recipes.
- In terms of pricing, Nourish may cause both synergies and trade-offs. Shifting to cooking from scratch requires adequate facilities for food preparation and storage and well-trained, costly kitchen staff. Increased labor costs maybe offset with the lower food costs from sourcing local, seasonal, whole ingredients. However, in order to take advantage of fluctuating prices and availability of seasonal ingredients, hospitals should plan food supply year-round, and purchase, process and freeze fresh fruits and vegetables when they are in season and available at their lowest prices.

However, from the perspective of recent approaches to social marketing—with an increased emphasis on wellbeing and sustainability as its transformative outcomes (Duane et al. 2016; Lefebvre 2012)—effects to be taken into account transcend "Innovators" and other members of the institutional food supply chain. From a holistic or transformative approach, Nourish encapsulates "the use of marketing techniques and principles to influence a target audience to voluntarily accept, reject, modify or abandon behavior for the benefit of individuals, groups or society as a whole" (Kotler et al. 2002: 5). Thus the third tier of Nourish' effects consists of QOL outcomes on end target beneficiaries (Rey-Garcia et al. 2017), both direct (patients) and indirect (professional and informal carers). In the case of patients (Murphy 2017):

- Sustainable food improves overall patient experience (*food satisfaction*): nutritious, flavorful food positively impacts patient satisfaction and may provide patients with control over their food experience (healthier and fresher food, more choice, dietary preferences such as gluten-free, vegetarian, vegan, etc.).

- Sustainable food contributes to the healing process (*food as medicine*): while healthy, nourishing food reinforces a patient's overall sense of well-being and hopefulness on the way to recovery, malnutrition costs patients their health, inside and outside hospital walls. Moreover, it creates unnecessary costs to the health care system, as malnourished patients stay 2–3 days longer in hospital than nourished patients, and are at higher risk of readmission within 30 days.
- Sustainable food that is familiar and acceptable to the traditions of diverse groups (*culturally sensitive food*) is a sign of respect, conveys a sense of dignity and helps to increase patient satisfaction and reduce waste. The cultural dimension is key in Canada, home of over 600 different indigenous peoples in need for reconciliation with Western institutions.

However, patients are not the only internal stakeholders being impacted by food for health innovations in the institutional food system, as retail food offerings in hospital cafeterias, gift shops, vending machines, and on-site franchises influence QOL outcomes of staff, informal carers (family, friends, neighbors) and other visitors (Murphy 2017).

Finally, the fourth tier of effects to be assessed would consist of impact on surrounding communities, society at large and the environment, in terms of both objective and perceived improvements in overall food governance—secure, just and sustainable food systems-, and attainment of Sustainable Development Goals (SDG). Fresh, in-season food that is sourced in proximity and traced for safety—as opposed to pre-packaged and highly processed food- positively impacts systemic change in the environment and local economies, particularly on the side of small producers such as farmers or fishers.

In order to assess this set of multi-tier effects, a developmental evaluation has been used: an evaluation approach specific for ongoing innovative initiatives under unpredictable environments. This type of evaluation is used not only to assess advances towards systemic, long-term change, but also to generate further "informed change" leading to future phases of an initiative.

Evaluation has resulted in seven key learnings: (1) Food matters to patients; (2) A whole-of-hospital approach is necessary; (3) Experiential learning and peer relationships are powerful; (4) Partnerships and a systemic approach reveal new sources of power; (5) Systemic change requires systems leadership skills, background infrastructure, coordination and financial resources; (6) Making significant change requires focus on specific issues; and (7) Policy innovation is crucial.

Furthermore, five emergent change pathways for the food-health system have been identified as promising venues for further action: (1) Patient and resident food experience; (2) Local and sustainable procurement; (3) Sustainable menus; (4) Traditional and cultural food programs; and (5) Preventative care (Hsu et al. 2019).

Some of the potential levels of effects and key performance indicators (KPI) of the food for health innovations that took place under Nourish' Innovators Program are illustrated in Fig. 13.3.

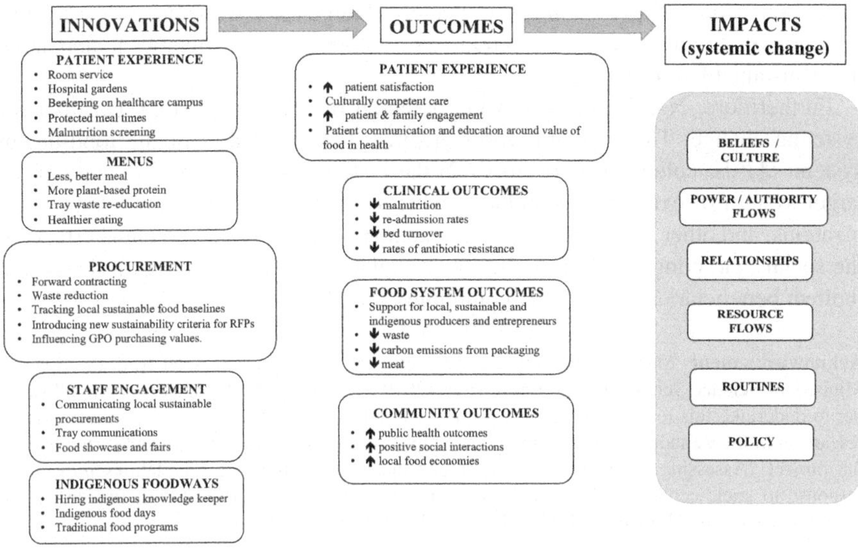

Fig. 13.3 Examples of effects and KPI of Nourish' innovations (2015–2019). Source: Adapted from Hsu et al. (2019: 40–41)

Conclusions

This case illustrates the contrast between the economic, social and environmental outcomes that may originate from different food governance systems. On the one hand, sustainable food systems call for stakeholder and relationship marketing approaches to understand the potential impact on QOL of people and planet (as exemplified by the goals of Nourish and other alternative initiatives around values-based institutional food supply chains); on the other hand, conventional food supply chains prevailing in most institutions respond to a transactional marketing orientation.

The Nourish initiative evidences that changing the governance of hospital food systems towards sustainability is of crucial importance for QOL of relevant stakeholders. The way hospital food is sourced, purchased, prepared, and delivered not only impacts health-related QOL of internal stakeholders (patients, staff and informal carers), but also other dimensions of QOL across local communities, the natural environment and society at large.

While extant literature has highlighted the potential contribution of end users as co-producers of social innovation, the first lever that Nourish activates in order to change ideas and behaviors about food for health in institutional food systems consists of nourishing individual leadership of intrapreneurs who are key decision makers in the supply chain of health institutions. From a marketing perspective, Nourish adopts a push approach to social innovation, rather than a pull one. It is on "Innovators" to push for new food for health ideas and behaviors along the institutional food supply chain and ultimately change the governance of the institutional food system; rather than on end users, customers or beneficiaries to demand a more sustainable hospital food.

Furthermore, Nourish embodies the potential of social marketing as a tool for systemic change. The program works at three different scales of the food-health system: (1) the cohort of innovators, (2) the institutions they work in, and (3) the larger system of external stakeholders, policymakers, healthcare networking organizations, and other influencers. From a systemic perspective, the potential effects of the social marketing program on health are enlarged to include QOL of direct and indirect beneficiaries, the broader community and the planet.

Acknowledgement Marta Rey-Garcia acknowledges the fellowship received from the Spanish Ministry of Science, Innovation and Universities (2019 Salvador de Madariaga Program), allowing her to undertake this research as visiting professor at UQAM, Canada, where she is international researcher of the Canadian Philanthropy Partnership Research Network (PhiLab) and participates in the project "Assessing the collective impact of Canadian grantmaking foundations projects in response to socio-economic issues and environmental challenges" (2018–2024), funded by the Social Sciences and Humanities Research Council of Canada (SSHRC).

Discussion Questions

1. Nourishing and leveraging the leadership of a cohort of "Innovators" is at the core of both the theory of change and the sequence of interventions of the social marketing initiative. Which are the strengths, weaknesses, opportunities and threats of this model of intervention across the market, social and policy dimensions? Explore commonalities and differences in your SWOT analysis for the case of private vs. public health organizations, and for developed vs. developing countries.
2. Large, mostly global food and beverage companies dominate both business-to-consumer and institutional food systems. These dominant actors are neither part of the grass-roots food movement nor members of the main alliances for food security and sustainability in Canada. To which extent can systemic change of food-health systems towards sustainability be achieved without them? Why? Which are the opportunities and risks of their involvement in initiatives such as Nourish?
3. End customers (i.e. patients, hospital staff, visitors) have a very weak standing in institutional food chains. Which internal marketing tools may be used at hospitals to get them more actively involved in the social marketing initiative?
4. Which key mechanisms/stakeholders should be activated in order to scale up the effects of Nourish towards enhanced security and justice of the broader regional or national food system?

Teaching Notes

1. **Nourishing and leveraging the leadership of a cohort of "Innovators" is at the core of both the theory of change and the sequence of interventions of a social marketing initiative that aims at enhancing QOL through changing the way hospital food is produced, sourced and consumed. Which are the strengths, weaknesses, opportunities and threats of this model of intervention across the market, social and policy dimensions? Explore commonalities and differences in your SWOT analysis for the case of private vs. public health organizations, and for developed vs. developing countries.**
The potential pedagogical interest of the Nourish initiative originates from its complex and versatile nature, and also from the fact that it is an ongoing process (this case focuses on its first phase of development, between 2015 and 2019). Thus, students may update its latest developments and results as part of case preparation; or instead search for similar initiatives in their own countries. The case can be useful for any type of marketing coursework where concepts from QOL, well-being, sustainability, ethical or transformative services marketing may be used to guide marketing mix decisions.

From a more traditional social marketing perspective, focus of case teaching could be on how the Innovator Program achieves its impact through its intermediate target, the cohort of innovators. This requires unbundling the effects that "Innovators" may have on the institutional food system, as decision-makers participating who are eager to accept, co-produce and promote new ideas about the relationship between food, health and QOL; and to implement them through their food sourcing, purchase, preparation and delivery decisions. From this point of view, the impact of this social marketing intervention depends on the capacity of these intrapreneurs to collaborate across sectors towards sustainability. These cross-sector partnerships echo SDG 17, Partnerships for the Goals, and encompass:

(a) First, collaboration within the community of practice of the Innovator Program, sharing previous knowledge and new learnings with other leaders in the cohort from either the demand or the supply side.
(b) Secondly, collaboration with other actors within institutional food supply chains, particularly between actors from the demand (other decision makers in the hospital or institution) and offer side (for example local producers).
(c) Thirdly, collaboration leveraging broader networks and relationships with policy makers and social movements (for example the food movement).

In order to assess the strengths, weaknesses, opportunities and threats of this model of intervention at the three different levels of cross sector collaboration, the Collaboration Continuum by James Austin and May Seitanidi (Austin 2000a, b; Austin and Seitanidi 2012a, b) provides a valuable framework. The framework, as synthesized in Austin and Seitanidi (2012a: 736), can be used to assess the development of collaborative relations between innovators and other relevant stakeholders along four different stages, and help identify the limitations and transformative potential of social marketing initiatives for sustainable food systems. The stages are: (1) Philanthropic; (2) Transactional; (3) Integrative; and (4) Transformational. Variables used to characterize the nature of the relationship include:

(a) Level of engagement
(b) Importance to Mission
(c) Magnitude of resources
(d) Type of resources
(e) Scope of activities
(f) Interaction level
(g) Trust
(h) Internal change
(i) Managerial complexity
(j) Strategic value
(k) Co-creation of value
(l) Synergistic value
(m) Innovation
(n) External system change

2. **Large, mostly global food and beverage companies dominate both business-to-consumer and institutional food systems. These dominant actors are neither part of the grass-roots food movement nor members of the main alliances for food security and sustainability in Canada. To which extent can systemic change of food-health systems towards sustainability be achieved without them? Why? Which are the opportunities and risks of their involvement in initiatives such as Nourish?**

The case can be used in the realm of commercial marketing in order to understand institutional food supply chains involving public and/or private (business or nonprofit) organizations that operate in the realms of health, social care or education. This approach can be used to illustrate the contrast between governance structures that take into account QOL, stakeholder and relationship marketing approaches (as exemplified by the goals of the Nourish initiative), and those with a transactional marketing orientation (e.g. the one prevailing in most institutional food systems).

In order to assess the risks and opportunities of partnering with global food and beverage companies, once again the Collaboration Continuum framework can be used. First, students may search for examples of successful and failed collaborative relationships with big corporations around sustainable food. A brainstorming on concrete ways to advance this type of relationship from the philanthropic towards the transformative stage may follow. Students should then assess the risk that these companies instrumentalize the partnerships and use the collaboration with intrapreneurs and social movements for greenwashing, i.e. to minimize reputational risks while at the same time keeping business operations within institutional food chains as usual.

3. **End customers (i.e. patients, hospital staff, visitors) have a very weak standing in institutional food chains. Which internal marketing tools may be used at hospitals to get them more actively involved in the social marketing initiative?**

   The Nourish initiative is about leveraging purchasing power, rather than consumer power, in order to improve QOL of relevant stakeholders through increased sustainability. However, it cannot succeed if patients do not come first in endorsing the idea of food for health and change their food habits, both inside and outside institutions. Students should identify levers that can be used to engage these relevant stakeholders, both market (mainly price and other marketing-mix mechanisms) and non-market (social marketing initiatives targeting patient activism, labor unions, food education, associations of physicians or nurses, social workers, etc.).

4. **Which key mechanisms/stakeholders should be activated in order to scale up the effects of Nourish towards enhanced security and justice of the broader regional or national food system?**

   The case can be used also to oppose traditional approaches to social marketing—with the novel focus on "ideas" as the product (Galan-Ladero and Alves 2019)—vs. more recent ones—with an increased emphasis on wellbeing, sustainability and QOL as its transformative outcomes (Duane et al. 2016; Lefebvre 2012).

   From a holistic or transformative approach, classroom discussion could focus on social marketing for sustainable food systems as a typical social innovation, with expected impacts on society at large and the environment, in terms of both objective and perceived improvements in food governance—secure and sustainable food systems-, and contribution to Sustainable Development Goals (SDG). Under this approach, the challenge consists of scaling up the innovation from the local level where it was born, to the national level. The framework provided by Robin Murray, Julie Caulier-Grice and Geoff Mulgan (2010) is useful to assess the different stages that a social innovation should experience in order to achieve the systemic change that is the ultimate goal of the Nourish initiative: (1) Prompts, inspirations and diagnoses; (2) Proposals and ideas; (3) Prototyping and pilots; (4) Sustaining; (5) Scaling and diffusion; and (6) Systemic Change. Students may use it to identify mechanisms to diffuse the innovation more broadly. The expected learning is that there is no short road for social marketing programs aiming at systemic change, as complexity and unintended and interaction effects (including trade-offs, tensions and paradoxes) should be taken into account.

References

Alves H, Vázquez JL (eds) (2013) Best practices in marketing and their impact on quality of life. Springer, Switzerland

Austin JE (2000a) Strategic alliances between nonprofits and businesses. Nonprofit Volunt Sect Q 29(1):69–97

Austin JE (2000b) The collaboration challenge: how nonprofits and businesses succeed through strategic alliances. Jossey-Bass, San Francisco, CA
Austin JE, Seitanidi MM (2012a) Collaborative value creation: a review of partnering between nonprofits and business: part I value creation spectrum and collaboration stages. Nonprofit Volunt Sect Q 41(5):929–968
Austin JE, Seitanidi MM (2012b) Collaborative value creation: a review of partnering between nonprofits and businesses. Part 2: partnership processes and outcomes. Nonprofit Volunt Sect Q 41(6):726–758
Barton A, Beigg C, Macdonald I, Allison S (2000) High food wastage and low nutritional intakes among hospital patients. Clin Nutr 19(6):445–449
Community Food Centres Canada (2019) Accessed March 19, 2020 from https://cfccanada.ca/en/Home
Cummins RA (2000) Objective and subjective quality of life: an interactive model. Soc Indic Res 52(1):55–72
Duane S, Domegan C, McHugh P, Devaney M (2016) From restricted to complex exchange and beyond: social marketing's change agenda. J Mark Manag 32(9–10):856–876. https://doi.org/10.1080/0267257X.2016.1189449
Edwards-Schachter ME, Matti CE, Alcántara E (2012) Fostering quality of life through social innovation: a living lab methodology study case. Rev Policy Res 29(6):672–692
Elkington J (2004) The triple bottom line: does it all add up. Routledge, London
Food and Agriculture Organization of the United Nations (FAO) (1996) Rome declaration on world food security and world food summit plan of action: world food summit, 13–17 November 1996, Rome, Italy. Accessed March 19, 2020 from https://digitallibrary.un.org/record/195568
Food and Agriculture Organization of the United Nations (FAO) (2017) Governance of food and nutrition security. Factors for viability and sustainability: case studies from seven Latin American countries Santiago Accessed March 19, 2020 from http://www.fao.org/3/a-i7529e.pdf
Food Secure Canada (2011) Resetting the table: a people's food policy for Canada. People's food policy project. Accessed March 19, 2020 from https://foodsecurecanada.org/sites/foodsecurecanada.org/files/FSC-resetting2012-8half11-lowres-EN.pdf
Food Secure Canada (2020a) Official website. Accessed March 19, 2020 from https://foodsecurecanada.org
Food Secure Canada (2020b) Growing resilience and equity: a food policy action plan in the context of Covid-19 (May 2020). Accessed June 30, 2020 from https://foodsecurecanada.org/sites/foodsecurecanada.org/files/fsc_-_growing_resilience_equity_10_june_2020.pdf
Galan-Ladero M, Alves H (2019) Case studies on social marketing. A global perspective. Springer, Switzerland
Hsu C, Hunter B, Lapalme H, Reynolds J (2019) Nourish: the future of food in health care phase 1 developmental evaluation (2016–2019). Accessed March 19, 2020 from https://static1.squarespace.com/static/58829365c534a576e10e3a5c/t/5d7bf27365fd1713e6526cee/1568404085673/Final+Nourish+Developmental+Evaluation+Report_2019Sept13.pdf
J.W. McConnell Foundation (2020) Sustainable food systems initiative. Accessed March 19, 2020 from https://mcconnellfoundation.ca/initiative/sustainable-food-systems/
Klein K (2015) Values-based food procurement in hospitals: the role of health care group purchasing organizations. Agric Hum Values 32:635–648
Kotler P, Zaltman G (1971) Social marketing: an approach to planned social change. J Mark 35 (July):3–12
Kotler P, Roberto N, Lee N (2002) Social marketing: improving the quality of life. Sage, Los Angeles
La Vía Campesina (2020) Official website. Accessed March 19, 2020 from https://viacampesina.org/en/
Land KC, Michalos AC, Sirgy MJ (eds) (2012) Handbook of social indicators and quality-of-life research. Springer, Dordrecht

Lefebvre RC (2012) Transformative social marketing: co-creating the social marketing discipline and brand. J Soc Mark 2(2):118–129

Murphy T (2017) The role of food in hospitals. HealthCareCAN, May 2017. Accessed March 19, 2020 from https://www.healthcarecan.ca/wp-content/themes/camyno/assets/document/Reports/2017/HCC/EN/RoleofFood_FinalEN.pdf

Murray R, Caulier-Grice J, Mulgan G (2010) The open book of social innovation. https://youngfoundation.org/wp-content/uploads/2012/10/The-Open-Book-of-Social-Innovationg.pdf

Nourish: The Future of Food in Health Care (2020) Official website. Accessed March 19, 2020 from https://www.nourishhealthcare.ca

Rey-Garcia M, Liket KC, Alvarez-González LI, Maas K (2017) Back to Basics. Revisiting the relevance of beneficiaries for evaluation and accountability in nonprofits. Nonprofit Manag Leadersh 27(4):493–511. https://doi.org/10.1002/nml.21259

Rey-Garcia M, Felgueiras A, Bauer A, Einarsson T, Cancellieri G (2019) Social innovation for filling the resource-needs gap in social services: new governance arrangements. In: Anheier HK, Krlev G, Mildenberger G (eds) Social innovation: comparative perspectives. Routledge/Taylor & Francis, New York, pp 104–129

Reynolds J (2018) Nourishing the future of food in health care. A Pan-Canadian Policy Scan 2018. Accessed March 19, 2020 from https://mcconnellfoundation.ca/wp-content/uploads/2019/05/Nourishing-the-future-of-health-care.pdf

Reynolds J, Hunter B (2017) PURCHASING POWER: 10 lessons on getting more local, sustainable, and delicious food in schools, hospitals and campuses. Food Secure Canada and the J.W. McConnell Family Foundation, March 2017. Accessed March 19, 2020 from https://foodsecurecanada.org/purchasing-power-report

Sirgy MJ (1996) Strategic marketing planning guided by the quality-of-life (QOL) concept. J Bus Ethics 15(3):241–259. https://doi.org/10.1007/BF00382951

Sirgy MJ (2001) Handbook of quality-of-life research: an ethical marketing perspective. Springer, Switzerland

Sonnino R, McWilliam S (2011) Food waste, catering practices and public procurement: a case study of hospital food systems in Wales. Food Policy 36:823–829

Sustain (2020) What is sustainable food? Accessed March 19, 2020 from https://www.sustainweb.org/sustainablefood/what_is_sustainable_food/

Tonon G (ed) (2015) Qualitative studies in quality of life: methodology and practice. Springer, Switzerland

United Nations (1961) International definition and measurement of levels of living. An interim guide. Accessed March 19, 2020 from https://digitallibrary.un.org/record/479794

Chapter 14
"Pakistan Without Waste": Improving the Quality of Life Through Corporate Social Marketing

Hina Y. Bhatti, M. Mercedes Galan-Ladero, and Clementina Galera-Casquet

Abstract Plastic has become an integral part of daily life, and it is practically used for everything, and in anywhere. However, plastic has also become a global pressing problem, both environmentally (due to the pollution generated by its waste, which affects climate change and takes a long time to decompose, remaining microplastics in the air, soil, and water) and healthily (due to its harmful effects on public health, especially when microplastics are introduced into the food chain). Thus, the objective is to reduce its use worldwide and this falls within the measures for the protection of the environment, which has been included in the Sustainable Development Goals for Agenda 2030 by the United Nations (UN). Social Marketing can be a useful tool to achieve this objective.

This case focuses on the successful "Pakistan without waste" campaign, a corporate social marketing (CSM) initiative which was launched by Coca-Cola Company Pakistan in 2019, with the collaboration of WWF-Pakistan. The two main goals of this CSM campaign were: (1) to create awareness about the problem of plastic pollution in Pakistan; and (2) to promote plastic recycling, to improve the people's quality of life in the country.

Keywords Corporate social marketing (CSM) · Quality of life (QOL) · Plastic pollution · Corporate social responsibility (CSR) · Pakistan

---

H. Y. Bhatti
University of Extremadura, Badajoz, Spain

Riphah International University, Lahore, Pakistan

M. M. Galan-Ladero (✉) · C. Galera-Casquet
University of Extremadura, Badajoz, Spain
e-mail: mgalan@unex.es; cgalera@unex.es

M. M. Galan-Ladero, R. G. Rivera (eds.), *Applied Social Marketing and Quality of Life*, Applying Quality of Life Research,
https://doi.org/10.1007/978-3-030-83286-5_14

Introduction

Corporate Social Responsibility (CSR) has acquired great importance in recent decades and has been adopted by many companies worldwide. One of the main CSR initiatives is Corporate Social Marketing (CSM), which also has significant implications for people's quality of life. Corporate Social Marketing is defined as "*the CSR initiative where a corporation (by itself or in collaboration with any public sector agencies and/or nonprofit organizations) supports the development and/or implementation of a behavior change campaign intended to improve public health, safety, the environment, or community well-being*" (Kotler and Lee 2005: 23). Consequently, its main distinguishing feature is the focus on behavior change. Thus, CSM is one of the first and foremost of the CSR initiatives that work on improving the quality of life (QOL).

CSR in general, and CSM in particular, can be very useful for Pakistan. As it is a developing country, CSM can help to improve the population's QOL and relieve its multiple demographic, economic, social, health, and environmental problems. The latter, the environmental problem, and specifically plastic pollution, will be the key issue to be addressed in this case.

Consequently, this case focuses on the successful "Pakistan without waste" CSM campaign, which was launched by Coca-Cola Company Pakistan in 2019, with the collaboration of WWF-Pakistan (Bhatti et al. 2020). The main goals of this CSM campaign were to create awareness about the problem of plastic pollution in Pakistan, and to promote plastic recycling, to improve the people's quality of life in the country.

The aim of this case study is to describe this successful CSM campaign and analyze its results in a developing country such as Pakistan.

Thus, the chapter will be organized in this way: first, the problem of plastic pollution in general, and in Pakistan in particular, will be explained; secondly, the collaboration between The Coca-Cola Company Pakistan and WWF—Pakistan, and specifically this CSM campaign, will be described; and, finally, the main conclusions of this campaign will be summarized.

Case Development

Societies are facing different environmental challenges worldwide. The climate change problems and the pollution (including caused by plastic waste) have a direct effect on public health and people's quality of life (QOL). For this reason, the protection of the environment has been included in the Sustainable Development Goals (SDGs) for Agenda 2030 by the United Nations. Exactly, SDG 13 focuses on "*taking urgent action to combat climate change and its impacts*", and SDG 14 focuses on "*conserving and sustainably using the oceans, seas and marine resources for sustainable development*" (UN 2020).

Specifically, the plastic pollution has become a serious global problem ("*an environmental catastrophe*"—UN 2020): "*plastic is polluting every corner of the planet, plastic pollution is everywhere*" (Greenpeace 2020). Thus, the United Nations (UN) have included plastic pollution as a priority and leaded the "Beat plastic pollution" global campaign in 2018, to reduce its use worldwide.[1]

But Pakistan joined the fight on this issue late. In 2019, the Government of Pakistan was enforced by profit and nonprofit organizations to take part in this UN social campaign. In this new context, Coca-Cola Company Pakistan, in collaboration with WWF-Pakistan, launched a pioneer campaign in the country, entitled "Pakistan without Waste".

The Problem of the Plastic Pollution: The Situation in Pakistan

Plastic has become an integral part of daily life, and it is practically used for everything, and in anywhere. However, plastic has also become a global problem, both environmentally (due to the pollution generated by its waste, which affects climate change and takes a long time to decompose, remaining microplastics in the air, soil, and water) and healthily (due to its harmful effects on public health, especially when microplastics are introduced into the food chain). The overproduction, overuse, and overconsumption of plastic continues uninterrupted (Greenpeace 2020), so the objective is to reduce its use worldwide.

Plastic is versatile and long-lasting, cheap and disposable (Greenpeace 2020). But plastic is also a non-biodegradable substance that does not get easily disposed-off in the soil or water, and it remains in the environment for hundreds of years, provoking air, water, and soil pollution. Plastic junk (e.g. bottles, bags, FMCG[2] packaging, single-use cutlery, glasses and dishes, etc.) "*is broken down into small particles*" (Parker 2019), "*gradually break into smaller and smaller pieces known as microplastics, which further damage ecosystems*" (Greenpeace 2020), because it is impossible to eliminate from soil, rivers, and oceans. Moreover, the toxic chemicals that are used in the manufacture of plastic, get transferred in the animal tissue and, finally, enter the human food chain, affecting health.

The most important action towards beating plastic pollution is to avoid the plastic products in general, and the single-use plastic packaging and the plastic bags in particular.[3] Unnecessary packaging could be removed, and essential packaging

---

[1] The United Nations are working together with Member States, UN Agencies, civil society groups, and the private sector, to help reduce plastic consumption, raise awareness and support efforts to find global, regional and local solutions (United Nations 2020).

[2] Fast-Moving Consumer Goods (FMCG).

[3] Fast-Moving Consumer Goods (FMCG) are usually packaged in single-use and single-portion plastic (Greenpeace 2020), generating an excessive amount of waste. And plastic bags, introduced in 1970 (Williamson 2003), became the most popular ones among retailers and consumers because of their quality (they were resistant, flexible, and they did not break), their price (they were the

could be made of a reusable and/or refillable eco-friendly material; and cloth bags and paper bags could be used as an alternative to plastic bags, because they are environment-friendly and biodegradable. Governments should enforce and make strict laws about the use of plastic in every shape or size. Thus, the United Nations ran the "Beat plastic pollution" campaign all over the world in 2018.[4]

The plastic industry produces a wide variety of plastics. World plastic production increased from 1.5 million tons in 1950 to 359 million tons in 2018 (Statista 2020)—Fig. 14.1.

That is, the total production of plastics, between 1950 and 2015, amounted to 8300 million tons, of which 6300 million tons corresponded to plastic used only once (World Economic Forum, in Planelles 2019). From this single-use plastic amount, 4977 million tons were abandoned, 567 million tons were recycling, and 756 million tons were incinerated (World Economic Forum, in Planelles 2019). And production is expected to double by 2050 (Parker 2019).

Thereby, the planet is facing serious environmental problems at the beginning of the twenty-first century, and one of the main global problems is the usage of plastic material ("*Up to 12 million tons of plastics are being swept into the oceans annually*"—UN 2020), which are very unsafe for the sea and other wildlife animals (National Geographic 2020). Thousands of these animals are killed by plastics (by entanglement or starvation) every year ("*from birds to fish to other marine organisms*"—Parker 2019).

But the plastic material is also very dangerous for other animals and human beings, because it is eaten by fish and other marine wildlife, "*quickly making their*

Fig. 14.1 Global plastic production, from 1950 to 2018. Source: Statista (2020)

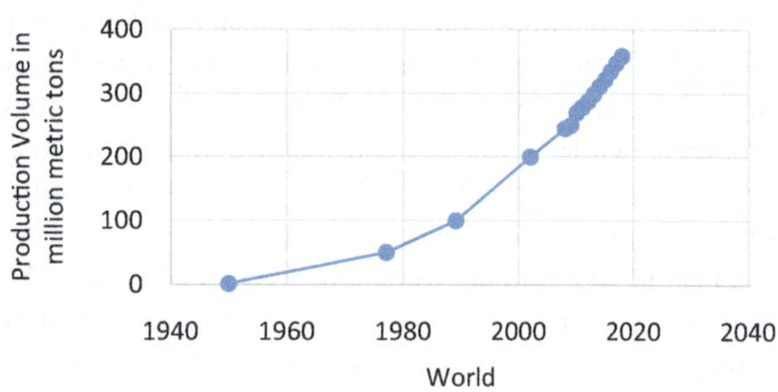

cheapest ones), their easy utilization (they were carried comfortably), and their duration (they could be reused for a long period of time). The problem is that single-use plastic bags were initially non-recyclable, so "*they constitute a massive problem both for land and oceans*" (Coca-Cola Journey 2019).

In 1994, Denmark was one of the first countries that took an active participation in the fight against the plastic bags. Later, other different countries from Africa, Australia, Europe, North America, South America, and Asia were also involved in this campaign, becoming a global movement.

[4]Also NGOs, such as Greenpeace or WWF, have similar campaigns ("Stop plastic pollution"—Greenpeace 2020; "No plastic in Nature"—WWF 2020).

way into the global food chain" (UN 2020).[5] Or, when the plastic is burned in open air, poisonous chemicals are added to the environmental pollution; or also when the plastic is dumped in the land, the hazardous chemicals seep underground, and this directly affects the quality of water. When people inhale this polluted air or drink this water, health problems increase. Thus, this threatening situation for human public health directly impacts on the quality of life. Some global data are summarized in Table 14.1.

On the other hand, and although recycling is a lucrative business (a $200 billion industry—Coca-Cola Journey 2019), in most countries it is still perceived as a governmental issue rather than a personal responsibility (Coca-Cola Journey 2019). Thus, and according to WWF (2020), "*over 70 percent of the households do not segregate their waste, which ultimately leads to lesser chances of it being recycled*". Globally, only 9% of plastic gets recycled (Greenpeace 2020). Consequently, "*91 percent of plastic waste is not recycled, eventually ending up landfill or oceans*" (Bureau of International Recycling, in Coca-Cola Journey 2019), or generating pollution through open burning or incineration (Greenpeace 2020). Even in the most developed countries, with the highest levels of awareness about the need to protect the environment, "*the recycling rate for plastics collected by households is often far less than 50%*" (Greenpeace 2020). Furthermore, "*most recycled packaging waste is down cycled into lower value or non recyclable products, meaning that the process is only delaying the plastic's inevitable journey to the landfill*" (Greenpeace 2020).

In addition, the effectiveness of recycling is limited by (Greenpeace 2020): (1) a poor flawed packaging design; (2) lack of infrastructure; (3) absence of a means to track plastic waste; and (4) lack of regulations (especially in developing countries).

Thus, plastic pollution is more visible in developing Asian and African nations, where garbage collection systems are often inefficient or nonexistent (Parker 2019).

Table 14.1 Some global data about plastic

500,000,000,000 plastic bags used each year
13,000,000 tons of plastic leak into the ocean each year
17,000,000 barrels of oil used for plastic production each year
1,000,000 plastic bottles bought every minute
100,000 marine animals killed by plastic each year
100 years for plastic to degrade in the environment
90% of bottled water found to contain plastic particles
83% of tap water found to contain plastic particles
50% of consumer plastics are single use
10% of all human-generated waste is plastic

Source: UN (2020)

[5]Microplastics have been found in more than 100 aquatic species, and also land-based animals (Parker 2019), many of them destined for human consumption.

Even worse, much of the plastics collected for "recycling" in developed countries are exported to developing countries (in Asia, mainly: China, until 2018; and also Indonesia, Malaysia, and the Philippines—Planelles 2019), "*where the lack of infrastructure and regulations make it difficult to manage the influx of trash from both domestic and foreign sources*" (Greenpeace 2020). Thus, only a very small percentage of this waste is recycled; the rest ends up incinerated, or simply abandoned and polluting the soil, rivers and oceans (Planelles 2019).

However, the Basel Convention, an environmental Treaty that regulates the transboundary movements of hazardous waste and which 187 countries participate in, launched a regulation for plastic in 2019 (which will be applied from 2021), to bring order to the chaotic international trade in plastic waste, one of the most polluting activities in international trade, characterized by the absence of rules (Planelles 2019). The new regulation establishes that (Planelles 2019): (1) waste must be classified and separated in many cases, having to be identified before being exported; (2) hazardous waste must be treated primarily in the country of origin; (3) non-recyclable waste cannot be exported; and (4) a prior permit from the receiving country will be required to be exported. In this way, "*traceability will be ensured and the uncontrolled export of plastic waste will be avoided*" (Planelles 2019).

In the case of Pakistan, the country is facing a lot of climatic and environmental issues (Kanwal 2018; CIA 2020):

- Global warming (weather becomes hotter—increase temperature).
- Increasing pollution: air pollution (Pakistan is one of the countries which suffer from poor air quality—according to EPI (2020)—, especially in fast-growing and overcrowding urban areas with a large number of motorized vehicles, uncontrolled solid waste burning, and a heavy use of polluting sources of energy—World Bank (2020); water pollution (from raw sewage, industrial wastes, and agricultural runoff; the Indus River has been declared as the second most polluted river in the world—Coca-Cola Journey (2019); noise pollution (in urban areas); and land pollution. Plastic pollution is specifically an outstanding issue nowadays (according to the 2020 Environmental Performance Index—EPI—, Pakistan ranks No. 142, out of 180).[6]

[6]The Environmental Performance Index (EPI) provides a data-driven summary of the state of sustainability around the world. Using 32 performance indicators across 11 issue categories, the EPI ranks 180 countries on environmental health and ecosystem vitality. These indicators provide a gauge at a national scale of how close countries are to established environmental policy targets. The EPI offers a scorecard that highlights leaders and laggards in environmental performance and provides practical guidance for countries that aspire to move toward a sustainable future.

High scorers exhibit long-standing policies and programs to protect public health, preserve natural resources, and decrease greenhouse gas emissions. They combate climate change with associated benefits for ecosystems and human health.

According to 2020 EPI, Denmark ranks No. 1, while Liberia ranks the last position (No. 180).

- Additional issues:
  - Related to water: limited natural freshwater resources, shortage of water (because of urbanization, ever-growing population, climate changes, lack of water management and the lack of political will to deal with the issue).
  - Related to soil: deforestation (because of energy crisis, urbanization, industrialization, and domestic use), soil erosion, and desertification.
- Natural disasters.

After India, Pakistan has the second-largest domestic market of plastics in South Asia. It grows at an annual average rate of 15% (Coca-Cola Journey 2019). But this increasing use of plastic has a negative side: its carbon footprint and its negative effect on ecosystems (Coca-Cola Journey 2019). Pakistan generates 250 million tons of garbage (WWF Pak 2020), which include plastic bags, food scraps, and PET bottles in a higher percentage than other countries of similar socio-economic development and income level (Coca-Cola Journey 2019). In addition, Pakistan has the highest percentage of mismanaged plastic in South Asia (CIA 2020).

However, this country also faces important economic and social problems (Table 14.2), such as (1) the constant and quick increase of population, with the consequent fast urbanization, and an increasing consumption; (2) a lack of education; and (3) poverty, affecting a significant part of the population.

Anyway, Pakistan has important strategic endowments and development potential (World Bank 2020). Pakistan has made significant progress, growing economically and regaining macroeconomic stability over the last years (World Bank 2020), and some progress in both security and energy (but there are still a challenging security environment and electricity shortages/power deficiencies)—CIA (2020), so the quality of life and the standard of living still needed to increase (Kanwal 2018).

Table 14.2 Main problems in Pakistan

Problem	Statistics (in 2020)
A "booming" population	• 233 million people • Population growth rate = 2% • More than 55% of the population: under 25 years • Urbanization rate = 2.53% • 2/3 of the population is settled in rural areas
A lack of education	Total literacy rate = 59% • 71.1% males • 46.5% females Very low in rural areas
Poverty	• Rate of the population below poverty line = 29.5% • Part of the population does not have access to: – Potable water – Electricity (52 million people without electricity in 2017; and only 64% of rural areas have electrification. Thus, there is a growing dependence on wood and other renewable energy resources)

Sources: World Population Review (2020), CIA (2020), and Statista (2020)

All these characteristics also have a significant impact on the environment. The garbage from rural communities is one of the big challenges for Pakistan: many people in rural areas are uneducated and they throw or burn garbage in the street. This behavior has, as consequence, that sewers system, waterways or rivers are blocked, and the hazardous gases of the garbage are added to the air.

According to WWF (2020), 65% of plastic garbage reached the beaches. And according to the Pakistan Environmental Protection Agency—PEPA (2020), 55 billion tons of plastic were being used annually, and plastic pollution rose 15% every year (Coca-Cola Pakistan 2020). Moreover, there were no laws or rules about plastic pollution in Pakistan.

Thus, although Pakistan did not take part in the "Beat plastic pollution" UN global campaign initially, the Government of Pakistan was enforced by profit and nonprofit organizations to participate in it in 2019. Therefore, since 14th August 2019, Pakistan has fully banned the single-use plastic bags. The plastic ban has been implemented in Pakistan capital city, Islamabad, and in Lahore and Karachi.

In this context, social marketing is one of the best ways to educate people and try to change their behavior about plastic pollution to improve their health and quality of life.

The CSM Campaign of Coca-Cola Company and WWF-Pakistan: "Pakistan Without Waste"

Some Pakistani companies are working on Corporate Social Marketing (CSM) campaigns. Basically, these CSM campaigns emphasize on issues such as health, injury prevention, environmental, and community. For instance, most of the companies in Pakistan that are collaborating and working together on improving the quality of life focus on environmental projects.

Specifically, this research focuses on analyzing the case of Coca-Cola Company Pakistan that, in collaboration with WWF-Pakistan, decided to launch a pioneer CSM campaign in the country in 2019. The chosen title was "Pakistan without waste". The aims of this program were two: on the one hand, to create awareness about the problem of the plastic pollution in Pakistan; and, on the other hand, to promote the plastic recycling to improve the people's quality of life in this country.

Coca-Cola Company Pakistan

The Coca-Cola Company is one of the best known and most valuable companies worldwide. This beverage company offers more than 500 brands and 4700 varieties, and in more than 200 countries (Coca-Cola Company 2020).

CSR plays a fundamental role in Coca Cola's strategy. Its current global CSR programs focus on these areas (Coca-Cola Company 2020): improving water access,

Table 14.3 The Rs in Coca-Cola Company Pakistan

Reduce	The material amount and energy used in manufacturing of packaging material and using recycled materials, as much as food safety principles and technology allow
Reuse and Recycle	Working together with various stakeholders to establish an environmentally friendly and economically sustainable infrastructure for post-consumer packaging recovery and recycling
Renewable	Exploring and testing alternative, renewable materials such as PlantBottle

Source: CCI (2020)

sanitation and hygiene, and supporting local communities (community development); empowering women, and offering equal opportunities, diversity and inclusion (human rights); creating socio-economic opportunities around the world (economic development); and contributing to the well-being of people (consumer well-being).

But Coca-Cola also works to reduce its environmental impact (its environmental footprint), and it also plays an active role in providing solutions for climate change—best practices to combat it, are part of the company's business sustainability strategy (Coca-Cola Journey 2019), and it is especially concerned about the global crisis of plastic waste management. As priorities, Coca-Cola focuses on minimizing the environmental impact by using fewer natural resources and generating less waste (CCI 2020). Thus, for example, the company shares with its bottling partners the "Climate Protection" strategy, which has the commitment of finding innovative ways to mitigate the environmental effects of their operations and products (e.g. using 100% recyclable packaging, putting into practice plastic recovery pilot studies from different NGOs, implementing awareness campaigns, etc.—Coca-Cola Journey 2019).

In this regard, the company launched its product packaging policy "World Without Waste" on January 19, 2018. The goal of this program was "*to collect and recycle a bottle or can for each one it sells in the market by 2030*" (Coca-Cola Journey 2019). This holistic plan, as part of the circular economy, also focused on the entire packaging lifecycle—from how bottles and cans are designed and made, to how they are recycled and repurposed (Coca-Cola Journey 2019). Thus, sustainable packaging and waste ensure sustainability during the production processes, and offer high quality beverages in a sustainable manner. That is, packaging innovation and resource minimization, recyclability, use of recycled and renewable materials (Table 14.3).

Nowadays, Coca-Cola's sustainable packaging vision includes (Coca-Cola Pakistan 2020): every bottle or can it sells by 2030, investing to make packaging 100% recyclable globally by 2025, and making bottles with at least 50% recycled content by 2030. Currently, the majority of the company's packaging is already recyclable (Coca-Cola Pakistan 2020).

Coca-Cola was introduced in Pakistan in 1953, in the city of Karachi. Later, several other plants were provided in different cities (UK Essay 2018). Its current products' portfolio is integrated by different brands (CCI 2020): Coca-Cola, Fanta,

Sprite, Coca-Cola Zero, Sprite Lemon Mint, Sprite Zero, Dasani, Rani Pulpy, Mutant, Cappy Joosi, and Monster. Local production offers employment opportunities for the local population (more than 3000 employees across Pakistan—Coca-Cola Pakistan 2020), and it is adapted to the style and taste of Pakistan. CCI Pakistan produces, distributes and sells beverages of The Coca-Cola Company in Pakistan.

Since the beginning of the twenty-first century, Coca-Cola Company Pakistan has been involved in different sustainable objectives. Some of them are related to several of the current Sustainable Development Goals (SDGs) established by the United Nations in the Agenda 2030.

Coca-Cola Pakistan is partnering with different organizations (e.g. nonprofit organizations such as WWF-Pakistan, the public sector, and other businesses such as malls) to sensitize citizens in general, and consumers in particular, about the benefits of recycling (Coca-Cola Journey 2019). An example is the initiative "Plastic Hut" (Recycling is Rewarding!, #PakistanWithoutWaste).

World Wildlife Fund (WWF) For Nature: Pakistan

World Wide Fund (WWF) is an environmental NGO, founded in 1961, in Gland (Switzerland). Nowadays, this NGO is globally spread in more than 100 countries (WWF 2020). The WWF mission is "*to conserve nature and reduce the most pressing threats to the diversity of life on Earth*", and its vision is "*to build a future in which people live in harmony with nature*" (Help. World Wildlife 2020). WWF organization is focusing on six main goals (Fig. 14.2).

WWF was established in Pakistan in 1970 because of the developing harmony environmental issues (WWF 2020). The total number of WWF offices in Pakistan in 2020 was 29 along with six regional offices. The main office is in Lahore (WWF 2020). Nowadays WWF Pakistan is one of the largest conservation organizations in Pakistan, working proactively against climate change and environmental degradation in the country (WWF 2020).

WWF Goal	Descriptions
Food	Drive sustainable food systems to conserve nature and feed humanity
Climate	Create a climate-resilient and zero-carbon world, powered by renewable energy
Freshwater	Secure water for people and nature
Wildlife	Ensure the world's most iconic species are secured and recovering in the wild
Forests	Conserve the world's most important forests to sustain nature's diversity, benefit the climate, and support human well-being
Oceans	A resilient ocean sustains marine life and functioning ecosystems that support rich biodiversity, food security and sustainable livelihoods

Fig. 14.2 WWF's six main Goals. Source: World Wildlife (2020)

Thus, it is concerned about the pollution issues in general, and plastic pollution in particular. The most significant problems are to eliminate the non-biodegradable materials, such as plastic. Therefore, this NGO acknowledges the need to create awareness among citizens; and the plastic recovery facility is just one of many manifestations. Its aim is to initiate more campaigns to promote cleaner Pakistan (Coca-Cola Journey 2019), in collaboration with different organizations (e.g. Governmental sector, private and civil societies, etc.).

At the end of 2019 (from 12th October to 12th November), WWF-Pakistan decided to collaborate with Coca-Cola Company Pakistan and started the social marketing campaign, entitled "Pakistan without waste" (WWF 2020), with the mission of cleaning Pakistan (e.g. "Recycling is rewarding!" initiative in Lahore).

"Pakistan Without Waste": A Corporate Social Marketing Campaign

For the first time, Coca-Cola Company Pakistan and WWF-Pakistan have formally collaborated in a project of these characteristics ("*Tackling Plastic Pollution in Pakistan*" project).

WWF-Pakistan was chosen by Coca-Cola Company Pakistan for this alliance because this NGO had conducted a previous campaign about the consumption, collection and disposal pattern of PET, and to quantify the amount of PET that was being recycled and also give knowledge regarding plastic pollution.

Thus, within its campaign "Pakistan without Waste", Coca-Cola Company Pakistan, in collaboration with WWF-Pakistan, developed the "Plastic Hut" initiative in Lahore. Both organizations partnered to install a plastic bottles collection hut across three malls in that Pakistani city, from October 12 to November 12, 2019 (Coca-Cola Journey 2019)—Figs. 14.3 and 14.4.

The aims of this activity were (Coca-Cola Journey 2019): (1) to spread awareness on the issue about plastic waste management in Pakistan, and (2) to engage the general public towards responsible collection and recycling of empty plastic PET bottles to tackle the issue of plastic waste pollution more effectively through public engagement and support.

Dates	Malls
October 12* – October 21, 2019	Packages Mall
October 23 – November 1, 2019	Fortress Square Mall
November 3 – November 12**, 2019	Emporium Mall

* Launch ceremony at Packages Mall Lahore

** Closing ceremony at Packages Mall Lahore, attended by senior officials from both entities.

Fig. 14.3 Dates for the "Plastic Hut" activity in the three malls in Lahore. Source: Coca-Cola Journey (2019)

Fig. 14.4 Coca-Cola & WWF Pakistan Launched Their First "Plastic Hunt" in Lahore, Pakistan. Source: Image Rights Reserved With The Coca Cola Export Corporation, Pakistan Branch

This public engagement activity was very successful. Some of the main results were (Coca-Cola Journey 2019):

- The audience was engaged in the "Pakistan without waste" campaign, and thousands of local residents were educated on the importance of plastic waste segregation and recycling.
- 1477 local residents were rewarded with special gifts and prizes through lucky draws for participating in the activity.
- 3932 bottles, which weighed 106 kg., were collected and recycled.

As a consequence of this, at the beginning of 2020, the Government of Pakistan fully banned single-use plastic bags and provided alternative cotton bags.

Conclusions

Plastic is the symbol of the throwaway culture (Greenpeace 2020). Plastic pollution is such a serious problem that it has to be considered in a global/worldwide context. Thus, solutions to beat plastic pollutions are:

- In the short term: making less plastic; reducing and eliminating plastic products in general, and avoiding especially unnecessary plastic packaging and single-use plastic (bags, cutlery, dishes, and glasses), offering alternatives such as "*reusable and refillable systems for transporting and storing goods, reusing sustainable materials instead of throwaway plastics*" (Greenpeace 2020); improving product design, when plastic is essential; and recycling plastic waste, and improving waste management systems.
- In the long term: changing consumption habits (Greenpeace 2020), into a more sustainable behavior.

Thus, two key elements are (UN 2020): (1) Global awareness and advocacy; and (2) Strong policies and leadership.

In Pakistan, plastic pollution is an increasing problem, especially in rural areas, because of a combination of different demographic and socio-economics characteristics (a fast population growth, with a quick urbanization and an increasing needs and consumption; a low literacy rate; and a significant level of poverty). In this context, social marketing can be one of the best ways to educate people and try to change their behavior to improve their health and quality of life.

However, Pakistan is starting to be concerned about plastic pollution, and the first legal measure has been to ban the single-use plastic bags.

The main purpose of Coca-Cola's "Pakistan without Waste" campaign was to build cohesion amongst the informal sector (composed by scavengers, junk dealers, and recyclers) and the formal sector, to identify the gaps in the enhancement of the collection and recycling efficiency. This campaign created awareness on the issue of plastic pollution amongst communities and educational organizations, and encouraged the plastic recycling to improve the quality of life in Pakistan.

"Plastic Hut", as part of the Coca-Cola's "Pakistan without Waste" CRM campaign, has been the first initiative of its kind in the beverage sector in Pakistan, to promote recovery and recycling of plastic bottles of beverages, while also getting a chance for participants to win prizes through lucky draws daily.

Because of its success, it is supposed that this type of initiatives will continue in the future, with more similar campaigns in more different cities, to promote cleaner Pakistan.

Discussion Questions

1. What do you think about the "Pakistan without Waste" campaign? Discuss its main strengths and weaknesses.
2. Has a similar campaign been carried out in your country? Why?
3. What differences are there when applying a corporate social marketing campaign in a developed country or in a developing country?
4. How else could this social marketing campaign have been carried out in Pakistan?
5. What other CSR campaigns or initiatives could be carried out in Pakistan to achieve the proposed objectives (raise awareness about the problem of plastic pollution and promote plastic recycling)?

Teaching Notes

1. **What do you think about the "Pakistan without Waste" campaign? Discuss its main strengths and weaknesses.**

This question is to invite students to think and give their opinions about the campaign, analyzing the possible strengths and weaknesses that they detect in it.

This campaign is already having positive outcomes, and it is sure it will help to improve the state of the environment in the country.

The main issue that Pakistan is currently facing, is the problem in the drainage system because of the litter. It needs to be disposed of and recycled properly.

However, some other issues are still intact. The major issue is the lack of awareness among the people of Pakistan. Many uneducated people usually dispose of their litter on the roads or wherever they see the heap of trash.

2. **Has a similar campaign been carried out in your country? Why?**

   This question is students to find out whether, or not, there have been similar campaigns to this one in their own countries, and explain why.

   (a) In case there have been similar campaigns, they could compare them and understand the methods used to solve this issue.
   (b) In case there have not been campaigns of this type, they could explain why they think these campaigns have not been developed, and analyze if they could be carried out in the future.

3. **What differences are there when applying a corporate social marketing campaign in a developed country or in a developing country?**

   The idea behind this question is students can compare this campaign in Pakistan with those carried out in other countries (developed or developing ones), analyzing whether there are similarities or differences in the results obtained.

   The corporate social marketing campaign could be more or less similar (especially if it is promoted by a multinational company, which could have a global program for all the countries where it operates), but probably the answer could be different depending on the country.

   The level of development of a country in general, and the economic and educational level of its population in particular, could influence whether the desired behavior is adopted or, on the contrary, not enough attention is paid to it.

4. **How else could this social marketing campaign have been carried out in Pakistan?**

   In Pakistan, this type of campaigns should be developed in eye-catching sites. Gaming sites or educational sites could be used for targeting young people (students, in particular). Online shopping sites could be another option to access the target audience.

   (If the students are from other countries, it would be advisable to give them prior information about the socio-economic characteristics and lifestyles in Pakistan, in order to propose alternative campaigns more adjusted to the Pakistani population).

5. **What other CSR campaigns or initiatives could be carried out in Pakistan to achieve the proposed objectives (raise awareness about the problem of plastic pollution and promote plastic recycling)?**

Campaigns should be focused on awareness about problems that are being faced by plastic pollution. First, people should be alerted about the current situation of excessive plastic pollution in the country. Secondly, people should be forced by law to use biodegradable bags. Thirdly, CSR initiatives should be focused on changing people's behavior. Fourthly, Green Development programs would be helpful to remove the plastic pollution in Pakistan.

In addition to Corporate Social Marketing, Cause-Related Marketing, Cause Promotion, traditional Corporate Philanthropy, Volunteering in the Community, or Responsible Socially Business Practices related to this topic could be useful initiatives for this. Multinational enterprises, such as Coca-Cola or Pepsi, could lead this cause ("fight against plastic pollution") in Pakistan, because of their international experiences in CSR initiatives worldwide and, specifically, in this issue (plastic pollution).

References

Bhatti HY, Galan-Ladero MM, Galera-Casquet C (2020) The role of corporate social marketing in improving the quality of life of the society: a case study of Coca-Cola Company Pakistan. II IAPNM LATAM Congress on Social Marketing. 9–10 September. Montevideo

CCI (2020) Official website. Retrieved from https://www.cci.com.tr/en/our-company/our-geography/pakistan. Accessed 10 Mar 2020

CIA – Central Intelligence Agency (2020) Pakistan. The World Factbook. Retrieved from https://www.cia.gov/library/publications/the-world-factbook/. Accessed 15 Aug 2020

Coca-Cola Journey (2019) Official website. Retrieved from https://www.coca-colajourney.com.pk. Accessed 10 Mar 2020

Coca-Cola Company (2020) Official website. Retrieved from https://www.coca-colacompany.com/. Accessed 10 Mar 2020

Coca-Cola Pakistan (2020) #PAKISTANWITHOUTWASTE. Coca-Cola and WWF-Pakistan's first ever Plastic Recovery Hut successfully concludes in Lahore. Retrieved from https://www.coca-cola.pk/news/events/coca-cola-and-wwf-pakistans-first-ever-plastic-recovery-initiati. Accessed 15 Aug 2020

Data World Bank (2020) Official website. Retrieved from https://data.worldbank.org/country/pakistan?view=chart. Accessed 26 Mar 2020

EPI – Environmental Performance Index (2020) 2020 global metrics for the environment: ranking country performance on sustainability issues. Retrieved from https://epi.yale.edu/. Accessed 15 Aug 2020

Greenpeace (2020) Official website. Retrieved from https://www.greenpeace.org. Accessed 15 Aug 2020

Helpwildlife (2020) Official website. Retrieved from https://help.worldwildlife.org/hc/en-us/articles/360007905494-WWF-s-Mission-Vision. Accessed 10 Mar 2020

Kanwal S (2018) The environmental issues in Pakistan. The Frontier Post, October 3. Retrieved from https://thefrontierpost.com/the-environmental-issues-in-pakistan/. Accessed 15 Aug 2020

Kotler P, Lee N (2005) Best of breed: when it comes to gaining a market edge while supporting a social cause, "corporate social marketing" leads the pack. Soc Mark Q 11(3–4):91–103

National Geographic (2020) Official website. Retrieved from https://www.nationalgeographic.com/environment/habitats/plastic-pollution/. Accessed 10 Mar 2020

Pakistan Environmental Protection Agency—PEPA (2020) Official website. Retrieved from http://www.environment.gov.pk/. Accessed 10 Mar 2020

Parker L (2019) The World's plastic pollution crisis explained. Retrieved from https://www.nationalgeographic.com. Accessed 15 Aug 2020

Planelles M (2019) Cerco al tráfico internacional de residuos plásticos que contaminant los océanos. El País, 20 May. Retrieved from https://elpais.com/sociedad/2019/05/19/actualidad/1558266684_100410.html. Accessed 15 Aug 2020

Statista (2020) Global plastic production from 1950 to 2018 (in million metric tons). Retrieved from https://www.statista.com/statistics/282732/global-production-of-plastics-since-1950/. Accessed 10 Mar 2020

UK Essays (2018) Coca Cola Company operations Pakistan marketing essay. Retrieved from https://www.ukessays.com/essays/marketing/coca-cola-company-operations-pakistan-marketing-essay.php. Accessed 10 Mar 2020

UN – United Nations (2020) Official website. Retrieved from https://www.un.org. Accessed 15 Aug 2020

Williamson L (2003) It's not my bag, baby! On Earth 25(2):32–34

World Population Review (2020) Pakistan. Retrieved from https://worldpopulationreview.com/countries/pakistan-population. Accessed 10 Mar 2020

World Wildlife (2020) How to help. Retrieved from https://www.worldwildlife.org/how-to-help. Accessed 10 Mar 2020

WWF (2020) Official website. Retrieved from https://www.worldwildlife.org. Accessed 15 Aug 2020

WWF Pakistan (2020) Official website. Retrieved from https://www.wwfpak.org/issues/plastic_waste_/. Accessed 15 Aug 2020

Chapter 15
La Hormiga Verde as a Case of Social Marketing to Improve the Quality of Life Through Recycling Waste Electrical and Electronic Equipment (WEEE)

M. Victoria Carrillo-Duran, Maria Garcia-Garcia, and Juan Luis Tato-Jimenez

Abstract La Hormiga Verde is a private company focused on applying social marketing to address an environmental problem—the processing of Waste Electrical and Electronic Equipment (WEEE). As the main objective of its activity, the company has the goal of explaining to young people that consumer electronic products can be transformed in the context of a circular economy. The reuse of WEEE can have a significant effect on the environment, and therefore on substantially improving people's quality of life. This case is significant because the company has put social marketing as the basis of its business model, and this is supported by an action—holding a contest to recycle e-waste. Through collaboration with all types of organizations, mainly educational institutions, the contest is the main entry point for the raw materials and the company's fundamental communicative action. As a result, La Hormiga Verde is a sustainable company that contributes to quality of life since it encourages the recycling of WEEE. In conclusion, this initiative brings with it a global dimension to Extremadura (Spain) in relation to improving the effects of WEEE recycling on a rural region's quality of life.

Keywords Social marketing · Circular economy · Quality of life (QOL) · Waste Electrical and Electronic Equipment (WEEE) · La Hormiga Verde

---

M. V. Carrillo-Duran (✉) · M. Garcia-Garcia · J. L. Tato-Jimenez
University of Extremadura, Badajoz, Spain
e-mail: vicduran@unex.es; mgargar@unex.es; jltato@unex.es

M. M. Galan-Ladero, R. G. Rivera (eds.), *Applied Social Marketing and Quality of Life*, Applying Quality of Life Research,
https://doi.org/10.1007/978-3-030-83286-5_15

Fig. 15.1 Linear economy. Source: Adapted from Ecoembes (2020)

Introduction

We currently live in a society with a model of production centred on a linear economy (Fig. 15.1) in which it is believed that there is a permanent supply of resources that can be used unlimitedly.

The desire to leave this type of model of production behind and move on to a circular economy is led by companies such as La Hormiga Verde.[1] According to Ecoembes (2020): "The circular economy is a model that prioritizes the careful use of resources and the reduction of raw materials. Thus this system becomes an alternative to the current model of extraction, production, consumption, and disposal, the linear economic model" (Fig. 15.2).

Since 2015 the European Commission has been interested in re-orienting the linear economy towards a circular economy, applying different measures on which the Commission estimates that it is necessary to continue acting in the years to come (MITECO 2020). At the moment, the measures taken are aimed at improving people's quality of life, and in this sense are related, on the one hand, to the different stages of the life cycle of the product—design and production, consumption, waste management, and use of resources contained in the waste through its re-introduction into the economy—and on the other, to the five areas that are considered priority to improve people's quality of life (MITECO 2020): (1) plastics, (2) food waste, (3) critical raw materials, (4) construction and demolition, and (5) biomass and products with a biological base.

Within this reference frame, it is essential to pay attention to what is defined as Waste Electrical and Electronic Equipment (WEEE), a concept that encompasses all types of electrical and electronic waste that are stored away without thinking about their utility for recycling, reuse. or repair. WEEE can be classified into different categories (Table 15.1).

The volume of WEEE has increased dramatically in Spain, reaching around 967 million tons in 2020, and exceeding 930 million tons in 2016 (Statista 2020) which represented an increase of more than 20 million tons compared to 2014 (Fig. 15.3).

However, in Spain, the WEEE management market is still just incipient, with this activity having begun around the year 2000. Currently, only around 20% of electronic waste is properly dealt with in the whole of the country (El Comercio 2020).

[1] La Hormiga Verde is the name of the company. In English, it would be "The Green Ant".

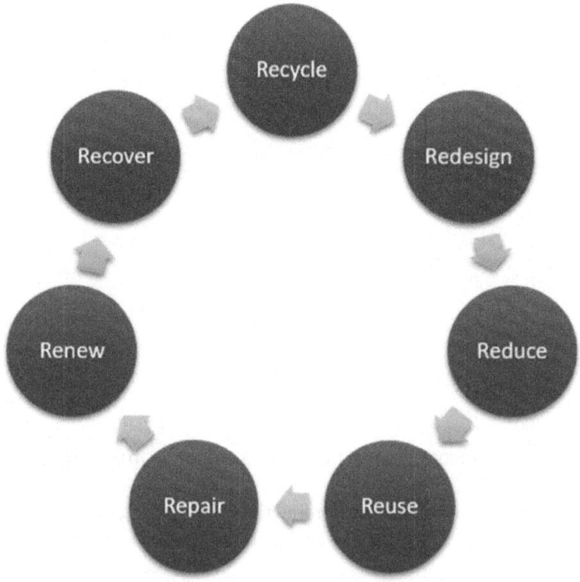

Fig. 15.2 Circular economy. Source: Adapted from Ecoembes (2020)

Table 15.1 Types of waste electrical and electronic equipment

Telecommunications equipment	Mobile phones, cordless phones, routers, modems, landlines, switchboards, telephone cable, ethernet cable, chargers,...
Computer equipment	Desktop computers, laptops, tablets, printers, computer cables, computer cards, USB cables, keyboards, mice
Small appliances	DVDs, stereos, video players, MP3 players, mixers, coffee makers, irons, toasters, vacuum cleaners, electric toys, video game consoles, cables of all kinds,...

Source: The authors, adapted from "La Hormiga Verde" (2020)

Problems of WEEE for the Quality of Life

This issue is not only a concern for Europe. It is a global concern which is reflected in decisions such as the 2030 Agenda on Sustainable Development, approved in 2015 by the UN. This document includes 17 Sustainable Development Objectives,[2] in which Objective 12 indicates that: "Currently, the consumption of natural resource materials is increasing, particularly in East Asia. Also, the countries continue to address challenges related to air, water, and soil pollution. The objective of sustainable consumption and production is to do more and better things with fewer resources. It is about creating net gain from economic activities while reducing the

[2] Available at: https://www.un.org/sustainabledevelopment/

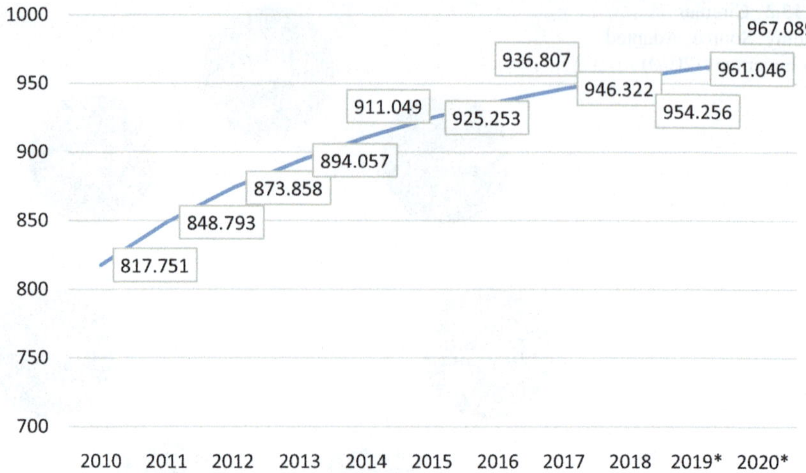

Fig. 15.3 Evolution of the production of waste electrical and electronic equipment in Spain from 2010 to 2020 (in metric tons). Source: The authors, adapted from Statista (2020)

use of resources, degradation, and pollution, at the same time as achieving a better quality of life" (United Nations 2020).

In line with the objective described, La Hormiga Verde works for sustainable consumption and production to promote the efficient use of resources through their reuse. It also wants to improve access to basic services, among which are the possibility of recycling from wherever one lives, no matter how isolated, and the creation of jobs with fair wages and good working conditions since it is a Special Employment Centre[3] for people with a disability.[4] All of this translates into a better quality of life in the work environment, helping to achieve general development plans that reduce economic, environmental, and social costs, and increase competitiveness.

The management team of La Hormiga Verde (2020) notes some difficulties in achieving this objective—difficulties which constitute an important brake:

[3]According to the Ministry of Employment and Social Economy of the Government of Spain, Special Employment Centres are companies whose main objective is to provide people with disabilities with inclusive work and wages appropriate to their personal characteristics, and that facilitate their integration into the ordinary job market.

[4]In this chapter, the United Nations definition of disability has been adopted (United Nations 2006, preamble) as well as the Americans with Disabilities Act concept of an individual with a disability (US Department of Justice 2009). According to Rivera, R.G., Arrese, A., Sádaba, C., & Casado, L. (2020: 37–38): "From those perspectives, diversity is an indicator of the level of variety in a myriad of people's observable and invisible dimensions, and inclusion refers to focused strategies and practices that facilitate meaningful interactions among persons". In this line, the term used in this study is people with disabilities instead of disabled people, and the term "inclusive work" when referring to people working in Special Employment Centres.

(a) Poor waste management: The lack of proper waste management leads to an increase in toxic elements found in scrap, such as lead, arsenic, cadmium, mercury, or phosphorus, among many other materials that are not biodegradable and that if not treated properly can end up in the land or water, with serious consequences for people's quality of life.
(b) The accumulation of WEEE in landfills: The presence of Recycling Disposal Points to dispose of the devices that are no longer wanted (which can be 70–90% recycled) would stop them having to be left in landfills.
(c) The illegal treatment of this waste: The application of cheap and illegal solutions for the treatment of waste is an environmental problem that causes great non-evaluable damage.
(d) Most developed countries do not have clear legislation in this regard: This legal vacuum can lead to damaging outcomes in the management of waste and problems in evaluating the future consequences of this waste on people's quality of life.

The Case of "La Hormiga Verde"

La Hormiga Verde began to function as a private organization in 2018 in Villafranca de los Barros, a town with 14,000 inhabitants located in the province of Badajoz (Spain) (Fig. 15.4). It has focused its recent activity at the regional level, in Extremadura, with the intention of managing a small part of the electronic waste market in this region. It tries to reach the closest homes and businesses, and has established as future short-term goals the possibility of additional growth into the border region of Andalusia (Spain) and Portugal (bordering country).

This company operates in a region with wide growth margins in terms of WEEE recycling. In 2017[5] in Extremadura, only 41% of the electrical and electronic equipment put on the market by producers over the previous 3 years was collected. Table 15.2 presents the evolution of the recycling of discarded electronic devices and components in the region.

The evolution of domestic WEEE recycling in Extremadura shows a decreasing trend, only partially corrected in 2016 when 259 tons of equipment were collected. In 2017, only 116 tons of the 54,599 tons recycled throughout Spain were collected in Extremadura, which represents 0.21% of the WEEE collected in the country (INE 2019). Therefore, the reality is that, despite the efforts that have been made, the region is clearly at the tail of recycling in Spain. In this sense, initiatives are needed to channel the European and state indications about the collection and recycling of WEEE.

Currently, there are two companies in Extremadura dedicated to the recycling of electronic waste. La Hormiga Verde, in addition to being an authorized manager and

[5] Latest data available.

Fig. 15.4 Location of La Hormiga Verde in Villafranca de los Barros (Spain). Source: La Hormiga Verde (2020)

Table 15.2 Tons of electronic equipment and components discarded in Extremadura

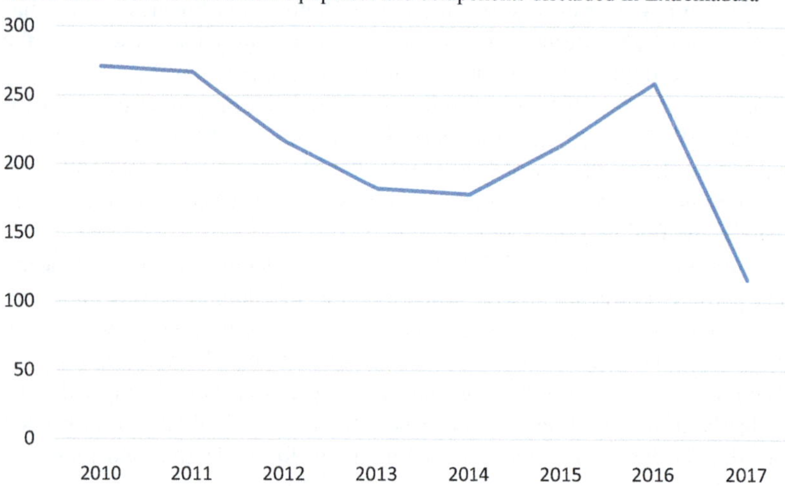

Source: The authors, adapted from INE (2020)

transporter of WEEE in Extremadura (Ref AAU 18/2332), has two differentiating values over the other company: it only employs people with disabilities, and it collects at the point of origin of the waste regardless of where it is located in Extremadura.

The Business Model

La Hormiga Verde follows a business model based on two fundamental pillars: the first is the circular economy, taking advantage of more than 90% of the waste to obtain new raw materials, and the second pillar is its social approach since it employs 11 people of whom 90% have disabilities. Therefore, it can be said that La Hormiga Verde is a special employment centre that is dedicated to the correct management of electronic waste (Waste Electrical and Electronic Equipment—WEEE), from collection to evaluation (weighing, classification, and calculation of its value for its new incorporation as raw material). According to the company itself, its objectives as an organization are the following:

1. Create a business model based on the management of electronic waste, that is expandable and replicable to border areas (in a first phase of development).
2. Generate benefits for social purposes, such as recycling plastic caps or collaborating with non-profit organizations.
3. Create stable employment for people with disabilities.
4. Offer solutions to better manage waste.
5. Help build a better future for the planet and for people's quality of life.

Regarding the services it offers, it helps individuals and institutions by collecting electronic waste from homes and businesses. It has its own means that allow it to organize and plan the collection of materials by optimizing travel routes and contributing to transport that is more sustainable.

The electronic waste collection is carried out through a network of "micro greenspots", i.e., micro recycling disposal points, in associated centres and establishments, in which the waste is collected from both the most central and the most remote towns of all of Extremadura. The objective of this service is that anyone can take their electronic waste to a spot near their home, even if they live in a remote area, and the company is committed to going to collect it, thus contributing to improving the quality of life of the people who wish to collaborate without this being a great inconvenience to them.

In addition, it offers a free warehouse cleaning service in which it helps to sort, to recuperate forgotten objects, and to recycle what is not useful, at no cost for the warehouse owner.

The income of this special employment centre comes from the sale of the different by-products extracted from the electronic waste, metals, electronic material, plastics, components, etc. These materials are supplied to end managers, who reintroduce

Table 15.3 SWOT analysis of La Hormiga Verde

Weaknesses	**Threats**
Few resources invested Scarcity of resources/size Little control over the results Limited experience Little promotion	Low awareness of the environment Lack of knowledge of the benefits of recycling
Strengths	**Opportunities**
Proper natural positioning Agreements with public entities Special Employment Centre	Little competition Increased social awareness Market growth Legislation favouring recycling

Source: The authors

them into the market. Operating expenses (personnel, equipment, supplies, financing, etc.) must be subtracted from these revenues.

This management model based on WEEE recycling is scalable, gradually increasing the processes with the increase in the number of products that are incorporated into the circular economy, in the collection spots, and in the number of new products and solutions that respect the environment.

The company's growth strategy is currently based on the reinvestment of profits in more services and improvements, and on its commitment to being an instrument for creating the maximum employment of which it is capable. Cooperation is believed to be a value with which to be able to achieve this goal, and La Hormiga Verde is very proactive.

Given its such recent creation, the company is in its initial phase and looking at future business projects with a view to growth and consolidation. As an outline of its situation, one can identify weaknesses and threats in this business, but, above all, great strengths and opportunities that the company seems willing to take advantage of (Table 15.3).

Among the weaknesses and threats are the scarcity of resources and size, and little investment and relative lack of control. These need definitive solutions for it to further develop its activity and offer an efficient service over what is a wide, disperse, and poorly communicated territory, as well as resources to strengthen the efforts to make the population aware of the need to recycle and the significance of the electronic waste that we all have at home.

The company's strengths and opportunities are summarized in its enjoying a model that, in addition to solving a social problem (generating profits to help people with disabilities), solves another environmental problem (helping to reintegrate waste into the production chain in the form of raw materials), always seeking for the common good and improving the quality of life.

La Hormiga Verde as a Case of Social Marketing

Given the recent creation of the company and the initial phase it is in, it has no budget assigned to dissemination actions or control systems since the procedure is eminently manual. Despite lacking a social marketing strategy as such, the key elements on which its main actions focus are the following:

1. ***The strategic objective***

   To raise awareness of the need to dispose of electronic waste correctly, indicating that it is necessary to find a sustainable solution so that it does not end up in landfills.
2. ***Principles of strategic action***

   To achieve this objective, the tool used above all is education through awareness campaigns so as to increase recycling, and consequently the quality of life. The means to do this do not involve a significant use of resources, but, at the same time, have a significant scope and impact. For this reason, the communication channels used are inexpensive, and the campaigns are creative and eminently educational.

   The educational content generates trust and loyalty among the public in addition to strengthening the company's prestige, helping expand its vision and values to increasingly lucrative markets.

   On the one hand, the guidance and instruction that the company offers its clients is a communication tool that serves to position them as market benchmarks and leaders in the sector. On the other hand, the effort to provide information to schools for the modification of everyday attitudes when it comes to disposing of waste involves strategies aimed at literacy, that is, the social actors involved need to know what types of electronic waste can be recycled. With this, the intention is to transform or create new behaviour in the social groups involved, who through that knowledge will be able to adapt their activity to achieve a more sustainable environment.
3. ***The target public***

   In the communication action plan, the objective is to reach as many people as possible. However, it can be said that the main public are young people between the ages of 12 and 18 years who are studying Secondary Education and living in Extremadura, which is where the company is located and is the territorial scope it covers. The proposal of La Hormiga Verde is to direct its communication actions mainly to younger people to turn them into active supporters of electronic recycling.
4. ***Planned communication channels***

   The media that the company uses to contact its target public are eminently digital. Currently the company has a strategy to disseminate its online activity which is focused on two websites (www.lahormigaverde.org and http://www.concursolahormigaverde.org/), and a corporate page on Facebook (La Hormiga Verde Centro Especial de Empleo).

The use of the websites as the main showcase of its cause allows it to have total control over the message that the company broadcasts, and in addition they are an instrument that gives the company credibility and reliability.

The idea of designing two differentiated websites in which to explain, on the one hand, the company and its identity and, on the other, a website that channels all the efforts related to its main marketing action, which is to hold a contest in schools, reflects the importance of this school contest for the company. Although the two websites are identical tools, they have different purposes.

On the corporate website, several aspects stand out very clearly: the fact that it contributes to the circular economy, the social economy, and all the certifications the company has to carry out its activity. These are the three axes on which its communication is based since they are the values that differentiate the company from its competition and makes it unique in the environment in which it is placed.

The contest website, which will be discussed below, focuses on disseminating the rules, prizes, and participation.

The Facebook corporate profile disseminates the work of the company, and regularly updates the information related to the contest. Tags such as the Spanish language versions of #CircularEconomy, #SocialEconomy, #Sustainability, and #Recycling are common. In this way it is possible to promote interaction, build a brand, and meet the potential public. The dissemination plan for its foreseen activities began to be implemented in September 2019. The action program is based on consolidating the content published on Facebook with frequent updating that reflects the company's offline activity.

La Hormiga Verde Contest

Highlighted among the main actions of La Hormiga Verde is the contest it organizes each school year for recycling e-waste, mainly in secondary schools that want to participate voluntarily.

The business objective of the contest is to encourage the collection of waste stored away in people's houses, as pupils take the waste in their homes to their school and deposit it in the micro greenspots placed for that purpose.

The educational objective of the contest is for the pupils to gain awareness of everything related to WEEE recycling as an example of a circular economy. In addition, the problem of sustainability is addressed to convey the importance of transitioning towards a model of production oriented to preventing waste generation, and in which the materials can be reused to avoid the depletion of what are finite natural resources. In this way, the pupils discover such aspects as:

- What things constitute WEEE.
- Where should this waste be deposited.
- How is its proper recycling carried out.

- Potential negative impact on the environment, on people's health, and, consequently, on the quality of life.
- The job opportunities that this represents.

The action mainly is conducted in secondary schools (with pupils of from 12 to 18 years in age). The number of schools participating was limited to 50 throughout Extremadura, in strict order of inscription. The focus of the hoped-for results of the action was on the development of ecological and social awareness within households, while expanding the market and increasing the number of types of waste collected. Finally, it was to develop knowledge about the circular economy and all of its benefits for society and the quality of life.

The Contest's Mechanics

The schools register through the website www.concursolahormigaverde.org, where the list of schools selected and the bases of the contest are also published.

The schools, for their part, must authorize the installation of a "micro greenspot" and a container for small and large batteries. A simple document is formalized which indicates that the recycling containers will remain in the school for a long time, and that the company promises to collect the material. As a complement, an informative talk is offered to explain some basic points:

1. What is electronic material, how is it made, and why is it recycled?
2. Objectives and operations of the contest.
3. Prizes.
4. Calendar and rules.

The contest lasts for a school year, and its progress is reported through the contest's website.

This medium provides information about the amount of WEEE collected in total in the form of the weight in kilograms (kg) and the points obtained. The quantification system is based on the fact that the company has assigned each type of device a value of points/kg, so that, for each type of device, the weight in kg is multiplied by that value to give the points per device. Then the points are summed for all the devices recycled. Also, the pupils in the school are counted to calculate the ratio of points per participating pupil, and thus not discriminate against schools with few pupils.

The bases of the contest are published on the website, with the table of points/kg for each type of WEEE collected, and the prizes to be distributed. At the end of the school year, and after the results of the contest have been determined, a simple awards ceremony is held. These prizes are quite attractive for both the schools and the pupils. They consist of robotics kits and 3D printers, which add visibility to the contest and reward the efforts of the top three classified schools.

Results

The results of the activity of this company can be grouped into different categories according to their nature.

Results in Terms of Quality of Life

Regarding the services offered and how they are offered, La Hormiga Verde contributes beneficially to sustainability by collaborating with different institutions (primary schools, secondary schools, town halls) in training and disseminating information about recycling with talks and visits.

It also helps with the employability of persons with disabilities, and aims at improving the existing knowledge concerning their inclusion and integration. The company can be defined as being socially responsible because of its creating stable employment for people with disabilities. La Hormiga Verde has added to the effects of its activity by obtaining a "Quantified Certificate of Corporate Social Responsibility" according to which it calculates the effects of the contributions of electronic waste from institutional suppliers in such aspects as CO_2 emissions, electrical energy saved, and work hours generated.

Table 15.4 lists the environmental savings generated by La Hormiga Verde (in line with its being a circular economy project) and job creation (in line with its being a social economy project).

Its contribution to improving people's quality of life and the sustainability of the planet is unquestionable since its work focuses exclusively on this activity.

Table 15.4 Environmental savings of La Hormiga Verde in 2019

CO_2 emissions	17,443 kg
Energy	812,290 kWh
Petroleum	357,611 l
Work hours generated	10,970 h
Material recovered	
Iron	7959 kg
Aluminium	381 kg
Copper	4893 kg
Plastics	17,077 kg
Electronic circuit boards	5508 kg

Source: The authors, adapted from the 2019 La Hormiga Verde annual report

Table 15.5 The types of waste electrical and electronic equipment (WEEE) collected by the secondary schools in the 2018–2019 school year

Material	kg	%
1—Old cables	2041	3.80
2—Desktop PCs (w/o monitor)	15,328	28.50
3—Aluminium	51	0.09
4—Mobiles, Tablets	203	0.38
5—Laptops	386	0.72
6—Switchboards	1129	2.10
7—Video	965	1.80
8—PC accessories	2393	4.50
9—Audio	671	1.20
10—Plastic plugs	911	1.70
11—Printers, Scanners	5649	10.50
12—Small household appliances	1158	2.20
13—Printer and toner cartridges	523	1.00
14—Kitchen appliances	2470	4.60
15—Cork stoppers (w/o bottles)	413	0.80
16—Monitors	19,461	36.20
Total	53,752	

Source: The authors, adapted from the 2019 La Hormiga Verde annual report

Results in Terms of Awareness

Its main source of fostering awareness lies in the contests it organizes, and their results are very satisfactory as a social marketing action. The data that justify the results relating to 2019 (Table 15.5) show that this action reached the following milestones:

The contest in secondary education schools.

- Coordinated with the Board of Education of the Junta de Extremadura.[6]
- Participants: 45 schools in the 2018–2019 school year, which have increased to 92 in the 2019–2020 school year.
- Amount of WEEE collected: 53,752 kg, the initial objective of the contest having been 25,000 kg.

As can be seen, the recycling of desktop computers and monitors stands out especially, followed by printers and scanners among other electronic computing and household devices.

[6]The Junta de Extremadura is the name given to the governing body of the region of Extremadura in Spain.

Table 15.6 WEEE inputs

Origin	Household and professional. The company's own network of Micro Green Points (MGPs), i.e., micro recycling disposal points. The demand for small, disperse points is attended to
Collection points	At schools, town halls, etc.
Providers of the waste	Recycling Disposal Points: practically nil Distributor: nil Managers: nil Individuals: dispersed, through the program's own MGP network installed in school, public, and similar buildings Producers of waste electrical and electronic equipment (WEEE): businesses, and public and private institutions
The total weight of WEEE managed by La Hormiga Verde in 2019 was 219.3 tons	

Source: The authors, adapted from the 2020 La Hormiga Verde annual report

Table 15.7 Output of waste managed

Description	Tons
Components	30.7
Electronic equipment	
Aluminium, copper, brass, stainless steel	14.6
Lead	
Cathode-ray monitors and televisions	48.6
Mix of batteries	2.2
Printer and toner cartridges	2.1
Rigid plastics from WEEE	6.2
Iron scrap	50.2
Silicon solar panels	2.8
Total	157.4

Source: The 2020 La Hormiga Verde annual report

Results in Economic and Recognition Terms

In relation to assessing the results of the activity of the company, Table 15.6 is a synthesis of the form of collecting the waste and the quantity achieved. These "inputs" represent whence the materials in the form of waste originate. It should be noted that the origin is mainly the company's network of "greenspots" and the public institutions with which it collaborates.

With respect to the amount of waste recovered and treated, this was 157.4 tons in 2019 (La Hormiga Verde 2019). Most of the waste collected is of a ferrous nature (iron scrap), computer monitors and television screens, and electronic components (Table 15.7).

With regard to the results in the form of awards and recognitions, in October 2018 the company received the Emprende 24 Circular award for the "Best Business Idea in Circular and Green Economy" awarded by in Extremadura. As reward, it received support to create and maintain its website and marketing actions, among other services.

Results in Terms of Communication

In terms of communication and promotion, La Hormiga Verde carries out a modest dissemination about its work, but with which it manages to promote values such as respect for the environment, the fight against climate change, and the generation of job opportunities in favourable conditions for people with disabilities.

From the data offered by the digital platforms on which it is present (the two websites and the corporate Facebook page), it can be seen that the community it manages to reach is mainly its closest geographical environment—the region of Extremadura. But it does manage to spread news of its activity in neighbouring areas such as the province of Seville. The scope of its messages in other regions is insignificant.

From that data, one can observe that the company manages to connect with a public of ages from 18 to 35 mainly, since its reach decreases as age increases. Undoubtedly, the spreading of the contest in schools contributes to connecting with the younger public (from 12 to 18 years in age), for whom the message already given on the Web is reiterated with their participation in the contest.

The evolution over its period of activity shows a slow but steady progression. La Hormiga Verde dedicates limited resources to publicising its cause, but the effects are positive and with a significant potential for growth. Nonetheless, there are major shortcomings, such as not managing social networks properly:

- It does not have a corporate presence on social networks such as Instagram that are especially aimed at its target public.
- There is little interaction, and just an eminently one-way use of communication on its corporate Facebook page.
- Its presence on other networks (as in LinkedIn) uses the name of the organization through the owner's personal profile.

Conclusions

In the case of La Hormiga Verde, some aspects stand out that make it different from other similar cases, even compared to other electronic waste recycling initiatives.

In general terms, La Hormiga Verde is a clear example of an organization created under the circular economy model to contribute to sustainability and the quality of life. Although it is a private for-profit initiative, it manages to combine the social and economic aspects in perfect balance in its activity.

In particular terms, there are some aspects that make this case stand out above others and that give it richness and originality:

1. La Hormiga Verde is a Special Employment Centre in which most of its workers are people with disabilities, this being another form of social contribution. These workers' desire to improve is an extra stimulus for the entire staff who strive daily to overcome their own limitations. This is certainly a differentiating element of this case study with the promotion of the integration of people with disabilities as well as boosting their job opportunities in good working conditions.
2. Given that the company is located in a geographical context, Extremadura, that is characterized as being a developing region, the work it does contributes to increasing the region's entrepreneurial projection and its business fabric. In the way the company carries out its work, it is also faithful to this principle since it is aware that it is situated in a rural and sparsely populated region in which its difference is to go to the most remote areas to guarantee that anyone who wants to contribute to the mission can do so, no matter where they are. Although Extremadura is not a developed region, initiatives like this champion the region's progress by contributing to the advance of society and the conservation of the planet. With its presence in schools and involving young people in the volume of waste they recycle, the company is thus committed to raising awareness of these issues.
3. Its social marketing strategy itself provides content to its business strategy, streamlining its tasks, giving it unique positioning and values as an entity that contributes with all of its actions to fulfilling its business mission, which above all is, being faithful to sustainability with the recycling of waste from a modern and excessively technical society.

The company stands out for the originality of its main action—the contest. Through this action, it achieves objectives that are economic (since it is the main source of revenue from raw materials), social (since it contributes its grain of sand to education and the awareness and promotion of socially responsible attitudes and behaviour towards the environment), and communicative (since it achieves the greatest impact through this action and its dissemination among its young public, who are potentially more proactive in benefit of the quality of life through caring for the planet).

Discussion Questions

1. How can WEEE affect the quality of life? What can be the solutions to the impact of WEEE on the quality of life?
2. What key aspects can be influenced to solve the WEEE problem and plan a social marketing strategy that helps to improve the quality of life?
3. What does the strategy of La Hormiga Verde contribute to solving the WEEE problem?

4. Can the strategy of La Hormiga Verde be considered to be helping to improve the quality of life?
5. What can be done to improve communication actions in La Hormiga Verde?
6. What are the keys to the success of the social marketing strategy of La Hormiga Verde?

Financing entities:

JUNTA DE EXTREMADURA
Consejería de Economía, Ciencia y Agenda Digital

Unión Europea

Fondo Europeo de Desarrollo Regional
Una manera de hacer Europa

European Regional Development Fund "A way of making Europe"

Teaching Notes

1. ***How can WEEE affect the quality of life? What can be the solutions to the impact of WEEE on the quality of life?***

WEEE poses a threat to the quality of life from a health and environmental point of view, since electronic and electrical devices contain polluting materials such as heavy metals (cadmium, lead, mercury, ...) and non-degradable plastics that are harmful to health and the planet. The reuse of these metals represents an economic and resource savings with the reduction of their environmental and health impact.

Electronic waste also poses a health risk since, once nature is contaminated, this can lead to DNA damage and diseases such as cancer.

Given the impact of WEEE on the quality of life, it is possible to act in different areas:

- Recycle: Any solution starts with the awareness of recycling. It is essential to make society see more the seriousness of the consequences of the negative impact that electronic waste has on the environment, and therefore on the quality of life.

Thus, promotion of awareness and education in this area are fundamental in all age groups, but fundamentally in young people.

- Renovate: The recycling of these materials is expensive and difficult, so another solution is to reduce the consumption of this type of devices. It is true that electronic devices have become essential in our lives, but changing or renewing them should respond to criteria of usefulness, not aesthetics or whim. That is, we must renew technological equipment only when necessary, thus extending the useful life of the devices already available in homes.
- Reuse. When it is necessary to purchase a new device, the old one can be taken to companies or organizations that can reuse it. There they will repair and re-sell the device, extending its usefulness. In addition, in this way one can contribute to helping less-favoured social groups.

Therefore, the main solutions can be presented under the premise of the three "Rs": "Recycle", "Reuse", and "Renew" (only when necessary).

2. ***What are the key aspects for solving the WEEE problem and planning a social marketing strategy that helps to improve the quality of life?***

This problem can be understood and therefore solutions to it undertaken, emphasizing different aspects or points of view.

Emphasis on Education

The need to integrate environmental education in the school curriculum or in the Educational Centre Project (training the teacher trainers). In the educational field, the importance is recognized of training pupils in environmental issues to allow the local and global environment to be improved. This is stated in Goal 4.7 of the Sustainable Development Objective on Education, which addresses the need to promote Education for Sustainable Development (ESD).

Environmental education is a cross-cutting content in the majority of teaching curricula at the different educational levels. Therefore, throughout pupils' academic stage, it is essential to include competencies related to proactive behaviour for the protection of the environment and which will improve the quality of life. This would contribute to internalizing respectful and sustainable behaviour towards the environment.

As part of education, small daily gestures respectful to the environment should be encouraged. Reflection on individual actions that can make a difference is fundamental, such as: completely unplugging electronic devices when not at home, extending the useful life of electronic devices, searching the second-hand market...

Emphasis on the Geographic Scope of the Problem

This is about transmitting the need to recycle in local environments to help minimize the global impact. Local authorities should do their bit by promoting recycling in proximity, as La Hormiga Verde does from the private sector.

With regard to this aspect, the European Union, in its Directive 2008/98/EC about waste, establishes that, in the European territory, waste must be disposed of as close as possible to the place in which it is produced (principle of proximity). The self-sufficiency of a territory in terms of recycling reduces economic costs and avoids unnecessary transport of materials.

Emphasis on Awareness

Much of society is unaware that, behind everyday objects such as a computer or mobile phone, there are highly polluting materials such as mercury, lead, or cadmium. It is necessary to make society aware of the impact of these materials not only on the environment, but also on health since prolonged exposure to these elements is highly damaging.

It would be appropriate to encourage debates and reflection through questions such as:

Did you know that . . .?[7]

- A refrigerator whose components are poorly recycled emits greenhouse gases into the atmosphere that are equivalent to the emissions of a car over 15,000 kilometres.
- A nickel-cadmium battery used in a mobile phone can pollute 50,000 litres of water.

It is also necessary to raise awareness in industry, given its important role in recycling electronic devices. It is necessary to encourage companies to conduct the controlled substitution of these materials, to promote policies that support the purchase of sustainable materials, to train human resources in energy and electronics savings, to favour contact with suppliers of sustainable materials, and to invest in the search for less polluting materials.

3. ***What does the strategy of La Hormiga Verde contribute to solving the WEEE problem?***

La Hormiga Verde contributes fundamentally because it favours the recycling of polluting components from electronic and electrical devices. It recycles the toxic components of the devices, and contributes to the recovery of the parts and components that can be reused in the production of future devices or to repair others.

It is committed to solving the problem in two ways not previously considered in similar contexts: it makes a great effort to raise social awareness on the one hand in households (since it focuses on providing a service that allows waste to be collected almost directly from homes), and on the other in young people (thanks to the contest it carries out in schools). This awareness-raising work in predominantly rural contexts contributes to the proper destruction of polluting devices while following the principle of proximity.

The visibility it adds to the activity it carries out, on the one hand, by giving talks in schools and, on the other, through the communication channels it uses, promotes the transmission of sustainable, recycling habits in daily life. In addition, it offers

[7] "The dangers of electronic waste". Available at: https://www.nationalgeographic.com.es/mundo-ng/peligros-basura-electronica_13239

information about polluting materials, thus increasing society's awareness of the problem of e-waste.

Through its business model, the company contributes to creating social value. One reason is that it hires people with disabilities. Another is its environmental work, with reducing the impact of electronic waste being the central axis of its activity and a principle of action that governs its development (for example, optimizing its travel routes and recycling all the office furniture in its facilities).

4. ***Can the strategy of La Hormiga Verde be considered to be helping to improve the quality of life?***

Its global strategy contributes to the improvement of local environments, with specific actions such as collecting WEEE at the point of origin (facilitating recycling in the most isolated areas) and employing people with disabilities, to whom it offers inclusive employment.

The work of raising awareness and sensitization in schools through the contest allows it to give visibility and diffusion to a problem that has a direct impact on people's quality of life. In addition, it manages to attract young people by encouraging their participation with prizes that are donated to the school, and supporting values such as group work as opposed to individualism. Through the contest, awareness is created of the need for individual recycling and its contribution to achieving the global objective. This behaviour, extrapolated to the daily context of each participant, also encourages family awareness, making homes places that are better protected against and more concerned about WEEE contamination.

5. ***What can be done to improve communication actions in La Hormiga Verde?***

Given the initial launching situation in which the company finds itself, improvement of its social communication plan should be consolidated. It should invest gradually and in coordination with its growth, until it is able to implement a professional plan of proper communication (which currently does not exist) that is solidly rooted in its social marketing strategy.

This path could begin with greater dedication to communication activities by the company's staff, since currently such dedication is very limited.

Likewise, it would be convenient to review the platforms and social media used in order to verify that they are relevant and adapted to the target public.

Professionalizing these activities should lead to content that is better prepared and of greater interest to the company's public. It would be pertinent to highlight and transmit its differentiating values (commitment to people who have a disability, being a certified entity, collecting at the point of origin...) since its current communications are eminently informative and lack interaction, which is not very motivating for its public to also move into action.

Subsequently, it would be convenient to invest in expanding the scope of communications through planned and paid communication actions on the platforms chosen (especially the online platforms). Traditional communications media are currently not a priority for the organization, so that promoting the online dissemination and reach would seem to be a strategy more in line with the reality of the company, as long as it is done in a planned way.

However, beyond such actions of online communications, those in charge of La Hormiga Verde could promote environmental education in a way that is more aligned with its business objectives and marketing strategy. This could be done through the talks already carried out in schools (which should be reinforced), and in using public relations (as a planned form of communication) in their contacts with suppliers, customers, and the media so as to spread a message based on the organization's social and environmental values.

Regardless of which platform or medium is used, the promotion of actions carried out in favour of recycling and environmental education should be based on spreading messages with a marked social content, in which respect for the environment and the use of sustainable materials constitute the fundamental pillar.

All this must be accompanied by the advice of communications professionals, and put into practice gradually and proportional to the company's business growth.

6. ***What are the keys to the success of the social marketing strategy of La Hormiga Verde?***

The key aspects that make La Hormiga Verde a unique company and that have provided the keys to its success, thus contributing to improving people's quality of life and reducing the waste's environmental impact, can be specified as the following:

- The school contest. The company's main tool and showcase is the contest carried out in collaboration with regional public administrations. This undoubtedly offers the company recognition among a young public and their families, which is very important for WEEE recycling. Involving and educating young people and households gives it a differential value compared with its competitors, in addition to positioning it more clearly as a benchmark in the sector at a regional level.
- The fact of being a Special Employment Centre makes La Hormiga Verde an organization concerned with the integration of people with some mental disability in the ordinary job market. This gives it added value that other companies in its sector do not have.
- The collection of electronic waste in institutions and organizations. The agreements with numerous businesses and institutions allows it to recycle large quantities of WEEE from which it subsequently obtains an economic benefit, and allows value to be created for the company in both economic and social terms, the latter because of providing society with strategies to improve its quality of life.
- Collection at the point of origin. The proximity to rural environments and its location in an area of marked geographical dispersion as is the case for the region of Extremadura (Spain) confers on the company full integration with the society in which it is inserted, and allows it to detect almost immediately deficiencies and possible market niches.

- Raising young people's awareness. The involvement of young people in the problem of e-waste is essential for the future evolution of the problem.
- The agreements with institutions and businesses also contribute not only to the company's own expansion but also to sensitizing the business fabric which is a major generator of e-waste. The establishment in many businesses and institutions of recycling protocols that include waste collection is a success for La Hormiga Verde.

In this way, La Hormiga Verde contributes to improving the quality of life of the society in which it carries out its activity since it facilitates recycling and offers information and education about this topic. In particular, it strengthens the quality of life of local rural environments in which WEEE is also a problem. It spreads values of respect for the environment and sustainability, while also promoting other values including the integration of people with disabilities and group work.

References

Ecoembes (2020) La economía circular en España. https://www.ecoembes.com/es/ciudadanos/envases-y-proceso-reciclaje/la-economia-circular-en-espana

El comercio (2020) La trastienda del CES: La búsqueda de una segunda vida tecnológica https://www.elcomercio.es/tecnologia/trastienda-busqueda-segunda-vida-tecnologica-20200107073917-ntrc.html

Instituto Nacional de Estadística, INE (2019) Estadísticas sobre recogida y tratamiento de resíduos. Available at: www.ine.es

Instituto Nacional de Estadística, INE (2020) Estadísticas sobre recogida y tratamiento de resíduos. Available at: www.ine.es

La Hormiga Verde (2019) Annual report 2019

La Hormiga Verde (2020) http://www.lahormigaverde.org/es/contacto

MITECO (2020) Economía circular en La Comisión Europea. https://www.miteco.gob.es/es/calidad-y-evaluacion-ambiental/temas/economia-circular/comision-europea/

Rivera RG, Arrese A, Sádaba C, Casado L (2020) Incorporating diversity in marketing education: A framework for including all people in the teaching and learning process. J Mark Educ 42(1):37–47

Statista (2020) Evolución de la producción de residuos de aparatos eléctricos y electrónicos en España de 2010 a 2020 (en toneladas métricas). https://es.statista.com/estadisticas/807066/evolucion-de-la-produccion-de-residuos-basura-electronica-espana/

U.S. Department of Justice, Civil Rights Division, Disability Rights Section (2009) The Americans with disabilities act: a guide to disability rights laws. Washington, DC. Retrieved from https://www.ada.gov/cguide.htm

United Nations (2006) Convention of the rights of persons with disabilities. Retrieved from https://www.un.org/development/desa/disabilities/convention-on-the-rights-of-persons-withdisabilities

United Nations (2020) Goal 12. Ensure sustainable consumption and production patterns. Available at: www.un.org/sustainabledevelopment/sustainable-consumption-production/

Online Resources

Facebook (La Hormiga Verde Centro Especial de Empleo)
http://www.concursolahormigaverde.org/
http://www.lahormigaverde.org

Chapter 16
Social Marketing for Flood Risk Management: A Local Communication Campaign in Spain

Juan A. Garcia, Jose M. Bodoque, Maria Amerigo, Belen Ruiz, and Andres Diez-Herrero

Abstract Most of the deaths and economic losses resulting from natural disasters that have occurred in Spain have been brought about by floods. The adequate management of flood risks is, therefore, a critical aspect as regards improving the quality of life of populations living in flood risk areas. Local communities' social resilience to floods is directly linked to the flood risk perception, the awareness of the actions to take before, during and after a flood, and the intention to be prepared and behave accordingly. These relationships provide enough evidence to support the suitability of designing social marketing (SM) campaigns that will improve the local community's risk perception, awareness and intention to be prepared and behave accordingly, thereby increasing people's quality of life.

This chapter presents a SM campaign that was implemented locally in a Spanish municipality and was composed of four types of activities (informative talk; quiz; storytelling session and photograph/video competitions; and intergenerational workshops). Research based on a survey was conducted before and after the communication campaign took place and was then used to evaluate its effectiveness.

Keywords Social marketing · Quality of life · Flood risk · Communication campaign

---

J. A. Garcia (✉) · B. Ruiz
University of Castilla-La Mancha, Talavera de la Reina, Spain
e-mail: Juan.Garcia@uclm.es; Belen.Ruiz@uclm.es

J. M. Bodoque · M. Amerigo
University of Castilla-La Mancha, Toledo, Spain
e-mail: JoseMaria.Bodoque@uclm.es; Maria.Amerigo@uclm.es

A. Diez-Herrero
IGME, CSIC, Geological Survey of Spain, Madrid, Spain
e-mail: Andres.Diez@igme.es

M. M. Galan-Ladero, R. G. Rivera (eds.), *Applied Social Marketing and Quality of Life*, Applying Quality of Life Research,
https://doi.org/10.1007/978-3-030-83286-5_16

Table 16.1 Number of natural disasters, deaths, total number of people affected, and economic losses according to disaster type: 2008–2018 annual average around the world (rank in parentheses)

Disaster type	Disasters[a]	Deaths[b]	Total affected (million)[c]	Economic losses (billion US$)[d]
Drought	17 (6°)	1822 (5°)	68.2 (2°)	8.4 (4°)
Earthquake	25 (3°)	32,476 (1°)	7.7 (5°)	41.8 (2°)
Extreme temperature	21 (4°)	6765 (3°)	8.2 (4°)	2.7 (6°)
Flood	151 (1°)	4843 (4°)	69.6 (1°)	34.8 (3°)
Landslide	18 (5°)	965 (6°)	0.3 (7°)	0.4 (7°)
Mass movement (dry)	1 (9°)	23 (9°)	<0.1 (9°)	<0.1 (9°)
Storm	100 (2°)	15,396 (2°)	32.6 (3°)	69.7 (1°)
Volcanic activity	4 (8°)	120 (7°)	0.4 (6°)	0.2 (8°)
Wildfire	9 (7°)	93 (8°)	0.1 (8°)	5.5 (5°)

Notes
[a]For a disaster to be recorded in the EM-DAT, at least one of the following criteria must be fulfilled: 10 or more people reported to be killed, 100 or more people reported to be affected, declaration of a state of emergency, and a call for international assistance
[b]People confirmed as dead and people missing and presumed dead
[c]Total number of people injured, homeless and affected
[d]Economic loss figures have been adjusted according to the current value (2019) of the US dollar
Source: Own elaboration from CRED (2019)

Introduction

According to the World Health Organization (WHO), a natural disaster is:

> An act of nature of such magnitude as to create a catastrophic situation in which the day-to-day patterns of life are suddenly disrupted and people are plunged into helplessness and suffering, and, as a result, need food, clothing, shelter, medical and nursing care and other necessities of life, and protection against unfavourable environmental factors and conditions. (Assar 1971, p. 14)

Natural disasters include, among others, droughts, earthquakes, extreme temperatures, floods, landslides, mass movements (dry), storms, volcanic activities and wildfires (Centre for Research on the Epidemiology of Disasters—CRED 2019). They have an immediate impact on human lives and often result in the destruction of the physical, biological and social environment of the people affected, thereby also having a longer-term impact on their quality of life (Wisner and Adams 2002).

Between 2008 and 2018, an annual average of 346 natural disasters were recorded in the Emergency Events Database (EM-DAT), which is maintained by CRED, with 62,503 deaths per year, over 187 million people affected per year, and US$163.6 billion in economic losses per year throughout the world. Table 16.1 shows that, when considering nine type of natural disasters, floods were the most frequent (annual average of 151 events) and affected more people than any other kind of disaster at a world-wide level (annual average of 69.6 million people affected). Floods were, moreover, the fourth greatest cause of deaths, surpassed only by earthquakes, storms and extreme temperatures; and the third greatest cause of economic losses, with an annual average figure below that associated with storms and earthquakes (CRED 2019).

Furthermore, and according to Alfieri et al. (2017), the intensification of the hydrometeorological extreme events resulting from global warming and the increasing exposure of the population raise concerns regarding future floods and their impacts. These authors explore three future scenarios for different warming thresholds and present a framework with which to estimate the population affected and the economic losses caused by floods on a global scale. They conclude that projected changes in flood risk are not homogeneously distributed around the world, with the largest increases being in Asia, the United States of America and Europe.

The type of natural disaster that led to the greatest number of fatalities in Spain between 1995 and 2017 was floods (342 deaths, which is 26% of the total). Furthermore, in the period 1971–2016, floods were an extraordinary risk and led to the highest economic losses in Spain. According to the Insurance Compensation Consortium (Consorcio de Compensación de Seguros—CCS, in Spanish), the financial figures associated with compensation for this type of event accounted for 62% of the total (Ministerio para la Transición Ecológica 2018). Various studies in Spain have also found a greater increase in the probability of damaging flood events when considering different levels of global warming above pre-industrial levels and socioeconomic scenarios, especially in the Spanish Mediterranean regions (e.g. Cortès et al. 2019).

All the above makes it clear that the adequate management of flood risks is, therefore, a critical aspect as regards improving the quality of life of populations living in flood risk areas (Borga et al. 2011). In this sense, based on the premise that absolute safety or zero flood risk does not exist, the Directive2007/60/EC concerning the assessment and management of flood risks includes the adoption of comprehensive risk management frameworks (Kubal et al. 2009). More specifically, Article 7 of the Directive 2007/60/EC states that "Flood risk management plans shall address all aspects of flood risk management focusing on prevention, protection, preparedness, including flood forecasts and early warning systems and taking into account the characteristics of the particular river basin or sub-basin". To this end, flood risk management plans must also considered the social dimension of risk (Amérigo et al. 2019) and, specifically, the characterisation of social resilience in order to reduce the negative effects of flooding on the quality of life of the communities affected (Khalili et al. 2015). Social resilience can be defined as "the ability of groups or communities to cope with external stresses and disturbances as a result of social, political and environmental change" (Adger 2000, p. 347).

Local communities' levels of social resilience to floods are directly linked to various psychosocial variables, such as: (1) the flood risk perception (Bodoque et al. 2019); (2) the awareness of the actions that should be taken before, during and after a flood (Bodoque et al. 2019); and (3) the intention to be prepared and behave accordingly (Amérigo et al. 2017). However, previous research in the field of risk analysis has identified the existence of a series of heuristics or perception biases, which are significant handicaps to any communication campaign. Some of these are risk normalisation, positive illusion, or environmental hyperopia. Related to the first of these is the risk normalisation effect, which consists of risk awareness owing to a greater exposure to it, which reduces the perception of risk owing to its effect on confidence in protective measures (Luís et al. 2016). Positive illusion is one way in which to psychologically cope with risk by relying on the ability of current mitigation measures to control the occurrence of hazards (Schmidt et al. 2014). According to Uzzell (2000), people tend to perceive environmental problems as more serious the farther away they are, and this has been termed as environmental hyperopia. Bodoque et al. (2019) found that people consider the probability of flood risk to be higher when it occurs further away than closer to them according to spatial (distance from their home) and temporal (far away in time) dimensions.

Bearing these findings in mind, the aim of this case study is to explore the appropriateness of designing and implementing a social marketing (SM) campaign in order to improve risk perception, awareness and intention to be prepared and behave accordingly in a Spanish municipality that is frequently exposed to floods, thereby enhancing this population's social resilience to floods and its quality of life.

Case Development: A Social Marketing (SM) Campaign with Which to Enhance Social Resilience to Floods

The SM campaign was designed and implemented by the research team responsible for the Projects entitled "Integration of Advanced Methodologies for the Improvement of Flood Resilience in Urban Areas" (MARCoNI, Reference: CGL2013-42728-R) and "Design of a Methodology to Increase Flood Resilience Compatible with Improved Status of Water Bodies and Sustainable Management of Water Resources" (DRAINAGE, Reference: CGL2017-83546-C3-R). It is an interdisciplinary research team in which professionals and academics in the fields of geology, hydrology, environmental sciences, psychology and marketing participate.

The municipality chosen for the implementation of the local communication campaign was Navaluenga (a village in the province of Ávila, in the Spanish region of Castilla y León). This municipality is located in central Spain on the banks of the Alberche River and the Chorrerón Stream; and had a population of 2027 inhabitants in 2014, according to the Spanish Statistical Office (Bodoque et al. 2016).

Navaluenga suffers from frequent flash floods, a kind of rapid flooding events. As shown in Fig. 16.1, in the last 100 years this municipality has experienced at least 34 floods, which is an average of 3.4 flood events per decade. The latest events, including the March 2018 one, led to huge economic losses and affected part of the population (Bodoque et al. 2016), with the consequent negative impact on the resident population's quality of life.

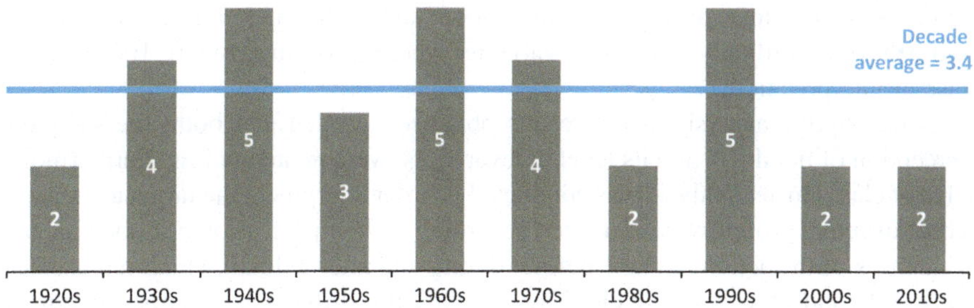

Fig. 16.1 Number of flood events per decade in Navaluenga: 1920–2019. Source: Own elaboration from Díez-Herrero (2001) and different mass media news

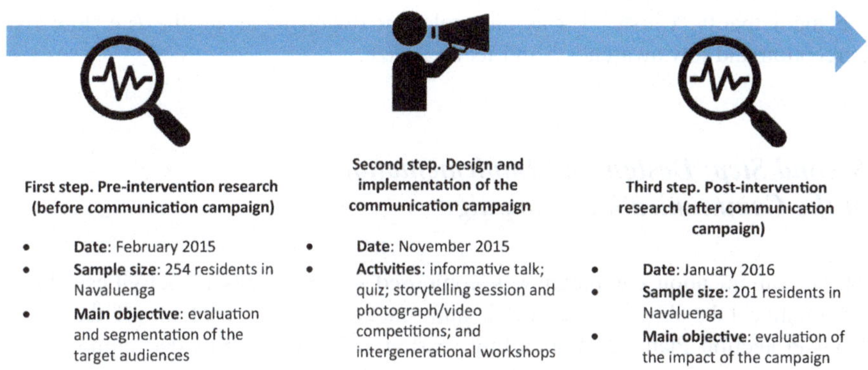

Fig. 16.2 Scheme for the development of the SM campaign. Source: Own elaboration

The SM campaign was developed by following three steps, which appear in the scheme presented in Fig. 16.2. The proposed process took 11 months. More details of what each of the proposed steps consist of are provided below.

First Step: Pre-intervention Research

The starting point was research based on a survey applied to a representative sample of 254 residents (i.e. more than 10% of the population of Navaluenga). An ad-hoc questionnaire was personally administered in order to collect information regarding: (1) the flood risk perceptions in Navaluenga and homes themselves, both in the short term (the next five years) and the long term (lifetime)[1]; (2) the awareness of the

[1] In the case of events related to natural disasters, the concepts of short and long term differ substantially from the periods considered in the economic disciplines. In these latter disciplines, the short term is usually associated with periods shorter than one year.

actions to take before, during and after a flood; and (3) the intentions to be prepared and behave accordingly.[2] All these variables were transformed to a 0–100 scale for ease of interpretation.

A descriptive analysis of the results obtained revealed that both, the sample's perception of flood risk and its level of awareness, were relatively low. Furthermore, a latent class cluster analysis was conducted in order to segment the target audience.[3] Three different groups were identified according to their perception of flood risk and awareness of the actions to take before, during and after a flood, which represented 61%, 24% and 15%, respectively. These groups also differed as regards age, family status, house type and flooded area, as shown in Fig. 16.3. This segmentation allowed us to establish an order of priorities in relation to the segments that the communication campaign should target. Cluster 2 was, therefore, a priority owing to its low level of awareness, even though 64% of them resided in the flooded area of the municipality. Cluster 1 was also relevant owing to its profile (i.e. low risk perception and low awareness) and its large size.

Second Step: Design and Implementation of the Communication Campaign

The communication campaign was composed of four types of activities: (1) an informative talk about floods; (2) a quiz on the different contents of the Local Civil Protection Plan; (3) storytelling session and photograph/video competitions concerning past floods; and (4) intergenerational workshops.

These four activities were designed by considering the groups identified in the first step. In order to reach cluster 2 (consisting mainly of couples with children over 12 years of age and who had a low level of awareness), the quiz on the different contents of the Local Civil Protection Plan was, therefore, proposed. This activity was published through collaboration with the local High School and was proposed to the children as a family activity in which everyone could participate by answering questions online once a week. In order to reach clusters 1 (made up of older people with low risk perception and low awareness) and 3 (made up of younger people), it was decided to include intergenerational workshops in which the older members of the population and young people could exchange their experiences regarding floods. The storytelling session and photograph/video competitions concerning past floods were mainly aimed at clusters 1 and 3 and allowed the photos and videos of historical

---

[2]The flood risk perceptions and the intentions to be prepared and behave accordingly were measured using four and five items, respectively, on a five-point Likert scale. The level of awareness was evaluated in five categories based on the percentage of correct responses in relation to the actions contained in the Local Civil Protection Plan.

[3]The number of groups was determined using the consistent Akaike information criterion (CAIC). The model parameters were estimated using Latent Gold® 4.5.

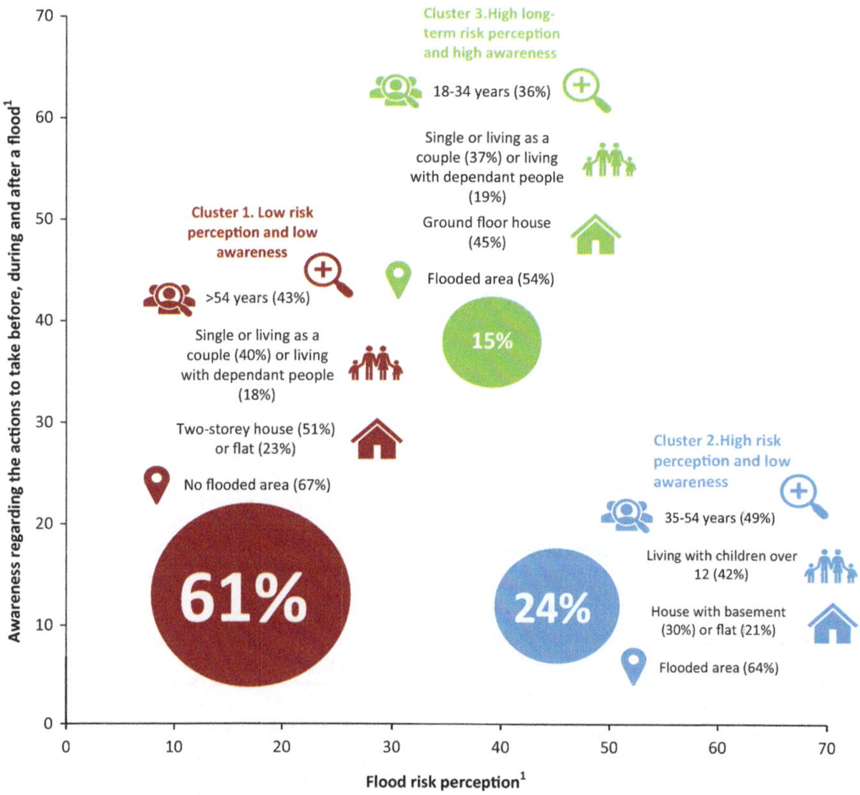

Fig. 16.3 Profiles of population groups. Notes: (1) X and Y axes of the bubble chart represent the average values. (2) All indicators were transformed to a 0–100 scale for ease of interpretation. Source: Own elaboration from Bodoque et al. (2016)

floods that had been collected by the older population to be released to the younger population. Finally, the informative talk about floods was addressed to the entire population of Navaluenga.

Different prizes were awarded, including participation certificates for all participants, and photo cameras and tablets for winners of the competitions and the quiz, respectively. The main communication tool used to promotion the different activities scheduled included both online (i.e. the municipal council's website and social networks, and email marketing) and offline media (i.e. posters and word-of-mouth communication). Less than 20% of the respondents in the post-intervention research stated that they did not know any of the activities in the communication campaign (Bodoque et al. 2019).

Table 16.2 Risk perception, awareness and intention to be prepared and behave accordingly before and after the implementation of the communication campaign

Indicators[a]	First step	Third step[b]	Mean differences[c]
Flood risk perception			
Navaluenga in the next 5 years	29	27	=
Navaluenga in their lifetime	48	60	Δ (12)
Their home in the next 5 years	10	10	=
Their home in their lifetime	18	19	=
Awareness of the actions to take before, during and after a flood			
Avoidance of negative consequences	4	10	Δ (6)
Evacuation routes and meeting point	10	19	Δ (9)
Self-protection behaviours	9	22	Δ (13)
Actions before leaving the home	39	54	Δ (15)
Actions after leaving the home	15	26	Δ (11)
Intention to be prepared for floods and behave accordingly			
Acquire an emergency kit	68	73	=
Find information about evacuation routes and meeting point	66	62	=
Know what to do when leaving the home	64	62	=
Know how to help family and neighbours	67	69	=
Take precautions at home	71	80	Δ (9)

Notes
[a]All indicators were transformed to a 0–100 scale for ease of interpretation
[b]The information in the third step was not available in a disaggregated way within each cluster
[c]Statistically significant mean differences between both periods, using t-test for paired samples ($p < 0.05$), are marked with Δ
Source: Own elaboration from Amérigo et al. (2017) and Bodoque et al. (2019)

Third Step: Post-intervention Research

In this third step, information was collected from 201[4] of a total of 254 adults who participated in the first step. The changes in risk perception, awareness and intention to be prepared and behave accordingly are shown in Table 16.2. Regarding the individual effectiveness of each action in the communication campaign, the informative talk allowed the awareness of evacuation routes and meeting points to be enhanced. Intergenerational workshops improved the awareness of evacuation routes and meeting points, along with the actions that should be taken before leaving home. Finally, the quiz was the most effective action, since it improved the awareness of three of the five categories considered (i.e. avoidance of negative consequences, self-protection behaviours and actions to take after leaving home).

[4]The sample distribution was as follows: (1) gender: female (55%), male (45%); (2) age: 18–34 (19%), 35–54 (45%), >54 (36%); and (3) education level: elementary education (52%), secondary education (29%), higher education (19%).

Conclusions

The paradigm shift as regards how flood damage mitigation studies should be addressed (Directive 2007/60/CE), implies a comprehensive analysis of hazards, demanding non-structural measures that include the community's participation in flood risk management, thus complementing or replacing structural strategies (e.g. river channels, dams, levees or reservoirs). The objective of this broad approach is to reduce the impact of the negative consequences of flooding by improving coping strategies and social resilience, thus leading to a positive impact on vulnerable people's quality of life. Enhancing social resilience to floods is, therefore, necessary in order to reduce future losses and to minimize any reduction in the quality of life of the communities affected. Social marketing campaigns could be a key strategy by which to improve the social resilience and quality of life of populations living in flood risk areas, thus increasing a community's ability to cope with a flood by minimizing damage and enabling them to return to their previous level of quality of life.

The traditional approach employed to improve the social resilience of populations exposed to floods is often focused exclusively on informative talks. In this case, a SM campaign based on four types of innovative activities was run. Moreover, the design and the implementation of these activities were carried out by considering the target audiences identified using a segmentation analysis. The involvement of the population in the activities designed was significant, as evidenced by the participation data collected in post-intervention research. The communication campaign impacted on the participants' awareness, thus making them more competent and resilient. However, the improvement in the perception of risks and the intention to be prepared and behave accordingly were much more limited.

Discussion Questions

1. How would you evaluate the impact of the social marketing campaign presented in this case study?
2. What elements explain the low effectiveness of the campaign as regards improving the flood risk perception and the intention to be prepared for floods and behave accordingly?
3. How could the SM campaign be enhanced? What additional activities and communication tools could be used to improve the results?
4. Identify a recent SM campaign aimed at improving social resilience to a natural disaster, and analyse its potential as regards improving the target audiences' quality of life.

Acknowledgements This work was funded by the projects MARCoNI (CGL2013-42728-R; MINECO) and DRAINAGE (CGL2017-83546-C3-R; MINEICO/AEI/FEDER, UE).

Teaching Notes

Answer to Question 1. How would you evaluate the impact of the social marketing campaign presented in this case study?

The SM campaign presented in this case includes: (1) pre-intervention research, which makes it possible to segment the target audience and has been used to design the activities proposed; and (2) post-intervention research, which makes it possible to evaluate the changes in risk perception, awareness and intention to be prepared and behave accordingly.

The data presented in Table 16.2, therefore, allowed an accurate assessment of the impact of the SM campaign.

- First, it will be observed that flood risk perception has only increased for the item that measures the flood risk perception in Navaluenga in the long term.
- Second, the SM campaign has been extremely effective as regards increasing awareness of the actions to be taken before, during and after a flood; especially with regard to the items related to self-protection behaviour and actions before/after leaving home.
- Third, in the case of the intention to be prepared for floods and behave accordingly, a significant increase has been observed after the SM campaign only in the case of the item regarding intentions to take precautions at home.

Answer to Question 2. What elements explain the low effectiveness of the campaign as regards improving the flood risk perception and the intention to be prepared for floods and behave accordingly?

Three main elements are useful to explain the low effectiveness of the campaign as regards improving flood risk perception and the intentions to be prepared for floods and behave accordingly.

- The first of these is the design of the SM campaign itself, since the most innovative activities, and especially the quiz, were mainly aimed at improving the awareness of the contents of the Local Civil Protection Plan. Moreover, the SM campaign was concentrated into a single month.
- The second element that helps explain the low effectiveness of the campaign as regards improving flood risk perception is linked to the heuristics or perception biases, especially those related to risk normalization, positive illusion, and enriching hyperopia. These biases could explain the fact that, despite having received information on flood risk, people tended to think that "these events occurred a long time ago", "they will not affect themselves or anyone else in their family" and, "in any case, they will affect the municipality but in the distant future".
- Finally, there is a third important element as regards understanding that the change in the intentions to be prepared for floods and behave accordingly are the existence of barriers that prevent the population from acting, one of the most important of which is the costs in terms of money, time and effort. If the population perceives that being able to act to be protected against floods requires

investing money and time and that they must make greater personal efforts than the benefits it brings, they will tend not to behave accordingly.

Answer to Question 3. How could the SM campaign be enhanced? What additional activities and communication tools could be used to improve the results?

Based on the elements discussed in the previous question, the SM campaign could be improved by acting on three aspects:

1. Planning the SM campaign by considering a broader time period, which would include periodic interventions evaluated individually;
2. Including interventions that are aimed at reducing the perceived costs to the population as regards the money, time and effort related to the different behaviours that will allow them to be prepared for floods; and
3. Proposing additional activities with a main recreational focus, since they have been found to be more attractive to the population.

As can been seen in Fig. 16.3, age segmentation is key aspect as regards identifying different groups based on flood risk perception and awareness. In this respect it would, for example, be possible to design additional activities for the younger population based on virtual reality, simulators, or computer/video/mobile games, which would be very attractive for this segment. Regarding the middle-aged population, new competitions could be proposed which, rather than focusing on awareness, are more oriented towards achieving changes in their flood preparedness behaviour. In this case, competitions or challenges through social networks could be used. Finally, for the older population, it may be appropriate employ more community-based interventions and, above all, more didactic activities aimed at informing dependent people how to act if they are involved in a flood event.

Answer to Question 4. Identify a recent SM campaign aimed at improving social resilience to a natural disaster, and analyse its potential as regards improving the target audiences' quality of life.

In relation to this question, there are many SM campaigns whose objective is to increase social resilience to a natural disaster that could be analysed by the students. One website that may be very interesting in order to answer this question is that of the Federal Emergency Management Agency (FEMA) of the United States Department of Homeland Security: https://www.fema.gov/. More specifically, FEMA provides a Flood Risk Communication Toolkit for Community Officials (https://www.fema.gov/media-library/assets/documents/179697) that includes templates and guides with which to design a communication plan and effective public meetings, along with a social media strategy that can be employed to address flood risk. It is backed by story maps and videos (Flood Risk Communication Video Series: https://www.youtube.com/playlist?list=PL720Kw_OojlIUiWw2bDc-On5MjQw13E6e). If the instructor considers that this question is very complex for the students, s/he could also simplify it by choosing one of the videos available on the YouTube channel of FEMA (https://www.youtube.com/user/FEMA/featured) that presents a specific communication campaign. Once the specific SM campaign has been chosen, it will be easier for students to assess its potential as regards improving the population's social resilience and quality of life.

References

Adger WN (2000) Social and ecological resilience: are they related? Prog Hum Geogr 24(3):347–364

Alfieri L, Bisselink B, Dottori F, Naumann G, de Roo A, Salamon P, Wyser K, Feyen L (2017) Global projections of river flood risk in a warmer world. Earth's Future 5(2):171–182

Amérigo M, García JA, Bodoque JM, Díez-Herrero A, Olcina J, Pérez-López R (2017) Efectos de la comunicación del riesgo de inundación sobre la percepción del riesgo y la intención de adoptar medidas preventivas. In: Bernardo F, Loureiro A (eds) Espaços e comportamento humano: do local ao global. Universidade de Évora, Évora, pp 237–238

Amérigo M, García JA, Pérez-López R, Talayero F (2019) Challenges to deal with climate change: analysis of flash flood risk perception. Papeles Psicól 40(3):197–204

Assar M (1971) Guide to sanitation in natural disasters. Retrieved from https://apps.who.int/iris/bitstream/handle/10665/41031/10678_eng.pdf. Accessed 23 June 2020

Bodoque JM, Amérigo M, Díez-Herrero A, García JA, Cortés B, Ballesteros-Cánovas JA, Olcina J (2016) Improvement of resilience of urban areas by integrating social perception in flash-flood risk management. J Hydrol 541:665–676

Bodoque JM, Díez-Herrero A, Amérigo M, García JA, Olcina J (2019) Enhancing flash flood risk perception and awareness of mitigation actions through risk communication: a pre-post survey design. J Hydrol 568:769–779

Borga M, Anagnostou EN, Blöschl G, Creutin JD (2011) Flash flood forecasting, warning and risk management: the HYDRATE project. Environ Sci Policy 14(7):834–844

Cortès M, Turco M, Ward P, Sánchez-Espigares JA, Alfieri L, Llasat MC (2019) Changes in flood damage with global warming on the eastern coast of Spain. Nat Hazards Earth Syst Sci 19(12):2855–2877

CRED (2019) Natural disasters 2018. Retrieved from https://www.cred.be/sites/default/files/CREDNaturalDisaster2018.pdf. Accessed 23 June 2020

Díez-Herrero A (2001) Geomorfología e hidrología fluvial del río Alberche: modelos y S. I. G. para la gestión de riberas (Doctoral dissertation). Retrieved from https://eprints.ucm.es/4329. Accessed 23 June 2020

Directive 2007/60/EC of the European Parliament and of the Council of 23 October 2007 on the assessment and management of flood risks. Retrieved from http://data.europa.eu/eli/dir/2007/60/oj. Accessed 23 June 2020

Khalili S, Harre M, Morley P (2015) A temporal framework of social resilience indicators of communities to flood, case studies: Wagga wagga and Kempsey, NSW, Australia. Int J Disaster Risk Reduct 13:248–254

Kubal C, Haase D, Meyer V, Scheuer S (2009) Integrated urban flood risk assessment—adapting a multicriteria approach to a city. Nat Hazards Earth Syst Sci 9(6):1881–1895

Luís S, Pinho L, Lima ML, Roseta-Palma C, Martins FC, Almeida AB (2016) Is it all about awareness? The normalization of coastal risk. J Risk Res 19(6):810–826

Ministerio para la Transición Ecológica (2018) Perfil ambiental de España 2017. Retrieved from https://www.miteco.gob.es/es/calidad-y-evaluacion-ambiental/publicaciones/pae2017_completo_reducido_tcm30-484531.pdf. Accessed 23 June 2020

Schmidt L, Gomes C, Guerreiro S, O'Riordan T (2014) Are we all on the same boat? The challenge of adaptation facing Portuguese coastal communities: risk perception, trust-building and genuine participation. Land Use Policy 38:355–365

Uzzell DL (2000) The psycho-spatial dimension of global environmental problem. J Environ Psychol 20(4):307–318

Wisner B, Adams J (2002) Environmental health in emergencies and disasters: a practical guide. Retrieved from https://apps.who.int/iris/handle/10665/42561. Accessed 23 June 2020

[illegible]

Chapter 17
We Stay Well Together: A Social Marketing Campaign

Filipa Almeida, Madalena Abreu, and Nuno Cadete

Abstract Coimbra Business School offers a well-shaped plan of education merging technical and social competencies and real training, and so giving strength to its student development for a better human society. One of the ways for doing so lies in Social Marketing, an optative discipline of the marketing graduation. Within this discipline, students are challenged to develop a real project, most of the times for the real benefit of a not for profit organization.

In 2020, on the top of the Covid-19 epidemic 'season', the students were invited to develop a campaign for a charity supporting homeless in the city of Coimbra (Portugal). The chosen team of students developed a social marketing (through social media) and developed other actions for this purpose as a crowdfunding campaign. They have been enrolled within this campaign for more than 3 months, struggling with the ups and downs a group of students has to face especially with the drawbacks of the state of emergency the country was dwelling with.

Overall the students gained tremendously with this experience learning how to do a social marketing campaign, including a fundraising campaign, and contribute to improve the quality of life of homeless people. Moreover, the outcome was most appreciated by the charity and also by other people that were enrolled with the project.

Keywords Social marketing · Fundraising campaign · Charity · Homeless · Higher Education Institution

F. Almeida · M. Abreu (✉) · N. Cadete
Coimbra Business School – ISCAC, Coimbra, Portugal
e-mail: iscac17434@alumni.iscac.pt; mabreu@iscac.pt; iscac4165@alumni.iscac.pt

M. M. Galan-Ladero, R. G. Rivera (eds.), *Applied Social Marketing and Quality of Life*, Applying Quality of Life Research,
https://doi.org/10.1007/978-3-030-83286-5_17

Introduction

Taking into account the context of the pandemic Covid-19, a time for serious involvement for the benefit of the most deprived ones, and within the scope of the Social Marketing discipline, we decided to join our efforts and take a real step to help the most needed at our city. The discipline of Social Marketing (Kotler and Roberto 1989) is an option of the marketing graduation course at Coimbra Business School, a Portuguese Higher Education Institution. We had, among other colleagues, chosen this discipline also for the passion of solidarity, culture of kindness and human rights we all share.

Our choice of what to do and each organization to choose was easy: actually, the situation of the homeless people has been vividly reported by social media all the time. In Coimbra, the city where we study, the most well-known charity for homeless support is the so called 'Cozinha Económica', *Associação das Cozinhas Económicas da Rainha Santa Isabel,* in its full name (ACERSI).[1]

This charity has been working hard, since the first moment, on the first line for homeless support, providing at least 900 meals a day. Before this time of crisis, ACERSI provided around 600 meals per day, but during this crisis the urgent need for food for homeless and poor families grew up fast. Moreover, the urgent needs have swollen in different directions. The pandemic has been aggressive prescribing other basic human needs for health, food, and safe shelter, such as cloth masks, personal protective equipment, disinfectant, medicines and other material.

Thus ACERSI has been waiting for every kind of help the city could give and we decided to increase awareness and support, organizing a social marketing campaign which also included to organize a fundraising campaign, a common practice within the scope of Social Marketing (Andreasen 1996).

What is more, this campaign would be the most important tool for being evaluated at a discipline within our studies at Coimbra Business School.

Case Development

Since the early beginning of this project we have been researching and studying information about the Portuguese's social and economic standards. One of the most striking cues is that, according to official data, the poverty rate is concentrated at 17.9% (INE 2020) in 2019. During the same year, it was found that the population living at risk of poverty or social exclusion was around 21.6% (PORDATA 2020a). Likewise, the risk of poverty rate before and after social transfers is at very high levels, accounting for 43.7% of the total Portuguese population (PORDATA 2020b). These values do indeed raise a huge concern because they reveal that more than a fifth of the population lives in a situation of poverty or social exclusion.

[1]Associations of the Economical Kitchens of the Holy Queen Isabel.

In the fight against different situations of poverty or social exclusion, different organizations provide social services in Portugal, being the most of them the so-called Private Institutions of Social Solidarity (IPSS), the most common type of charity in Portugal. These organizations are private, non-profit institutions, with the aim of granting goods and providing solidarity and justice support services to those who essentially lack it, in the social, health and education fields. These institutions celebrate protocols with the District Social Security Centres, in their area of operation, through which they are guaranteed financial support for the acquisition of equipment and the provision of these support services to the populations.

In Coimbra district it is possible to find more than 100 associations of social solidarity, one of which is our main target, ACERSI. The crisis caused by the pandemic has led to an increasing number of families turning to ACERSI, who previously served an average of 600 meals a day. During the time of the first wave of the pandemic crisis (Spring 2020), the numbers skyrocketed, reaching more than 200 the number of families being supported on a daily basis and more than 900 meals served daily. It should be noted that the increase in meals served was due to what we can call 'new poverty' (people who previously had precarious jobs and lost them, having no savings to face this new situation).

In the context of the Social Marketing discipline, which promotes field work as part of the assessment, a group of 12 students decided something had to be done concerning this new poverty, also seeking to increase awareness and support for social responsibility. Since the beginning, we had all the support of our Higher Education Institution and also the support of the União de Freguesia de Coimbra (a branch of the city council). As already mentioned, we chose to support ACERSI, being this charity the one that had the biggest number of people begging for food in Coimbra.

Developing the so called Effects on Quality of Life (QOL), a common concept for describing people's lives conditions, there are multiple aspects being tackled within this campaign; such as Health (maybe the most important and persecuted aspect); material comfort (apart from the most important issue, food itself, also the way the food is offered by a friendly organization within a cosy atmosphere, is a very appreciated aspect); relationship is also an important aspect as the people that come to have a meal at ACERSI also enjoy meeting other people in the same condition. It is important to think that for some of the people that go daily to this charity, socialization just happens here and in a very safe and ordained situation.

Project Planning and Execution

Early at the beginning, there were three levels of needs identified:

- Being a charity, one of the basic needs of ACERSI is located in the financial plan. Having liquidity for its obligations and for its common operation was a real need,

and moreover at this time in order to cope with the increased operational costs that the pandemic would bring.
- A second plan was related to the humanitarian mission provided by ACERSI: the provision of food to needy citizens and families. Thus it was also defined that the second level would be the collection of non-perishable food.
- At the third level, taking into account the health, safety and reduction of the spread of Covid-19, it was essential to obtain disinfectant products for employees, material resources and facilities, and PPE's (Personal Protection Equipment) for both employees and users.

We then established objectives and goals, in order to move on to the operational plan (Henley et al. 2011). The campaign had three main objectives: (1) to alert and turn out the community more aware of the growing number of people with food deprivation in Coimbra; (2) to raise awareness, knowledge and confidence around ACERSI (it's worth to remind that charities serve as intermediaries' between donors and beneficiaries, but they also have to being transparent and gain trustworthiness); and (3), the last but not the least, to raise donations. Our goal was to raise awareness of 10% of the population of Coimbra city, being this achieved by the period of 2 months, to raise 5000 euros in donations and to gather as much food, disinfectants and equipment as possible. For the collection of goods, a tangible target was not determined taking into account both the punctual occurrence of the campaign and the moment of confinement that made the logistic part more complex.

After these initial steps, who looked for the support of entities that could leverage our project. As a matter of fact, we did achieve to obtain the support of a regional media partner that guaranteed us a maximum exposure and visibility. The daily newspaper 'As Beiras', a regional newspaper, with a circulation of 12,000 copies and more than 30,000 subscribers, alone could guarantee the fulfilment of the community's awareness objective.

Moreover, we were also able to count with support from other departments of the School.

First Step: The Definition of Teams and Tasks

The cornerstone of any project is the definition of the work team and what each element will do and when. With a total group of 12 people, it was decided that we should be divided into three divisions: Content, Network and Business Management (West and Worthington 2017).

The *Content division*, made up of six elements, was responsible for all the production of communication and creativity for the campaign. They were also in charge of the study and monitoring of "competition", something that is always essential for a plan of this scope to be successful. A list of campaigns and similar entities was prepared to support us for creative decisions and choices. This division was also responsible for contacting individuals who supported the campaign and gave their faces to maximize visibility, recognition and guarantees of transparency and suitability. There was also the responsibility of contacting all the media that could, in parallel with our media partner, disseminate and help with the social impact intended for the campaign. In creative terms, the responsibility fell on the creation of images and videos for the campaign. This was a division relevant to the success of the campaign and could only be developed by those who are in love with the project.

The *Network division* was responsible for managing social networks (Hui et al. 2014). This group was responsible for each publication and stick to it, to study and analyse data on the social networks used to maximize the visibility of the campaign as well as the connection and interaction with the target audience. They should also provide the analysis of traffic and interactions so that the content division could direct its production of videos and photos to the preferences of our audience. They were also responsible for the creation of an additional way to fundraising, creating and managing a parallel digital crowdfunding campaign in partnership with a website (www.ppl.pt).

The *Business Management division* was responsible for contacting the business environment with the aim of directly collecting donations, food and individual protective equipment. Their tasks included mailing and telephone contact, personal contacts and all the logistics for acquiring and delivering the goods collected. After choosing the operational collaborators, a database of contacts was built, establishing relationships with more than 200 companies in the municipality of Coimbra. Moreover, a plan was developed to send personalised emails and follow-up contacts. It was a key division for the success of the campaign and was responsible for the largest share of fundraising in cash.

Second Step: The Choice of the Social Media

Research was made about the most efficacious networks to work with. The main social networks were analysed, as well as their users, hours of higher traffic, preferences, tastes, needs, and so on. Thus, the choice for our project was on Facebook and Instagram. Although most of the times falling attendance figures, Facebook remains the most impactful social network with the greatest use worldwide and nationally. It also has an algorithm easy to understand, and the interaction is facilitated and "user friendly". The use of Instagram, like Facebook, allows for low complexity usage, management and interaction, and it is a growing network with a very high spread of messages among the younger community.

Third Step: The Campaign Launching and Operationalization

The campaign officially began on April 8, 2020 and lasted roughly 2 months, until mid-June 2020.

The *content group* was responsible for the image treatment area and for all image content presented on social networks: photos, newspaper clippings, thanks, videos and other ways of mass communication. The local press turn out to be an important way for reaching potential donors and, so, this group managed to reach almost all regional newspapers ('Diário As Beiras', 'Diário de Coimbra', 'Campeão das Províncias' and 'O Despertar') with articles, reports and interviews and also reaching local radio broadcasts ('RUC' and 'Rádio Regional do Centro'). Among the work developed, the production of a logo for the campaign stands out, and the definition of the 'signature' for the campaign ("Juntos Ficamos Bem"—it means "We Stay Well Together", in English), as well as the creation of templates for publication on the social networks Facebook and Instagram.

The *network group* was responsible for publishing the content developed on the Facebook and Instagram social media pages and was also in charge for creating and managing the campaign's crowdfunding. On Facebook, the page reached 1546 likes and 1555 followers of the so-called "Juntos Ficamos Bem" campaign, on June 17, 2020. Overall, 63 publications were made in the 2 months of work, with 8 videos, and dozens of photos, motivational phrases, messages for calling attention for the need of help, messages of gratitude, and information of contributions. The total reach of publications during the 2 months was 28,619, which generated 4624 impressions and 3127 interactions. On Instagram we had 108 followers and a total of 51 publications, publishing newspaper clippings, 43 photos, thanks, 8 videos and other creative content, of which 8 were videos and images. Regarding crowdfunding, the campaign was on for 1 month reaching a total amount of 689 euros.

The *business group* established contacts in the business network of the central area of the country, in order to raise money for ACERSI. An online survey was made to find out which companies were already doing. After the research was done, an email was sent, with the campaign brochure, to all email addresses. In total 356 corporate emails were sent, and the subsequent telephone contact reached more than 100 companies. After these operation, 17 donations were received from companies and individuals, consisted of foodstuffs and non-foodstuffs: palletizing film, toilet paper and napkins, fabric for social masks, masks, visors, gloves, PPE, olive oil, rice, sweets for meals, oil, potatoes, cabbages and various food items. Some of these products were delivered by us personally at ACERSI, being these deliveries documented through photos, and subsequently sent to donors as well as to the colleagues who managed social networks.

Monitoring

The campaign ran without major obstacles and those who were able to provide some feedback were quite pleased with our creativity, resilience and flexibility. Communication evolved with a certain cadence, and social media followers grew and interactions were also raising.

The written media was attentive to our operations and up-to-date, and collaborated with articles, reports and interviews with some of the entities being part of the campaign. In fact, regional and local newspapers were following the campaign and emphasizing ACERSI, their growing difficulties, increasing demanding conditions and, at the same time, willingness and real ways to help the most deprived. This was one of our goals and was being fully achieved.

One of our biggest joys was the moment ACERSI received a telephone from the Portuguese President of the Republic, which shows that our message reached not only the Coimbra community, but went beyond the borders of our local community and reached the top of the national hierarchy. We could say we were working well in terms of awareness.

The local radio stations followed the written press and gave some prominence to the operations as well. However, they could have been more effective and we encountered some resistance in this channel. In the future, the radio will be a channel to dig more as we believe it is important to be close to the community through the voices that we hear daily. It will be another way of ensuring visibility and awareness for a campaign.

The biggest threat that we had to face was unexpected: group work brings friction, internal obstacles and turbulence. And even if everyone knows that this is normal in working groups, we were far from this "snow monster". As a matter of fact, when we work in order to help others, with a quasi-altruist motivation, no one is expecting heavy discussions around the best way to help. The different perspectives on donations, sometimes extreme perceptions of fairness and ethical procedures, or opposite perceptions of how and when to communicate, caused a big turmoil and washed out the good team atmosphere. Actually, we went through some periods of chaos and wasted hours and days of work, which should be quite useful for the good of the fundraising campaign. Slippages are important to grow and learn and their correction is required but, at some moment, we felt we could not make the situation worse. Working in groups is fruitful and has many advantages, but it is an enabler of greater complexity and problems of which we must be aware and know how to solve. And so there have been some days that we did not manage properly the fundraising campaign due to interpersonal conflicts. These were big challenges for the group and the general mood of the group was not the best until the end. The discussion went on via web meetings and we then compromised to do our best taking into account the solidarity aim everyone was pursuing.

Outcomes

The campaign, as initially planned, had three major objectives: (1) To make the community more aware of the growing number of people with hunger in Coimbra, (2) To create more awareness for ACERSI and (3) To get real results with the campaign for goods and money.

We can say that we have been able to help ACERSI getting more friends and general support.

At this time of pandemic, it was not easy to obtain the needed products and contacts with companies especially because the general volume of sales had declined, and also companies have been on the spot to provide help.

At the end, we managed to raise 5309 euros in cash transfer and various food items, PPE's, disinfectants and protective material, among others. The total value on donated goods was estimated by all partners involved by more than 7000 euros, clearly exceeding the target of 5000 euros. We were unable to accurately measure the impact of the campaign at the level of awareness, but it seems to us that due to the number of interactions on social networks, we fell short of the initially proposed target of 10% of the population (more than 10,000 people were needed).

Conclusions

In operational terms, we had the opportunity to draw important conclusions for the future. We realize how viral a publication on social networks is and how we can create, manage and monitor them. We learned to understand the analytics and algorithms of the social networks being used on this campaign, new ways to raise awareness through social networks, and how important can be for any project to use channels such as the press, radio, television and the so-called "word of mouth", apart from the digital channel. Moreover, we realized the importance of heterogeneous needs of different target segments in terms of social marketing and how to adjust positioning statements and communication tools.

We also concluded that personal contact is always valued by various groups, bringing a hilly valuable commitment for both parts that normally interact and engage in some sort of exchange. We could understand that personal contact brings other results and achievements, being the digital channel also fundamental in order to maximize visibility, recognition, awareness and, of course, fundraising. Moreover, the key to success lies in the equilibrium of tools in use and a permanent monitoring for the right and timely corrections.

However, the biggest and most fulfilling achievement reached by all of us happened with the final report of the campaign showing we have been able to help ACERSI, and made some people's' lives better, improving their quality of life.

As a final conclusion all the work done has been a valuable case of a social marketing campaign increasing the quality of life of our so close fellows.

Discussion Questions

1. What were the best ways to handle a successful social marketing campaign, including a fundraising campaign, like this one? Are there other methods that were forgotten? And taking into account that the main goal was improving people's quality of life overall?
2. Which are the more important groups for the success of a fundraising campaign like this one? Were the tasks the proper ones?
3. Could the team of 12 students be coordinated in other ways? What kind of divisions/departments could be more efficacious for a social marketing campaign?
4. How could the team of students be evaluated? Would it be also admissible to ask people from the charity for their opinion? Should there be a discussion at the end of the project?
5. What are the advantages and drawbacks of a social marketing campaign, including a fundraising campaign, solely via web?

Teaching Notes

Answers to Discussion Questions

1. **What were the best ways to handle a successful social marketing campaign, including a fundraising campaign, like this one? Are there other methods that were forgotten? And taking into account that the main goal was improving people's quality of life overall?**
   The success of a fundraising camping lies very much in a definition of a fundraising potential based on real facts. The students did not develop a plan based on evidence and past similar cases. Also these kinds of campaigns should begin with Brainstorming, with possible strategies. Moreover, the people's quality of life was not studied and the benefactors should have been interviewed at least.
2. **Which are the more important groups for the success of a fundraising campaign like this one? Were the tasks the proper ones?**
   The biggest problem the team had to tackle was the lack of leadership. The team faced various problems that needed almost an iron figure. The team lost energy, time and personal trust because every project needs rules, decisions, and authority, resources that were not well planned.
3. **Could the team of 12 students be coordinated in other ways? What kind of divisions/departments could be more efficacious for a social marketing campaign?**
   Working in groups is fruitful and has many advantages, but it is an enabler of greater complexity and of which we must be aware and know how to solve. And so there have been some days that we did not manage properly the fundraising

campaign due to interpersonal conflicts. Every project with the participation of different people needs a clear division.

4. **How could the team of students be evaluated? Would it be also admissible to ask people from the charity for their opinion? Should there be a discussion at the end of the project?**

   The team of students should have been evaluated by the charity staff. This could be indeed a very good way for self-development and a powerful source of knowledge about each one's capacities. Moreover, the discussion at the end should discuss the most appropriate ideas, messages, and action developed.

5. **What are the advantages and drawbacks of a social marketing campaign, including a fundraising campaign, solely via web?**

   A social marketing campaign via the web can miss a great part of the target audience. Social marketing asks for personal contact with who you want to influence, and using solely the web can damage the more personal messages.

References

Andreasen A (1996) Marketing social change. Jossey-Bass, San Francisco

Henley N, Raffin S, Caemmerer B (2011) The application of marketing principles to a social marketing campaign. Mark Intell Plan 29(7):697–706. https://doi.org/10.1108/02634501111178712

Hui JS, Gerber EM, Gergle D (2014) Understanding and leveraging social networks for crowdfunding: opportunities and challenges. DIS 2014, June 21–25. https://doi.org/10.1145/2598510.2598539. Accessed 24 June 2020

INE (2020) Sobre a pobreza, as desigualdades e a privação material em Portugal, Ano de Edição: 2010. 27 June 2020. Retrieved from https://www.ine.pt/xportal/xmain?xpid=INE&xpgid=ine_publicacoes&PUBLICACOESpub_boui=100334100&PUBLICACOESmodo=2

Kotler P, Roberto EL (1989) Social marketing. The Free Press, New York

PORDATA (2020a) População em risco de pobreza: total e por grupo etário (%). Retrieved from https://www.pordata.pt/Europa/Popula%C3%A7%C3%A3o+em+risco+de+pobreza+total+e+por+grupo+et%C3%A1rio+(percentagem)-2331

PORDATA (2020b) Taxa de risco de pobreza: antes e após transferências sociais. Retrieved from https://www.pordata.pt/Europa/Taxa+de+risco+de+pobreza+antes+e+ap%c3%b3s+transfer%c3%aancias+sociais-1940

West LL, Worthington A (2017) Handbook of research on emerging business models and managerial strategies in the nonprofit sector. IGI Global, USA

Part III
Inclusion and Interpersonal Relationships

Chapter 18
Case Mosca Hnos.: Breaking Gender Stereotypes Through the Game

Patricia Correa, Stefanía Yapor, and Oscar Licandro

Abstract This chapter gives an account of the case study conducted by the Uruguayan company Mosca Hnos., who jointly with the social organization Girls in Tech and the communication agency ALVA, developed a campaign of social marketing encouraging the inclusion and promotion of STEM (Science, Technology, Engineering and Mathematics) skills through educational games for girls. From this perspective, the campaign aims to promote the improvement in women's life quality by involving the objective of changing the perception that people have of their life position vis-à-vis their cultural context and the value systems that prevail in Uruguayan society associated with the feminine or masculine gender. This campaign promoted a change of interests, expectations, future achievements of women, and gender inclusion.

Through social marketing, a change of behavior is promoted in reference to the social problems the communities in which the companies operate face, influencing an improvement in the quality of life of its members, in this case, in relation to gender equality. The campaign was a pioneering experience in Uruguay aimed at modifying the choice of stereotyped purchase of toys for girls or boys, enabling the development of STEM skills in girls and giving them the opportunity to expand their future horizon.

Keywords Social marketing · Gender inclusion · Quality of life · Education · STEM skills

P. Correa (✉) · S. Yapor
Catholic University of Uruguay, Montevideo, Uruguay
e-mail: macorrea@ucu.edu.uy

O. Licandro
CLAEH University, Montevideo, Uruguay
e-mail: olicandr@claeh.edu.uy

M. M. Galan-Ladero, R. G. Rivera (eds.), *Applied Social Marketing and Quality of Life*, Applying Quality of Life Research,
https://doi.org/10.1007/978-3-030-83286-5_18

Introduction

Throughout history, companies have become key actors who are called upon to play a leading role in the search for effective solutions to the social problems faced by humanity. Currently, private companies cannot look aside. Thus, the tendency to work in the development of collaborative networks with the State, organizations and people from civil society, demands the commitment of companies to get involved, identify and develop improvement opportunities in key issues such as poverty, pollution, access to drinking water, gender inequality, gender violence, social conflicts, among others. It is not by chance that different authors have made reference to this topic recently. Thus, Austin and Chu (2006: 3) argue that "*to seek effective solutions, the world's attention has gradually shifted towards private companies, a sector whose ability to execute is acknowledged even by its detractors*". On the other hand, Porter and Kramer (2011) indicate that, from an updated position, companies generate profits when they solve social problems. In this sense, these authors promote the concept of "shared value" as the basis of the development of a business model where important needs are met, social value and economic value are created at the same time, and the business environment of the community in which the company operates is improved.

In this way, companies are constituted as relevant agents to promote the improvement of the quality of life, towards their stakeholders. Regarding their employees, through socially responsible practices, companies can contribute to the quality of life at work by having fair and adequate compensation, implementing healthy and safe working conditions, opportunities for fulfilment, growth and use of human capacity, social inclusion, spaces for interpersonal relations and recognition, balance between the professional and work environment, among other actions (Alves Corrá et al. 2013). These factors promote companies' productivity and competitiveness (El País 2015). In turn, companies can contribute to the quality of life of their stakeholders and the community through social responsibility practices aimed at supporting, proposing and participating in cultural, sports and local-development activities, generating training opportunities for the society, responsibly managing waste, resources used and all the elements that make up the value chain to ensure decent working and production conditions, among others (Alves Corrá et al. 2013).

Companies must take the lead that drives a synergy between business success and the progress of society (Porter and Kramer 2011). Social marketing has contributed to the development of this trend from companies. With a slow but constant evolution, it has gradually been positioned as a discipline of relevance for such purposes. Within this perspective, MOSCA Hnos. S.A. was identified. A Uruguayan company in the stationery and toy sector that, since 2017, has developed a campaign focused on gender equity, whose axis is to stimulate the purchase of toys linked to the STEM disciplines (Science, Technology, Engineering and Mathematics) for girls. These disciplines have made important achievements possible in fields such as health, agriculture, infrastructure, renewable energy and education among others. Nevertheless, according to the report "Cracking the code: girls' and women's education in science, technology, engineering and mathematics (STEM)" made by UNESCO (2017), only 35% of the students registered in careers related to STEM at world-wide level are women. This fact gives an account of the limited opportunities that girls and women may have for their development and quality of life as these careers are increasingly demanded for countries' well-being.

From its strategy, the company offers a value proposal that considers aspects of social relevance and, beyond its core business, aims to encourage reflection on current topics related to childhood, education, the parent-child bond in learning through play, among others. In this way, through its marketing campaigns, it seeks to convey a message that stimulates a change in behavior in adults responsible for the education of children and adolescents.

The research focused on identifying and describing "inspiring practices" of the company Mosca Hnos. that contribute to the use of social marketing and to the promotion of gender stereotypes deconstruction.

Based on the general objective set, the specific objectives were defined:

1. Get to know and describe the proposal of Mosca Hnos. as an inspiring practice of social marketing.
2. Identify the role of the different actors who participated in the development of the campaign.
3. Analyze the different variables of the marketing mix that were at stake in the campaign.
4. Analyze the impacts of the campaign on the parties involved and their potential contribution, and how it can contribute to improve their quality of life.

The research was within the framework of the Research Program on Corporate Social Responsibility of the Catholic University of Uruguay. The methodological design developed is exploratory-descriptive in nature for its objectives, and focused on the perspective of three universes: (1) the company, (2) the communication agency and (3) the organization. A qualitative approach was developed, where the technique used was the semi-structured interview, and it was applied to the following target population: (a) Mosca's General Manager, (b) company sellers, (c) Director of the communication agency ALVA and (d) one of the social organization Girls in Tech (GIT)'s directors for Uruguay. The field work was carried out in the period August-October 2019. Also, secondary information regarding several aspects of the advertising campaign and the organization GIT was used.

Case Study Development

A Look at the Social Cause

Gender differences in participation in STEM education to the detriment of girls begin at an early stage in cares, early childhood education, and in games related to science and math. This is most evident in the early years of secondary education (when specialization begins and students decide which subjects to study) and sharpens as the educational level increases (e.g. in terms of master's and doctorates), in research and professional careers (UNESCO 2017).

The 2030 Agenda for Sustainable Development adopted by the United Nations General Assembly in 2015 indicates the relevant role of STEM areas and education on them, as well as the importance of gender equality (in Sustainable Development Goals 4 and 5) as drivers that can provide students with the knowledge, skills, attitudes and behaviors needed to achieve inclusive and sustainable societies.

Girls' interest, commitment and performance on STEM disciplines may be affected if they are immersed in a family environment that perpetuates gender stereotypes in terms of considering that "boys are better at math and science than girls" and that "science and engineering are male careers" and that treat girls and boys unequally.

On the contrary, from early childhood, families and schools can stimulate the development of spatial, linguistic and numerical skills in girls through playful learning, as it has been proved that access to resources for scientific experiments is associated with their performance and interest in science (UNESCO 2017). Girls' exposure to STEM experiences can also be increased through role-playing games that allow approaching other women who work on and/or teach these disciplines, programs that aim to empower, motivate and encourage girls to pursue these careers, among others.

Situation of Women and STEM Disciplines in Uruguay

As in the international level, women are also underrepresented in STEM areas. At the educational level, women graduate mainly from careers linked to social, human and health sciences, while a much smaller percentage do so from basic sciences and technologies. Women studying ICT (Information and Communication Technologies) at university are below 20% (MIMCIT 2018). In the workplace, there is also a predominance of 83.6% of males in STEM occupations (Uruguay Transforma 2019).

In Uruguay, a number of actors are committed to achieving gender equality. In 2016, the Inter-Agency Panel Women in Science, Innovation and Technology (MIMCIT) emerged with the aim of strengthening and proposing public policies for scientific and technological development and innovation with a gender focus (CUTI 2019). It is a panel composed of various actors related to education, research, ministries and government agencies, business sector, among others. On the other hand, the "National Strategy for Gender Equality" proposes the promotion of cultural transformation, stereotypes deconstruction and the advancement of the normative framework towards gender equality (Presidency 2018). In turn, the "National Development Strategy 2050", which lays the foundations for Uruguay to move towards sustainable development, considers gender as one of its three cross-cutting axes and as key to moving the country's economic and social development forward (OPP 2016).

A Different Perspective: Quality of Life

Quality of life contributes to the study of people's well-being, from a physical and psychological perspective, relating material needs with socio-affective needs and integrating psychological and social measurements of perception and evaluation of the subjects' own experiences (Casas 1996).

The effect of social relations and relations with the environment is mediated by the particular view of each subject, that is, the way in which each one interprets their context and situation, so this view is the key that determines their quality of life (Patrick et al. 2002). Casas gives these perceptions and evaluation of the subjects' experiences as much or even more value than to the material or objective conditions defined by the experts as adequate (Casas 1996; in Tonon 2008).

In this sense, the cultural messages and stereotypes that girls may perceive from an early stage can affect their self-perception of what society expects from them, what they consider they can or should do at the job level in terms of choosing a career linked to STEM disciplines or not, etc. A girl at 4 years old already learns to adjust her behavior according to the stereotypes she is internalizing (Lippa 2005). This is linked to Ferris's (2006) statement about the forces that produce quality of life. In this case, the endogenous force, linked to girls' mental, emotional and physiological living conditions, can be influenced by exogenous force in terms of social influence and cultural patterns on the gender stereotypes present.

The philosophy of marketing oriented to quality of life should improve clients' well-being, but also preserve the well-being of other stakeholders and society (Alves and Vázquez 2013: 4). Although the bibliography indicates the contribution made by women working in STEM disciplines to improving the quality of life in society, in terms of, for example, advances in the prevention of cholera and cancer, the expansion of the understanding of brain development and stem cells, among other discoveries (UNESCO 2017), no specific studies have been found that address the promotion of STEM skills in girls, articulating the perspective of social marketing with that of quality of life.

In this sense, this case is a contribution to the approach to this subject, where a gap has been found to investigate. It can be seen how MOSCA jointly with GIT and ALVA seek to generate a change of attitude and behavior that improves girls and women's quality of life providing information on the importance of their participation in STEM disciplines, and how the choice of toys from childhood can be a factor that influences their student and career path to obtain better opportunities and contribute to the progress of society. This differs from the toy sales strategy of other competing companies that perpetuate gender stereotypes. It is considered that this campaign can have an impact on improving the society's quality of life and on achieving the Sustainable Development Goals, in terms of gender equality.

The Company

MOSCA Hnos. is a Uruguayan company born in 1888, working on the stationery and toy sector. Currently, it employs more than 300 people focused on serving and advising its clients as a service premise. The company has 15 stores, an online sales service (www.mosca.uy), and a shopping center for corporate clients: Mosca Office. Its philosophy includes the commitment to offer practical solutions aimed at accompanying playful, intellectual and cultural development at all stages of people's development. Mosca Hnos. takes on the constant challenge of updating, innovating and being a permanent reference in the life of the Uruguayan society.

Every year, it reviews its value proposal integrating relevant topics from the community. In this sense, it has a strong component of innovation in the selection of its products for the "childhood" segment, integrating its concern for issues such as children and adolescents' consumption and appropriate use of technology to the commercial trend. From this place, MOSCA Hnos. identified the worldwide trend of the interest of parents and academia on giving more participation to girls in games related to hard disciplines such as science, technology, engineering and mathematics, where there is a male predominance. In 2017, the company took on the mission to encourage girls to participate in this type of games from early childhood, promoting gender inclusion from different disciplines and promoting their continuity in secondary and tertiary education.

The Social Organization

Girls in Tech (GIT) is a nonprofit organization focused on strengthening the commitment, training and empowerment of women in technology, as seen in their name: "Girls in Technology". It was born in San Francisco (United States) and its work is currently present in over 50 "localities" in different parts of Asia, Europe, Africa, Australia and South America.

It arrived at Uruguay in 2016, from the work of a group of women who voluntarily make their time, ideas and potential available, and work on program projects that arise in the United States, adapting them to local reality or incorporating other projects that can strengthen work in that social cause. In Uruguay, according to surveys carried out by the Uruguayan Chamber of Information Technology, the fact that women are encouraged to carry out certain soft-skills jobs, but not to study or work in the field of STEM sciences was detected as a social problem. For this reason, GIT Uruguay decided to work on projects that stimulate those skills related to technology in girls from an early age. As one of the interviewed directors of GIT Uruguay expressed, the problem "*is much more complex than just education, right? It has to do with play, with culture and family, there are multiple dimensions, but that is where there is an opportunity to break certain paradigms down*". Among the activities carried out by GIT Uruguay is the Campaign "*STEM Toys: I learn by playing*" ["*Juguetes STEM: Aprendo jugando*", in Spanish] developed jointly with MOSCA and ALVA.

The Communication Agency ALVA

It is not by chance that this project has been promoted and proposed by the agency ALVA, since its organizational purpose has a strong orientation towards social marketing. ALVA is an independent communication agency from Uruguay, founded in 2014, and made up of collaborators from different disciplines. It defines itself as "*an independent, innovative and responsible communication agency*" (ALVA 2019). As part of its strategic objectives, it comprises four dimensions, which determine its competitive advantage: advertising, sustainability, gender, and innovation. Since 2017, ALVA has been the management support team of UN Women and they are the founders of the "Gender Observatory on Advertising" in Uruguay, which, as expressed by the director of ALVA, "*inspired by social sustainability... we are in an advertising industry immersed in a generation of culture with a gender vision of a healthier society regarding stereotypes and inclusion*".

The Campaign

Since the 2nd semester of 2017, MOSCA Hnos. has developed its marketing strategy aimed at achieving a different position from the competitors, with creativity and innovation, but above all, taking the institutional philosophy of having a look towards the needs of the community as a reference and committing to it from a social perspective. So, the proposal to work on a campaign for Children's Day arises from ALVA, its communication agency, promoting STEM toys in order for girls to join the "hard" disciplines—such as Science, Technology, Engineering and Mathematics—from early childhood, thus promoting gender inclusion. ALVA visualized the opportunity to generate a social differential and new behaviors through cultural change, through the Children's Day brief, by uniting the reference in the toy sector in Uruguay with the GIT organization, specialized in training and empowerment of women in technology. The three parties joined forces and developed the STEM campaign, identifying the opportunity to create a new category with exclusive spaces for toys that promote STEM skills with the aim of breaking gender stereotypes down from play.

The **main objective** of the campaign was including and promoting STEM skills in girls; to achieve a change in behavior from educational play promoting that from early childhood they incorporate STEM skills, since in Uruguay there are three men for every woman in the STEM fields. In this sense, it is sought that adults responsible for children promote the development of these skills in girls too from their role as educators. The final objective is to have an impact on the choice of STEM-related areas in secondary and higher education made by women based on early childhood experience. On the other hand, generating reflection on these issues was also an implicit purpose of the campaign; in some way, communication compromises the questioning of gender equality.

The STEM space brings together in a single place (shelf within each of the Mosca Hnos. stores) games and toys that promote the development of these skills, giving both boys and girls the opportunity to expand their horizon in the future. It is made up of about 200 toys, among which there are games of robotics, laboratory, anatomy, assembling and disassembling pieces, among others.

The **target audience** of the campaign were adults, especially women from 30 to 50 years old in their category of shoppers, main buyers in this season, and children from 5 to 12 years old in their category of consumers, level ABC1 + C2.[1]

The campaign was called "*Playing for a better future*" ["*Jugar para un mejor futuro*", in Spanish] and the communication was focused on conveying the following message: "*playing can be the key for a better world*", "*#I learn STEM by playing*" ["*#Jugar puede ser la clave para un mundo mejor*" and "*#jugando aprendo S*TEM", in Spanish].

Campaign management initially included a process of awareness by the work team. MOSCA Hnos. knew its products, its suppliers, and the market; the social organization was the one who had the knowledge of how to approach this subject jointly with the agency's communication work. Mosca Hnos's General Manager defines the role of GIT in the campaign as the leading organization and specialist in the subject of the participation of girls in STEM disciplines in Uruguay. In this way, GIT and the agency provided training to the staff of MOSCA Hnos. on gender and the importance of not naturalizing stereotypes constructed at a social level on this subject, with the aim of raising awareness in the actors involved. GIT worked with the purchases, marketing and sales team, involving the sales managers of the stores, sharing the knowledge learned with the rest of the staff. Then, it was the turn for product selection, for which GIT carried out a curatorship identifying which ones could be part of the STEM gondola and which ones could not, from the experiential-learning approach based on the contributions of educational references such as Montessori and Naranjo. They selected the products, and grouped and identified them with a STEM badge. Sales staff also participated in this process.

The **external communication** of the campaign was carried out through all the channels developed by the company, both online and offline, covering all the dimensions of the promotional mix. Public relations actions were carried out, with press releases for the campaign launch event, in which the Minister of Industry, Energy and Mining—GIT's godmother—, and the director of Ingenio—the Technological Laboratory of Uruguay's incubator—participated, two key references for

[1]Level ABC1 + C2: It refers to the upper and middle levels of the social strata, according to the demographic and socio-economic profile of society, through which households are classified according to their consumption capacity and, in this way, the population is segmented and characterized in relation to their income levels.

the campaign, one on her role as a female engineer and the other as a precursor of innovation. Simultaneously, digital content was launched explaining the capabilities that different games promote, and activations were carried out in events for girls and boys to experience them.

Impacts of the Campaign

For the Company

Both the General Manager of the company, and the Director of GIT and the Director of the agency ALVA agree on the fact that, from the campaign, there was an increase in sales of that category of toys—exceeding the proposed objectives—which continued to be verified in relation to the level it had prior to its implementation. This increase was 300% in the first year of its launch, according to data provided by the company. As stated by its General Manager: "*it is clear that prior to launch,* [STEM toys] *had almost no participation on sale and once we developed the category it became a relevant family of products within the toy store*". This represents a contribution to the social cause of achieving equal access to STEM disciplines for girls, where the company puts into practice its role as an agent of social change in an issue other companies in the sector are not addressing, while benefiting from increased sales. Currently, as its General Manager highlighted, the STEM gondola is already part of the company's proposal, which is why in each store it has become a sector that has gradually incorporated more toys and that has reinforced the purchase of some others.

For Society

Although MOSCA Hnos. has measured the impact in relation to the level of sales, so far, there has not been a survey linked to the public's reaction to the campaign, nor at the level of the stores in the direct approach of sellers with the customer, nor through social networks measuring their response to the advertising pieces generated.

At the beginning of the campaign, according to the testimony of the sellers, customers asked what STEM is, and currently, through advice, some decide to buy these toys as presents and break down with gender stereotypes; while others, even if they are considering buying them, keep those stereotypes incorporated (mainly in not accepting a pink packaging for boys or in giving away certain types of toys that "are associated with girls"). This may lead to the reflection that while this campaign is taking an important first step (which had not previously been taken) in the domestic market regarding the participation and inclusion of girls in STEM disciplines through play, it is necessary to work at the society level to overcome these gender stereotypes and continue to improve girls and women's quality of life in Uruguay.

For Employees

The sellers interviewed affirmed to support the social cause of the campaign, promote, offer customers such toys in the first instance, and explain that they foster skills for children. They add that they would like to have more information so they can advise customers more. This last point in the planning between the company and GIT is addressed for the next stages of the campaign, focused on enhancing their communication at the internal level of the company (with a "STEM Decalogue" so that staff has more information, is sensitized and can transmit to customers), and at the external level with events that bring girls closer to women that are references in these disciplines.

For the Social Organization Involved

From this campaign, GIT has managed to have a partner in the business field that allows it to show society the importance of this social cause through a leading toy shop in the country, and that contributes to achieving equal access and participation of girls in STEM and improving their quality of life by having and perceiving that they may have greater possibilities in their personal and professional development. This is the beginning of what can be an alliance that may enhance its impact by continuing to work together.

For the Agency

For the agency it also represented an opportunity to promote a social cause in which they believe and to strengthen work towards it through the bond they developed by linking the company MOSCA Hnos. with GIT. It is one of the works that they liked the most, of which they are proud when they see that the STEM gondola is still in the toy shop, as indicated by its Director. In addition, thanks to this campaign, the agency won a Golden Bell ["Campana de Oro", in Spanish], an award given to the best advertising pieces of the year in Uruguay.

Conclusions

This case study identified and analyzed the practices developed by the company MOSCA Hnos. as a contribution to social marketing and the promotion of the deconstruction of gender stereotypes, through the generation of a "STEM space". From that place, it is concluded that the company was a pioneer in encouraging the participation of girls in this type of games from early childhood, which may be a potential to promote gender inclusion in different disciplines and promote its continuity at higher levels of education and job placement. The campaign was also aimed at changing the choice of purchasing stereotypical toys for girls or boys, enabling the development of STEM skills and giving them the opportunity to broaden their horizon to the future and a better quality of life.

The strategic alliance between the actors involved in the campaign (MOSCA Hnos. as a market leader in the toy sector; GIT as the leading social organization in Uruguay on the subject of women inclusion in STEM disciplines; and ALVA as a communication agency whose pillars are sustainability, gender and innovation), promoted the generation of a positive externality to the extent that promoted reflection on breaking down stereotypes and encouraging a change in behavior.

The management of the campaign is part of the four dimensions of social marketing (Hasting and Domegan 2014). First, it integrates the *customer* dimension, as it identifies the needs, aspirations, values and priorities of the target audience. Second, it has a *creative and innovative* dimension, through which the components of a marketing integrated communication were developed. It then comprises the *collective dimension,* as it recognizes the social problem in the Uruguayan community, implementing an alternative that contributes to its mitigation. Finally, the *competitive dimension*, with a relative scope, insofar as, although different price levels were included in the selection of products, their average does not include all the socio-economic levels, an aspect that is relevant for social marketing oriented to quality of life.

The impacts of the campaign are visualized towards the actors involved. On the one hand, for the company, it allowed the development of an innovative and permanent proposal throughout its commercial chain, integrating the interests of its clients, the community due to the social problem, and its staff. The impact measured was the sales indicator, far exceeding the stated goal. On the other hand, for both GIT and ALVA, it represented an opportunity to continue working and spreading the social cause in the community. For society, a space for questioning the problem of gender stereotypes was generated, finding as a weakness the fact that there is no evaluation from the client's perspective, necessary to know how this campaign has managed (or not) to influence its quality of life. This impact could be measured with the various indicators that have been developed from the quality of life perspective (e.g. see Tonon 2016). What kind of toys do MOSCA customers choose when deciding on a gift for a girl? And for a boy? How does society see this campaign? These are just a few questions that appear. Although its impact is not measured, it is considered a very important contribution to promote a change that bets on gender equality and the improvement of quality of life.

In this sense, aspects are identified that could enhance the achievement of a greater scope and impact of the results, such as the need to generate different approaches to the customer community, evaluating their perception of the campaign, as well as new inputs regarding needs, preferences and interests to work in the future. In addition, developing indicators is recommended in order to monitor, evaluate and generate new action plans. Strengthening the training of the staff involved in the campaign in order to achieve greater efficiency in customer awareness and communication is also considered important.

Regarding the research, it is relevant to point out that it has the methodological limitation of not considering representativeness in the number of sellers interviewed, as well as on the impact of the campaign on customers.

Finally, the case study shows the global trend towards social marketing, posing the challenge of strengthening the progress made and solving the weaknesses of this discipline, seeking sustainable effects for the community.

Discussion Questions

Question 1. What do you think drives companies to join this type of campaign?
Question 2. What factors do you think limited other companies in the Uruguayan market to join this campaign?
Question 3. What is your opinion on the interaction of the three actors of the campaign? What strengths and weaknesses are seen?

Teaching Notes

Question 1. ***What do you think drives companies to join this type of campaign?***

A space for reflection is opened regarding the role of companies as agents of change and regarding the fact that, if they wish to be sustainable, they cannot limit themselves only to obtaining benefits, but also be responsible for their negative impact and generate positive impact. In this sense, they can commit themselves to contribute to the development of opportunities for improvement in social problems, thinking of generating a win-win relationship between the parties involved by promoting behavioral change focused on achieving gender equality, necessary for the social and economic development of the countries. Gender equality allows companies to benefit by strengthening their work environment, better taking advantage of the talents of their staff and increasing their commitment and predisposition to collaborate in improvement and quality processes.

Question 2. ***What factors do you think limited other companies in the Uruguayan market to join this campaign?***

From the point of view of the social organization GIT, MOSCA Hnos. is the only company in the market that has the right toys to promote STEM skills in girls and boys. This is linked, for example, with the decisions about the products to be imported, with the knowledge and commitment towards this social cause and with the capacity of in-house toy production. The Director of GIT stated that "*it would be a dream for us to produce a line of STEM toys*", but they have not yet been able to generate an alliance with a company that carries out this purpose, so an opportunity opens up to continue supporting and spreading the participation of girls in STEM skills from childhood, as well as a market opportunity could be developed.

Question 3. ***What is your opinion on the interaction of the three actors of the campaign? What strengths and weaknesses are seen?***

It is necessary to visualize the contribution of each party involved: knowledge, experience, resources that are extremely valuable and different and allow creating the necessary synergy and achieving a greater result than each of the parties would have achieved if they had proposed to develop this campaign only with their means. Opening the debate to analyze the highlights of the campaign, the limitations framed in social marketing practices and what factors are considered necessary to sustain this joint work over time is intended.

References

ALVA (2019) Una agencia de comunicación independiente, innovadora y responsable. https://www.alva.com.uy/. Accessed 12 Oct 2019

Alves Corrêa D, Cirera Oswaldo Y, Carlos Giuliani A (2013) Vida con Calidad y Calidad de Vida en el Trabajo. Invenio 16(30):145–163

Alves H, Vázquez JL (eds) (2013) Best practices in marketing and their impact on quality of life. Applied Research in Quality of Life. Springer Netherlands, Dordrecht

Austin J, Chu M (2006) La empresa privada y los sectores de bajos ingresos. Rev Harv Rev Latin Am 6(1):3–5

Casas F (1996) Bienestar social. Una introducción psicosociológica. PPU, Barcelona

CUTI (2019) Mesa Interinstitucional Mujeres en Ciencia, Innovación y Tecnología. Cámara Uruguaya de Tecnologías de la Información. Industria TICs, 06/08/2019

El País (2015) Calidad de vida y competitividad van de la mano en la empresa. El País, Empresas, 03/08/2015

Ferris A (2006) A theory of the social structure and the quality of life. Appl Res Qual Life 1 (1):117–123

Hastings G, Domegan C (2014) Social marketing: from tunes to symphonies, 2nd edn. https://doi.org/10.4324/9780203380925

Lippa RA (2005) Gender, nature and nurture, 2nd edn. Lawrence Erlbaum Associates, Mahwah, NJ

MIMCIT (2018) Claves para el desarrollo: más mujeres en ciencia, tecnología, ingeniería y matemáticas (STEM). Mesa Interinstitucional Mujeres en Ciencia, Innovación y Tecnología. https://www.anii.org.uy/upcms/files/listado-documentos/documentos/doc-stem-1-.pdf. Accessed 12 Oct 2019

OPP (2016) Sobre los Sistemas de Género. Oficina de Planeamiento y Presupuesto, Presidencia de la República Oriental del Uruguay, 02/01/2016

Patrick D, Edwards T, Topolski T, Walwick J (2002) Youth quality of life: a new measure incorporating the voices of adolescents. QOL Newsl 28:7

Porter M, Kramer M (2011) Valor Compartido. Cómo reinventar el capitalismo y crear una oleada de innovación y crecimiento. Harv Bus Rev (Edición América Latina) 89(1):33–49

Tonon G (2008) Investigar la calidad de vida en Argentina. Universidad Nacional Lomas de Zamora. Rev Psicodebate Psicol Cul Soc 8:141–151

Tonon G (ed) (2016) Indicators of quality of life in Latin America. Appl Res Qual Life 13:255–256
UNESCO (2017) Descifrar las claves: la educación de las niñas y las mujeres en ciencias, tecnología, ingeniería y matemáticas. https://unesdoc.unesco.org/ark:/48223/pf0000366649. Accessed 15 Sept 2019
Uruguay Presidencia (2018) Consejo Nacional de Género presentará estrategia para la igualdad de género con perspectiva 2030. Uruguay Presidencia. Compromiso, 06/03/2018
Uruguay Transforma (2019) Mujeres y niñas en ciencia, tecnología e innovación. Sistema Nacional de Transformación Productiva y Competitividad, 25/04/2019

Chapter 19
Quality of Life Marketing, Innovation and Change Management: The Rasti Robotics and Education Team

M. Elena Ordóñez y Revuelta, Daniela Nicole Rodríguez Mincey, Jazmín Nogaró, and Reynaldo G. Rivera

Abstract "ERRE"'(Equipo Rasti de Robótica y Educación, or Rasti Robotics and Education Team, in English) is an example of good practice in terms of innovation, social marketing and development through networking processes between the corporate world and education system. The proposed case focuses on quality of life improvement for school communities and families, through change management based on digital advances.

Rasti is an Argentine company specialized in toy brick production. In 2019, the ERRE department was created to sell kits and services for education, in order to teach educational robotics and create digital opportunities for students. However, the 2020 SARS-CoV-2 pandemic forced ERRE to redesign and implement a new communication and relationship management strategy. This case study shares innovation, communication and marketing practices to show how the company remained resilient through complexity via a social marketing strategy which improved teachers and student's quality of life during mandatory lockdown.

Keywords Social marketing · Education and innovation · Quality of life · Digitization and robotics · Networking · Pandemic and lockdown

---

M. E. Ordóñez y Revuelta
Universidad Empresarial Siglo 21, Cordoba, Argentina
e-mail: maria.ordonez@ues21.edu.ar

D. N. Rodríguez Mincey · J. Nogaró · R. G. Rivera (✉)
Austral University, Buenos Aires, Argentina
e-mail: dnrodriguezmincey@mail.austral.edu.ar; jnogaro@mail.austral.edu.ar; rrivera@austral.edu.ar

M. M. Galan-Ladero, R. G. Rivera (eds.), *Applied Social Marketing and Quality of Life*, Applying Quality of Life Research,
https://doi.org/10.1007/978-3-030-83286-5_19

Introduction

Educational robotics is defined as a multidisciplinary and meaningful learning environment: a tool by which children, teenagers and adults may learn to build simple or complex buildings and machines. The process includes planning, theory, strategy, practice and pedagogical curricula; all from a perspective of "genuine digital inclusion" (Maggio 2012). In recent years, there have been many countries—including Argentina—which have included digital education, programming and robotics training in their curricular content, involving Elementary through High School level students. From a pedagogical point of view, educational robotics is a strategy and practice that aims to develop students' abilities to develop their curiosity and motor skills during the learning process, while simultaneously preparing them for adequate proficiency in Information and Communication Technologies (Barrera Lombana 2015). According to Karaman and Giuriati (2019), educational robotics is an inclusive practice that completely transforms teaching/learning methods from within the classroom, as it blends a variety of topics spanning various academic disciplines, their ecosystems, roles, expectations, particularities and abilities related to mechanics, design, electronics, collaborative work structures, creativity and imagination. Collaborative work through trial and error is one of the main methods used by educational robotics to learn *with* others, while attempting to solve problems *for* others.

Tonon claims that "quality of life" is the perception of each individual on their position in life, amid their own cultural context and value system, related to their specific expectations, interests and achievements (2015). Robotics has proven to be an excellent tool when trying to harness students' interactions between the physical and virtual world, and to ease socialization so that the entire educational community can also get involved in the experience. It generates a high level of motivation in students and promotes curiosity, analysis and experimentation. Countless benefits converge in this method of project-based learning, such as the posing of challenges, teamwork and learning from mistakes, which favor students' personal independence. From this view, educational robotics is a fundamental instrument of empowerment and development that could improve today's youth's quality of life.

Case Development

Lockdown and the Digital Gap

During 2020, Argentines became confined to their homes due to the SARS-CoV-2 pandemic, giving rise to a social, personal and psychological experience like never before. The situation was especially unprecedented for Argentina, as the federal government ordered mandatory household confinement from March through November. Faced with this new reality, digitization was crucial in the education system's efforts of facing deep socio-cultural change, since digital tools immediately allowed for alternative communication methods. Research indicates that the pandemic practically forced the digitization of education, but widened the digital gap and provoked the isolation of particular groups of students and education professionals (Fernández et al. 2020; Murillo et al. 2020). Considering these circumstances, Rasti was able to transform the lockdown into an opportunity to reduce the digital divide and promote educational transformation through a social marketing strategy for quality of life.

From Blocks to Robots

Rasti was created in 1968 with pedagogical principles in mind: the goal was to allow children to intuitively experiment with scientific and mechanical principles through their toys, by offering mechanical pieces such as bricks, pulleys, gears and motors. Until 2018, Rasti almost exclusively produced and sold these toys. It was in that year when two robotics and educational management experts—Juan Manuel Zamora and Gastón Jeger—presented the option of jointly developing a differential value proposition for educational robotics with Rasti, to be subsequently offered in the education market.

The company soon discovered that the educational robotics market involved different products, services, communication channels and strategies than what they were accustomed to in the regular toy market. For this reason, the Rasti Robotics and Education Team (Equipo Rasti de Robótica y Educación—ERRE) was created, composed by an interdisciplinary work team of both external professional partners and the Rasti company, with the aim of developing an attractive, innovative and "fun" proposal to bring students closer to the new technological paradigm. Programmers, pedagogical consultants, industrial designers, an electronic engineer, and a copywriter were brought into the team, with the purpose of designing and implementing educational robotics kits that worked both from within the classroom as well outside of it, such as in extracurricular classes. ERRE developed robotics kits built with durable equipment and open-source software, along with a pedagogical plan that could be easily articulated with the regular curricular contents of Elementary through High School levels, a training program for teachers adjusted to schools' needs, and an *ad-hoc* advising branch. One of the key axes of Rasti's proposal was based on instructing school faculty into managing innovative learning environments that host critical hands-on thinking for the development of digital education.

ERRE: Why Robotics?

From a global perspective, the spread of Information and Communication Technologies (ICTs) is part of the United Nations' 2030 Agenda for Sustainable

Development (2015). In the United States, organizations such as the US National Research Council and the National Science Foundation consider science, technology, engineering and mathematics as fundamental disciplines for technologically advanced societies (also known as the STEM movement), and addresses the concern to include these subjects in a more integrated school curriculum. In Spain, programming and robotics are already curricular subjects in some autonomous communities. France also joins the group of countries that have introduced programming into their curriculum. As of 2015, the Argentine Federal Council of Education declared that technological education is of strategic importance to the National Educational System. For this reason, the National Ministry of Education proposed learning objectives for compulsory programming and robotics education to lay the path towards its formal inclusion in Argentine schools, which were later regulated in 2018 as a priority learning focus. Given this outlook and opportunity, Rasti identified that the skills they could instill through ERRE would enhance the quality of life of students at an early age by exposing them to disciplines that they could come into contact with later in adulthood.

From Marketing as Exchange to Social Marketing for Quality of Life

Value creation is marketing's main objective, through the exchange of valuable goods and/or services between parties (Lee and Kotler 2015). From this point of view, from 2019 ERRE sought to generate value by teaching technological skills and creating a community of institutions oriented towards inclusive education for the twenty-first century.

Before ERRE, Rasti's sales channel was focused on toy wholesalers (large distributors), medium-sized toy stores or chains and department stores such as local companies Coppel or Falabella. Their communication strategy considers both adults, who are decision makers of the purchase, and children, who influence and use the acquired product. As Daniel Dimare (Rasti's Director of Marketing and Communication) explains: "*We have to consider both the young and the old when we communicate*".

In 2019, ERRE designed and implemented a new communication and marketing strategy, the components of which can be seen in Table 19.1, showcasing the differences between the business units. ERRE's marketing strategy involved:

- Designing products for student's skill development in the long-term, and training services for a leap in the educational community's technological progress.
- Prices defined to facilitate access of all educational communities into the program.
- Channels that would also include non-conventional sectors such as schools, government ministries and educational centers.

Table 19.1 Rasti business lines

Business Line	Brand Product	Purchase decider and age target	Sales channel Consumer
Toys	**Bimbi** Toys for babies	**Decision-maker** Adult **Target** 0 a 24 month-olds	**Sales channel** Toymaker channels Wholesale distributors Retail stores (Coppel and Falabella) Non-exclusive sellers **Consumer** Children Adults and families
	Blocky Large themed blocks for simple assembly.	**Decision-maker** Adult **Target** 3 to 6 year-olds	
	Rasti Themed or unthemed smaller blocks for complex assembly	**Decision-maker** Adult **Target** Mixed between children and adults	
ERRE robotics	**IKO, OKI 1** and **OKI2** Programming and robotics kits that include: Portable case with building equipment Educational online platform Rastiblock (programming system) and mobile app Teacher training workshops Access to the ERRE educational community	**Decision-maker** School directors Legal representatives or owners Teachers Ministerial authorities (to reach public and rural schools) **Target** 3 to 17 year old students, teachers.	**Sales channel** Educational system Reference and exclusive distributor An online store exclusive to schools in the Rasti community (for expansion or replacement of parts) **Consumer** Schools and other educational institutions

Source: Authors' own elaboration

- Assembly of an exclusive network of mentors knowledgeable in education to be the institutional and commercial link between ERRE and schools.

Using Kotler and Keller's 4Ps of Marketing as a guide, "people, processes, programs and performance" (2012), ERRE implemented a marketing mix oriented by social objectives. The company set up a team of interdisciplinary professionals (marketing mix component: people) as part of a new business unit that took advantage of Rasti's previous experience and educational robotics (processes), which included services such as robotics kits, pedagogical programs, training and free software (programs), for achieving financial and and sociocultural performance indicators. A shift towards social marketing implied the implementation of a new corporate business model, focused on social innovation, that would add to the current supply of toys.

The ERRE value proposition aimed to adapt to the unequal reality of schools in Argentina, in the most comprehensive and flexible way possible. A year after ERRE launched, over 130 schools were incorporated into the "ERRE Community", 80% located in the Province of Buenos Aires, and 20% in other provinces, such as Córdoba and Santa Fe. Internationally, four educational centers were located in Ecuador and another two in Uruguay. 2019's second semester and January and February of 2020 were very active months, focused on pedagogical advising and teacher oriented workshops in programming and robotics, preparing for the 2020 academic year that would begin in March. Most schools in the ERRE community took part in at least a few training workshops led by educational robotics specialists, 100% of which were held in person until February 2020. Each program was adapted and planned based on the faculty's level of prior knowledge on each subject, and aimed to form collaborative work teams with a "Project-Based Learning" (PBL) approach, with the possibility of applying robotics and programming to exercises with social impact.

Lockdown's New Challenges

The SARS-CoV-2 pandemic meant that schools and other training centers had to create and design new communication alternatives between teachers and students. However, by mid-April 2020, educational institutions that provided blended learning formats (face-to-face and online) were a minority. When the mandatory lockdown decreed by the national government began, private and public educational institutions at all levels had to reinvent themselves and implement various tools such as e-learning platforms, virtual classrooms, online messaging systems, among others, and shift class contents to an online format. The lockdown also led ERRE into rethinking, analyzing and creating new ways to articulate familiarity between schools and new ICT tools. For this, Rasti iterated over its previous plan to account for an innovative course of action, to be implemented over the following months.

The first action carried out in April was the arrangement of focus group styled virtual meetings with Technology or Robotics teachers in the ERRE Community. These aimed to identify needs that teachers were having in different schools, and to decide how Rasti could collaborate and support them with new initiatives and training activities. It was then possible to verify that schools were lacking simple materials and tools for the implementation of ICT programs.

Second, a web page was created on Rasti's site, "#YoMeQuedoEnCasa" (I Stay at Home), under the category #RastiEduca (Rasti for Education) with open and free content so teachers, students and families could access and use pedagogical and recreational materials related to programming and robotics. ERRE opened its services to the community with themes such as: "Install RastiBlock software for free", "Computational Thinking from home"; "Dare to put these great ideas together with Rasti!"; "See what you can do with Rasti Robotics Kits"; among others. Activities for the development of computational thinking from home were added to the contents previously developed by ERRE. The company launched the following marketing campaign on Facebook in March:

"#StayAtHome with #Rasti: Quarantine invites us to stay at home ... It may be difficult to stay entertained at home, but we have the solution. #BuildWithRasti Upload or share everything that you're building so that we inspire each other to make new constructions with our favorite building blocks: Rasti".

As can be seen in Fig. 19.1, the families responded positively.

The third action of collaborative innovation was the creation of a webinar cycle for educators. Conferences were organized with prestigious partners such as IBM and Google, addressing interests of the educational field. Between April and July 2020, 14 open and free webinars were held on topics such as: home schooling, neurosciences, psychology, artificial intelligence, future jobs and public speaking, among others. A total of 4500 educators, academic experts and professionals from international corporations participated, in order to share knowledge, tools and good practices that could enrich educational skills. They were hosted by various national universities such as the Universidad del Salvador, Universidad FASTA, and Universidad Siglo 21 and the Association of Private Schools of the Province of Buenos Aires.

Fourth was a set of paid online workshops for school faculty on "Computational thinking to implement robotics and programming", where basic and advanced topics were addressed to develop entertaining projects for the classroom. No prior knowledge or specific programming equipment or material was required to participate. The first workshop event was held in August 2020, and with the experience gained, four more were launched in October.

Fifth came the launch of an educational robotics product for families directed to the end consumer: a simpler kit with fewer parts was created that did not compete with the one prepared for schools, but that did open a new possibility for the home as an innovative market proposition. The Rasti online store was redesigned, both for regular toys and robotics kits, allowing for the direct purchase of products.

In an interview conducted in August 2020 with Juan Manuel Zamora, Commercial Director and Partner of ERRE, and Gabriel Dimare, Commercial Manager for Rasti, it could be verified that the social marketing strategy for quality of life involved lessons learned towards organizational changes:

1. New found importance of adapting the focus from in person to virtual relationships with customers.
2. Accelerating digitization and innovation can increase ERRE's strategic positioning.
3. Relevance of sharing content to those who need it, attempting to make programming go viral so that any person can learn to do it in a simple and free way.
4. The webinars forged alliances with companies and universities to co-create new ideas and services for improving inclusion in education.
5. Reputation improvement and generation of new business ideas based on the results of the webinars. This allowed for the creation of a new online training format for schools and the opening of courses for children.

Translation: *"Inti's little animals (3 years-old). Fabrizio builds everything with Rasti. Laureano, from Salta".*

Fig. 19.1 *Families participation in Facebook campaign.* Source: Rasti (2020) [https://www.facebook.com/JuguetesRasti]

Conclusions

A disruptive crisis like a pandemic moves people and organizations towards innovation to help those who suffer most from its consequences. In the case presented in this chapter, Rasti, a Latin American family business which has managed to survive the transformations of its industrial sector and the multiple challenges of international competition, used social marketing strategies to increase its stakeholders and clients' quality of life. This strategy facilitated change implementation, which started with a focus on education, and proceeded with the company's digitization by incorporating activities in digital spaces. This perspective sought to merge Rasti's objectives with those of its stakeholders, which revealed the importance of cooperation and participation in the product experience and the importance of sustaining channels to achieve those goals.

The case allows us to conclude that social marketing with a quality of life perspective not only serves to direct the goals of change management and digitization, but also betters the positioning of companies in their markets. Rasti's strategy increased the brand's popularity by 227% and organic search traffic by 337% in less than one year. In 2020 Rasti became the most important national brand in Argentina, measured by organic search traffic and keywords. Maximizing quality of life of children, families and educators is a viable way to adapt companies to new sociocultural paradigms.

Discussion Questions

1. Analyze the importance of robotics programs in schools for quality of life of students, families, teachers, schools and society.
2. The quarantine accelerated the need to learn to use and implement digital communication tools and social marketing, especially regarding social media, in order to generate a communication channel between the Company (Rasti), schools, teachers, families and students. Discuss the pros and cons of this accelerated organizational process and the importance of social marketing in that process.
3. What do you think about the decision taken by ERRE to transform its social marketing proposition?
4. Based on the ideas developed by ERRE, what other proposals do you think could have been developed to increase quality of life through social marketing?

Teaching Notes

1. **Analyze the importance of robotics programs in schools for quality of life of students, families, teachers, schools and society.**
   Given that digital technologies are rapidly and consistently advancing in every aspect of everyday life, it is important for children and teenagers to be able to adapt via the formal educational spheres they inhabit. ICT development is even part of the United Nations' 2030 Sustainable Development Agenda, and many countries have already incorporated curricular content on robotics, programming and other STEM fields in their school's classes.

Regarding students, Karaman and Giuriati (2019) claim that educational robotics blends a variety of topics spanning various academic disciplines, their ecosystems, roles, expectations, particularities and abilities related to mechanics, design, electronics, collaborative work structures, creativity and imagination. Collaborative work through trial and error is one of the main methods used by educational robotics to learn with others, while attempting to solve problems for others. In this way, educational robotics can be a holistic discipline for schools to teach children the skills they will need to confront a digitalized future, while bettering their current quality of life and, potentially, that of their adulthood as well.

Families may see benefit in these programs not only due to the strengthening of their children's education, but also in the possibility of sharing entertaining and pedagogic activities from the comfort of their own homes. Implementing programming and robotics courses by Rasti can educate children in complex competencies, while operating as a means of entertainment to stimulate their attention: especially since mandatory quarantine prohibited recreational in person activities that children used to attend before the SARS-CoV-2 outbreak. Taking advantage of time spent as a family using these resources, their quality of life might be benefited transgenerationally.

Finally, teachers may broaden their knowledge on robotics and programming, not only for use in the classroom but also for their own lives and self-gratification extracurricularly.

2. **The quarantine accelerated the need to learn to use and implement digital communication tools and social marketing, especially regarding social media, in order to generate a communication channel between the company (Rasti), schools, teachers, families and students. Discuss the pros and cons of this accelerated organizational process and the importance of social marketing in that process.**

Pros	Cons
Students may acquire skills in areas which are becoming more present in social and work life, in an innovative and entertaining way. Families may benefit from such learning and the quality time spent with their children.	Technological overload and a broadened span of entertainment options may distract children from activities such as educational robotics. If children don't find the proposal fun, they may not commit themselves to it in the long term.
Teachers may acquire knowledge in groundbreaking areas, allowing them to develop personal and professionally.	Difficulty of passing on "know how" on robotics to teachers with little to no exposure to technological tools.
Teachers may offer alternatives to traditional learning methods which might spark student's attention, when prepared to lead innovative classes.	Lack of face-to-face interaction makes following through with students difficult, especially regarding hands on activities
ERRE's iterative strategy process allows for growth on successful implementations, and the chance to work on its flaws.	Elaborating a strategy without prior testing may incite risk that could end in corporate loss, which could have been prevented with more elaborate planning.

3. **What do you think about the decision taken by ERRE to transform its social marketing proposition?**

   According to the student's view on the subject, an answer may follow one or a mix of the following guidelines:

   (a) Positive, adequate

   ERRE's social marketing strategy oriented towards quality of life improvement strengthens and benefits students and teacher's learning experience during pandemic times. It executes actions with social impact that evidences Rasti's commitment to social development as one of its main objectives as a company. Its collaborative innovation axes effectively prove Rasti's value system and mission as well, which evidences a positive strategy for the creation of value and that may work as a basis for future ideas that may be implemented.

   (b) Decent, improvable

   Although the actions implemented by Rasti are partly valid to justify success in teaching useful resources in schools, there are some attributes that may be modified to benefit the community even further. These changes include ________________. By incorporating this idea into the social marketing plan, student, teacher and family's quality of life may be considerably benefited, leading to a more informed society, ready to tackle the challenges of globalization, digitalization, or whatever may come next.

   (c) Negative, must be re-evaluated

   ERRE did not make the right decision to favor children's skill development and the formation of a network between families and schools because ________________. The social marketing plan must be reevaluated as a whole, as it hinders the learning process. Changes suggested as an alternative to the current plan include ________________.

4. **Based on the ideas developed by ERRE, what other proposals could have been developed to increase quality of life through social marketing? Research actions put forth by similar companies to answer.**

   To answer this question, students should elaborate their own benchmark analysis exploring strategies used by other market players. Examples may include Lego (https://www.lego.com/en-gb/categories/robots-for-kids), Sphero, (https://sphero.com/pages/socially-distanced-with-sphero) or others.

References

Barrera Lombana N (2015) Uso de la robótica educativa como estrategia didáctica en el aula. Praxis & Saber, vol. 6, núm. 11, enero-junio, 2015, pp. 215–234. Universidad Pedagógica y Tecnológica de Colombia. https://www.redalyc.org/pdf/4772/477247215010.pdf

Fernández NG, Moreno MLR, Guerra JR (2020) Brecha digital en tiempo del COVID-19. Hekademos: revista educativa digital 28:76–85

Karaman M, Giuriati S (2019) Robótica inicial: hablar de juego, ciencia y robótica en la infancia es posible. Villa María, El Mensú Ediciones

Kotler P, Keller KL (2012) Dirección de Marketing, 14a edn. Pearson Educación

Lee NR, Kotler P (2015) Social marketing: changing behaviors for good. SAGE Publications

Maggio M (2012) Enriquecer la enseñanza. Los ambientes con alta disposición tecnológica como oportunidad. Buenos Aires, Editorial Paidós

Murillo FJ, Duk C, Murillo FJ, Duk C (2020) El Covid-19 y las Brechas Educativas. Revista Latinoamericana de Educación Inclusiva 14(1):11–13. https://doi.org/10.4067/S0718-73782020000100011

ONU (2015) Resolución A/RES/70/1 Transformar nuestro mundo: la Agenda 2030 para el Desarrollo Sostenible

Rasti (2020) #EnCasaConRasti Facebook Campaign. Rasti. https://www.facebook.com/JuguetesRasti/. Accessed 20 Apr 2020

Tonon G (2015) Qualitative studies in quality of life: methodology and practice. Springer International Publishing. https://www.springer.com/gp/book/9783319137780

Chapter 20
Promoting Inclusive Education in Nigeria: Diary of a Special Needs Mum Initiative

Ogechi Adeola, Vanessa Burgal, and Oserere Ibelegbu

Abstract In some parts of Africa, there are certain indigenous social and religious perceptions about children living with disabilities. People believe that disability is contagious and disabled people are jinxed; hence, they should not interact with people in the community who have disabilities. Consequently, caring for children living with disabilities is a herculean task. Disabled people are denied access to a good life, quality education and quality healthcare, amongst others. This chapter discusses quality of life (QoL) and how it pertains to people living with disabilities, particularly in Nigeria. We also highlighted the essence of inclusive education to accommodate those living with disabilities. We, thereafter, tell the story of Bukola Ayinde, a lawyer and mother of an eight-year-old girl living with cerebral palsy, who has been faced with many challenges in the process of caring for her child. In her quest to ensure that her daughter has access to rehabilitation therapies, quality education and is accepted in her community, she became a disability advocate through social marketing activities and founded the *Diary of A Special Needs Mum* Initiative. This chapter concludes by encouraging sensitisation programs that will change the perception of people about those living with disabilities.

Keywords Disability · Quality of life · Inclusive education · Social marketing · Social acceptance

Introduction

Disability is a body impairment, which restricts an individual's ability to engage in certain tasks. These impairments could be physical, intellectual, cognitive, mental, developmental, sensory or even a combination of multiple conditions (Government of Western Australia Department of Communities n.d.). People living with

O. Adeola (✉) · V. Burgal · O. Ibelegbu
Lagos Business School, Pan-Atlantic University, Lagos, Nigeria
e-mail: oadeola@lbs.edu.ng; vburgal@lbs.edu.ng; oibelegbu@lbs.edu.ng

M. M. Galan-Ladero, R. G. Rivera (eds.), *Applied Social Marketing and Quality of Life*, Applying Quality of Life Research,
https://doi.org/10.1007/978-3-030-83286-5_20

disabilities are also referred to as those with special needs. According to the World Health Organization's (WHO) 2011 World Disability Report, about 15 percent of the world's population live with one form of disability or the other. Also, in sub-Saharan Africa, and Nigeria in particular, over 25 million of its over 200 million people are estimated to be living with disabilities (Ewang 2019). Many of them lack equal access to health care, education, employment and housing opportunities; they lack special care and are invariably excluded from the society. They are faced with one form of discrimination or another, even from public institutions. Just recently, the bill for the Discrimination Against Persons with Disabilities (Prohibition) Act, 2018 was passed into law and signed by the Government of Nigeria; this was after nine years of persistent advocacy from the disability rights group and activists (Ewang 2019).

Disability cuts across gender, age, race, social status, religion, economic and political positions (Haruna 2017). Some people are born with impairments, while others are impaired as a result of either illnesses or accidents, or even war. Regarding babies born with impairments, this is often attributable to the state of health and nutrition of the mother, particularly during pregnancy, to genetic and chromosomal conditions of the parents, as well as to environmental factors such as pollution, chemicals in food and water, and poor health care systems. For instance, German measles (rubella) in a pregnant woman causes deafness in the child when he/she is born. Similarly, other sexually transmitted diseases such as HIV and syphilis may lead to a deformity in the unborn child. Likewise, a malnourished pregnant woman can give birth to a child with deformity due to vital nutrients lacking in her system, which should contribute to the proper development of the fetus. Also, some babies in their infancy who suffer from illnesses such as meningitis, measles, and polio may end up having one form of disability or another (Maxwell et al. 2007).

According to Maxwell et al. (2007), poverty is being considered one of the major causes of disability. As a result of a low standard of living, such as unhealthy working conditions, inaccessibility to basic social amenities, and poor sanitation, amongst others, poor people become highly prone to disability. They invariably contract diseases such as polio, and tuberculosis, amongst others, which could render them incapacitated. It is, however, disheartening that most people and the society at large have superstitious beliefs and myths about disability. Some people believe that it is a form of punishment from their gods and ancestors probably because of the sins or abomination committed by either the individual, the individual's parents or grandparents. Others also believe that disability is caused by witchcraft, and some people are of the opinion that it is a curse. Consequently, other people see those with special needs as different from them and thus must be criticised, mocked, and excluded. Amongst other challenges faced by special needs individuals include lack of access to public amenities and discrimination because of the belief that they are associated with bad luck or that their disability is infectious.

Globally, education is considered as the driver to human capital development; hence, every child has the right to education, irrespective of their disabilities. This has become a global practice as it is indicated in the United Nations Sustainable Development Goal (SDG) 4, which states thus: "To ensure inclusive and equitable

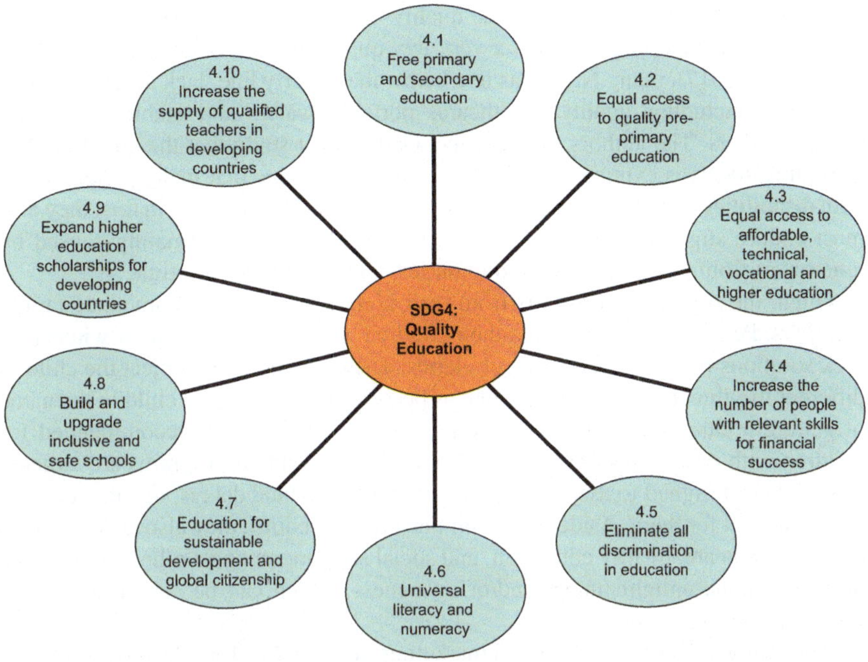

Fig. 20.1 Ten targets of UN SDG4. Source: Sustainable Development Goal Education 2030 Steering Committee (n.d.)

quality education and promote lifelong learning opportunities for all." Importantly, the SDG 4 has ten targets embedded in it, in a bid to achieve the goal. This is represented in the chart (see Fig. 20.1). In line with this goal, the Government of Nigeria has designed a training manual for Special Education Needs and Disabilities (SENDs), which will be used by teachers. Therefore, it is important to understand that in pursuing access to inclusive and quality education, the wellbeing of individuals with special needs is improved, thus leading to attaining a good quality of life.

According to WHO, quality of life is defined as "an individual's perception of their position in life in the context of the culture and value systems in which they live and in relation to their goals, expectations, standards and concerns." Although there is no universal definition of the concept, it is a multidimensional concept since it may be understood from economic, psychological, and social perspectives (Leitao and Alves 2016). Succinctly, quality of life is defined as the total wellbeing of an individual (Meule et al. 2013). It is understood as a person's complete satisfaction with every facet of his/her life, including social, cultural, health, physical, environmental and the value systems (Badiora and Abiola 2017).

Quality of life (QoL) is a very relevant concept, as it allows for measuring progress towards attaining improved wellbeing, thereby helping to realise the sustainability goals and targets. Some dimensions of quality of life include healthcare, satisfaction of needs and material wealth (Muhammad 2016). It is the responsibility of a government to help improve the quality of the life of its citizens. One of the features of a developing nation is a very low quality of life. According to Badiora and Abiola (2017), many Nigerians live below the poverty line, lack access to social amenities, including quality healthcare, portable water, and stable electricity, amongst others. The authors further concluded in their study that the quality of life of rural residents is extremely poor. It is important to state that many people living with disabilities do not have access to a high quality of life. Apart from this, they also must endure stigmatisation, despicable and wrongful attitudes (mainly caused by ignorance) from people in their communities, all through their lifetime.

Often, the stigmatisation starts from their homes, among their immediate family members. People who believe that their children are disabled because of witchcraft, seek solutions from native doctors or clerics. They would rather subject the child to different life-threatening activities such as beating and starving the child in the name of getting a cure, than key into early intervention programmes recommended for children with disabilities (Ayinde 2019a). Early intervention programs are targeted action plans designed to assist children with developmental delays, to catch up with milestones set for them. Aside from their personal afflictions, they also lack access to quality healthcare, quality education, and social support, amongst others. Hence, the need for public enlightenment and/or awareness, which can be achieved through social marketing.

According to Dann (2010), social marketing can be defined as "the adaptation and adoption of commercial marketing activities, institutions and processes as a means to induce behavioural change in a targeted audience on a temporary or permanent basis to achieve a social goal" (p. 151). It involves the use of marketing tools for the accomplishment of socially desirable goals, rather than commercial gain or achieving certain organisational goals (Chin and Mansori 2018). Simply put, social marketing is the use of campaigns targeted towards improving the wellbeing of individuals in a community; in this case, those with special needs. During such campaigns, all relevant stakeholders are called upon to have a change of attitude towards people living with disabilities, and also to provide them with basic necessities of life, thereby granting them access to a high quality of life in terms of quality healthcare, inclusive education and employment, amongst others.

The concept of social marketing in Nigeria has long been adopted, particularly by the Government, to curb corrupt practices, with the goal of encouraging citizens to cultivate the right attitudes. The Government of Nigeria has established various agencies and institutions saddled with the responsibility of social marketing campaigns, to propagate social change, given the level of deterioration in the economy (Izogo and Chukwuemeka 2013).

In the same vein, at various levels of Government, there have been social marketing campaigns such as public health awareness against drug abuse, HIV/AIDS, and smoking. There have also been campaigns for family planning, immunisation, and road safety, amongst others. Non-governmental organisations also carry out humanitarian services to the society in the form of clubs, voluntary organisations, and community development associations (Izogo and Chukwuemeka 2013).

Case Development: Diary of a Special Needs Mum Initiative

Meet Bukola Ayinde

Bukola Ayinde is the founder of Diary of a Special Needs Mum Initiative, which is a project under P4:13 Foundation (Philippians Four Thirteen Foundation). She is a lawyer, social entrepreneur, author, facilitator, counsellor[1] and a young mother of an eight-year-old girl living with cerebral palsy in Lagos, Nigeria.

Her daughter, Oluwalonimi Ayinde (Nimi) was born premature, and as a result, she was kept in an incubator for the first six weeks of her life. According to Bukola, the doctor told her Nimi would not be discharged until she was able to breathe independently and also add an extra 1 kg, as her birth weight was 1.2 kg. While Nimi was in the incubator, she developed apnea and mild jaundice.

All through the incubation period, Bukola was always worried at the sight of very little Nimi, but the doctors and nurses kept assuring her that Nimi would be fine. After a turbulent experience in the incubator, Nimi's health improved, she weighed 2 kg and was certified to go home with her parents. It was a beautiful and joyous day for Bukola and her husband, realising that their daughter eventually made it, after staying several weeks in the incubator.

The Experience

Eight months later, it took a family member to reiterate what Bukola and her husband had suspected, but had not acknowledged, about their precious daughter. Nimi had not met most of her development milestones. She was not able to sit and control her head and had no control of her hands and legs. Bukola's relative insisted that Bukola and her husband should take Nimi to the hospital and get all tests carried out, and they did just that.

After Nimi had undergone a series of tests, the paediatrician broke the news to Bukola and her husband that Nimi has cerebral palsy. Cerebral palsy is damage to the part of the brain that controls movement. The doctor said that the damage might have been caused by a sickness called pre-eclampsia, which Bukola had during pregnancy. He also stated that it could have been caused by Nimi's low birth weight or even the fact that Nimi experienced series of apnea[2] attacks while in the incubator.

After some months, Bukola and her husband visited a pediatric neurologist who narrowed the cause of the cerebral palsy to the very initial apnea Nimi experienced while in the incubator. It was a life-threatening apnea, and it took over four minutes before she was resuscitated. This was the beginning of a new reality in Bukola's life. She felt helpless, desperate, devastated and depressed about Nimi's condition.

[1] https://www.linkedin.com/in/bukola-ayinde-489186138/?originalSubdomain=ng

[2] Apnea is defined as the cessation of respiratory airflow, which is common to premature babies

According to Bukola, being a first-time mum and now a mum of a special needs child in Nigeria was like walking blindfolded through a maze.

She had to brace up to take care of Nimi and became more encouraged when she realised she was pregnant, Nimi was going to have a sibling. The joy of expecting a second baby erased some of the dark clouds that crowded Bukola's head about her daughter's diagnosis.

In a bid to understand how to get support for her daughter, she read a few books written by other Nigerian mums who have children living with disabilities. That led her to register Nimi in a special needs school in Lagos, Nigeria. Thereafter, Bukola and her husband enrolled Nimi in a summer school at Peto Institute in Budapest, Hungary. The institute is a special school for children with cerebral palsy, and the facilities are specially designed to suit the special needs of the children. According to Bukola, there is no institution in Nigeria to be compared to the Peto Institute. After the summer programme, she decided to homeschool her daughter. She employed a speech therapist, an occupational therapist, a physiotherapist, and a professional caregiver to work with Nimi at home. While on this journey, one of the therapists suggested that Nimi should go to a mainstream school so she could interact with her peers.

When Nimi was a little over two years old, Bukola searched for a mainstream school that her daughter could attend. Some doors were shut in her face, as most school owners said they did not have the facilities to take care of Nimi. Eventually, through a reference from another mum who had a special needs child, Bukola found a school that accepted Nimi. Nimi started attending a mainstream school, together with children without disabilities. At this point, Nimi was still fully dependent. She could neither sit, stand nor write by herself, and she was non-verbal. Therefore, she had to rely on her caregiver for everything.

Although it was easier for Bukola to allow her daughter to attend a mainstream school, she found out that she was more reluctant to allow her to attend the Sunday school at her church. She was sceptical about the teachers and how other children in the class will accept her. When she was growing up, she met some religious people who felt that children with disabilities had spiritual issues. Bukola decided to take a chance and Nimi settled down at Sunday school, although not without a few glitches. There was a day she went over to pick her daughter after church service, and she noticed that most of the children were gathered around her, looking at her like she was a rare specimen. Her heart was broken for her child, as she knew it was a painful thing to be different from others. The teacher asked the students to sit down, although Bukola felt it would have been better if the teacher had explained to the children, why Nimi was different from them.

The Aftermath: Inclusive Education

As Nimi progressed with her education in a mainstream school, she became more aware of her environment, and she started attempting to say a few words. The proprietress of the school was very helpful, as well as the teachers. Nimi was allowed to undergo physiotherapy sessions at school. At a point, Bukola withdrew Nimi from the school and decided to homeschool her, when she discovered that she was not properly taken care of by her private physiotherapist, while at school. After a few months of homeschooling Nimi at home, Nimi was eager to go to school, and she would cry each morning when she saw her younger sister in her school uniform going to school. This made Bukola to be on the look-out for another mainstream school for Nimi.

After Nimi had spent a few years attending a mainstream school, Bukola described her as a very intelligent girl, even though she could not speak well and clearly. Nimi was given the privilege to participate in a spelling bee competition in her school, and she was able to memorise each word that was given to her, and she spelt them correctly. When Nimi had to move to a third school because the owner of her present school relocated from Nigeria, she was placed in year one, even though her mum knew she could fit into year two class. Her new school did not believe she could learn, but after a few weeks in her class, her teacher realised how intelligent she was and immediately decided to move her to year two. However, by this time, Nimi refused to move to year two as she had bonded with her year one classmates. That problem was solved by teaching her year two and year one subjects, while she stayed in the year one class.

Nimi's potentials would not have been discovered if the proprietress of the school she attends did not accept her. She would not have been able to attain this height of learning if her parents did not go the extra mile to get her educated. Not only is Nimi succeeding in her educational pursuit, but she is also a favourite with her classmates. They love her dearly, and they always look out for her wellbeing. Unconsciously, her classmates have learnt how to love persons different from them. This shows that acceptance is one of the benefits of inclusive education.

Outcome (Social Marketing: Getting the Conversation Started)

Owing to Bukola's experience as a special needs mum, she became a voice for families who have children with special needs in Nigeria. Bukola uses her foundation to sensitise the public about children living with disabilities aiming at:

- changing the mind-set and pre-conceived beliefs of disability as emanating from evil acts of parents or generational curses
- ensuring all children, regardless of physical or mental ability, are given access to quality education.
- generating debates or discussions amongst stakeholders on effective disability management, to improve the quality of life of those who are living with disabilities.

To reach these objectives, Bukola started by writing for national newspapers with articles such as *Decoding Disability Management in Africa* and *Inclusive Education for Children With Disabilities,* written in Guardian Newspaper, *Embracing*

Disability Inclusion in Africa, Fight For Your Mind (A letter to special needs mums) written in Punch Newspaper, and she also wrote a series of articles on *Benefits of Inclusive Education* on an online blog, BellaNaija. She made two documentaries about inclusive education and acceptance of special needs people. One of the documentaries was about her daughter, Nimi. She speaks in public gatherings, encouraging school owners to adopt inclusive education. She urges church leaders to encourage their members to show love to people living with disabilities.

Bukola has used different fun platforms to educate students about disability and how to show love and acceptance to people that are different from them. This includes an art class where elementary students were taught to paint; they watched a documentary about inclusive education and spoke with an adult who is living with a disability. Bukola also organises essay competitions for students to write about disability inclusion, as well as Think Tank Competitions, where students listen to different people living with disabilities, talk about their lives. The students thereafter make suggestions to the state government on how disability can be managed better in the state. All her programs are documented on video and the highlights shared on many social media networks. Bukola has written three storybooks and a colouring book about disability inclusion.

Her fifth book, *Naked And Not Ashamed*, is a thirty-day journal about her experiences as a special needs mum. Bukola, in that book, wrote letters to different stakeholders, including the Nigerian Church, School Owners, Parents-Teachers Association, The Government and Special Needs Mums (Ayinde 2019b).

Letter to the Nigerian church leaders: Bukola acknowledged the fact that no doubt, many churches are involved in reaching out to those in the hospitals, prisons, and the unsaved, through missions. However, the people living with disabilities are being ignored; there are no wheelchair ramps at the entrance of church buildings, and some Sunday Schools do not accept them. Therefore, only a few parents take their special needs children against all the odds, to churches. Some church members even warn their children not to associate with those living with disabilities, having the belief that these people are cursed. Bukola, in her letter, further implored religious leaders to begin with a disability awareness campaign that preaches showing love and acceptance (not pity) to special needs individuals. She beckoned on religious leaders to sensitise their members, telling them that these people with special needs are not cursed, not stupid, idiots or imbeciles, rather they are human beings, just like every other person.

Letter to School Owners: Bukola noted that children living with disabilities have a right to mainstream education, and advocates for inclusive education, as is being practised in Finland. She highlighted a few things to be done, to get started. These include: seeking knowledge, educating the teachers, partnering with non-profit organisations that focus on disability inclusion, teaching students about children with disabilities via storytelling, stage plays and the likes, educating the parents of children in their schools, and not extorting parents who have children living with disabilities, amongst others.

Letter to Parents-Teachers Association: She acknowledged the fact that parents are very careful about what and who their children are being exposed to. Hence, there are different beliefs ranging from the fact that disabilities are infectious, or that the special needs kids are possessed with demons, to the fact that if their children learn in the same classroom with a child living with disability, then their children may imitate the behavioural pattern of the disabled child. She assured parents that all these beliefs are only fallacies, and there is nothing to worry about. She advised them to choose to be kind. In like manner, she called on teachers to learn more about prevalent forms of disabilities in children and thus have loving hearts and patient minds towards children placed under their care.

Letter to the Government: Bukola specifically wrote to the Lagos State Government, appreciating the Government for efforts made to ensure that those living with disabilities are not left out, even though, a lot is yet to be done. She appealed that urgent decisions need to be made, to improve the welfare of those living with disabilities, thereby providing them access to a high quality of life. Bukola highlighted three areas the Lagos State Government can be involved. These include advocacy in terms of prevention, early detection and re-orientation, provision and availability of therapy clinics and empowerment through education for people with disabilities.

Letter to Special Needs Mums: Bukola encouraged mothers who have children with special needs, to get busy with other activities, aside from taking care of their special children. She further advised them to ensure they rest and exercise, as a form of therapy. She encouraged them to keep hope alive, despite the challenges.

Furthermore, Bukola has made it a point of duty to mentor other mothers who have children living with disabilities. She has a support group for some of these women. She organises training programs where they can learn skills, so they can become financially empowered. Because of Bukola's boldness in telling her story and sharing her experiences with her daughter within her community, more and more women have come out to share their own stories. It is comforting to see that more schools are willing to embrace inclusive education in Nigeria. Disability discussions are no longer shrouded in secrecy, as people are becoming more informed, thereby, increasing their acceptance of people living with disabilities.

Conclusions

This chapter has been able to demonstrate the importance of social marketing in the Nigerian society, through the lens of Nimi's story. Disability is not a disease; neither are those who live with disabilities cursed or abnormal. Certain medical conditions have resulted in their disabilities, either during birth or by accident. People living with disabilities are also human beings and thus have the right to enjoy everything a person living without disability enjoys. People living with disabilities should be considered when projects and policies are to be implemented in any society since their wellbeing is very paramount. They deserve the right to quality education, access to quality healthcare, access to social amenities, the right to socialise and interact with every other person around them and they deserve love and care as well.

Bukola considered the fact that if she, an educated and middle-class individual could face such challenges caring for Nimi, it would be worse for those low-income earners who have children living with disabilities and do not have a support system. At this point, Bukola saw the need for social marketing. She decided that the people, the Government, religious bodies, schools, organisations, hospitals should be made aware of the needs of those living with disabilities, in our societies. It is important that an enabling environment is created to include the needs of those living with disabilities. The responsibility does not only lie on the Government but also every individual. It is essential that everyone begins with a change of attitude and acts nicely towards people living with disabilities. Parents and teachers can tell their wards about children with special needs, teaching them to treat them like their fellow human beings, interacting with them, rather than avoiding, stigmatising, and humiliating them.

Discussion Questions

1. In your own opinion, what should be the role of the Nigerian Government towards people living with disabilities? Discuss the Social Marketing Campaign programmes and other tools the Government could use.
2. What are the challenges that Bukola faces in an emerging market like Nigeria, with high levels of illiteracy, and a large number of citizens living below the poverty line?
3. Discuss the target groups identified by Bukola and evaluate her Communication Strategy for each of them.
4. Some children with disabilities have been bullied in schools. How can schools promote love and acceptance?
5. How can organisations promote disability inclusion in their recruitment processes?
6. Describe the concept of inclusive education and its importance to a society, comparing the Nigerian perspective with other countries'.
7. Define Quality of Life (QoL). How can social marketing programmes improve the quality of life of people living with disabilities, such as Nimi in the case study? Compare the situation of disability inclusion in Nigeria vs. other advanced countries and identify social marketing campaigns developed in those countries to improve QoL of people with disabilities.

Table 20.1 Examples of Policy Instruments, classified by Principal Governing Resource that can be used

Modality/ Information	Authority	Treasure	Organisation
Information collection and release	Command and control regulation	Grants and loans	Direct provision of goods and services and public enterprises
Advice and exhortation	Self-regulation	User charges	Use of family, community and voluntary organisations
Advertising	Standard setting and delegated regulation	Taxes and tax expenditures	Market creation
Commissions and inquiries	Advisory committees and consultations	Interest group creation and funding	Government reorganisation

Source: Hood (1986)

Teaching Notes

Promoting Inclusive Education in Nigeria: Diary of a Special Needs Mum Initiative

This case has been developed for use in Marketing Management, Integrated Marketing and Communications, as well as entrepreneurship courses. It is also appropriate for MBA and Executive Development Programs, as well as advanced undergraduate courses. The subject matter makes it suitable for courses that relate to social marketing strategies, governmental policies and non-profit organisations management. This true-life story provides a description of the design process of a non-profit association that can prove especially useful for start-ups, entrepreneurs, and non-profit organisations, that desire to create environmental and social value.

Answer to question 1: In your own opinion, what should be the role of the Nigerian Government towards people living with disabilities? Discuss the Social Marketing Campaign programmes and other tools the Government could use.

To answer this question, we recommend that students take into consideration the reality of African countries and conduct a PESTEL (Political, Economic, Socio-Cultural, Technological, Environmental & Legal) analysis, to help them understand the operating environment and limitations the Nigerian Government may encounter in ensuring acceptance of people living with disabilities.

Before discussions on Social Marketing commence, students may wish to explore how the Government can develop and use Communication Policy Tools. See Table 20.1 below:

To learn more about this resource, see:

Hood, C. (1986). *The Tools of Government*. Chatham, Chatham House Publishers.

When discussing the use of Social Marketing campaigns to change the perception of Nigerians and get the conversation started amongst stakeholders—citizens, non-profits and government agencies, students should begin by:

1. describing the target audience
2. determining the communication objectives
3. designing the messages and the content of the message
4. choosing the appropriate communication channels and media.

Target Audience

Students should prioritise and focus on

- Families and communities
- Public institutions
- The educational system

Communication Objectives

- Changing the mind-set and pre-conceived beliefs of disability as emanating from evil acts of parents or generational curses.
- Ensuring all children, regardless of physical or mental ability, are provided access to quality education.

Content of Messages

- Doctors explaining the major causes of disabilities.
- Health experts and educators describing the advantages of inclusive education.
- Successful people living with disabilities.
- Public places accessible to people living with disabilities.

Potential Channels

- Radio and TV campaigns in local dialects about how people become disabled, debunking myths about disabilities. Target: low-income areas and rural areas, particularly areas with a high incidence of disabilities.
- Social media: Facebook & Instagram. Target: middle-class, urban areas, the southern part of Nigeria.

Other Governmental Actions & Tools

- To ensure that all public places are accessible to people living with disabilities. In Nigeria, for instance, this resolution is already contained in the Disability Rights Law. However, the Government must encourage all stakeholders to implement it. Government must begin with making available these appropriate public infrastructure, before other organisations can follow.

Answer to question 2: What are the challenges that Bukola faces in an Emerging Market like Nigeria, with high levels of illiteracy, and a large number of citizens living below the poverty line?

The first phase of a marketing plan is analysing the Market, also named Situation Analysis, to understand the micro and macro environment of the company or organisation. To answer this question, students can start looking at the PESTEL analysis, from question 1, to help them identify the challenges any entrepreneur, as well as non-profit organisations, may encounter when trying to develop a project in Africa. According to the World Bank, "in Africa, an estimated 6.4% of children in this age range have moderate or severe disabilities; and less than 10% of all children with disabilities under the age of 14 are attending school."[3]

A good source of information on Situation Analysis is:

Steenburgh, T., Avery, J. (2010). *Marketing Analysis Toolkit: Situation Analysis*. Harvard Business School, 9-510-079.

Students will probably discuss the difficulties of low-income families who live with a special needs child or adult, and how to fight the traditional beliefs that a child's disability is as a result of witchcraft activities, pushing these families to seek for a solution from native doctors or religious clerics.

Students may suggest:

- Providing counsellors to support families through their journeys
- Providing free medical and rehabilitation services
- Financial support

Answer to question 3: Discuss the target groups identified by Bukola and evaluate her Communication Strategy for each of them.

Bukola selected the following targets:

- Church leaders
- School owners
- Parents-teachers associations
- Government
- Special needs mums

Students will discuss the different strategies and channels used by Bukola to reach those targets and should try to recommend additional options or strategies.

Bukola writes and develops a significant amount of social marketing content through newspaper articles, letters, books, videos and social media. Eventually, she can use Public Relations events and influencers as additional tools, if not already doing so or increase the use of that channel. She can, in addition, target more public and private organisations as a source of sponsorship and communication tools.

[3] https://www.worldbank.org/en/topic/disability/brief/disability-inclusive-education-in-africa-program

Answer to question 4: Some children with disabilities have been bullied in schools. How can schools promote love and acceptance?

Students will suggest the information and resources schools need to solve this type of problems, as well as the best medium to convince the schools' stakeholders and to educate teachers and students.

Suggestions

- Promotion of love and acceptance through discussions, fun platforms like drama, songs and essay competitions.
- Giving students the right information about disabilities.

Answer to question 5: How can organisations promote disability inclusion in their recruitment process?

Students will mention that many international companies have already included this policy in their recruitment rules and processes. What is needed is to convince local companies and institutions to follow this example. Looking at the target (organisations) and after the analysis of question 1 and 2, students, can discuss key strategies of inclusion, such as the recruitment of disabled employees. Governments can also provide incentives and encourage employers to have inclusive hiring practices and policies that will not discriminate against persons with disability in the recruitment process and also make provisions for facilities where they can effectively carry out their duties.

Other suggestions can be:

- organising career development programmes for people living with disabilities.
- organising disability inclusion awareness and sensitisation programmes for employers, government officials and other stakeholders.
- setting aside a special day, perhaps in line with International events on disability, to celebrate persons with disabilities, and engender inclusion.

Answer to question 6: Describe the concept of inclusive education and its importance to society, comparing the Nigerian situation with other countries'.

- Students to provide definitions in their own words.
- Importance to society will include:
  - People with disability will have the same opportunity to succeed in life, as their peers.
  - Children in classrooms will become more tolerant of people who are different from them.
  - The best place to integrate people with disabilities into society is through the school system.
- Students can list differences and similarities between Nigeria and countries when defining the role of inclusive education.

Answer to question 7: Define Quality of Life (QoL). How can Social Marketing programmes improve the quality of life of people living with disabilities, such as Nimi in the case study? Compare the situation of disability inclusion in Nigeria vs. other countries and identify social marketing campaigns developed in other countries to improve QoL of people with disabilities.

Define Quality of Life.

- Quality of Life definition. Students should provide definitions in their own words and include the following concepts:
  - Psychological and physical health
  - Individual's perception
  - Individual's expectations.

The World Health Organisation (WHO) defines Quality of Life as "an individual's perception of their position in life in the context of the culture and value systems in which they live and in relation to their goals, expectations, standards and concerns. It is a broad-ranging concept affected in a complex way by the person's physical health, psychological state, personal beliefs, social relationships and their relationship to salient features of their environment."[4]

- For people living with disabilities, Quality of Life implies Social Acceptance, especially by their peer groups (especially by other children for the young ones and other employees, in the workplace), and their recognition as an individual with equal rights (economic, educational, health, etc.)
- To improve the Quality of Life of people with special needs, Social Marketing programmes can change the narrative by sharing the right information in the society. The leading cause of stigmatisation and bias is ignorance.
- When comparing developing countries to more advanced economies, students may argue that the former faces more challenges with disability inclusion, particularly in poor communities with limited resources. Students are expected to search for and provide examples of measures that could be adapted to encourage disability inclusion in developing countries like Nigeria.

References

Ayinde B (2019a) Embracing disability inclusion in Africa. https://punchng.com/embracing-disability-inclusion-in-africa/

Ayinde B (2019b) Naked and not ashamed: 30 days journal. Philippians Four Thirteen Foundation, Lagos, Nigeria

Badiora AI, Abiola OB (2017) Quality of life (QoL) of rural dwellers in Nigeria: a subjective assessment of residents of Ikeji-Arakeji, Osun-state. Ann Ecol Environ Sci 1(1):69–75

[4]World Health Organization (2020) WHOQOL: measuring quality of life. https://www.who.int/healthinfo/survey/whoqol-qualityoflife/en/.

Chin JH, Mansori S (2018) Social marketing and public health: a literature review. J Marketing Manag Consumer Behav 2(2):48–66
Dann S (2010) Redefining social marketing with contemporary commercial marketing definitions. J Bus Res 63(2):147–153. https://doi.org/10.1016/j.jbusres.2009.02.013
Ewang A (2019). Nigeria passes disability rights law: offers hope of inclusion, improved access. https://www.hrw.org/news/2019/01/25/nigeria-passes-disability-rights-law
Government of Western Australia Department of Communities: Disability Services (n.d.) What is disability? http://www.disability.wa.gov.au/understanding-disability1/understanding-disability/what-is-disability/
Haruna MA (2017) The problems of living with disability in Nigeria. J Law, Policy Globalization 65:103–113
Izogo EE, Chukwuemeka AE (2013) The Nigerian perspective of social marketing campaigns: a study of Ebonyi state action committee on Aids (EBOSACA). J Inf Knowl Manag 3(3):93–109
Leitao J, Alves H (2016) Entrepreneurial and innovative practices in public institutions. A quality of life approach. Springer, Switzerland
Maxwell J, Belser JW, David D (2007) A health handbook for women with disabilities. California: Hesperian. http://hesperian.org/wp-content/uploads/pdf/en_wwd_2008/en_WWD_2008_Community.pdf. Accessed April 6 2020
Meule A, Fath K, Real RG, Sutterlin S, Vogele C, Kibber C (2013) Quality of life, motion regulation, and heart rate variability in individuals with intellectual disabilities and concomitant impaired vision. Psychology of Well-Being: Theory, Res Practice 3(1):241–266
Muhammad Z (2016) Improving quality of life through community-based participatory development in Nigeria: explanatory factors for success and failure. Procedia Soc Behav Sci 222:151–159
Sustainable Development Goal–Education 2030 Steering Committee (n.d.) Sustainable development goal 4. https://sdg4education2030.org/the-goal
World Health Organization (2011) World report on disability. https://www.who.int/disabilities/world_report/2011/report/en/

Chapter 21
Disability, Labour Inclusion and Social Marketing in Spain: The ONCE Foundation Case

Marco Antonio Cruz-Morato and Carmen Dueñas-Zambrana

Abstract Labour inclusion for people with disabilities and its impact on the quality of life of this group, in economies such as Spain, is still a problem. In spite of the previous efforts carried out by policy makers based on regulation, the situation persists and it seems necessary to confront it in a different way. Thus, in this work, Social Marketing and Behavioral Economics are presented as powerful tools to overcome the problem, fighting against the social stigma usually suffered by people with disabilities, and it also describes how NGOs, associations and society as a whole can participate in finding the solution. The ONCE Foundation campaigns "Don't be my limit" and "Working is a story" are described according to this model. The study of successful cases and the potential of Social Marketing (from a Behavioral Economics approach) to tackle the exclusion of people with disabilities in the labour market could be a very interesting starting point to promote actions oriented in this sense, and to ensure a more sustainable and prosperous future for everyone in terms of quality of life.

Keywords Disability · Labour inclusion · Social marketing · Behavioral economics · Social exclusion

---

M. A. Cruz-Morato (✉)
Faculty of Tourism, University of Málaga, Málaga, Spain
e-mail: mcruz@uma.es

C. Dueñas-Zambrana
Faculty of Social and Labour Studies, University of Málaga, Málaga, Spain
e-mail: cdz@uma.es

M. M. Galan-Ladero, R. G. Rivera (eds.), *Applied Social Marketing and Quality of Life*, Applying Quality of Life Research,
https://doi.org/10.1007/978-3-030-83286-5_21

Introduction

There is an increasing concern about the situation of social exclusion (and the lack of quality of life) generally suffered by groups such as people with disabilities. However, there is still a lot to be done in different areas of life, and one of them is the labour market. The situation of labour inclusion of this collective in economies such as Spain seems particularly dramatic, with low activity rates (see INE 2016, 2019; Cruz-Morato and García-Lizana 2011).

The need for using all the marketing tools for social issues is perfectly reflected in the research carried out by Karl et al. (2018). Thus, Social Marketing, defined as "[...] *the application of commercial marketing technologies to the analysis, planning, execution, and evaluation of programs designed to influence the voluntary behaviour of target audiences in order to improve their personal welfare and that of their society*" (Andreasen 1995: 3), aims to facilitate social change both by adopting positive behaviour, and by decreasing a negative one (Dann 2010).

Social Marketing can therefore promote the inclusion of people with disabilities in the labour market through campaigns that seek to raise awareness within society and normalise their labour situation, combating the social stigma suffered by the collective (Cruz-Morato and García-Lizana 2011; Cruz-Morato et al. 2017a).

Any initiative to change behaviours implicitly assumes the need to integrate Psychology into the model (see Carvalho and Mazzon 2013; or Thaler 2016). It is for this reason that it is not possible to talk about Social Marketing without mentioning Behavioral Economics (the field of knowledge that studies the economic behaviour of human economic agents which involves economic decisions, as well as its determinants and consequences, Van Raaij 1981).[1] In this way, Behavioral Economics would be the basis of Marketing and especially Social Marketing.

This case aims to delve into the Social Marketing actions that have tried to promote the integration of people with disabilities into the labour market in Spain, based on the theoretical model set out above, looking at the specific campaigns "Don't be my limit" and "Working is a story" carried out by the ONCE Foundation (among a wide range of activities), a well-known association for people with disabilities in this country. Thus, the case development is divided into four sections: the first one briefly presents the problem regarding labour inclusion for people with disabilities in Spain; in section 2 the Social Marketing and Behavioral Economics model is described as an effective strategy to face the problem; next, the ONCE Foundation campaigns: "Don't be my limit" and "Working is a story" are reported and, in the last section, the effects on quality of life are related.

As it was said before, this case study could be a very interesting starting point to promote actions oriented in this way and improve the quality of life of people with disabilities, as well as that of the whole society. It is necessary to remember that the

[1]This field is especially relevant since the publication of "Nudge" (Thaler and Sunstein 2008), which defined Behavioral Economics as "nudging".

fight against social exclusion also has a positive impact on economic growth itself (and not only in terms of greater equity or social justice, see Cruz-Morato et al. 2017b).

Case Development

The Problem Regarding Labour Inclusion for People with Disabilities in Spain

In this section, the main figures concerning the problem of inactivity among people with disabilities in Spain will be highlighted, according to the latest data (year 2018) published by INE (Spanish National Statistics Institute) at the end of 2019. It will be considered labour inclusion of this group to be a specific social exclusion problem and a situation of decrease in their quality of life.

Therefore, in 2018 there were 1,899,800 people with disabilities of working age (from 16 to 64 years old), which represented 6.3% of the total population of working age (INE 2019). According to INE (2019, p. 3): "*The most remarkable thing about the group of people with disabilities is their low participation in the labour market. In 2018, its activity rate was 34.5% (half a point less than in 2017), that is, more than 43 points lower than that of the population without disabilities*". In Fig. 21.1, the activity rates of people with disabilities and people without disabilities can be found, showing that low activity figures of people with disabilities are fluctuating around 34% and those of people without disabilities around 78%.

Delving into the situation, in Fig. 21.2 the activity, employment and unemployment rates of people with and without disabilities during the year 2018 are shown by gender. In summary, not only the labour inactivity is the main labour problem for people with disabilities, but also the situation for women is even worse than men, especially in activity rates (although the difference between the activity rates of women without disabilities and those with disabilities is smaller than for men, due to the worse situation of women without disabilities compared with men without disabilities).

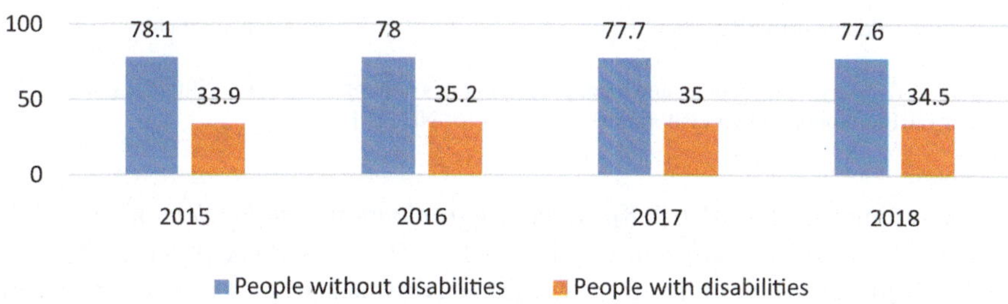

Fig. 21.1 Activity rates per year of people with disabilities and people without disabilities. *Source: Own elaboration, according to INE* (2019)

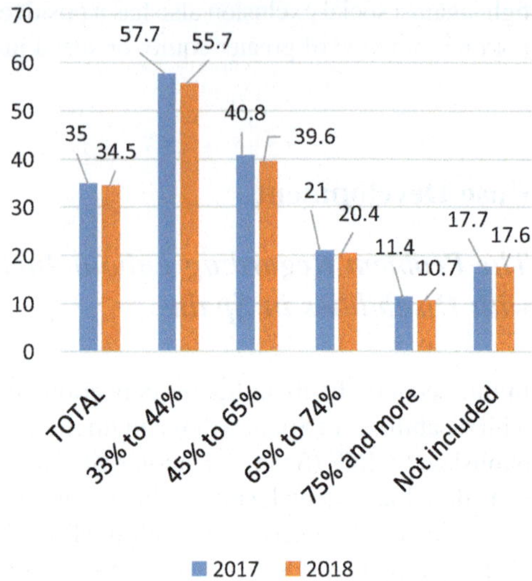

Fig. 21.3 Activity rates by degree of disability. *Source: Own elaboration, according to INE* (2019)

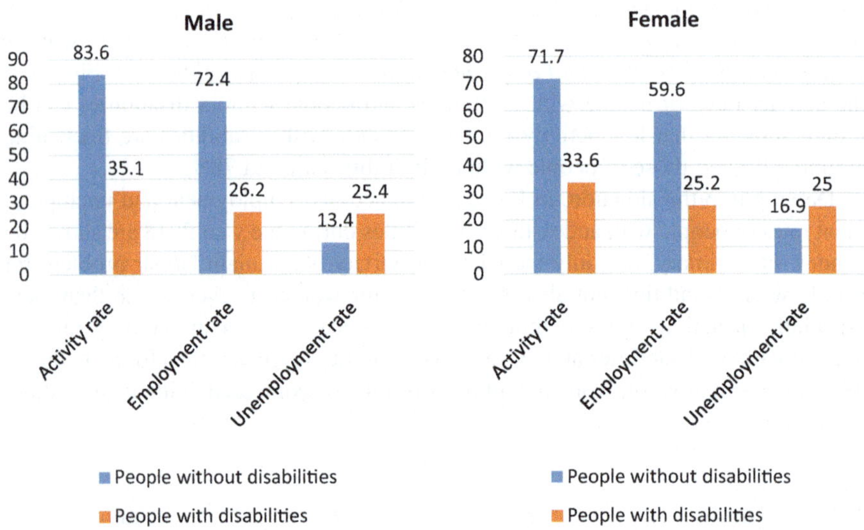

Fig. 21.2 Activity, employment and unemployment rates of people with and without disabilities by gender (2018). Source: Own elaboration, according to INE (2019)

According to INE (2019, p. 5): "*Labour participation is highly determined by the type and intensity of the disability*". Thus, in Fig. 21.3, it could be observed that, the higher the degree of disability, the lower the activity rates, resulting in a difference of 45 points between the 33% to 44% degree of disability group and the 75% and more degree of disability group.

In relation to the type of disability, people with hearing impairments showed the highest activity rates (58%) as opposed to people with mental deficiencies who showed the lowest ones (29.1%, INE 2019). Thus, although the situation for people with disabilities is negative in terms of labour inclusion, it is necessary to point out the importance of carrying out a detailed segmentation in order to analyse the problem correctly. See INE (2019) to delve into the labour market situation for people with disabilities in more detail.

Social Marketing and Behavioral Economics to Face the Problem

According to the previous research quoted, people with disabilities, as well as other groups of population such as women, suffered from some kind of social discrimination in the labour market. This provokes a social stigma in this group and could explain the low activity rates presented in the previous section. Thus, the implementation of a Social Marketing intervention, from a Behavioral Economics perspective, could be useful in fighting against this social exclusion. In this section, how and why this should be implemented will be explained.

Social Marketing aims to change the target behaviour to benefit general population or those who are at a disadvantaged situation. In our case, the social issue would be the fight against labour exclusion of people with disabilities, an action desirable to the community as well as to this particular group (improving their options to escape from this situation) and to raise awareness of the issue (of possible determinants, implications, etc.), changing the mentioned behaviours on private companies and non-profit organisations at a micro level, and also governments at a macro level.

Regarding labour inclusion of people with disabilities, it is essential to include Psychology into the model (Behavioral Economics). This is not only to get a better development of the Social Marketing intervention (see Lefebvre and Kotler 2012; or French 2013, among others), but to also deal with other elements previously analysed, to delve into society behaviours (people with disabilities and the rest of the population, who could be developing, consciously or not, discrimination/stigmatisation processes towards this group) and to boost the empowerment of this collective in an effective manner.

According to Miller and Major (2000), having a social stigma is a potential source of psychological stress. Such stress could lead the stigmatised person (a person with disabilities in this case) to prefer not to participate in economic activities and the labour market, restricting their empowerment. In accordance with Mandiberg and Warner (2012, p. 1736), quoting Corrigan and Watson (2002): "*Stigma leads some to reduce their exposure to discrimination from the larger community by restricting their activities in it*".

Thus, from a psychological perspective, the person with disabilities could be suffering from stress, but whether they decide (consciously or unconsciously) to participate or not in the labour market depends on how they can or want to face the previously mentioned stress. Compas et al. (2001) made a complete classification of possible coping strategies. In summary, these strategies could be positive (functional) or negative (dysfunctional). Most of these coping strategies are dysfunctional, finding not participating in economic activities to be the less risky behaviour. Nevertheless, functional coping strategies also exist and some people with disabilities opt to participate in the labour market, usually related to higher human capital provision and resources (empowerment).

Concerning Social Marketing, Calderwood and Wellington (2013) exposed some Social Marketing strategies for stigmatised people. Thus, Social Marketing campaigns are normally oriented to the general public, but stigmatised people should also be taken into consideration as audience targeting, in order to avoid the negative consequences that these communication campaigns could have for them (their special circumstances have to be considered, in order to not perpetuate the stigma).

To summarise, a Social Marketing/Behavioral Economics approach can be useful to face the situation, focusing on people with disabilities (increasing functional coping strategies), and also on the rest of society (reducing the discrimination of these people that generates the social stigma; and also promoting generosity, which would help this group access to productive resources and enhance their empowerment, according to previous research quoted before).

The ONCE Foundation Campaigns: "Don't Be my Limit" and "Working Is a Story"

Related to the previous framework, in this section two Social Marketing campaigns carried out by the ONCE[2] Foundation in Spain ("Don't be my limit" in 2016 and "Working is a story" in 2019) will be described, among other actions developed by this association related to this issue. Content analysis has been carried out, focusing on the following aspects of these campaigns: the message of the campaign, tone used, purpose, graphic design, broadcasting media and the target audience (based on Galan-Ladero and Galan-Ladero 2019).

The ONCE Foundation for the Cooperation and Inclusion of people with disabilities was created in 1988, by agreement of the ONCE association and the main organisations for people with disabilities in Spain. It was conceived as an instrument of cooperation and solidarity of the Spanish blind towards other groups of people with disabilities to improve their quality of life. CERMI[3] is also a member of the Foundation, which brings together more than 3000 associations, representing the 3.8

[2]"Organización Nacional de Ciegos Españoles" (National Organisation of the Spanish Blind, in English).

[3]"Comité Español de Representantes de Personas con Discapacidad" (Spanish Committee of Representatives of People with Disabilities, in English).

million people with disabilities who exist in Spain. This foundation obtains its main source of funding from ONCE gambling (which basically means that ONCE dedicates 33% to social services). Among its main objectives, is "*the promotion of full employment integration of disabled people*", and, since its creation until December 2017, the ONCE Foundation has supported 41,245 projects, submitted by individuals and legal entities (which represents more than 1902 million euros—ONCE Foundation, 2020).

"Don't Be my Limit"

Presented at the end of 2016, in this campaign people with different disabilities call to occupy the place that corresponds to them in the workplace (as well as in other aspects of life). The campaign uses the slogan "Don't be my limit", which is intended to make people understand that, on many occasions, it is the rest of society who (consciously or unconsciously) became a limitation to their possibilities for personal and professional development. Furthermore, these situations of discrimination limit their empowerment and affect, for instance, the labour inclusion of this collective.

As it is said in the spot: *"I want to be the one to heal you; I want to be the one to teach you; I want to be your son's girlfriend; I want to be your dance partner; I want to be your best friend; I want to be the one to defends you; I can be her mother; I can be the one who listens to you; I can be your co-worker, or, why not, your boss. 74% of people with disabilities do not have a job. I am prepared to be what I want to be. Don't be my limit".*

The spot has a solemn, serious and emotive tone (as well as being informative, positive and encouraging), with classical music in the background, and an elegant cinematographic design in black and white (with clear accessible staging and language: subtitles, sign language, etc.) The different people with disabilities (a blind physiotherapist, a teacher in a wheelchair, a deaf girl, etc. real people with different realities regarding disability) appear one by one, expressing what they want to do or be. As stated before, the objective is to bring the discrimination that these people could be suffering from in different aspects of life and work to the attention of the target audience (the rest of society). It also aims at trying to highlight the fact that they are as capable as the rest of society.

This campaign was broadcast on the most important mass media. In addition to a television and film spot (45″, 30″ and 20″), the campaign has pieces for the written press and the internet. As well as social networks such as Facebook, the video can also be found in YouTube,[4] with more than 5000 views. A website was also created during this campaign in which a series of videos called "More than a casting" were

[4]See https://www.youtube.com/watch?v=kmFawJXzVA8, https://www.youtube.com/watch?v=TutWL0nLviA

Fig. 21.4 "Don't be my limit" campaign. *Source:* ONCE (2016)

collected, with the aim of paying a small tribute to all the people with disabilities who showed up to the casting (Fig. 21.4).

"Working Is a Story"

This campaign took place at the end of 2019. It has been developed together with the European Social Fund for labour and social inclusion of people with disabilities. "Working is a story" presents a story made by other stories, those of people with different disabilities who face the same daily problems that anyone would experience at work during their usual workday. It tells the stories of different people (Rubén, María, Nieves and Domingo) through a series of videos, which pursues their labour inclusion (normalising the workday and labour activity of people with disabilities, fighting against their usual discrimination by the rest of society) while positioning the training and employment programs of the ONCE Foundation as a tool to achieve a quality job.

As it is said in the spot: "*The problem is not that I have a physical disability or that I have experienced a toxic relationship. It is not having Down Syndrome or living in a town in the middle of nowhere. The problem is not that I am blind or that I am over 45 years old. Not that I'm deaf or too young and inexperienced. The problem is . . . that this helmet is rubbing a lot! Or having to explain everything a thousand times because they don't pay attention. Or convincing the gentleman that these shoes cannot be changed. Or that the Internet crashes! At ONCE Foundation we work so that you can work and so that your only work problems are these ones. Program for the labour inclusion of people with disabilities. Co-financed by the European Social Fund*".

Fig. 21.5 "Working is a story" campaign. *Source:* ONCE (2019)

The tone of this campaign (whilst being informative, positive and encouraging) is casual and with an undeniable sense of humour, especially when the first person reveals what the real problem is for him. It is in that moment when some subtle, fun music starts in order to reinforce the humour of the scene. In terms of graphic design, the scene is shown in colour in an informal manner, the four people with disabilities explain their situation one by one (also with subtitles and sign language).

The purpose is to normalise the activities in the workplace of people with disabilities, and the current problems they face, fighting against the usual discrimination they suffer from the rest of society, as it was remarked on before. The target audience is also the general public. However, the strategy is based on humour and irony.

And in relation to broadcasting media, the campaign contains 5 spots (the general one of 40″, and the 4 stories of each person, 20″ each one). The campaign also contains a website, social media and banners. The adverts that make up the campaign can be seen on television, as well as on the website www.trabajaresunahistoria.es (which centralises and integrates the ambitious online media plan for this campaign[5]). The spots can be also found on YouTube,[6] with the general video having reached 782,170 views (Fig. 21.5).

Effects on Quality of Life

There is no doubt that this issue (the high labour inactivity of people with disabilities) relates to and negatively affects the quality of life of people with disabilities.

[5] For instance, the Instagram presence: https://www.instagram.com/explore/tags/trabajaresunahistoria/

[6] See https://www.youtube.com/watch?time_continue=6&v=JZaM2_bOZ4Y&feature=emb_logo to watch the 40″ one.

Not only in a quantitative and objective way (not having a job, money, etc.) but also in a qualitative and subjective manner (status, self-esteem, self-realisation...), also according to the Behavioral Economics approach developed. As Myrdal (1944) states, it is necessary to not forget about the psychological effects of discrimination. In Simões and Santos (2017), a study can be found about the impact of personal and environmental characteristics on the quality of life of people with disabilities (but focusing on the case of intellectual disability).

Quality of Life (see Tonon 2015, to go into more depth) encompasses different approaches (such as economic, social or psychological- Leitao and Alves 2016). According to Hagerty et al. (2001), within the subjective dimension, people give a different specific weight (importance) to the different areas of their lives.

Thus, from a subjective point of view, the quality of life of people with disabilities will also depend on the importance they attach to their need for job inclusion. Given the importance that they seem to give to labour integration (in light of the data), the situation of low quality of life of the group is evident. In this way, from the intervention framework developed, it would be necessary to promote positive coping responses for people with disabilities in order to turn this importance into action and undertake measures that allow them to increase their quality of life. However, it would also be necessary to reduce discrimination from the rest of society through Social Marketing/Behavioral Economics to tackle the situation of people with disabilities.

To sum up, this case study ("Don't be my limit" and "Working is a story" campaigns developed by the ONCE Foundation in Spain) is an important starting point to study and develop practical actions to improve the quality of life of people with disabilities, but also that of the whole society. It is necessary to remember that, at least in the quantitative dimension, fighting against social exclusion also has a positive impact on economic growth itself. In any case, the real impact on the quality of life by these campaigns (in terms of labour inclusion) is difficult to encompass and should be measured in the future (the last campaign dates from 2019 and there is not any more current data available yet). That being said, in regard to the impact of the first campaign in terms of labour inclusion (as it was developed in 2016), it seems that it did not achieve great results. Some analysis must be carried out (perhaps the different approach developed by the second campaign would contribute to change the situation). Moreover, according to the previously shown YouTube viewings figures, for instance, the second campaign has had much more views and more social media presence.

Conclusions

The main outcomes of this case are the following:

- The situation of labour inclusion of people with disabilities in Spain is very negative, with low activity rates, despite the previous public and private efforts developed to overcome the situation.
- Different groups present different data; lower activity rates have been observed in women with disabilities, those with a higher degree of disability or people with intellectual disabilities (among others). Thus, it points to the need for segmentation if more effective interventions are pursued.
- Social Marketing and Behavioral Economics are powerful tools to face the problem, fighting against the discrimination/stigmatisation suffered by people with disabilities in the labour market, causing a decrease in their labour participation.
- In line with the conceptual framework carried out, the two different cases of Social Marketing/Behavioral Economics campaigns previously described ("Don't be my limit" and "Working is a story", by ONCE Foundation) shed some light about practical interventions in that sense.
- The low participation rates of people with disabilities affect their quality of life in a negative way, both in the quantitative and qualitative dimension.
- The social exclusion of people with disabilities in the labour market also produces a limitation in the quality of life of the general society, at least in the quantitative dimension, as it is a constraint on economic growth.
- In light of the data, it seems that the first campaign did not achieve an improvement in labour inclusion of people with disabilities. The second campaign also presents more views in YouTube and a wider Social Media presence. Therefore, it is necessary to analyse the impact of the second campaign on labour inclusion and to improve it in order to really achieve a sustainable development for all the society.

Discussion Questions

1. Do you consider that labour exclusion affects the quality of life of people with disabilities? Explain why and provide strong reasons according to the case information.
2. What do you think about the Social Marketing/Behavioral Economics model of intervention developed? Do you consider it to be useful in tackling the situation? Explain why, giving a full explanation.
3. What type of Social Marketing strategy do the two ONCE Foundation campaigns studied mainly correspond to (a reinforcement strategy, an induction strategy ...)? Base your answer on firm reasoning.

4. What similarities and differences exist between the two campaigns ("Don't be my limit" and "Working is a story")? Which one do you consider more appropriate depending on the information provided by the case? Why do you think the "Don't be my limit" campaign did not achieve greater results? Reason why.
5. Based on the case information, how do you think you could improve these campaigns?

Teaching Notes

1. Do you consider that labour exclusion affects the quality of life of people with disabilities? Explain why and provide strong reasons according to the case information.
   According to the case information, labour exclusion negatively affects the quality of life of people with disabilities. This is not only in a quantitative and objective way (not having a job, money, etc.), but also in a qualitative and subjective manner (status, self-esteem, self-realisation. . .). As this issue seems to be important to them (under the subjective perspective, it is necessary to take into account the importance that people attach to the issue). Nevertheless, the most important thing is that the student adequately substantiates his/her answer.
2. What do you think about the Social Marketing/Behavioral Economics model of intervention developed? Do you consider it to be useful in tackling the situation? Explain why, giving a full explanation.
   There could be many different answers and it depends on how the student develops their argument, as long as they substantiate it in a solid way. However, with regard to the model exposed in the case, there are many reasons to understand how the Social Marketing/Behavioral Economics model of intervention developed is a good strategy to face the problem of labour inclusion of people with disabilities. Thus, it could be useful to fight against social stigma that people with disabilities usually suffer in the labour market, in trying to change negative prejudice in the general population and boosting a positive positioning of people with disabilities as capable workers, in order to increase empowerment and functional coping strategies of people with disabilities.
3. What type of Social Marketing strategy do the two ONCE Foundation campaigns studied mainly correspond to (a reinforcement strategy, an induction strategy. . .)? Base your answer on firm reasoning.
   It is necessary to remember that, according to Santesmases (1999) or Galan-Ladero and Alves (2019), different Social Marketing strategies can be applied: (a) A reinforcement strategy (using awards, incentives, legal norms, etc. to reinforce attitudes); (b) An induction strategy (providing economic incentives, social controls, etc. to induce a desirable behaviour); (c) A rationalisation strategy (giving more information, trying to persuade with advertising, etc. to generate a change of a negative attitude regarding a desirable social behaviour); and (d) A

confrontation strategy (using coercive actions or economic sanctions to generate a change in behaviour.

Regarding this case study, especially a rationalisation strategy seems to be developing; giving more information, trying to persuade with advertising, etc. to generate a change of a negative attitude about a desirable social behaviour (in this case, labour inclusion of people with disabilities). Nevertheless, as stated before, the student could appropriately substantiate another strategy, so it is necessary to take this issue into account.

4. What similarities and differences exist between the two campaigns ("Don't be my limit" and "Working is a story")? Which one do you consider more appropriate depending on the information provided by the case? Why do you think the "Don't be my limit" campaign did not achieve greater results? Reason why.

   The main similarities between these two campaigns are: the objectives, target, broadcasting media, promotor, etc. In regard to the differences, it has to be highlighted the tone of the campaigns (serious and emotional in "Don't be my limit", humorous and informal in "Working is a story"), the graphic design (black and white and solemn in "Don't be my limit", colourful and casual in "Working is a story"), the message (the first directly appeals to the general public: "Don't be my limit", the second is not as direct), the music (elegant and emotive in the first campaign, fun in the "Working is a story" campaign), etc.

   Regarding which one the student considers more appropriate, the most important thing is that they adequately justify their answer. Nevertheless, regarding the results, the "Don't be my limit" campaign seems to have failed to have a real impact on labour inclusion and had poor views on YouTube, so perhaps it is not the most appropriate strategy. The reasons for this could be an improvable communication plan (especially in social media) and/or a negative and overly direct message (blaming the rest of society, in an imperative way, for the labour situation of people with disabilities), among other possible reasons.

5. Based on the case information, how do you think you could improve these campaigns?

   Although there could be different possible answers to this question, possible ideas could be: Segmentation (considering the differences in activity rates by gender, degree of disability or type of disability); developing a positive reinforcement message (instead of a critical, blaming negative one); or taking into account what was commented by Calderwood and Wellington (2013) that stigmatised people should also be taken into consideration in audience targeting in order to avoid the negative consequences that these communication campaigns could have for those people (their special circumstances have to be considered in order to not perpetuate the stigma). Furthermore, there are other points that the student could make, as long as they make sense with the situation described.

References

Andreasen A (1995) Marketing social change. Jossey-Bass, San Francisco, CA

Calderwood KA, Wellington WJ (2013) Social marketing strategies for stigmatized target populations: a case example for problem gamblers and family members of problem gamblers. Qual Rep 18(97):1–19

Carvalho HC, Mazzon JA (2013) Homo economicus and social marketing: questioning traditional models of behavior. J Soc Mark 3(2):162–175

Compas BE, Connor-Smith JK, Saltzman H, Thomsen AH, Wadsworth ME (2001) Coping with stress during childhood and adolescence: problems, progress and potential in theory and research. Psychol Bull 127(1):87–127

Corrigan PW, Watson AC (2002) The paradox of self stigma and mental illness. Clin Psychol Sci Pract 9(1):35–53

Cruz-Morato MA, García-Lizana A (2011) La economía y la psicología ante el problema de la inactividad de las personas con discapacidad. Revista de Fomento Social 262(66):251–284

Cruz-Morato MA, García-Lizana A, García-Mestanza J (2017a) "El problema de la exclusión social en la Unión Europea: ¿Puede el Marketing Social resolver la situación? Una perspectiva desde la Economía del Comportamiento", *Revista de Gestão dos Países de Língua Portuguesa, Special Issue "New Dimensions in Social Marketing",* 16 (3):28–43

Cruz-Morato MA, García-Lizana A, García-Mestanza J (2017b) El Impacto de la Exclusión Social sobre el Crecimiento Económico en la Unión Europea. Revista de Economía Mundial 45:43–64

Dann S (2010) Redefining social marketing with contemporary commercial marketing definitions. J Bus Res 63(2):147–153

French J (2013) Social business, social behavior and social marketing: three cornerstones of future social development. Social Business 3(4):285–296

Galan-Ladero M, Alves H (2019) Case studies on social marketing. A Global Perspective, Springer, Switzerland

Galan-Ladero MM, Galan-Ladero MA (2019) The importance of social Marketing in Global Health Emergencies: the case of Zika virus infection. In: Galan-Ladero M, Alves H (eds) Case studies on social marketing. Management for Professionals. Springer, Cham

Hagerty MR, Cummins RA, Ferriss AL, Land K, Michalos AC, Peterson M, Sharpe A, Sirgy J, Vogel J (2001) Quality of life indexes for National Policy: review and agenda por research. Soc Indic Res 55:1–96

Instituto Nacional de Estadística (2016) El Empleo de las Personas con Discapacidad. Notas de prensa. Retrieved from: https://www.ine.es/prensa/epd_2016.pdf

Instituto Nacional de Estadística (2019) El Empleo de las Personas con Discapacidad. Notas de prensa. Retrieved from: https://www.ine.es/prensa/epd_2018.pdf

Karl FM, Smith J, Piedt S, Turcotte K, Pike I (2018) Applying the health action process approach to bicycle helmet use and evaluating a social marketing campaign. Inj Prev 24(4):288–295

Lefebvre RC, Kotler P (2012) Design thinking, Demarketing and behavioral economics: fostering interdisciplinary growth in social marketing. In: Hastings G, Angus K, Bryant C (eds) The SAGE handbook of social marketing. SAGE Publications Ltd, London, pp 80–94

Leitao J, Alves H (2016) Entrepreneurial and innovative practices in public institutions. A Quality of Life Approach, Springer, Switzerland

Mandiberg JM, Warner R (2012) Business development and marketing within communities of social service clients. J Bus Res 65(12):1736–1742

Miller CT, Major B (2000) Coping with stigma and prejudice. In: Heatherton TF, Kleck RE, Hebl MR, Hull JG (eds) The social psychology of stigma. Guilford, New York, New York, pp 243–272

Myrdal G (1944) An American dilemma. McGraw-Hill, New York

ONCE Foundation (2016). Retrieved from: https://blog.fundaciononce.es/articulo/2016-12-02/no-seas-mi-limite

ONCE Foundation (2019). Retrieved from: https://www.trabajaresunahistoria.es

ONCE Foundation (2020). Retrieved from: https://www.fundaciononce.es/es/pagina/mision-vision-y-valores

Santesmases M (1999) Marketing. Conceptos y Estrategias, Pirámide, Madrid

Simões C, Santos S (2017) The impact of personal and environmental characteristics on quality of life of people with intellectual disability. Appl Res Qual Life 12(2):389–408

Thaler BRH (2016) Behavioral economics: past, present, and future. Am Econ Rev 106(7):1577–1600

Thaler RH, Sunstein CR (2008) Nudge. Penguin Books, New York

Tonon G (2015) Qualitative studies in quality of life: methodology and practice. Retrieved from https://www.springer.com/gp/book/9783319137780

Van Raaij WF (1981) Economic psychology. J Econ Psychol 1:1–24

Chapter 22
Corporate Activism and Quality of Life: Starbucks Corporation Case Study

Joaquin Sanchez Herrera, Teresa Pintado Blanco, and Carlota Lopez Aza

Abstract This case study explores Starbucks' social marketing campaign through a corporate activism strategy. Our aim is to gain a perspective of this problem based on the quality of life theory. This led to our study of Starbucks' social activism campaign for the hiring of 10,000 Syrian refugees in the US between 2017 and 2022 with three basic objectives in mind: (i) help one of the most vulnerable groups in the context of wars and terrorism, giving them a second chance to rebuild their lives and that of their families, (ii) materialise their social commitment in those areas where the company operates, and (iii), from a social marketing perspective, contribute to the change of attitude of citizens towards this group in particular.

Starbucks' economic indicators, as well as the social, economic and demographic conditions in the United States with respect to refugees, are shown for this case study and analysis. So far, the campaign has managed to recruit 2100 refugees (data updated to December 2019), from 12 different countries, in its establishments in the United States, Canada and Europe.

Finally, readers are invited to reflect on whether the arrival of Syrian refugees in the US can have a positive impact on the quality of life for the nation and for Starbucks workers.

Keywords Corporate activism · Quality of life (QoL) · Refugees · Social marketing · Starbucks

Introduction

This case study reflects on the relationship between social marketing, corporate activism and quality of life. It also presents the problems of the Syrian people and the consequences of an immigration policy such as that established by President

J. Sanchez Herrera · T. Pintado Blanco · C. Lopez Aza (✉)
Complutense University of Madrid, Madrid, Spain
e-mail: joaquins@ucm.es; tpintado@ucm.es; carlop14@ucm.es

M. M. Galan-Ladero, R. G. Rivera (eds.), *Applied Social Marketing and Quality of Life*, Applying Quality of Life Research,
https://doi.org/10.1007/978-3-030-83286-5_22

Trump in the United States. Following Executive Order 13769,[1] signed in January 2017, which limited refugee access to the country, Starbucks announces its intention to hire 10,000 Syrian refugees over the next five years. This case study analyses the current social marketing campaign[2] from the perspective of social marketing and corporate activism, based on the Corporate Activism Decision Matrix (CADM). Finally, it shows how the Starbucks refugee recruitment plan affects the brand and the attitude of its current and potential consumers, as well as an improvement in the quality of life, serving as a topic for discussion in the classroom to understand the dimensions and consequences of these types of decisions.

Social Marketing, Corporate Activism and Quality of Life (QoL)

Social marketing is the design, implementation and control of programs seeking to increase the acceptability of a social idea or practice in a target group (Bloom and Novelli 1981). Social marketing tactics persuade individuals to alter their individual behaviour in order to improve their own health and welfare (Andreasen 2005). Over the years, it has also evolved towards a broader concept in which it produces changes on an individual and institutional level (Lefebvre 2011).

Within social marketing, corporate activism is defined as those business activities that promote, impede or direct social, political, economic and/or environmental reform or stasis with the desire to promote or impede improvements in society (Kotler and Sarkar 2018). Likewise, it is usually presented through communication campaigns and/or statements made by CEOs positioning a company for or against an issue that polarises society, such as immigration, abortion or feminism. The key to activism is the triangulation between identity, consumption and values (Manfredi-Sánchez 2019), a strategic movement nowadays given that society requires companies to take public positions, which can improve business profits (Kotler and Sarkar 2018) and at the same time come into closer alignment with stakeholder values.

Furthermore, the social marketing campaign being studied here deals with a highly controversial issue: immigration and Starbucks' public posture on this matter. This can generate changes in attitude and behaviour, mainly through confrontation strategies although, in practice, rationalisation or reinforcement strategies have also been used.

Ultimately, if social marketers want to achieve substantial improvements in public health and welfare, they need to expand the boundaries of the concept (Wymer 2010). One way of doing this is to introduce corporate activism as a

[1]The full text of the executive order is available for consultation at: https://www.whitehouse.gov/presidential-actions/executive-order-protecting-nation-foreign-terrorist-entry-united-states-2/

[2]The company's message can be analysed at: https://www.starbucks.com/responsibility/community/refugee-hiring

technique in their social marketing campaigns. It is within upstream social marketing, defined by Andreasen (2005) where it has more space, since it consists of encouraging different organisations to participate in order to achieve a positive social purpose. In the current context, more and more companies are realising that they have a broader responsibility with consumers and with society in general (Polanski, cited in Dibb and Carrigan 2013). This is why the option of an activist marketing strategy from the perspective of social marketing makes sense to better identify with its audiences and provide added value as a differentiator.

This makes companies focus more on how they can improve citizens' quality of life and address consumers' personal goals/motivations (Polanski, cited in Dibb and Carrigan 2013). According to Sirgy and Lee (1996), quality of life marketing is aimed at improving the well-being of consumers without harming other stakeholders in the organisation. This objective is common to social marketing and corporate activism, since both try to achieve a positive change in attitude, aimed at solving social, political, environmental and other problems.

The Syrian Issue and Trump's Immigration Policy

The civil war in Syria is one of the most dramatic conflicts of the last decade. According to United Nations data, approximately 400,000 Syrians have lost their lives in this war, the consequences of which are still very present today, with the massive influx of Syrian citizens to the Greek border (BBC, 2020). Their goal is to reach countries that guarantee safety and a prosperous future for their families. One of the destinations where Syrians and other Muslim-majority countries settle is the United States (Ward 2019).

Quality of life (QOL) indicators for the United States are well above those of Syria. OECD data on well-being in the United States in 2017 show above-average values in most indicators, such as access to housing (8.5 points out of 10), education (7), civic engagement (7), health (8.9), or safety (7.5) (OECD Well Being Report 2017), but it is not possible to compare them with those of Syria, because the OECD does not include this country in its reports. However, the Happy Planet Index (2019), an initiative promoted by the Gallup group, provides indicators that bring together several sources that include many more countries. These sources include data from the OECD itself, but also others from the United Nations Department of Economics and Social Affairs, the Global Footprint Network, or World Bank indicators. Table 22.1 shows the quality of life indicators for the United States and Syria, in which the enormous distance that separates both countries can be seen in most factors.

However, upon arrival, refugees are confronted with different perceptions from the host country: (i) they may be seen as vulnerable individuals who migrate involuntarily due to persecution in their country of origin; (ii) or as individuals who put the safety of the country of destination at risk by coming from conflict zones (Adida et al. 2019). If the refugees are also Arabs or Muslims, previous studies have

Table 22.1 Happy planet index: United States vs. Syria

Country	Life Expectancy	Average Well-being (0-10)	Inequality of Outcomes	Inequality-adjusted Well-being	GDP/capita ($PPP)
US	78.8	7.0	13%	6.5	51,457 $
Syria	70.4	3.2	30%	2.6	2080 $

Source: Happy Planet Index (2019)
The full report is available for consultation at http://happyplanetindex.org/

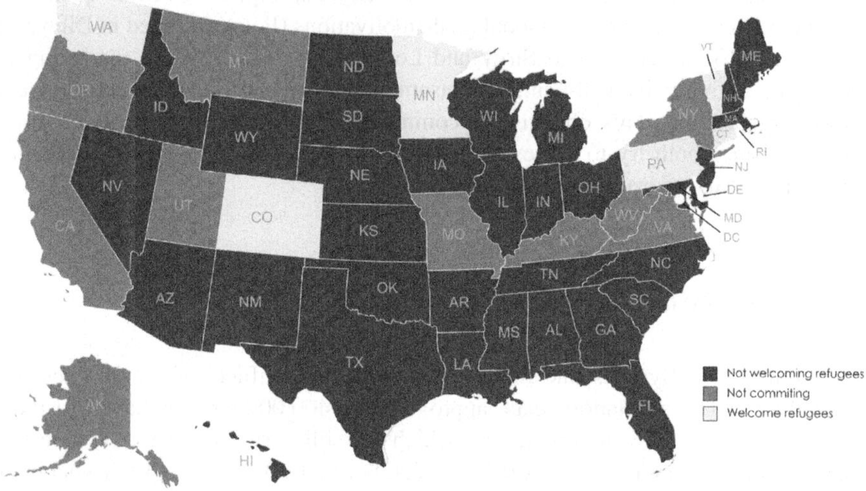

Fig. 22.1 States for or against the entry of refugees into their territories. Source: Fantz and Brumfield, CNN (2015)

shown that most Americans have negative impressions of them, especially after the terrorist attacks of 2001, whose media coverage has since focused on acts of violence and religious extremism (Setthamalinee 2006).

In fact, the North American social context does not particularly favour the entry of Syrian refugees into the country. According to data collected by CNN (2016, 2020) governors of 31 states have declared that they are against the admission of Syrian refugees into their territories (Fig. 22.1).

The American public also has a significant anti-Muslim bias that decreases somewhat among Democrats, and Americans specifically prefer Syrian refugees and those who are highly skilled, English-speaking and Christian (Adida et al. 2019).

This context and the takeover in the US of the Republican, Donald Trump, led to the signing of Executive Order No. 13769 on 25 January 2017, which imposed a minimum 90-day ban on refugee immigrants to travel to the US from seven countries, the majority of which being Muslim (including Syrian citizens, because their entry was considered detrimental to national interests and a national security threat). Its main objective was to ensure the protection of US citizens against terrorist

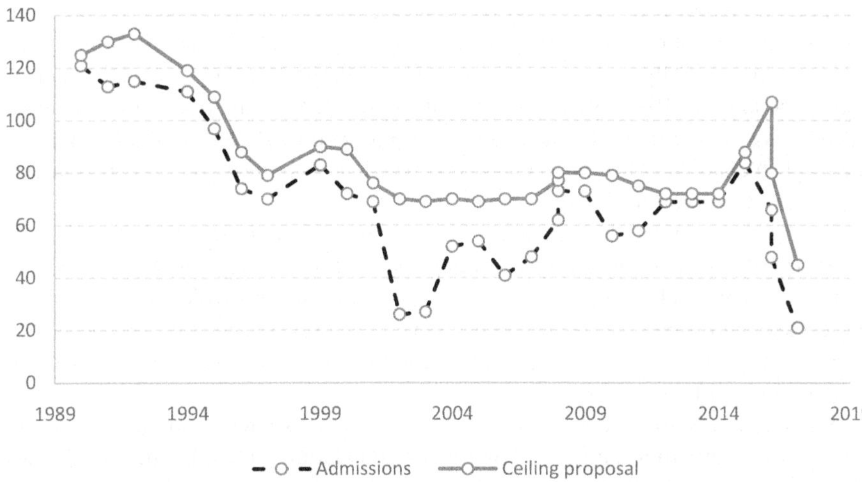

Fig. 22.2 Refugee Admissions and Admission Ceiling in the United States (1990-2018) (Data in thousands). Source: United States Department of State (2019)

attacks and to prevent the exploitation of its immigration laws for malicious purposes (Executive Order 2017).

The order has caused much criticism since its entry into force. For example, many saw the same discrimination based on religion and place of origin. Even CEOs of large US companies such as Tesla, Facebook, Apple and Microsoft publicly expressed their displeasure. Others, such as Starbucks CEO Howard Schultz, decided to act by promising to hire 10,000 refugees in the next five years (until 2022) in the 75 countries where Starbucks operates (Rosen 2017; Starbucks 2017). The order was appealed, and therefore paralysed, until the United States Supreme Court considered Donald Trump's immigration veto legal in 2018 (BBC 2018).

Data from the State Department, as of 2019 (latest report available), reflect a decrease in the number of refugees since Trump's takeover (Fig. 22.2). In 2018, the United States admitted 22,405 refugees, a decrease of 58 percent from the previous year in which the Immigration and Nationality Act (INA) was enacted and a 73% decrease compared to 2016 (Annual Flow Report 2018).

The Starbucks Case

Company History

Starbucks was established in 1971 in Pike Place market (Seattle, US) with the objective of selling coffee beans and ground coffee, tea and spices. Years later, in 1982, Howard Schultz joins Starbucks as sales and marketing director, offering coffee to restaurants and bars; shortly afterwards, Schultz travels to Italy where he became impressed with the quality of Milan's espresso and was the inspiration for the current concept of Starbucks coffee. From that moment on, the company started to grow exponentially, and in 1992 it was listed on the NASDAQ stock market. A short time later, in 1996, the first establishment outside North America was inaugurated in Tokyo and internationalisation was expanded in 1998 with the purchase of the English chain Seattle Coffee Company, which at that time had 60 establishments (Starbucks Corporation, 2020).

Today, the company has branches in more than 75 countries, with over 26,000 stores (partly owned and partly operating under license), and more than 300,000 employees (Starbucks Corporation, 2020). Starbucks offers a wide variety of different coffees and mixes, as well as other beverages prepared on the spot or bottled (iced drinks, teas, juices, among others), food (cakes, sandwiches, salads, etc.) as well as cups, gifts or books.

Starbucks' responsible behaviour has been demonstrated from the very start through different programmes: (i) "Starbucks Foundation" created to finance literacy programmes in the United States and Canada, currently supporting the cultivation of coffee, tea or cocoa, providing clean water, or promoting educational programmes; (ii) the "Starbucks ™ Shared Planet ™" commitment to conduct business responsibly since 2008; (iii) the "Business Ethics and Compliance Programme"; (iv) the "Mission statement on the environment" reducing the environmental footprint, or (v) "Starbucks Community Service" programmes for community participation (Starbucks 2020), among others.

Starbucks Social Marketing Campaign: Syrian Immigration

In response to Trump's anti-immigration laws, Starbucks initiated a social marketing campaign to hire 10,000 refugees by 2022, an indirect blow to the US President's executive order (Maze 2017; Rosen 2017; Starbucks 2017).

Starbucks has always supported the creation of opportunities for all types of audiences from the very beginning, and refugees seek an opportunity to rebuild their lives, always starting from difficult circumstances.

The Starbucks campaign proposed that the hiring of 10,000 refugees would enrich their corresponding communities. 2500 of them would come from Western Europe, and 1000 from Canada, while in the United States the campaign would focus on holders of Special Immigrant Visas (SIVs), as well as participants (and their families) who served alongside US troops abroad. Recruitment would take place in markets with the greatest need for refugees, and where there was a base camp to meet that need; like the rest of the company's employees, applicants would need work permits and would have to pass the same background check. Ultimately, Starbucks' goal with this campaign was to provide tools, resources and support to address the needs of refugee claimants, as well as their hiring managers.

To reinforce its campaign, Starbucks partnered with the UNHCR (UN Refugee Agency) action #WithRefugees and the Association of Refugee Tents, in order to have a greater joint impact on the lives of refugees. It also partnered with refugee resettlement agencies as well as several non-governmental organisations: the International Rescue Committee –UNHCR–, the UN Refugee Agency, Hire Immigrants, and the organisation No One Left Behind. The Starbucks Foundation also played a significant role in funding refugee job training programmes.

This led Kelly T. Clements (UNHCR High Commissioner for Refugees) to mention that "Starbucks' commitment shows how companies can tangibly help refugees. People who are forced to flee often arrive in new countries with specialised knowledge and the willingness to work hard. Above all, they want the dignity that comes with being able to support their own families. Through their jobs, refugees also integrate more quickly into their communities and bring tangible economic and social benefits to them".

The letter Starbucks sent to company staff arrived a day after CEO Howard Schultz expressed "confusion, surprise and opposition" to Executive Order No. 13769, a sentiment he said he shared with many in the organisation, who were seeing the promise of the American dream being questioned (Rosen 2017). It should be taken into account that, eleven years earlier, Starbucks had problems with part of the Muslim community because it decided to open new stores in Israel, which was interpreted as an attack on the Palestinians and their historical rights (Setthamalinee 2006).

Days later, and aware of the risks involved in social activism, Scultz also said that his action was a statement about personality, not politics (Maze 2017). Starbucks also informed its employees that it would offer them and their families free legal services on immigration matters (Rosen 2017). In short, Starbucks initiates a strategy of confrontation with the national government, along with a strategy of reinforcement towards its employees that, in this case, is supported by this social marketing campaign.

The move was praised by its advocates, as Trump supporters urged a boycott of the company (#BoycottStarbucks). However, criticism also came from within the company at the annual shareholders meeting in March 2017. One of them asked Schultz why he was willing to risk Starbucks' reputation and why he failed to react in a similar way to travel bans imposed by Democratic presidents. Schultz responded by insisting that the plan was based on core values of compassion and humanity, not politics (Maze 2017; Rosen 2017).

On the other hand, Schultz also urged his workers to be politically active and responsible. "*Starbucks is doing its part; we need them to use their voices to do the same while respecting the diverse views of the 90 million customers who visit our stores in more than 25,000 locations around the world*" (Maze 2017). These statements have been accompanied by palpable results, as shown by the Global Social Impact Report (2018): so far, the campaign has managed to recruit 2100 refugees (data updated to December 2019), from 12 different countries, in its establishments in the United States, Canada and Europe.

Starbucks Social Marketing and Activism as a Contribution to Quality of Life (QoL)

Starbucks' social marketing towards refugees is more closely related to the lifetime values of its customers, which, in turn, can positively influence a higher purchase probability (Corcoran et al. 2016). Once the campaign has come to an end in 2022, the effect that this social marketing campaign has had on consumer behaviour can be more accurately assessed. It could also improve the quality of life of refugees, accessing legal and dignified work in countries that are safe for them and their families. On the one hand, these types of actions can also have a positive impact on current Starbucks employees, who see how the company they work for tries to improve society and makes them part of it. Management must ensure that the organisation offers satisfactory working conditions and relationships. Management can thus promote the quality of working life (QWL) (Sirgy et al. 2001). Employees in favour of the QWL are likely to show positive results (Lee et al. 2015) and have a closer relationship with their organisation.

It is also interesting to reflect on whether the arrival of refugees could have a positive effect on the quality of life in the country, and it seems that their contribution has been very positive in terms of productivity and the work environment at least. According to one of the first studies published on this matter, refugee employees are more loyal to the companies that hire them, which reduces training costs associated with turnover, and they tend to be tremendously efficient in their professions (Tent Research Report, 2018). On the other hand, it is important to consider the quality of life that attracts residents. This measure includes "third places" that foster community and communication between people outside home and work. The results show that coffee shops and bars are the best third places (Jeffres et al. 2009) and more specifically McDonald's and Starbucks (Burnett et al. 2017), which favour a better perceived quality of life. Previous studies have shown that respondents with higher education and income prefer Starbucks whose impact is positive on quality of life (Land et al. 2012).

However, it must be borne in mind that many Starbucks restaurants in the United States are located in some of the US states that were against the admission of refugees. Fig. 22.3 shows the ten cities in the United States in which Starbucks has the most establishments, and the posture of the states in which those cities are located with respect to the admission of refugees into their territory (Fig. 22.3).

The graph only reflects one state that was in favour of the admission of refugees (Seattle), while California, New York and Oregon have a neutral posture, and finally it highlights those that reject the presence of refugees (Illinois, Texas, Nevada and Arizona). These ten cities are the most important to Starbucks from a business point of view, but four of them are in states opposed to admitting refugees.

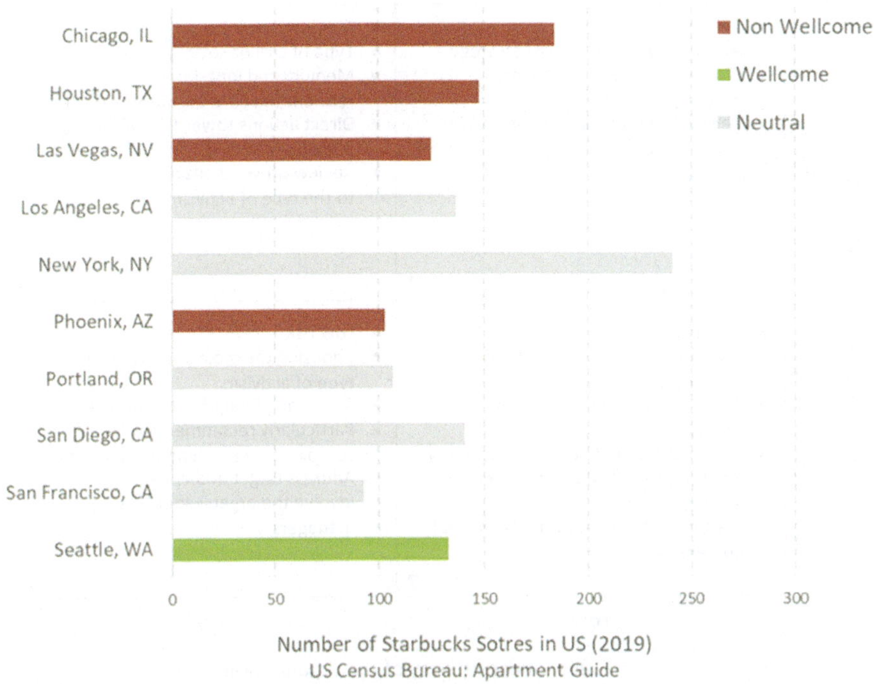

Fig. 22.3 The ten cities with the majority of Starbucks establishments, and their posture regarding acceptance or rejection of refugees. Source: Own elaboration based on data from the US Census Bureau (2019)

Did Starbucks Follow the Right Strategy?

When it comes to decision-making regarding corporate activism, there are two questions that are not easy to answer:

(a) What type of corporate activism should be adopted and what degree of involvement should the company show?
(b) Have they had a positive effect on people's quality of life?

The answer to the first question can be found in the principles defined in the Corporate Activism Decision Matrix (CADM) (Sánchez et al. 2020), and a multitude of social and quality of life indicators provided by official bodies (OECD, Migration Policy Institute (2020), US Census Bureau, etc.) can be used to evaluate the impact that corporate activism actions may have had.

The CADM matrix isa tool that provides useful guidance to companies on how they should make decisions regarding corporate activism. The matrix is made up of two relevant variables: (i) the degree of controversy in industry, and (ii) the level of consistency of the organisation (the difference between what it says and what it

Fig. 22.4 Corporate activism decision matrix (CADM). Source: Sánchez et al. (2020)

does). These two variables can result in four different scenarios that have important implications in the process of adopting a corporate activist strategy (see Fig. 22.4).

The first quadrant (1) considers the situation in which the level of controversy in the sector is high (for example, the tobacco sector, or the gaming sector), and the level of consistency of the organisation is low. In these cases, the risk of taking activist positions is very high, and it would not be advisable to follow these lines of action.

The second quadrant (2) shows an organisation that operates in a sector with a low level of controversy, as well as a low level of consistency. In these cases, the risk of adopting activist strategies is high, and the choice of this type of initiative would only be justified if aggressive competitive postures are to be taken with respect to an established leader.

The third quadrant (3) shows the location of organisations that operate in controversial sectors, as well as their high consistency. It is therefore possible for responsible, honest and socially engaged companies to find themselves in controversial sectors that are frequently criticised. In these cases, the adoption of activist strategies implies a medium risk and, unlike the previous scenario (2), here postures focusing on social or civil aspects should be adopted.

Finally, the fourth scenario (4) is the best for the adoption of activist initiatives, since industry's low level of controversy converges with the organisation's high level of consistency. In these cases, the risk is low, and they can be integrated into companies as part of their corporate identity, especially if the organisation has a leadership position in its sector.

In which quadrant is Starbucks located? According to the Edelman report (Edelman Trust Barometer 2020), in 2017 the food and beverage sector had a score of 68 points out of 100 (maximum confidence), well above other sectors, such as the financial sector, which showed a score of 55 points, and slightly above leisure and motor industries, or the telecommunications sector. Therefore, Starbucks would be at the bottom of the vertical axis, since it belongs to a sector with a low level of controversy.

Regarding the organisation's level of consistency, Starbucks appears to have been consistent with its posture regarding the recruitment of refugees from Syria, based on its statements and other behaviours observed that reinforce its posture on this matter. For example, Starbucks is part of the United Nations Refugee Agency (UNHCR), and actively collaborates with non-governmental organisations such as the "International Rescue Committee" (IRC), or the US organisation "No One Left Behind". According to local media and company employee statements, Starbucks' commitment was firm, and its 2017 refugee recruitment programme is currently running according to schedule. It can therefore be stated that the level of commitment of the organisation is high, placing it on the right side of the horizontal axis.

Based on these two parameters (level of controversy and level of consistency), Starbucks would be placed in quadrant 4 (see Fig. 22.5), whose most important general recommendations are as follows:

(a) Low risk: For Starbucks, adopting an active posture with regard to refugees from Syria did not pose a high risk as did some its customers who see immigration from troubled countries as a threat. Although there were movements calling for a boycott of their products, their impact was zero or very small, judging by the company's revenue figures (see Fig. 22.6). On the other hand, it does not appear

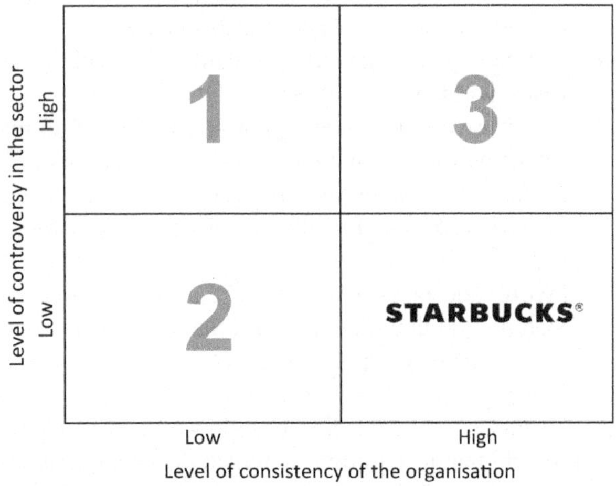

Fig. 22.5 Starbucks' posture in the Corporate Activism Decision Matrix (CADM)

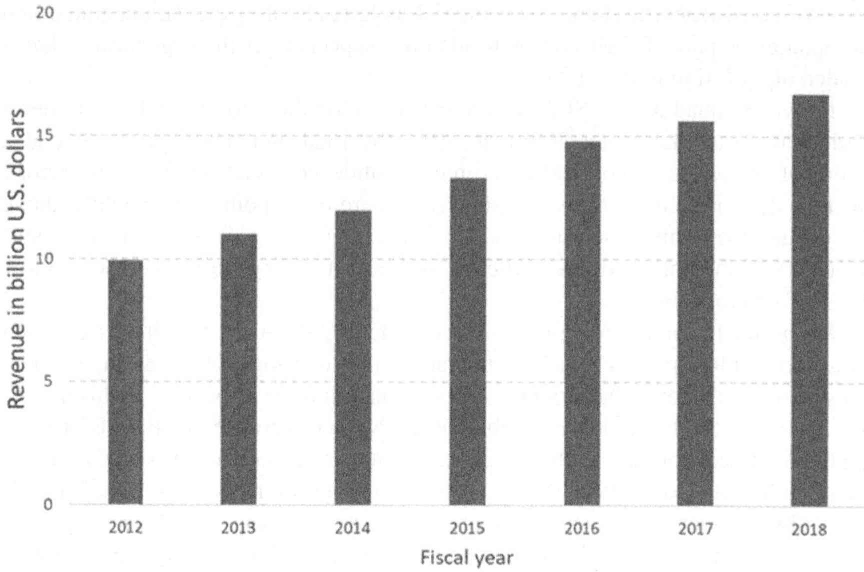

Fig. 22.6 Evolution of Starbucks' revenue (2012-2018). Source: Own elaboration based on Starbucks Annual Reports (2019)

that the announcement of the initiative had a negative effect on the price of its shares, as can be seen in Fig. 22.7 attached.

(b) Choice of the type of most socially engaged activism: Starbucks did indeed choose a type of social activism, trying to improve the living conditions of a group that fled their country of origin in search of a future for themselves and their families.
(c) Adoption of long-term postures: Starbucks announced this initiative in January 2017, and is committed to carrying it out over the next five years (2017-2022), so it is not just a one-off action, but a line of action sustained over time, which implies a constant concern for this cause.
(d) Particularly recommended in companies with a leadership position: Starbucks was a world leader in its sector, but today it is even more so thanks to its alliance with Nescafé. Its leadership position allows it to make these types of corporate activism decisions with less risk and greater authority.
(e) Address all audiences involved: Starbucks made its announcement public through all kinds of media, reaching out to customers, employees, shareholders and suppliers.
(f) Involve the main managers of the organisation: in this case, the president of Starbucks at that time, Howard Schultz, was the one who led this initiative, and was its main promoter, not only within the company, but also abroad as a spokesman to all social media.

Therefore, Starbucks closely follows the principles of the CADM matrix, and it can be said that its corporate activism decisions were correct from a technical point of view.

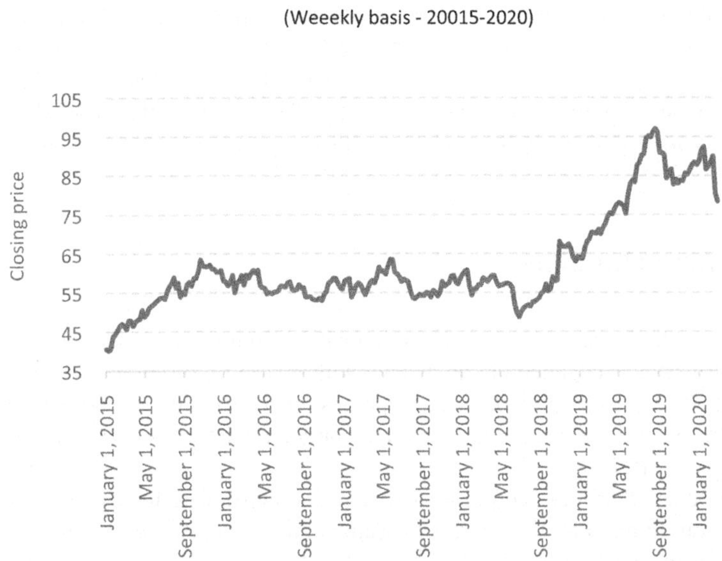

Fig. 22.7 Evolution of the price of Starbucks shares. (Weekly basis - 2015-2020). Source: Own elaboration based on Starbucks share price data (2015-2020)

Conclusions

This case study highlights the use of corporate activism as a social marketing strategy to improve the quality of life of refugees in particular and of society in general. The corporate activism decision matrix (CADM) that has been applied can be used as a guide to make decisions of this nature, depending on the level of controversy in the sector and organisational consistency; it can therefore be used by other companies that conduct activist campaigns from the perspective of social marketing. As seen in this case study, Starbucks' location in the fourth quadrant of the matrix meets all the technical requirements that ensure proper adoption of a corporate activist strategy.

The main effects of this social campaign on quality of life indices are as follows:

(a) The quality of life in the host country improves in terms of productivity as refugees are more loyal and efficient workers.
(b) The quality of work life improves because Starbucks employees feel they have a closer relationship with the company as it involves them in its campaigns and ensures legal, satisfactory and dignified working conditions.
(c) The quality of life for residents improves thanks to third places that include coffee shops like Starbucks.
(d) The quality of life of customers with the same social postures as Starbucks improves and will lead to higher purchase probabilities.

Social marketing in general, and corporate activism in particular, have become an essential tool for companies to connect with their audiences, achieve unity between business and personal values, and cause a change in attitudes and behaviours regarding social issues that polarise the population, as is the case of refugees, which involves improving their quality of life.

Discussion Questions

1. Do you think the perception, attitude or behaviour of Starbucks customers and employees has changed or can change with regard to Syrian refugees?
2. Look for other social marketing campaigns related to refugees and compare them to the Starbucks campaign (message, target audience, success, influence on quality of life).
3. Do you see Starbucks corporate activism as opportunist? Justify your answer.
4. Do you think that the Starbucks campaign improves the quality of life of employees, customers and investors? How?

Teaching Notes

This case study was written for a 60-90 minute discussion. In most cases it might be more helpful to divide the students into small groups so that they can discuss among themselves and come up with alternative solutions. Students should read the case study before class without answering the questions raised. If the teacher does not have enough time, the questions can be assigned well in advance, making it clear that the analysis needs to be completed before coming to class, possibly requiring parts of it to be submitted individually. Later in class, and regardless of the method chosen, the session will develop in the same way. Different aspects of this case study can be highlighted depending on the type and characteristics of the course.

Suggested Calendar

First part. 30 minutes: introduction

In addition to clarifying the elements of the case study analysis and the central idea of social marketing strategies, reference is also made to other concepts. The teacher can invite the students to comment on their vision of immigration, in particular of refugees. Then the teacher can explain the different types of activism and ask the students for real examples.

Second part. 45 minutes: analysis

The students are organised into groups and must answer the questions (reread the case study if necessary). The teacher can go through and solve the discussion questions in order, or choose those that best suit the course and their learning objectives. Discussion questions help students think about the key issues raised by the case study. Discussion questions help students think about the key issues raised by the case study. In relation to the questions posed, the answers should be similar to the following:

1. ***Do you think the perception, attitude or behaviour of Starbucks customers and employees has changed or can change with regard to Syrian refugees?***

   Students' reflections should refer to what social marketing can do to change the behaviour of North American society, considering the influence of a company like Starbucks. Students are expected to comment and discuss these and other aspects: (i) Educating consumers or employees about the positive influence of immigration; (ii) Developing a social movement for the integration of immigrants into the labour market; and/or (iii) Convincing the government to change the immigration policy.
2. ***Look for other social marketing campaigns and compare them to the Starbucks campaign (message, target audience, success, influence on quality of life).***

   Students must be clear about the topics that social marketing addresses to find other campaigns (smoking, obesity, diseases, social problems, etc.).
3. ***Do you see Starbucks corporate activism as opportunist? Justify your answer.***

   Students must identify the differences between an opportunistic strategy and the development of a long-term activist strategy, which is related to stakeholder values. To do this, they must start by defining corporate activism (sect. 1.1) and applying the CADM matrix (sect. 2.4) to justify Starbucks' activist strategy as non-opportunistic.
4. ***Do you think that the Starbucks campaign improves the quality of life of employees, customers and investors? How?***

   Arguments in favour must be based on increased productivity, satisfaction, loyalty, efficiency, etc. using data in sect. 2.3 of this chapter. The arguments against must gravitate around the possibilities of a boycott suffered by the company, the reduction of its reputation by stakeholders contrary to the position of Starbucks, or the CEO's own declaration as an action of personality without using the concept of political and/or social activism (sect. 2.2).

Third part. 15 minutes: close

The summary discussion should focus on what Starbucks has done so far and what the organisation faces in the future, as well as key quality of life indicators. The teacher could ask other questions for a final discussion: What specific steps should Starbucks take next? How can Starbucks inspire other companies to innovate in activism? Do you think Starbucks is likely to try and launch new social marketing campaigns?

References

Adida CL, Lo A, Platas MR (2019) Americans preferred Syrian refugees who are female, English-speaking, and Christian on the eve of Donald Trump's election. PLoS One 14(10):e0222504. https://doi.org/10.1371/journal.pone.0222504

Andreasen AR (2005) Social Marketing in the Twenty-first Century. Sage, Thousand Oaks, CA

Annual Flow Report (2018) Refugees and Asylees. Office of Immigration Statistics:1–10

BBC (2018) La Corte Suprema de Estados Unidos considera legal el veto migratorio de Donald Trump a varios países de mayoría musulmana. Disponible en: https://www.bbc.com/mundo/noticias-internacional-44608203

Bloom PN, Novelli WD (1981) Problems and challenges in social marketing. J Mark 45(2):79–88

Burnett P, Brooks T, Bassett P (2017) Estimating quality of life and place with location theory: the McBucks index. Soc Indic Res 134:455–472

Corcoran M, Newman K, Devasagayam PR (2016) Consumer perception of corporate activism: strategic implication for marketing. Int J Acad Res Bus Soc Sci 6(10):52–61

Dibb S, Carrigan M (2013) Social marketing transformed: Kotler, Polonsky and Hastings reflect on social marketing in a period of social change. Eur J Mark 47(9):1376–1398

Edelman Trust Barometer (2020) Disponible en https://www.edelman.com/trustbarometer

Executive Order (2017) Executive order 13769: protecting the nation from foreign terrorist entry into the United States. Presidential Documents 82(20):8977–8982

Happy Planet Index report (2019) Disponible en http://happyplanetindex.org/resources

Jeffres LW, Bracken CC, Jian G, Casey MF (2009) The impact of third places on community quality of life. Appl Res Qual Life 4:333–345

Kotler P, Sarkar C (2018) Brand activism: from purpose to action. Idea Bite Press

Land KC, Michalos AC, Sirgy MJ (eds) (2012) Handbook of social indicators and quality-of life research. Springer Publishers, Netherlands

Lee JS, Back KJ, Chan ESW (2015) Quality of work life and job satisfaction among frontline hotel employees: a self-determination and need satisfaction theory approach. Int J Contemp Hosp Manag 27(5):768–789

Lefebvre RC (2011) An integrative model for social marketing. J Soc Mark 1(1):54–72

Manfredi-Sánchez JL (2019) Brand activism. Commun Soc 32(4):343–359

Maze J (2017) Starbucks plans to hire 10,000 refugees. Nation's Restaurant News, NY

Migration Policy Institute (2020) Disponible en https://www.migrationpolicy.org/

OCDE (2017) Better life initiative: measuring Well-being and Progress. Disponible en: http://www.oecd.org/statistics/better-life-initiative.htm

Rosen B (2017) In swipe at Trump's travel ban, Starbucks sells its brand of social responsibility. The Christian Science Monitor, Boston, Mass

Sánchez J, López-Aza C, Pintado T (2020) Activismo Corporativo: ¿Moda o estrategia de comunicación de marca? Harvard Deusto 162:6–13

Setthamalinee S (2006) The construction of collective identity of Muslims in America after September 11, 2001. Prajñā Vihāra, 7(1)

Sirgy MJ, Efraty D, Siegel P, Dong-Jin L (2001) A new measure of quality of work life (QWL) based on need satisfaction and spillover theories. Soc Indic Res 55(3):241–302

Sirgy MJ, Lee D (1996) Setting socially responsible marketing objectives: a quality-of-life approach. Eur J Mark 30(5):20–34

Starbucks (2017) Starbucks makes global commitment to hire 10,000 refugees by 2022. Disponible en: https://www.starbucks.com/responsibility/community/refugee-hiring

Starbucks (2018) Global Social Impact Report. https://stories.starbucks.com/stories/2019/2018-starbucks-global-social-impact-report/

Starbucks (2019) Starbucks Annual Reports. https://investor.starbucks.com/financial-data/annual-reports/default.aspx

Starbucks Corporation (2020) Starbucks Coffee Company. http://www.starbucks.com/
US Census Bureau (2019) United States Census Bureau. https://www.census.gov/
Ward DG (2019) Public attitudes toward young immmigrant men. Am Polit Sci Rev 113(1):264–269. https://doi.org/10.1017/S0003055418000710
Wymer W (2010) Rethinking the boundaries of social marketing: activism or advertising? J Bus Res Elsevier 63(2):99–103

Chapter 23
Enhancing Women's Quality of Life and Empathy through a Micro-Learning Social Marketing Strategy

Reynaldo G. Rivera and Jazmín Nogaró

Abstract This chapter presents the case of a university and an international NGO that developed, executed, and evaluated a protocol (EduQualitas SM) and a social marketing campaign—*Orientación Familiar Digital* or Digital Family Orientation, in English (DFO). These endeavors intended to improve the quality of life in the area of Argentina with the highest poverty and violence levels: Buenos Aires' suburban area.

The campaign sought to develop empathy—an ability that plays a fundamental role in the quality of intra-family relations and the development of people's pro-social behavior, leadership, and decision-making capability—in 56 women.

The case is the first to be developed in and for a Latin American country, through an interdisciplinary consortium of actors, which uses digital micro-learning and instant messaging technologies (WhatsApp) in a context of social isolation to improve the quality of life.

The research shows that the protocol and methodology used increased women's empathy in its critical dimensions. The social marketing campaign became a tool for the digitalization of a civil society organization, facilitating the continuity of its activities amidst pandemic preventive isolation policies.

Keywords Social marketing · Micro-learning · Empathy · Women · Quality of life

Introduction

From a political, social, and cultural standpoint, the Buenos Aires conurbation or Greater Buenos Aires includes the first and second suburban areas of the city's Metropolitan Region, where 34.1% of its population can be characterized as poor and 49.6% of children and adolescents live below the poverty line.

R. G. Rivera (✉) · J. Nogaró
Austral University, Buenos Aires, Argentina
e-mail: rrivera@austral.edu.ar; jnogaro@mail.austral.edu.ar

M. M. Galan-Ladero, R. G. Rivera (eds.), *Applied Social Marketing and Quality of Life*, Applying Quality of Life Research,
https://doi.org/10.1007/978-3-030-83286-5_23

The Greater Buenos Aires area is the Argentine region with the highest negative impact of the compulsory isolation policies and mortality rates caused by COVID-19. Since March 2020, when the quarantine began, more than a third of the people in Buenos Aires' suburbs have struggled to access food. There has been an increase in problematic consumptions, too.

Several Civil Society Organizations (CSOs) focus on efforts to reduce poverty and women's exclusion in this area. One of them, ANSPAC, an organization founded in 1974 in Mexico with branches across fourteen countries in the Americas and Spain, promotes women's overall empowerment. Its 112,306 members are distributed in units managed by female coordinators, who give courses on self-knowledge, emotion management, and interpersonal relations. During the COVID-19 pandemic, ANSPAC Argentina found itself, like many other organizations, lacking a methodology that would allow it to quickly adapt its training to the virtual world.

This case analyses the application of a social intervention protocol based on a dialogic relational model (EduQualitas SM) developed by Universidad Austral (Argentina) and InterMedia Social Innovation (Italy). This intervention improved the quality of life of a group of women from the Greater Buenos Aires area, partially digitizing ANSPAC's training activities through a social marketing program that used digital micro-learning strategies to increase empathy and social engagement.

Social Marketing, Quality of Life and Empathy: A Theoretical Framework

Recent studies show that poverty and women's exclusion in the Greater Buenos Aires area is not only material, but also emotional and relational (Rivera et al. 2019).

Psychological distress levels are three times higher among people belonging to a marginal working social-occupational stratum (Rodríguez Espínola and Salvia 2019). Negative coping with stress is also influenced by precariousness: 40% of poor people show an avoidant/negative style (Rodríguez Espínola and Salvia 2019).

Recent research (for a review of the literature, see Rivera et al. 2019) indicates that the prevention of conflict and violence against women requires changes in social attitudes, norms, and relational processes. From a multidimensional perspective of the theory on quality of life that includes both objective and subjective aspects (Tonon 2016, 2017), women's quality of life would increase if relational skills were improved. Relational and spiritual dimensions are as important for well-being and life satisfaction as material resources and other objective indicators of development such as security or transparency: empathy, compassion, care and understanding are relational assets that contribute positively to quality of life (Tonon 2017, pp. 17, 21). As Sen and Nussbaum's theory on the quality of life and capability approach indicate, empirical evidence confirms the importance of empathy as a relational good. Empathy facilitates compassion and the development of scripts, attitudes, and behaviors that favor positive moral action (Deane-Drummond 2017) and the reduction of poverty in society (Lane 2001; Segal 2007).

Consequently, a social marketing strategy based on a relational model and aimed at improving interpersonal relations through the development of empathy abilities could increase the quality of life of women living in social exclusion such as those in the Buenos Aires conurbation.

EduQualitas SM Protocol Implementation

Outside the field of health promotion, there are few validated protocols for social marketing and improving the quality of life of people at risk of exclusion (Rivera et al. 2019). Considering the growth of violence against women in Argentina, Universidad Austral and the Italian CSO InterMedia Social Innovation agreed to develop, validate, and disseminate the EduQualitas SM protocol. Including six stages (see Fig. 23.1), EduQualitas SM provides a path to implement and assess social marketing programs aimed at promoting women's well-being and overall health.

Although the protocol's stages are sequential, the process is a continuum, and its phases are interconnected.

In March 2020, the project team identified a specific target audience (women participating in ANSPAC training activities) to implement the protocol. After two initial interviews with ANSPAC coordinators, the project's partners established the central goal of the social marketing strategy: to increase the quality of life and empathy of women experiencing social exclusion.

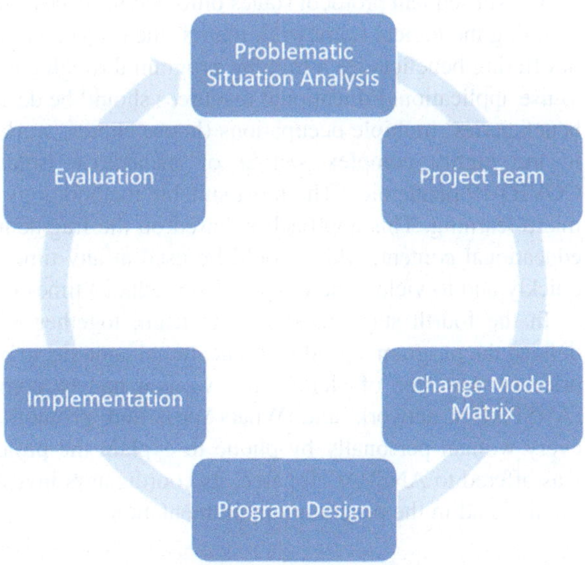

Fig. 23.1 EduQualitas SM Protocol. Source: own elaboration

Table 23.1 EduQualitas SM Protocol

Analysis	Project partners identified a dire need: To help women in a period of preventive isolation via a daily use channel (the free WhatsApp platform). The alternative was Facebook, but WhatsApp ensured confidentiality and the possibility of one-on-one connections between coordinators and beneficiaries. This would improve women's empathy and their relationship with ANSPAC through personalized training.
Team	The project team held virtual training meetings with ANSPAC coordinators to analyze its theoretical model as compared to the CSO's existing programs. The project team prepared some guides with detailed instructions for the tasks to be carried out during protocol execution.
Matrix	Based on the project's theoretical model and the previous stages, the project team developed a logical framework matrix with four modules (family relations, emotion management, empathy as an emotion, and empathic disposition), a methodology (digital micro learning), as well as a monitoring and an evaluation procedures.
Design	Previous research on empathy development and measurement (McLaren, 2013; Richaud 2008) and ANSPAC coordinators' engagement served as the basis to design educational materials.
Implementation	The program was implemented between May 13 and June 8, 2020. The project manager remained in permanent contact with the coordinators, which proved vital to ensure execution quality.
Evaluation	The project team used a QuestionPro platform to set up an online questionnaire. Beneficiaries answered it, and responses were used to determine women's empathy levels before the intervention. In addition to a weekly follow-up with coordinators, a post-test evaluation was carried out in the first week of June, via the same platform and using the same pre-test scales.

Source: Elaborated by the authors

The subsequent protocol stages unfolded in successive meetings (see Table 23.1).

Using the logical framework matrix, the project team determined the importance of offering beneficiaries a training program through a mobile platform and an easy-to-use application. Educational resources should be designed to be compatible with beneficiaries' multiple occupations (house chores, work, children's education, etc.) in the highly complex setting of mandatory isolation or quarantine during COVID-19 pandemics. The most suitable methodology for that context was digital micro-learning. This approach is based on the fragmentation and delivery of short educational content, which could be used at any time and place, to be consumed quickly and to yield concrete results in reduced times (Salinas and Marín 2015).

In the fourth stage (design), the team, together with ANSPAC coordinators, defined the program's product (educational contents to promote women's empathy), price (it was free of charge, but women had to complete weekly tasks), place (ANSPAC's network and WhatsApp), and promotion (coordinators contacted every woman personally by phone to explain the project). Although the program was offered to ANSPAC for free, its coordinators invested time and efforts in their training and in the program's implementation.

The program's promotion among beneficiaries included the opportunity to secure an official certificate from Universidad Austral upon completing the last module and the final evaluation survey.

The program designed was digital and usable by other CSOs as well. Indeed, the Digital Family Orientation (DFO) program, the theoretical model, and the EduQualitas SM protocol would serve as standards and procedures for the digitization of CSOs' training activities.

The DFO included four weeks or modules, with four interventions each, every one of them demanding an engagement of one hour per week. Each intervention consisted of micro text messages, videos, images, and activities. Messages between coordinators and beneficiaries were personalized to ensure privacy and continuous support. In fact, the personalization of micro-learning contents facilitated their acceptance and increased women's commitment levels.

In terms of content, following the theory of change based on persuasion (Prochaska and DiClemente 1982), the first module intended to raise women's awareness on the importance of empathy, while the second aimed at promoting emotional intelligence growth; the third showed how to develop emotional and cognitive empathy as well as putting change into action, and the fourth focused on planning and turning change into concrete actions.

Coordinators collected and consolidated participants' weekly responses, sending the resulting data to the project's team for impact evaluation.

Results of the Digital Family Orientation Program

Both coordinators and participants widely welcomed and strongly supported this campaign at the two locations where it was implemented (San Miguel and Bancalari). The educational contents' simplicity and accessibility, as well as their customization to the target public's specific needs and weekly progress raised participants' commitment and progress.

Beneficiaries acknowledged having greater self-control when facing difficult situations, as well as experiencing more care and compassion for the suffering or unfair treatment of others, especially children, respecting them as such and giving them room for dialogue at home. As a participant put it, they learned "*to be more tolerant and to look at every situation from different standpoints, as well as to listen in order to make better decisions.*"

Table 23.2 summarizes the main results achieved in the empathy dimensions influenced by the campaign.

The relationships among coordinators, beneficiaries, and project team members proved essential for the program's impact. The closer coordinators were to beneficiaries, and the more convinced they were of the training program, the greater the commitment and compliance shown by participants. In fact, the beneficiaries' group that completed the post-test online survey had a very committed team of

Table 23.2 Qualitative impact analysis

Dimension and module	Beneficiaries' phrases that show program' impact (translation from Spanish to English try to reflect original style)
Empathic concern Modules 1 and 3	They were asked to describe a situation where they could be more empathetic: *"To share something with a person you don't like, but doing your best and treating him with respect. The truth is that respect comes first"* They were asked to analyse their arrangements in relations with others: *"I greet others whether I know them or not .... Some people greet me very kindly .... The answers are always positive .... When I upload a positive msj* [message] *I feel very good... Anxious to what they will tell me. For me it's super important.... I'm always aware of the need of people more than family members I try to be and contribute in what I can ... I am not accustomed to say whether it is right or wrong ... Only on some occasions when it is possible. But it would be nice to try and say it every day."* Empathy with children: *"Children are a reflection of their parents if I, as a mother, bring up my children under violence... Or bad habits my children will grow up the same way... that's what I think.* *I have my own self-criticism .... And I was raised on sticks* [using punishments] *as they say... And the truth is I don't do what they did to me sometimes I have people who tell me that I am doing wrong by talking sweetly to the children... That they will never obey me... That I have to beat them up from time to time so that they grow up strong... I tell them it's not my way of life."* On sending positive messages to the family on WhatsApp: *"I always say hello and am greeted in the same way ... Generally. They always put a heart as emoticon. It's always important to be more attentive to everyone if a person is having a bad time or a good time you have to accompany him/her always."*
Perspective taking Modules 1, 2 and 3	*"I let* [children] *argue if it makes sense, maybe they don't fight about anything, always because oneself feels that he is failing to the other and they talk to each other from the pain of their hearts, I never let them go overboard with words anyway . . . besides brothers they are friends. I make silence until I can speak from the heart and not from anger. Words, if misused, are weapons that leave terrible marks."* *"Sometimes it's a little easier to understand each other's position even though we are hurt for no apparent reason and sometimes it hurts so much that it becomes very difficult. It is also difficult to identify the reason, many times".* *"I don't argue with my family, thank god. I argued with*

(continued)

Table 23.2 (continued)

	a neighbour a few months ago. I had a bad time because I didn't expect her to attack me in this way. And I may have had a bad time not because I felt bad, but because I was not what she expected me to find. I learned that to solve a problem we can always dialogue as civilized people".
Fantasy or possibility of transposing oneself into fictional situations Modules 1, 2 and 4	Reaction to a fight with your partner in front of their children: *"I try to avoid fights in front of the children. If happens, I explain to them that they are different from adults and that it is not serious. Don't let them be sad... that everything is fine and they have nothing to do with it. I apologize for the moment."* They were asked to write a short diary about their emotions. Negative emotions: *"One negative situation that I get is because of my mother, for example, that we disagree on many things. For example, she was upset about things that happened to my younger brother and she passed that feeling on to me. Because I see that she gives a lot of importance to things that happen to him, that happened to me also and she did not give importance."* Positive emotions: *"A positive energy, it happened when saying to a friend that I was helping my neighbour she told me that she wanted to help too. And she brought me some goods for him. · I was very happy with that gesture and even more so knowing that it serves him."* In the final online survey they wrote phrases like: *"I learned that little things can change my life or my day-to-day life and that of others. That we don't need too many things to be happy."* *"I learned that we must consider more the person we have aside, that we must have more consideration to ourselves, that we must help more, that the world needs many more good people, that I must enjoy my children, who are the driving force of my life, and thank god I have met many beautiful people, and I thank god and life for putting good people on my path."* *"In the program it appears how to identify, control and share empathy and to think about things that I didn't think about before or didn't take into account that also made me settle in a different reality from the one I was there, I proposed myself to understand and help people with little or a lot of empathy."*
Personal distress Modules 1 and 2	*"Very nice reflection... It touched me and something made me cry just now..."* *"I put the theme of emotions into practice several years ago. With my children every day we ask ourselves how we feel today and despite what each one of us feels we talk about it. Later I will see how to put the rest into practice, even if it costs a lot at first."*

(continued)

Table 23.2 (continued)

	"I learned to be clear about my emotions and to show more of myself."

Source: Own elaboration

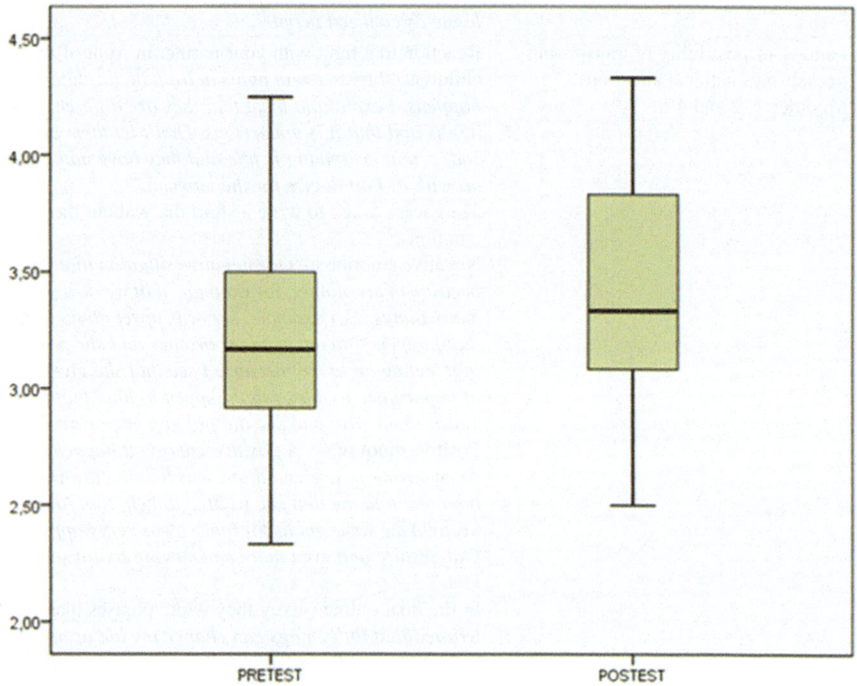

Fig. 23.2 Impact of the campaign. Source: Own elaboration

coordinators. Therefore, CSO coordinators did not only provide information or support, but they also served as participants' advisors.

In addition to the qualitative data collected during program's implementation, its impact was measured through a quasi-experimental design without a control group, using an abridged, 12-item version of the Argentine adaptation of the Interpersonal Reactivity Index or IRI (Richaud 2008), which relies on a scale validated with different types of subjects and cultures. The items were selected according to their loading scores on the key empathy dimensions or factors (empathic concern, perspective taking, distress, fantasy). The beneficiaries completed an online survey via the QuestionPro platform at the beginning and at the end of the intervention.

Considering that only a limited number of participants completed both measurements (24 for the pre-test and 23 for the post-test), the scale showed a high level of internal consistency (Cronbach's Alpha = .704). From the 12 variables on the IRI scale, a simple index was drawn to indicate empathy levels, which proved higher (see Fig. 23.2) at the end of the intervention (Mpretest = 3.19, Mpostest = 3.42).

To analyze the significance of the campaign's impact on the specific dimensions empathy, we applied the Student T-test for independent samples (for ethical reasons, we did not record respondents' identities in the surveys). Levene's Test was used to determine the homogeneity of variances. Considering the significance level of the test that allows rejecting the Null hypothesis (.05), the project team concluded that the DFO program increased women's empathic concern and self-control.

Conclusions

The results of the DFO training program based on a relational model show that the social marketing strategy pursued and the protocol used increased women's quality of life, improving their empathy capabilities.

Simultaneously, EduQualitas SM protocol favored participants' digital engagement by designing, implementing, and evaluating a micro-learning methodology through an accessible, easy-to-use, and well-known mobile platform. The project helped ANSPAC to continue providing services to its beneficiaries by means of a digitalized training process.

Therefore, evidence-based and theoretically oriented social marketing strategies can improve the quality of life of target groups when, in addition to developing an appropriate mix of product, price, place, and promotion, they focus on social innovation based on beneficiaries' and actors' ongoing participation. However, social marketing protocols and models would fail to achieve positive results without the commitment of CSOs' volunteers and social workers. Careful strategic and process planning would increase their effectiveness and social impact.

Social marketing can be a tool for change management, organizational transformation and quality of life promotion, especially in contexts of social exclusion such as those of the Buenos Aires conurbation.

Discussion Questions

1. Integrated marketing and communication considers that an effective strategy requires planning a series of processes, which generate content to be communicated through specific channels. These contents have an impact on organizations' brands. Could you identify these four elements (processes, channels, contents, and brand) in this case?
2. Applying the EduQualitas SM protocol and taking into account the evaluation of its first implementation, how would you improve the DFO program?
3. What would you add to the program to make it sustainable in your community?
4. What aspects of ANSPAC's organizational design and management would you improve based on the results of this intervention?

Teaching Notes

Question 1. Integrated marketing and communications consider that an effective strategy requires planning a series of processes, which generate content to communicate through specific channels. This content has an impact on the organisation's brand. Could you identify its four elements (processes, channels, contents and brand) in the case?

Processes:

EduQualitas SM implied a disruptive transformation of ANSPAC's processes, since it includes situation analysis, a logical framework matrix and a design based on a theoretical model.

Processes were developed in a participatory way following the different stages of the protocol (see Table 23.1—EduQualitas SM Protocol in case study).

It is important to highlight the fourth stage (design) in which the team, together with ANSPAC coordinators, defined the program's product (educational contents to promote women's empathy), price (free of charge, but women have to accomplish weekly tasks), place (ANSPAC's network and WhatsApp) and promotion (coordinators contacted every woman personally by phone to explain the project).

Channels:

The project used a key channel for promoting women's participation (WhatsApp), critical for defining the micro-learning methodology.

Contents:

DFO includes four weeks or modules, with four interventions each, which demand participation of one hour per week. Each intervention consists of micro text messages, videos, images and activities. It is critical to point out the importance of the theory of change based on persuasion.

Brand:

The project success was influenced by the power of partners' brand. Austral University and ANSPAC are well-known organizations. Their brands position may facilitate women's participation in the program.

Question 2. Applying the EduQualitas SM protocol and taking into account the evaluation of its first implementation, how would you improve the DFO program?

An effective way to improve DFO program is to increase CSO's coordinators training, particularly regarding micro-learning and WhatsApp as an educational tool. CSO's volunteers and social workers may be able to experience the program before its implementation in beneficiaries. Although data collection was participatory, CSO's would be more effective and accurate with an initial training in research methodologies.

Finally, DFO should be longer, offering women more content that would increase their identification with fictional characters and opportunities to participate through an exchange of ideas and experiences with beneficiaries from other contexts.

Question 3. What would you add to the program to make it sustainable in your community?

To discuss this question the professor should introduce students to change management, particularly the Logical Framework: a way of planning a process of change at implementation level in a sequential way. After defining the theoretical model of change, the project designer defines inputs or resources, initiatives or activities, outputs and outcomes, impact and results. More information on the model may be found in van den Dool and van den Dool (2005).

Question 4. What aspects of ANSPAC's organizational design and management would you improve based on the results of the implementation?

Some aspects to improve on are:

- Inclusion of new quality of life indicators that would influence women's empathy.
- Long-term coordinator training in beneficiaries' quality of life and relationships.
- The digitalization of processes, so that they can be deeply in touch with their communities and adapt their programs to the new normal after the COVID-19 pandemic.
- Design and develop new social marketing-oriented strategies to increase participants' quality of life.
- Planning processes to increase effectiveness and social impact.

References

Deane-Drummond C (2017) Empathy and the evolution of compassion: from deep history to infused virtue. Zygon 52(1):258–278. https://doi.org/10.1111/zygo.12317

Lane RE (2001) Self-reliance and empathy: the enemies of poverty: and of the poor. Polit Psychol 22(3):473–492. JSTOR

McLaren K (2013) The art of empathy: a complete guide to life's most essential skill. Edition: 10/16/13. Sounds True, Boulder, Colorado

Prochaska JO, DiClemente CC (1982) Transtheoretical therapy: toward a more integrative model of change. Psychotherapy: Theory, Research & Practice 19(3):276–288. https://doi.org/10.1037/h0088437

Richaud MC (2008) Evaluación de la empatía en población infantil argentina. Revista de investigación en psicología 11(1):101–115

Rivera RG, Castro Sanchez M, Dimier de Vicente MD (2019) Marketing social y violencia interpersonal. Un modelo aplicativo para el desarrollo de programas de prevención. Quaderns de Polítiques Familiars 05:50–65

Rodríguez Espínola S, Salvia A (2019) Malestar subjetivo (2010–2018). Asimetrías sociales en los recursos emocionales, afectivos y cognitivos. (Observatorio de la Deuda Social Argentina. Barómetro de la Deuda Social Argentina. Documento de trabajo.). Universidad Católica Argentina. https://repositorio.uca.edu.ar/bitstream/123456789/8300/1/malestar-subjetivo-asimetrias-sociales.pdf

Salinas J, Marín VI (2015) Pasado, presente y futuro del microlearning como estrategia para el desarrollo profesional. Campus Virtuales 3(2):46–61

Segal EA (2007) Social empathy: a new paradigm to address poverty. J Poverty 11(3):65–81. https://doi.org/10.1300/J134v11n03_06
Tonon G (2016) Indicators of quality of life in Latin America. Springer International Publishing. https://www.springer.com/gp/book/9783319288406
Tonon G (2017) Quality of life in communities of Latin countries. Springer
van den Dool L, van den Dool LT (2005) Making local government work: an introduction to public management for developing countries and emerging economies. Eburon Uitgeverij B.V

Chapter 24
Social Marketing Actions in Small-Format Convenience Stores: The Case of Oxxo in Mexico

Rafael Fabricio Matos-Cámara, Magda Lizet Ochoa-Hernández, and Pilar A. Huerta-Zavala

Abstract Oxxo is a Mexican chain of small-format convenience stores owned by FEMSA. Over the course of 30 years, it has managed to satisfy the daily needs of its customers with stores in the Mexican Republic and in other Latin American countries. Corporate social responsibility and social marketing actions are part of its business culture: investing in communities, respecting cultural diversity and reducing environmental impacts through sustainable business practices—all of these activities are part of the chain's objectives. In this continuous effort to be a more environmentally and socially responsible organization, they have developed social marketing actions with programmes aimed at serving three strategic areas of action: collaborators (employees), society and the environment.

In this case, we will focus on a strategic area of society: improving the quality of life of people through an environmental awareness programme called 'Good Neighbour'. Although the programme involves activities focused on ecological education, reforestation, recycling, rehabilitation of public spaces and the promotion of health and sports, we focus here on reforestation, which seeks to reduce environmental problems and generate an awareness of change while improving the current conditions in the society where it operates. The main achievements of Oxxo are shown, together with the active role of the community involvement in this type of action.

Keywords Quality of life · Environmental impact · Social marketing · Retail · Awareness raising

---

R. F. Matos-Cámara
La Salle University Cancun, Cancun, Mexico
e-mail: fabricio.matos@upn042.edu.mx

M. L. Ochoa-Hernández
Autonomous University of Tamaulipas, Tampico, Mexico
e-mail: mlochoa@docentes.uat.edu-mx

P. A. Huerta-Zavala (✉)
University of Burgos, Burgos, Spain
e-mail: phuerta@ubu.es

M. M. Galan-Ladero, R. G. Rivera (eds.), *Applied Social Marketing and Quality of Life*, Applying Quality of Life Research,
https://doi.org/10.1007/978-3-030-83286-5_24

Introduction

The company and society seek to create value and generate trust in both directions. The company does not depend only on the product or service it offers, it also depends on the community where it is located. Thus, companies that invest in their community also learn from that community, because such companies have the opportunity to better understand the needs of their consumers and design strategies to satisfy them (Weller 2020).

Identifying what organizations can do and how they can act to improve social reality has emerged as a vital strategy for companies to survive beyond the actions they undertake, generating positive or negative impacts that create favourable or unfavourable opinions. Being attentive and respectful of social and environmental causes is a way of showing what path the company is willing to follow to serve its customers, contribute to society and stay focused on a sustainable future (Giuliani 2012).

Climate change is widely acknowledged as a major problem and aggravating the effects on air pollution is one of its many manifestations. In cities, people produce more per capita emissions of greenhouse gases due to the demand for residential services and electricity consumption (Kahn 2009), and climate change has significant effects on the temperature of cities. The climate influences human activity, including diet, recreation and chores (Albouy et al. 2016). Interventions by governments, companies and individuals can help cities reduce the problems caused by climate change.

Oxxo, a convenience store network owned by the Mexican beverage company FEMSA COMERCIO with more than 18,000 stores in Latin America, assumes that the generation of economic value today depends in part on initiatives aimed at promoting environmentally and socially responsible activities. These initiatives are based on five strategic lines of action: ethics and corporate values, quality of life in the company, health and well-being, connection with the community and care for the environment. Implementing campaigns focused on these strategic axes is a form of influence in favour of the acceptance of ideas that converge with these axes and that seek to change consumer behaviour (Giuliani et al. 2012).

In its reforestation campaign, which we present in this case, Oxxo seeks to reduce environmental problems and generate an awareness of change while improving living conditions in the society where its chain of convenience stores operates. Through interaction with the community, with competent bodies, with government support, as well as with adequate infrastructure, future expectations seek to mitigate the consequences of climate change, which is a principle consistent with the values identified in Oxxo.

Corporate Social Responsibility and Social Marketing

Corporate social responsibility and social marketing have benefits that translate into economic and social value for employees and the community, as well as activities that help preserve the planet. Cooperation and interaction between all the agents involved are thus fundamental, because from the cooperation and interaction between the different audiences, the company seeks to achieve business objectives for the benefit of. This has a positive impact on the quality of life for society at large and stakeholders in particular.

Stakeholders are all those key agents interested in the organization such as customers, employees, partners, investors, financial institutions, suppliers, distributors, civil associations and environmental groups that can affect the achievement of a company's objectives (Heikkurinen 2018). Companies must therefore reward these stakeholders to achieve the expected benefits from both sides of the relationship.

For Oxxo, its performance as a corporate entity appears in a commitment based on ethics and values, and its efforts are directed towards those causes in which the organization can have a strong impact based on three axes: its people, the community and the planet. The strategic plan operated by Oxxo consists of activities closely related to the three corporate axes, which are identified with the most important values for the company and for all of its stakeholders. These actions that Oxxo has implemented and which appear in FEMSA's annual sustainability content report (2018) are described below.

1. *Collaborators (its people): Oxxo Institute and agreements with higher education institutions that provide the opportunity for their employees to finish secondary school/undergraduate degree, health programmes and labour inclusion for vulnerable groups.*

    - Oxxo Institute: In 25 positions at Oxxo, more than 460 employees have had the opportunity to complete their baccalaureate studies in semi-open systems taught at the Oxxo Institute.
    - Agreements with higher education institutions: Through the Oxxo-TEC Milenio agreement, 90% scholarships are offered to the children of leaders of commercial commission agents.
    - Health programmes:
        - The Occupational Health and Safety Administration System (SASSO) offers 16 occupational health programs to all FEMSA COMERCIO (Oxxo) personnel; and
        - 20% reduction in days lost due to illness and disability, due to the implementation of the actions of the Risk Prevention Manual in the 13 Oxxo Distribution Centres (CEDIS) and 21 Oxxo positions, benefiting more than 21,500 employees.
    - Labour inclusion: It is estimated that more than 730 Oxxo employees in Mexico are people with disabilities. The company is committed to promoting

their professional development and inclusion in a balanced work environment. Therefore, in 2018 Oxxo opened a new Oxxo Directed Labour Training Centre in the town of Ciudad del Carmen, Campeche, adding to its list of nine training centres in Mexico. The initiative, launched simultaneously with the National System for the Integral Development of the Family, expands opportunities for employees with some type of disability, providing them with three months of job training in a simulated operating environment, which prepares them to work successfully in any Oxxo store.

2. *Society (the community): "Redondeo" [rounding], "Buen Vecino" [Good Neighbour] (ecological education, reforestation and recycling, rehabilitation of public spaces, promotion of health and sports) and Food Bank.*

   - Rounding Oxxo customers: The rounding programme, which started in 2002, is a link between clients and local institutions and creates a bond of mutual support. Currently, this programme operates throughout Mexico through Oxxo and other FEMSA corporate business formats. With the participation of collaborators, who invite customers to participate rounding the total of their purchase, 83.56 million Mexican pesos (US $4.26 million) were collected in 2018, which benefited 276 institutions. The programme allocates proceeds to institutions that work to benefit the community and environment in which they live. They seek to become agents of change and contribute to the construction of more supportive societies with formal non-profit charitable organizations that promote integral development and a dignified life. Through the rounding programme, non-profit Civil Society Organizations (CSOs) are supported, including Civil Associations (AC), Private Charitable Associations (ABP), Private Assistance Institutions (IAP) and Foundations, which mainly serve children, the young and the elderly who live in situations of vulnerability, whether due to illness, disability, poverty, abuse and/or abandonment. To receive benefits from the PRO Redondeo Programme, organizations must meet a series of requirements, including being constituted as authorized grantees.
   - Good Neighbour: This programme (which promotes community-based actions) is an initiative that emerged at the end of 2009, with the objective of involving Oxxo stores in their communities through activities that can be classified into the following types:

     – Ecological Education, Reforestation and Recycling: educational programmes and socialization activities that seek to reduce environmental problems and generate awareness of change and improvement of current conditions.
     – Rehabilitation of public spaces: programme focused on promoting spaces for coexistence and recreation, in support of the work carried out by public services. Activities include work in parks, plazas, gardens, streams, streets, and other community locations.

- Health and sports: activities aimed at promoting sports practices and healthier lifestyles.

- Support to Food Banks: To combat hunger in Mexico, Oxxo began its food programme in 2010 in collaboration with the Food Bank of Mexico (BAMX), a civil association dedicated to rescuing food to address the problem of hunger in the population. Together, the objective of this programme is to channel surplus food in good condition for human consumption, which is distributed through Food Banks—located throughout the country—in coordination with the Oxxo Distribution Centres (CEDIS), helping them to reach different civil society organizations. During 2018, more than 64 million pesos (US $ 3.26 million) were channelled in products that benefited more than 21,800 Mexican families.
- Health and Sports: The company carried out health and sports promotion activities for neighbouring communities, including sporting events, vaccination modules and cancer detection in stores. In 2007, the Majalca Challenge was developed, which is a project that promotes a healthy environment through mountain biking along the Reliz–Majalca route. The project arose based on the initiative of Oxxo, which was in charge of drawing up an 80-km ecotourism route to highlight the natural beauty of Chihuahua. More than 1000 cyclists have participated in the most recent events.

3. *Environment (the planet)*: Ecological Clubs, Renewable Energy and Green Stores.

- Ecological Clubs: Oxxo is committed to sustainable development. Through environmentally friendly processes, it positively affects the environments in which its stores operate and the communities that surround those environments, activating projects to solve their current and future needs. These projects ensure the competitiveness, profitability and permanence of their business through the sustainability of their operations and guarantee the involvement of their business partners, as well as increasing the value of the brand, making them jointly responsible as a good neighbour.
- Renewable Energy: This is a fundamental issue for the operation of the business; year after year it incorporates new technologies, as well as processes and tools that contribute to diversify the energy portfolio and optimize its use, reducing the environmental footprint of its operations. The company supplied renewable energy to more than 600 pharmacies, more than 6100 Oxxo stores, 15 manufacturing plants and 53 distribution centres at the end of 2018 (FEMSA COMERCIO 2018).
- Green Stores: To contribute to a healthier environment and increase the number of green spaces, the Oxxo chain plants trees in front of its stores where possible. By the end of 2018, Oxxo had planted more than 19,234 trees near their stores in Mexico. Trees mitigate climate change by absorbing carbon dioxide from the air and releasing oxygen. They also reduce the risk of

flooding by absorbing rain, controlling erosion and creating more permeable soils.

Once the panorama of actions congruent with Oxxo's values has been shown, we will focus on the partnership axis with the Good Neighbour programme and specifically on the reforestation campaign, which we will address in the next section.

Case Development: Reforestation: The 'Good Neighbour' Initiative

Background of the Social Marketing Campaign

The community reforestation campaign seeks to get Oxxo stores to participate in reforestation activities in the places where they operate. The actions of the Oxxo reforestation campaign are focused on making people aware of the importance of preserving the environment and participating with the environment in a favourable way, and promoting the development of green areas in the territories, as well as creating friendly environments where the Oxxo chain is present to help improve the air quality.

To ensure reforestation, the efforts of this commercial chain are focused on preserving the environment through cooperative actions with its collaborators and provide guidelines for reflection on the development of an environmental culture. To carry out the reforestation initiative, Oxxo also invited residents to add their time, talent and effort and to participate in preserving existing trees and planting others. This campaign has a visible presence and is communicated through annual forums and billboards. This translates into the reduction of environmental pollution and the good management of the natural resources of their communities.

In its 2014 annual report, FEMSA COMERCIO (2014) indicates that Oxxo contributed to the development of a healthy environment by promoting around 69 reforestation actions in schools, parks and mountain ranges. In 2016, 500 varieties of trees were planted at 134 Oxxo chain stores in Mérida, which made the chain a part of the municipal green infrastructure project developed by the City Council of that city to plant 60,000 trees with the aim of improving residents' quality of life (Reporteros Hoy 2016). Likewise, reforestation is circumscribed in an educational programme that, through community-assisted activities, aims to reduce environmental problems due to scarcity of trees and develop a mentality of change and environmental improvement.

Oxxo is concerned about the implementation of reforestation projects in the community, as in the state of Quintana Roo, where Oxxo has opted for reforestation actions to protect the environment and held the Forum of Encounters Add to Multiply 2019 in this region (FEMSA COMERCIO 2019). Oxxo thus invests year after year in Quintana Roo through activities such as the reforestation campaign. In its 40-year presence in the market, the Oxxo chain has developed collaborative actions in its business and in the community with the aim of managing shared economic and social value (FEMSA COMERCIO 2019).

The Social Marketing Campaign

For the development of the social marketing campaign, Oxxo has used advertising posters in its stores to generate public awareness through thematic images that show young people, adults and society in general planting trees in places where practically no tress exist, in a climate of camaraderie, joy and friendship. Oxxo has also organized forums with opinion leaders who express their concern for the preservation of the environment through cooperative actions with Oxxo workers and the community, giving guidelines for reflection on the development of an environmental culture. To motivate the audience for the Oxxo reforestation initiative, the opinion leaders in the forums invite the community to add their time, talents and efforts to participate in preserving the existing trees and planting others on a field day.

The target audience of the reforestation social marketing campaign is specifically limited to customers by location, as Oxxo is geographically segmented by city size and local area. The campaign targets people between 18 and 60 years of age, with an average monthly income level between US $1300 and US $1500 (middle class in Mexico). Most are made up of people with at least an undergraduate education, including engineers and skilled workers. In general, these people live in residential urban areas. Safety and balance in life are important to one's needs as an individual. This market segment stands out for having an outgoing personality and a perception of facing risks, and they are aware of the social problems, and care about the preservation of the environment (FEMSA COMERCIO 2019).

Analysis and Results Obtained

In this section, the results obtained from the social marketing campaign are analysed, in which people from the company, the community and the initiative that, as a Good Neighbour, join forces to take part in the reforestation programme actively promoted by the Oxxo chain of stores. Oxxo workers were an important part of the campaign, as were the neighbours who joined in the reforestation actions, thus contributing to the preservation of the environment. Employees are motivated above all to get actively involved in solidarity with the community, so that neighbours, acquaintances, friends and family also actively participate and contributing their time to reforestation actions in public spaces, thus contributing to the environment.

In this sense, communications are established so that people come together with determination to improve the context of the communities where they live and work. It is important to note that participation in this type of volunteering allows growth as an individual, enables the development of close ties with the population and

Table 24.1 Evolution of the Oxxo Reforestation Programme

Year	2011	2012	2013	2014	2015	2016	2017	2018	2019
Trees planted	7561	8493	9944	13,393	16,954	17,164	17,367	20,000	22,063
Year	2011–2013			2014–2015		2016–2017		2018–2019	
Trees programme	6600			8906		15,880		19,423	

Source: Own elaboration based on FEMSA COMERCIO (2019)

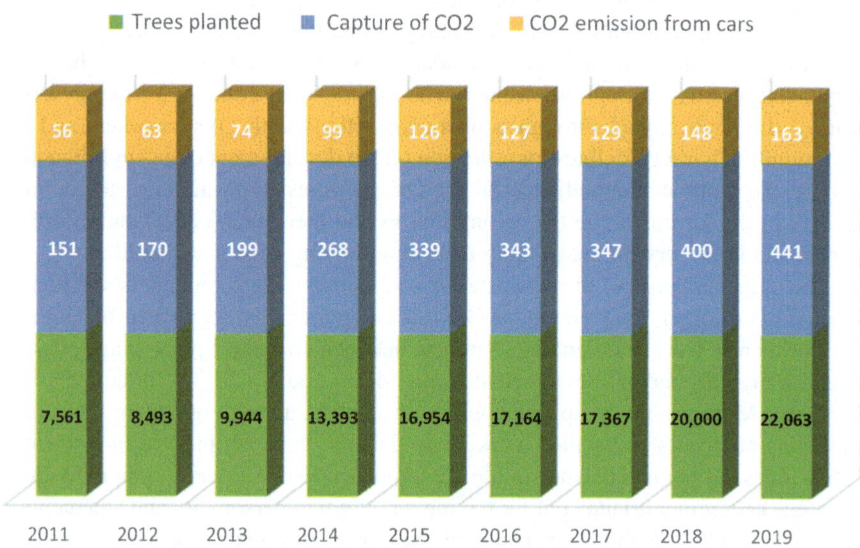

Source: Own elaboration based on FEMSA COMERCIO (2019)

Fig. 24.1 Evolution of the Oxxo Reforestation Programme and its Impact on the Environment

improves the quality of life of all residents who live in the community. In this type of volunteering, the neighbours also share their concerns and generate proposals according to the needs observed in the place. Under these ideas, alliances with institutions and government support as key actors are important in this network of initiatives (FEMSA COMERCIO 2019).

Based on the cooperative work of neighbours and local organizations, Oxxo's reforestation campaigns have achieved an exponential increase in tree planting. In 2011 approximately 7561 trees were planted, and in 2019 there were 22,063 trees planted, which represents an increase of 300% from 2011. A large percentage of these trees planted are part of the store tree-planting programme promoted by the Oxxo chain. Between 2018 and 2019, a total of 19,423 trees were part of this programme (See Table 24.1). This is reflected in the decrease in air pollution, as shown in Fig. 24.1.

According to the evolution of Oxxo's reforestation programme, we can say that, thanks to the fact that 7561 trees planted in 2011, 151 tonnes of CO_2 were captured (absorbed), which is estimated to be equivalent to the emissions of 56 cars. In 2019, the CO_2 capture was 441 tonnes, which represents the CO_2 emissions of 163 cars—all thanks to the planting of 22,063 trees (See Fig. 24.1). This is a clear example of this company's concern for the environment, expressed through the planting of these trees.

In line with these results, it is reported that in 2019, a total of 17,000 volunteer actions were carried out, with some 65,000 people who work within Oxxo collaborating in activities for the reforestation programme in stores (FEMSA COMERCIO 2019).

Conclusions

Oxxo seeks to transform the world around them and to improve the quality of life of its employees and communities, thus generating economic and social well-being. The intention of the social marketing campaign carried out by Oxxo was fulfilled, as it achieved the participation and cooperation of collaborators and neighbours, who contributed to preserving the environment and improving the local air quality. The chain thus ensures its competitiveness, profitability and positioning in the commercial sector through actions to preserve the environment and, at the same time, achieves the participation of its stakeholders, such as collaborators, neighbours and local institutions. These cooperative actions lead to an increase in the value of the brand. Finally, for Oxxo and organizations throughout the world there are challenges to carrying out new business projects, among which contributions to the environment and society by pursuing a balanced, understandable, flexible and friendly relationship are particularly significant (FEMSA COMERCIO 2019).

The contribution of the reforestation campaign in reducing environmental impacts can be observed through some of its efficacy indicators. This contribution has had a positive impact on consumers seeking responsible consumption, and it also helps retain talent, because workers identify with the objectives and want to be part of the social and environmental values promoted by the company. Oxxo's social marketing thus helps improve the corporate reputation and generate higher profitability and real social impact. The Oxxo commercial chain thus appears to be one of the companies that places the greatest emphasis on social marketing work, with this factor being a unique value that identifies and differentiates Oxxo from other companies.

Discussion Questions

1. What is the impact of social marketing in Oxxo convenience stores?
2. What behaviour does Oxxo's reforestation campaign for its convenience stores promote in the society in which it operates?
3. What other social marketing strategies could be implemented in this type of business?

Teaching Notes

1. **What is the impact of social marketing in Oxxo convenience stores?**
   The impact of Oxxo's social marketing campaign for reforestation contributes to the retention of talent, because workers identify with and want to be part of the social and environmental values that the company promotes, which, in turn, impacts consumers and affects the corporate reputation, thus generating greater profitability and a real social impact.

   Analyse in a discussion forum the importance of Oxxo's social marketing. Reflection will allow us to understand the impact that social marketing has on Oxxo's cooperative actions.
2. **What behaviour does Oxxo's reforestation campaign promote in the society in which it operates?**

   The behaviour promoted by the campaign is one of cooperative action and awareness, as well as the promotion of an environmental culture.

   Investigate three online newspaper articles about the behaviours promoted by the reforestation campaign and, in a team of three, compare and contrast the opinions expressed.
3. **What other social marketing strategies could be implemented in this type of business?**

   This type of business should implement all corporate social responsibility actions that are consistent with the values promoted by the company itself.

   Think of five social marketing strategies that Oxxo could develop and share them with your colleagues.

References

Albouy D, Graf W, Kellogg R, Wolff H (2016) Climate amenities, climate change, and American quality of life. J Assoc Environ Resour Econ 3(1):205–246

FEMSA COMERCIO, Fomento Económico Mexicano (2018) Sustainability Content 2018. FEMSA Annual Report, 1–36. Available in: https://femsa.gcs-web.com/static-files/1d4c39a2-bc4b-4a89-b981-738d74e9ddc2

FEMSA COMERCIO (2019) Annual Report, 1–12. Available in: http://annualreport.femsa.com/

FEMSA COMERCIO, Fomento Económico Mexicano (2014) Social Responsibility Report, 1–55. Available from: http://www.annualreport.femsa.com/2014/pdf/FEMSA_SR14_Eng.pdf
Giuliani AC (2012) Marketing of Varejo Contemporâneo. Ottoni Editora, Itu
Giuliani AC, Zambon MS, Monteiro TA, Betanho C, Faria LHL (2012) Social marketing, marketing related to social causes and corporate responsibility: the case of the Pao-de-Açúcar supermarket, Brazil. Invenio: J Acad Res 29:11–27
Heikkurinen P (2018) Strategic corporate responsibility: a theory review and synthesis. J Global Respons 9(4):388–414. https://doi.org/10.1108/JGR-06-2018-0020
Kahn ME (2009) Urban growth and climate change. Ann Rev Resour Econ 1(1):333–350
Reporteros Hoy (2016) Sembrará Oxxo 500 árboles en sucursales de Mérida. Available from: https://reporteroshoy.mx/wp/sembrara-oxxo-500-arboles-sucursales-merida.html
Weller A (2020) Exploring practitioners' meaning of "ethics," "compliance," and "corporate social responsibility" practices: a communities of practice perspective. Bus Soc 59(3):518–544. https://doi.org/10.1177/0007650317719263

Chapter 25
The Power of Color in Communities: The Social Impact Program 'Comex for a Well Done Mexico'

Luis M. Cerdá-Suárez and Pablo Cardona-Soriano

Abstract Positive social change is possible when communities join forces, giving rise to a greater sense of belonging and prompting public spaces to be recovered. By harnessing creativity, murals create links between local residents, evoke their identity, act as social marketing and promote key quality of life indicators such as the existence of public spaces providing a meeting place for members of the community, participation, and satisfaction with community life.

Designing social marketing interventions with an impact on quality of life is just one of the many achievements made by Comex, a Mexican paint manufacturer and distributor of waterproofing products, through the social impact program 'Comex por un México Bien Hecho' (Comex for a Well Done Mexico, in English). Since 2016, the program's designers have been working closely with Colectivo Tomate, a multidisciplinary civil society organization that facilitates encounters and social connection experiences through art and plural dialog. The program has empowered 25 neighborhoods in 16 cities and villages including Mexico City, La Paz, Puebla and Monterrey. The 2020 'Comex for a Well Done Mexico' program thus brings about community-based change by offering new opportunities to change lives and places through the power of color.

Keywords Communities · Planned social change · Social marketing · Quality of life · Mexico

Introduction

The concept of community quality of life in Latin America is particularly useful in reflecting local voices, drawing on the construction of a collective scenario and artistic engagement to communicate with local communities and social

L. M. Cerdá-Suárez (✉) · P. Cardona-Soriano
International University of La Rioja, Logroño, Spain
e-mail: luis.cerda@unir.net; pablo.cardona@unir.net

M. M. Galan-Ladero, R. G. Rivera (eds.), *Applied Social Marketing and Quality of Life*, Applying Quality of Life Research,
https://doi.org/10.1007/978-3-030-83286-5_25

organizations. A recent example of a successful citizen participation experience is the 'Programa Comunitario de Mejoramiento Barrial' (Community Neighborhood Improvement Program) in Mexico City, which had a direct impact on the quality of life of the beneficiaries (Valverde and Gutiérrez 2017). The main objective of the initiative was to develop an ongoing, integrated program to improve public spaces in the capital's neighborhoods, especially those with high levels of violence, degradation, and marginalization. In doing so, the program would promote public spaces as meeting places and enhance their impact on quality of life, strengthening community life and reinforcing the counseling delivered by diverse civil organizations. Other examples of similar programs include the 'Programa para el Mejoramiento de Viviendas en Lote Propio' (Housing Improvement Program on Individual Property, in English) and the 'Programa de Apoyo a Pueblos Originarios' (Indigenous People Support Program, in English).[1]

The ultimate goal of social marketing is social good, or in other words, making the world a better place through actions such as mitigating poverty and improving quality of life (Costanza et al. 2008). Moreover, quality of life and the impact of public space upon it can inspire practitioners to implement new tools and strategies for effective social marketing campaigns (Constantinescu 2012).

There is a tendency for social marketers to use persuasion to target their audiences instead of instigating a process whereby the target group itself comes to acknowledge that change is required (Perez-Mujica et al. 2014). Yet in order to forge lasting relationships with local residents, people need to make desired choices rather than having decisions imposed upon them (Andreasen 2002). While there is no guarantee that a change of attitude will produce the desired behavior, it is an important step towards it (Stead et al. 2007).. The general rule, of course, is that people's behavior reflects their attitudes, although a positive attitude is not in itself a predictor of behavior (Chamhuri et al. 2015).

Comex is a Mexican paint manufacturer and distributor of waterproofing products, while Colectivo Tomate is a multidisciplinary civil society organization based in Puebla that creates social experiences through art. Comex and Colectivo Tomate travelled around Mexico together as part of the Mural City project, which seeks to change the social narrative of places with high levels of segregation and violence through the collective design and creation of murals by artists and local residents. Drawing on this case study, this chapter examines how a future scenario might be constructed to reflect where a local community is heading and explore ways of discerning the potential impact of actions aiming to create social value for traditional neighborhoods.

[1]From 2000–2006, the Federal District Government implemented several programs to improve public spaces. These included the 'Programa para el Mejoramiento de Viviendas en Lote Propio' (Housing Improvement Program on Individual Property, in English), which had a far-reaching impact, as well as the 'Programa de Apoyo a Pueblos Originarios' (Indigenous People Support Program, in English). Both programs included housing and land use actions based on community organizing, self-empowerment initiatives relating to land, design, construction, housing allocation, and other activities not constrained by government policy or reliant on the housing and land markets.

Case Study

Changing Social Values through Commitment

Social marketing aims to influence behaviors, not just to change attitudes. Central to this mission is the desire to change values and attitudes as a way of influencing social habits and behaviors among the population. Exploring the relevance of these changes, this case study provides an introduction to social marketing ideas and skills as applied in neighborhoods or local communities. Additionally, the actions of local actors are analyzed as their role can shed new light on the concepts examined here.

Empowerment to act is a motivating factor in achieving commitment among local populations (Leung et al. 2004). It involves collective training, communication, motivation, and social recognition and requires actors to accept responsibility for their own actions. In this context, Colectivo Tomate is a Mexican civic organization that encourages communities to take action for transformation. Since 2009, they have taken their Mural City project to many cities and villages around Mexico, creating bonds between visitors and residents and capturing the essence of the community.

A place is much more than a mere geographical term: it also communicates something of its culture. One way in which communities express their culture and make a neighborhood their own is to name it themselves, while another method is to paint murals around the neighborhood. The case of Mexico is particularly interesting. The Mexican mural movement has created public murals in palaces, courthouses, mansions, and public buildings. The historical role of the arts in the lives of Mexican communities is indicative of the extent to which murals foster empowerment and improve quality of life.

Colectivo Tomate began painting murals in the neighborhood of Xanenetla in Puebla, Mexico, to rescue muralist heritage and use it as a tool to render the facades of the historical city center more representative of the community's identity. In 2010, the Xanenetla community decided that the images on the murals should reflect 'who we were', 'who we are', and 'who we want to be'. For this reason, the designs co-created with local artists described the community's past, present and future. Prior to the community mural project in strategic and operational collaboration with Comex, Colectivo Tomate had spent many years working on different mural projects with painters, architects, photographers, graphic designers, environmentalists, and artists, painting cities and empowering their historical identities with colorful facades, smiling faces, dripping paintbrushes, restored houses, and mural art as a tool for social cohesion.

Meanwhile, Comex, a company owned by PPG but founded in Mexico, is a registered trademark of Consorcio Comex, S.A. de C.V. Comex Group is one of the most prominent paint manufacturers and distributors of paints and waterproofing products in the sector, with 3300 sites in North America (PPG 2019). By the end of 2018, the Mexican company employed 4500 people at its company-owned stores, four training centers, seven manufacturing facilities, and three research centers in

Mexico. Celebrating its anniversary in 2018, Comex is a market leader in the production, distribution and sale of decorative paints, waterproofing products, wood care products, accessories and industrial coatings, serving clients in the construction, industrial and transportation industries and aftermarkets (PPG 2018).

In recent years, Colectivo Tomate and Comex have formed an alliance to encourage the work of local artists in towns like Puebla, La Paz, Guadalajara, Monterrey, and many more, focusing largely on urban mural projects. Colectivo Tomate has worked in various neighborhoods, while Comex has donated money and paint to communities for mural projects. The social marketing initiative was developed by Comex and Colectivo Tomate through a multi-step procedure (surveys, workshops, interviews, and focus groups) involving citizens, users, and experts in the field of social change. The initiative targeted men and women from low and middle-income groups, as social marketing strategies typically target specific audiences (PPG 2019).

Understanding the Impact of Social Marketing Campaigns on Communities: A Quality-of-Life Approach

Studies have shown that safe neighborhoods are crucial for community satisfaction and that violence and low social capital have a huge impact on quality of life (Valverde and Gutiérrez 2017). Crime has become a major driver of wellbeing deprivation in Mexico by reducing satisfaction with community life (Rojas 2017).

Social marketing is not the only way to target people on important matters such as health or environmental campaigns (Domegan 2008). The discipline can often be integrated with other activities, including training, education, community mobilization or research used to identify issues and provide a focus for a planned social change strategy (Brennan et al. 2015). The main advantage is that it can reach large numbers of people simultaneously and that it offers an opportunity to inform the public about a particular issue (Sanclemente 2017).

Focusing on an issue of social relevance is likely to be the most productive way of bringing about planned change in local communities, but it is important to find a way to specify the desired outcome and action required in the imagery used, and, if possible, to provide a means by which positive reinforcement can be effected (Whitehead and Stroope 2015). A useful strategy for maintaining connections with residents and knowing how best to improve their quality of life would combine social marketing with community participation, seeking to resolve problems such as violence and low social capital (Doucet and Lee 2015).

Fig. 25.1 The 'Bird of Dreams' mural in Monterrey. Source: Colectivo Tomate (2019)

Links Between Relationship Marketing and Social Marketing: Experiences and Results from the 'Comex for a Well Done Mexico' Program

Several authors observe that relationship marketing represents a social systems paradigm within which social marketing may be analyzed (Kashchuk and Ivankina 2015). That is, adopting a relationship approach to social marketing is more likely to enable change to be effected (Peñaloza 2018). The paradigm shifts from viewing social marketing within a transactional framework to a relational one, with implications for practice. It represents a new approach to thinking about social problems (Tonon and Rodriguez 2016).

Frequently, social marketing focuses on the operational level and neglects the strategic level (Gordon et al. 2018). If a system is conceptualized as an entity that interacts with the environment, a systems approach to social marketing means employing strategies not only at an individual level but also at a multiple level, such as collective action, engagement, social interaction, and co-created approaches to social change (French et al. 2010). One example of a systems approach to social marketing is community-based social marketing, which identifies barriers to desired behaviors, designs appropriate strategies using behavioral change tools, pilots strategies within the community, and evaluates the final program once it has been implemented (French and Gordon 2020). In this case study, system social marketing in the context of relationship marketing may be described in this way.

Working in collaboration, Comex and Colectivo Tomate created the 'Bird of Dreams' mural in the Campana-Altamira neighborhood in Monterrey, Mexico. The mural, which is the first of its kind in the world, was painted on the facades of 300 homes as part of the 'Comex for a Well Done Mexico' program (Fig. 25.1).

In 2018, the Secretary for Social Development of the State of Nuevo Leon, the Sub-Secretariat for Crime Prevention of the State of Nuevo Leon, Monterrey's municipal government, and the Monterrey Institute of Technology (also known as Tecnológico de Monterrey, in Spanish) launched actions aiming to improve public spaces. The initiative impacted 1500 people living in the Campana-Altamira neighborhood directly and another 6300 indirectly.

Public space has been traditionally viewed as the responsibility of the state, although the current situation in Latin America calls for citizen participation in community issues (Tonon 2015, 2017, 2019). "By revitalizing public spaces, we encourage neighbors to get involved and participate actively in bringing harmony, security and a sense of belonging to the area", said Gilberto Alcaraz, director of the 'Comex for a Well Done Mexico' social impact program. A methodology based on active community participation and social-artistic intervention played a key role in achieving this social change. Besides painting walls in various locations, the program's core vision and mission are to help strengthen the community's social fabric and improve people's quality of life.

The social impact program 'Comex por un México Bien Hecho' (Comex for a Well Done Mexico), based on a relationship marketing paradigm and the creation of community murals, involved the following activities: (1) imagining the picture, (2) mapping elements, (3) considering multiple perspectives, (4) facilitating reflexive practice, (5) understanding interactions, (6) thinking creatively, and (7) fostering engagement, empowerment, and consensus. Part of the specific methodology used in this evaluation consisted of interviewing institutional agents and actors, communities and artists in order to assess the changes implemented.

In the context of the program, the overall objective of the Mural City initiative was to develop an integrated framework for improving public spaces in cities, especially those with high levels of violence. A set of indicators was designed for the project, relating to:

1. resilience criteria;
2. diagnosis of community issues;
3. establishment of a mechanism based on interpersonal relationships; and
4. the role of commitment in communicating with communities.

The approach used to analyze the program drew on a classical analysis methodology using both qualitative and quantitative data. The sample consisted of a total of seven cities in Mexico, evaluated between November 2018 and February 2019. Sixteen interviews were held with relevant actors in the community, including beneficiaries with similar characteristics to the final target group, as well as 16 interviews with institutional authorities, 11 in-depth interviews with operational managers, and 8 participatory sessions with 132 participants as part of a community development strategy. Additionally, 35 online questionnaires were completed by artists and around 729 residents were asked to make a judgement on certain perceptions in order to grasp the potential impact of the initiative.

The results presented in the following paragraphs derive from the methodology used in the program and described above. Adopting a broad perspective to operationalize this integrative framework, the focus was on subjective and objective quality of life indicators reflecting community residents' satisfaction with a number of aspects linked to social and political matters, as well as to the services operating within the community (a summary of the main results is displayed in Table 25.1).

Table 25.1 shows the main results relating to perceptions of quality of life in Monterrey, Zacatecas, Saltillo, Culiacán, La Paz, Villahermosa, and

Table 25.1 Selected results of the 'Comex for a Well Done Mexico' program: the Mural City project

Criterion	Dimension	Indicator	Positive impact
Resilience	Collective confidence Sense of community belonging	Satisfaction with life in the community	83.2%
		Satisfaction with neighborhood's features	62.1%
Diagnosis	Empowerment	Solving of community problems	86.4%
	Positive externalities	Effect on people's perceptions of public space	82.6%
Interpersonal relationships	Appropriation of public space	Public spaces for encounters	61.8%
Commitment	Commitment and participation	Participation in community	76.2%

Source: The authors, using data from Comex-Colectivo Tomate (2019)

Tuxtla-Gutiérrez based on a descriptive analysis. In Table 25.1, the fourth column indicates the percentage of informants perceiving a positive impact for each indicator summarized in the table. The results of this analysis provided additional evidence and suggested that significant findings could be found for the main dimensions and variables. Specifically, respondents were asked to indicate the extent to which the initiative had improved quality of life in their communities since the project was completed on the following four-point scale: did not enhance, slightly enhanced, somewhat enhanced, and greatly enhanced.

Regarding satisfaction with life in the community and with the neighborhood's features, most responses were positive (that is, quality of life was somewhat enhanced and greatly enhanced, with 83.2% and 62.1%, respectively). Additionally, Table 25.1 presents the results for the empowerment and positive externalities dimensions. Here, 86.4% and 82.6% of respondents observed a positive impact following the intervention in terms of its contribution to solving community problems and impact on people's perceptions of public space.

Finally, perceptions of the relevance and use of public spaces as meeting places by members of the community and community development after the initiative (measured by participation in the community) showed an increase of 61.8% and 76.2% respectively.

Just like other social impact programs, both regional and local, the resilience criterion explored benefits to vulnerable groups in terms of indicators such as satisfaction with life in the community and satisfaction with neighborhoods (Su et al. 2019). In this case, Monterrey's municipal government, in collaboration with the Tecnológico de Monterrey, designed a preliminary scale to measure overall perceptions of safety based on satisfaction in two domains: satisfaction with life and satisfaction with the neighborhood's social, economic, and physical features. Additionally, in accordance with the Secretary for Social Development of the State of Nuevo Leon and the Sub-Secretariat for Crime Prevention of the State of Nuevo

Leon, projects in the neighborhoods were to be based on a diagnosis of social issues and specify the physical space that they would impact upon. The projects had to be designed in such a way as to include community participation in terms of participants and percentage of participation; that is, a description of the participatory process was to be submitted as part of the project planning process.

In this initiative, a rise in social capital over the 2016–2018 period can be seen in certain criteria, dimensions, and key quality of life indicators in the results. That is, improvements in quality of life were achieved through stimulation of the community organization's decision-making process, creation and use of public spaces for encounters among the members of the community, organization for solving community problems in the neighborhoods, and community development (opportunities, inclusion, and motivation to improve skills and competences).

According to a survey carried out in cities such as Zacatecas, Saltillo, Culiacán, Monterrey (Altamira), Villahermosa, Tuxla Gutiérrez and La Paz, following this social project, 76.2% of respondents said that they were committed to taking part in actions to improve their local community. In particular, the number of people who considered it possible to carry out social and public projects rose to 82.6% (i.e., positive externalities derived from this initiative).

In the specific context of the 'Bird of Dreams' mural, 22 artists and 23 facilitators from Colectivo Tomate painted the mural and Comex contributed USD $135,000 to the program, including 9000 liters of paint. "*The mural extends its wings, generating connection, community and trust while also narrating the adversities and resistance faced by early residents of the neighborhood*", said Tomás Darío from Colectivo Tomate. The program has reached 3.5 million people around the country and after three years, the results are more than evident.

To summarize, the project involved approximately 300 volunteers and 1500 residents supporting more than 50 workshops that helped people to develop skills in conflict resolution, communication, interpersonal relationships, and resilience. A mentoring program run by the Autonomous University of Nuevo Leon enhanced residents' skills in recovering public spaces and implementing urban art programs, as shown in Fig. 25.2.

Conclusions

This study evaluated the effects of the social impact program 'COMEX for a Well Done Mexico' on local communities, behaviors, and attitudes towards social values among the target population in Mexico. It found that awareness of the social benefits related to the program was associated with positive attitudes towards local communities with social problems and that social media provided a productive means to disseminate information about the specific campaign described. The program was designed to promote, develop, and consolidate citizen processes through participatory planning and citizen organization works. The idea was to implement sustainable

Fig. 25.2 'Mexican Allegory' in Piedras Negras. Source: Colectivo Tomate (2019)

projects and strengthen the ideal of constant community involvement among the community.

The social impact of these interventions has been evaluated by the Monterrey Institute of Technology and Higher Education (ITESM) and the organizations *Camino Colectivo* and *Acciones para el Desarrollo Comunitario A. C.* (Adeco). The results are very positive: not only did the project result in spectacular murals designed at a number of workshops, it also generated social change that can be felt in interactions between residents and renewed pride in their neighborhoods and places. Moreover, the cities and villages targeted by the program have become appealing tourist destinations and fertile locations for experimental art.

This study reflects the findings of previous research studies and other social and cause-related marketing programs, demonstrating that campaign awareness in local communities is one of the most significant predictors of the efficacy of the campaign itself. Furthermore, our results support findings obtained by social and cause-related marketing campaigns aiming to change attitudes, behaviors and social habits, reinforcing the evidence that recall of the campaign was the most important attribute in evaluating the efficacy of programs in local communities in Mexico.

Discussion Questions

1. Describe the various stakeholders and their interests in this case study. What potential sources of conflict of interest can you identify? Draft a report indicating how social marketing might help to facilitate communication with community stakeholders.
2. Social marketing actions can improve urban image as a key quality of life indicator. How would you seek to establish a brand image for a local community? Examine how a brand image creates value for people in a neighborhood of your choice.
3. How might one evaluate the usefulness of social communication to stakeholders in a local community? Illustrate your answer with examples showing how a social marketing program might address the indicators identified in this case study.
4. You have been asked to design and plan a social marketing campaign to address vandalism within the various communities in your city. Draw up a plan indicating the main objectives and messages of the campaign and how it will be portrayed in your local media.

Acknowledgments The authors would like to express their gratitude to Comex and Colectivo Tomate for providing access to the pictures and data used in this study. We are especially indebted to Fania de la Vega, Mai Hernandez, and Maribel Benitez.

Teaching Notes

Answer to Question 1. Describe the various stakeholders and their interests in this case study. What potential sources of conflict of interest can you identify? Draft a report indicating how social marketing might help to facilitate communication with community stakeholders.

Stakeholders are held to be those individuals or groups that can affect or are affected by the achievement of a purpose or have a legitimate claim. In our case, stakeholders often include residents, investors, local groups, funding agencies, government inspectors, the press, and the wider community in general.

Focusing on relationships can bring about behavioral change and this can be viewed as a key social marketing goal. Strategic alliances are very important in order to facilitate different forms of service provision but it is important that policies and guidelines are in place. For example, the advent of partnerships between Comex and social actors brings social marketing into contact with commercial enterprise. This situation can give rise to differences of opinion and conflicts of interest, as only long-term campaigns can produce measurable changes (with a few rare exceptions). Moreover, funders, investors, and the private sector always seek short-term results.

Campaigns often place excessive emphasis on behavioral change (individual rather than community), instead of creating a consensus conducive to social change.

For this reason, it should be remembered that communication with community stakeholders and residents can in many cases be more important than the message itself. To sum up, an important consequence of this consideration is that the standards and criteria by which social and political issues are assessed should be developed as part of a process of social change involving citizens to enhance their welfare rather than treating them as recipients of efforts to change their behaviors and attitudes.

Answer to Question 2. Social marketing actions can improve urban image as a key quality of life indicator. How would you seek to establish a brand image for a local community? Examine how a brand image creates value for people in a neighborhood of your choice.

Organizations possess different media channels through which they can communicate with their various audiences and stakeholders. Drawing the attention of a specific audience may prove to be quite a difficult task, so it is helpful to creatively adapt an image to appeal to specific audiences. Messages and imagery should portray people with whom members of the target group can identify, and, in this respect, it is crucial to pre-test the appeal of a social marketing communication or whatever marketing mechanism is to be used.

Using our imagination, we can think of a brand image for a local community as a cluster of purposeful and expressive values. In the case of neighborhoods, the brand image communicates the idea that local communities are value-driven and is delivered by social actors in their interactions with residents and other stakeholders. Brands reflect reputation and make it easier to position communities in people's minds. They can also create value and provide emotional, hedonic and symbolic benefits to residents.

Answer to Question 3. How might one evaluate the usefulness of social communication to stakeholders in a local community? Illustrate your answer with examples showing how a social marketing program might address the indicators identified in this case study.

In quality of life studies, this term as a construct can be conceptualized as an individual's subjective perception of their objective conditions of life and wellbeing in terms of the two main approaches in quality of life theory: subjective and objective. Combining these two approaches, quality of life can be defined as 'the extent to which objective human needs are fulfilled in relation to personal or group perceptions of subjective wellbeing'. That is, while objective needs refer to security, subsistence, affection, etc., subjective perception relates to life satisfaction, happiness, and personal usefulness in order to understand the value that people place upon public goods, things and ideas.

The most relevant studies on subjective perceptions of quality of life are based on surveys. The reason for this is that those involved in marketing must familiarize themselves with people's perceptions, attitudes, beliefs, values, wants and needs. Using this information, social marketers can influence consumers' and citizens' behaviors as members of a community or as public goods and services users. Additionally, using a quantitative approach, they must also find out how personal, social and psychological factors influence behavior so that they can use this information to good effect in the marketing of public goods, services, and other relevant societal messages.

However, surveys pose two main problems for marketers: lack of interest in collaborating in research and uncertainty surrounding sampling and non-sampling errors in the data provided by respondents. These two types of errors may be eliminated through observation, which reflects participants' true behavior as they are not usually aware they are being analyzed and cannot manipulate the information given to the interviewer. However, the specific nature of research based on observation gives rise to numerous ethical concerns. In terms of quality of life studies, observation is found not only in medical studies regarding patients' health, but also in social research to avoid disturbing participants with further questions.

Answer to Question 4. You have been asked to design and plan a social marketing campaign to address vandalism within the various communities in your city. Draw up a plan indicating the main objectives and messages of the campaign and how it will be portrayed in your local media.

A social marketing plan is designed and developed to cover an institution's relationships with its stakeholders, other groups of interest, and, where appropriate, its competitors and intermediaries. It should list specific actions relating to the social marketing mix. Although the traditional 4 Ps are also proposed in social marketing, some authors such as Weinreich (2011) extend the model to the 8 Ps, adding people/public, partnership, purse strings and policy to product, price, promotion and place[2]:

1. Product: what does the stakeholder receive? What is the stakeholder offered?
2. Price: how much will it cost the stakeholder? Not only in monetary terms, but also in terms of time, effort, energy, emotional cost, etc.
3. Promotion: what package of incentives can be offered that will be valued by the stakeholder?
4. Place: where does the relevant behavior take place?
5. People/public: for instance, people could refer to specific external groups including the target audience, policymakers, and gatekeepers, while the internal groups would comprise the actors or agents trained to implement the social marketing program.
6. Partnership: identifying common goals and working together in genuine partnership through the co-creation of a market. That is, the nature of the behavior targeted for change is of interest to the community as a whole. It offers an opportunity for collaborative partnership between several social bodies, helping to defer the cost of social marketing campaigns.
7. Purse strings: for example, considering ways to maximize resources including human resources as well as financial.
8. Policy: using marketing to connect different policy agendas and maximizing their impact across the whole social system.

---

[2]Weinreich, N. K. (2011): Chap. 3. The Social Marketing Mix. In Weinreich, N. K.: *Hands-On Social Marketing: A Step-by-Step Guide to Designing Change for Good (second Edition).* London, United Kingdom, SAGE Publications, 13–23.

Through dedication and creativity, a social marketing campaign can solve residents' biggest challenges, collaborating with them closely to find the right path forward. Actions should include all those necessary to paint murals, including restoration of facades, coordination of workshops with artists at the mural painting festival, and documentation of the entire creative process on video and on paper. In this context, according to Weinreich (2011),[3] three elements relating to social marketing commonly emerge: (1) its main purpose is to achieve a specific social good through particular behavioral goals; (2) it is a comprehensive process designed in phases to address short, medium and long-term perspectives; and (3) it employs marketing methods.

For this reason, the planning and implementation process should be designed to ensure that appropriate actions are taken to enable the partnership between private and nonprofit institutions to meet its marketing objectives within the context of the environment in which it operates. Working together, it is possible to celebrate the voice of cooperation and the power of color.

References

Andreasen A (2002) Marketing social marketing in the social change marketplace. J Public Policy Mark 21(1):3–13

Brennan L, Fry M-L, Previte J (2015) Strengthening social marketing research: harnessing "insight" through ethnography. *Australas Mark J AMJ* 23(4):286–293

Chamhuri NH, Hamdan H, Ahmah P, Ismail F (2015) Conceptual framework of public participation in ensuring quality of life of the urban poor in Malaysia. Procedia Soc Behav Sci 168:349–356

Comex-Colectivo Tomate (2019) Resultados de la evaluación del programa Ciudad Mural en el marco de México Bien Hecho impacto. Comex-Colectivo Tomate, CDMX

Constantinescu M (2012) Using marketing research in quality of life theory and practice. Procedia Soc Behav Sci 46:754–759

Costanza R, Fisher B, Ali S, Beer C, Bond L, Boumans R, Danigelis NL, Dickinson J, Elliott C, Farley J, Gayer DE, MacDonald Glenn L, Hudspeth TR, Mahoney DF, McCahill L, McIntosh B, Reed B, Rizvi AT, Rizzo DM, Simpatico T, Snapp R (2008) An integrative approach to quality of life measurement, research, and policy. SAPIENS 1.1:2008, Online since 19 December 2008

Domegan CT (2008) Social marketing: implications for contemporary marketing practices classification scheme. J Bus Int Mark 23(2):135–141

Doucet JD, Lee MR (2015) Civic communities and urban violence. Soc Sci Res 52:303–316

French J, Blair-Stevens C, McVey D, Merritt R (2010) Social marketing and public health: theory and practice. Oxford University Press, Oxford

French J, Gordon R (2020) Strategic Social Marketing for Behaviour and Social Change, 2nd edn. SAGE Publications Ltd, London

Gordon R, Dibb S, Magee C, Cooper P, Waitt G (2018) Empirically testing the concept of value-in-behavior and its relevance for social marketing. J Bus Res 82:56–67

[3]Weinreich, N. K. (2011): Chap. 1. Social Marketing Basics. In Weinreich, N. K.: *Hands-On Social Marketing: A Step-by-Step Guide to Designing Change for Good (second Edition).* London, United Kingdom, SAGE Publications, 3–6.

Kashchuk I, Ivankina L (2015) Marketing approach to the research of older adults' Well-being. Procedia Soc Behav Sci 214:911–915
Leung KK, Wu EC, Lue BH, Tang LY (2004) The use of focus groups in evaluating quality of life components among elderly Chinese people. Qual Life Res 13(1):179–190
Peñaloza L (2018) Ethnic marketing practice and research at the intersection of market and social development: a macro study of the past and present, with a look to the future. J Bus Res 82:273–280
Perez-Mujica L, Duncan R, Bossomaier T (2014) Using agent-based models to design social marketing campaign. Australas Mark J AMJ 22(1):36–44
PPG (2018) Celebrating Our 135th Anniversary. 2018 Annual Report. Available online at: http://2018annualreport.ppg.com/. Accessed on 25 December 2019
PPG (2019) Creating our future. 2019 Annual Report. Available online at: http://2019annualreport.ppg.com/. Accessed on 25 March 2020
Rojas M (2017) Crime and failure of community life in Mexico. In: Tonon GH (ed) Quality of life in communities of Latin countries. Springer, Cham, Switzerland, pp 83–94
Sanclemente JC (2017) Marketing and corporate social responsibility (CSR). Moving between broadening the concept of marketing and social factors as a marketing strategy. Spanish J Mark - ESIC 21(Supplement 1):4–25
Stead M, Gordon R, Angus K, McDermott L (2007) A systematic review of social marketing effectiveness. Health Educ 107(2):126–191
Su L, Huang SS, Nejati M (2019) Perceived justice, community support, community identity and residents' quality of life: testing an integrative model. J Hosp Tour Manag 41:1–11
Tonon G (ed) (2015) Qualitative studies in quality of life methodology and practice, Social indicators research series, vol 55. Springer, Dordretch, New York
Tonon GH (2017) Rethinking community quality of life in Latin American countries. In: Tonon GH (ed) Quality of life in communities of Latin countries. Springer, Cham, Switzerland, pp 3–14
Tonon GH (2019) The importance of Teaching quality of life theory and methodology in social sciences programs. In: Tonon GH (ed) Teaching quality of life in different domains. Springer, Cham, Switzerland, pp 1–14
Tonon GH, Rodriguez L (2016) Measuring quality of life and inequalities in South America. In: Tonon GH (ed) Indicators of quality of life in Latin America. Springer, Cham, Switzerland, pp 3–18
Valverde K, Gutiérrez E (2017) The community program for neighborhood improvement in Mexico City. In: Tonon GH (ed) Quality of life in communities of Latin countries. Springer, Cham, Switzerland, pp 95–116
Weinreich NK (2011) Hands-on social marketing: a step-by-step guide to designing change for good, 2nd edn. SAGE Publications, London
Whitehead AL, Stroope S (2015) Small groups, contexts, and civic engagement: a multilevel analysis of United States congregational life survey data. Soc Sci Res 52:659–670

Chapter 26
A Marketing Contribution to the Recognition of Regional and Local Brands: "Portugal Sou Eu" Case Study

Ana Cardoso and Bruno Sousa

Abstract This case study aims to understand the importance of attachment in social marketing contexts, analysing the affectivity to the program "Portugal Sou Eu" (i.e. an initiative of the Portuguese Ministry of Economy). The main objective of this Portuguese program is to increase informed consumption and foster the valorisation of national supply through the involvement of all civil society. "Portugal Sou Eu" is important to increase competitiveness and job creation in Portuguese companies (especially to SMEs) and quality of life (Qol) for citizens. The program seal is attributed to products and services based on national incorporation criteria, brands and patents, national employment and added value for the country. This case study emphasises the decision process of purchase and quality of life (i.e. to understand the importance of government initiatives and programs in promoting national brands and quality of life for citizens). Actions are a tool that can contribute to improving the quality of life of the population of a national territory.

Keywords Attachment · Brand · "Portugal Sou Eu" · Quality · Recognition

Introduction

Government initiatives and programs to promote national brands are decisive in the operational domain of a country. They can influence the purchasing decisions of citizens (and even visitors). Actions are a tool that can contribute to improving the quality of life (QoL) of the population of a national territory. The evolution of marketing also brought with it the development of the brand concept, whose interest

A. Cardoso
University of Minho, Braga, Portugal

B. Sousa (✉)
Polytechnic Institute of Cávado and Ave(IPCA), Braga, Portugal
e-mail: bsousa@ipca.pt

M. M. Galan-Ladero, R. G. Rivera (eds.), *Applied Social Marketing and Quality of Life*, Applying Quality of Life Research,
https://doi.org/10.1007/978-3-030-83286-5_26

lay in perceiving ways to influence consumer behaviour (Lee and Kotler 2020). According to the American Marketing Association (AMA), a brand is a name, term, sign, symbol, or design, or combination thereof, for the "purpose of identifying the goods and services of a seller or group of sellers and differentiate them from those of competition" (Keller 2013, p. 2).

Ghodeswar (2008) enhances the identification function by stating that a trademark is a distinctive name and/or symbol with the intention of identifying the goods or services of a seller or a group of sellers, and to differentiate those products or services from competitors. The degree of brand loyalty will be determined by the success or failure of the strategy adopted. To be efficient and to deliver positive results, a brand identity must be in tune with its customers (Malär et al. 2011), differentiate the brand from competitors and represent what the organization can do and effectively do over time (Ghodeswar 2008; Aaker and Joachimsthaler 2012).

Looking closely at Portugal's case, the country and its economy are currently experiencing a phase of re-emerge from a serious economic crisis (with particular relevance to pandemic effects and consumption habits), quality of life and social concerns that has shaken not only this country, but also most European countries. The markets experienced this negative phase, causing the population to lose some purchasing power, especially in Portugal.[1] Due to the decrease in purchasing power, the price sensitivity of consumers increased significantly, meaning that concerns about the valuation of domestic production were in the background. Therefore, it is important to highlight the attachment theory as an element that may cause changes in the population's consumption habits (and, consequently, in the citizens' quality of life). The attachment theory emphasizes an affective bond between people and specific places, brands or certain products (Hidalgo and Hernandez 2001).

The brand attachment refers to the link or bond that is shared by certain people with certain brands or products (Scannell and Gifford 2010). This affection often refers to a sensation, a feeling (including symbolic and emotional expressions). As such, the motivation for choosing this theme finds its justification on this point. The goal is to understand the extent to which the «Portugal Sou Eu» Program aims to boost and enhance Portugal's offer with remarkable national incorporation, that is, national added value and the promotion of informed consumption, through an active and national production with an impact on the population's quality of life (Boateng et al. 2020). In crisis situations, consumption habits tend to be different. Sometimes, consumers tend to favour national, regional or local products (sometimes due to price sensitivity) or affective ties to products of national origin (driven by government programs). This situation affects the quality of life of the population (who purchases the products) but also of the professionals of the companies (who manage to maintain jobs and working conditions for employees).

[1] Due to the economic crisis that affected European Union, that lasted between the years 2011 to 2017, Portugal had to be rescued by the Eurozone, through a 78 billion loan financed by the European Stability Mechanism, the European Financial Stabilization Fund and the International Monetary Fund, being under the control of Brussels for several years. This situation did not happen in Spain or Italy, but that also happened in Greece and Ireland, although with different results.

Fig. 26.1 Logo of the program "Portugal Sou Eu". Source: Portugal Sou Eu (2020)

Case Development: "Portugal Sou Eu" Program

Contextualization and Mission

The program "Portugal Sou Eu" is an initiative of the Ministry of Economy, approved by the Resolution of the Council of Ministers 56/2011, designed to be particularly addressed to small and medium-sized enterprises (SMEs), and aims to boost and enhance the national offer through an active brand that represents the national production. The main objective of this program is to increase informed consumption and foster the valorisation of national supply through the involvement of all civil society, increasing competitiveness and job creation in Portuguese companies, especially to SMEs.

The "Portugal Sou Eu" initiative is available to any citizen and/or entity, and there are various forms of participation, broken down on the program's website (www.portugalsoueu.pt). The project under study is intended for all end consumers and needs to be sensitized by promoting and identifying the origin of products and services, providing informed and sustainable choice of consumption (IAPMEI 2020). It is also important to include SMEs in the primary, secondary, retail and catering sectors, as for them there are advantages and benefits of joining the "Portugal Sou Eu" network of companies. Finally, the program in question also includes large companies and large retailers and institutional buyers. These are sensitized to the promotion of supply and demand platforms that facilitate interaction with national SMEs.

Always aiming at enhancing national identity, promoting conscious consumption and fostering the competitiveness of Portuguese companies (e.g. people's salaries, employment, health and not only on companies' competitiveness), the program has strategic and operational objectives. Regarding the strategy, the "Portugal Sou Eu" program was designed to stimulate the economic recovery of the economic fabric, making it more competitive, always with a view to enhancing the national supply. By boosting the market, it is intended to assist companies so that they are able to increase their export potential. Nowadays, this program has been gaining more importance, as exemplified by the two agreements reached between Associação Empresarial de Portugal (AEP), the coordinating entity, Makro and the SONAE MC group. These two agreements aim to include products with the "Portugal Sou Eu" seal, in order to encourage consumers to buy them. Still in relation to the context, through contact with the company Nacional, another company whose adhesion to the program is also recent, there are advantages related to the reinforcement of portugality provided by the seal acquired in the adhesion (Fig. 26.1).

Strategic and Operational Objectives

The team responsible for the "Portugal Sou Eu" program outlined two types of objectives (i.e. strategic and operational). The strategic objectives are related to the stimulation of the competitiveness of national companies, the incentive to production with increased incorporation of value in Portugal (contributing to the revitalization of the national productive fabric and creation of jobs) and the sustainable recovery of economic growth (Quintela 2020), with the effort to ensure the articulation and coherence between public and private actions that fit these objectives. The operational objectives refer to the actions to be implemented in order to achieve the desired results. These objectives are, once again, spelled out on the official website of the "Portugal Sou Eu" Program.

Therefore, they refer to the increase in publicity and notoriety of the "Portugal Sou Eu" brand and to create conditions that allow consumers to make an informed choice, fostering the importance attributed by the Portuguese to the consumption of products and services originating in Portugal, stimulating a change in the attitude of consumers and companies.

Initiatives and Promotion

Thus, through the website of the program under study, the initiatives related to the member companies refer to their mobilization, using various activities of member mobilization such as visits, meetings, workshops, seminars, in order to clarify the companies about membership of the "Portugal Sou Eu" seal and its requirements.

Focusing now on initiatives aimed at consumers, the program under analysis also develops several actions that favour the adhesion to "Portugal Sou Eu". Therefore, the first initiative concerns the dissemination of information through the portugalsoueu.pt. portal. In this portal the qualified products and services "Portugal Sou Eu" are disseminated and on social networks and through smartphones, shows in each place where the same products, services and participating establishments can be found. Another initiative relates to the use of prescribers in the promotion of "Portugal Sou Eu". Some personalities from the most different spheres of society, designated as "Portugal Sou Eu" ambassadors, are used, who contribute publicly to boost the brand, promoting the initiative and promoting the informed choice of products and services that adhere to their activities (Fig. 26.2).

The program values, through a seal, the production of products, services and crafts. The "Portugal Sou Eu" seal is attributed to products and services based on national incorporation criteria, brands and patents, national employment and added value for the country. Products and services that meet the requirements for joining the Program are identified by the consumer through the "Portugal Sou Eu" brand. The society of the twenty-first century has seen how the influence of economic, socio-cultural, political and technological factors has managed to redesign to our

Fig. 26.2 Acreditar em Portugal começa comigo (Believing in Portugal starts with me). Source: Portugal Sou Eu (2020)

lives and our working conditions (Tonon 2015). It is possible to include big changes that have resulted in a remodelling of the work and personal environments in which we interact. Regarding Quality of Life (QOL), the program presented here "Portugal Sou Eu", the initiative is more than a program, This program is a collective expression of pride, a responsible attitude, a simple way of creating difference in the country and everyone (i.e. a different country in terms of quality of life). Whenever consumers and companies prefer, advertise and give a voice to Portuguese products and services, they are not only promoting quality and authenticity. They are also helping to strengthen the national economy and generate wealth. And that is guaranteed return for everyone. "Portugal Sou Eu" and much more. "Portugal Sou Eu" studied the impact of membership for participating companies 82.6% of companies consider that sales benefited from joining the program. According to IAPMEI (2014), and regarding the buying habits of products with national incorporation, more than 60% of consumers purchase Portuguese products very frequently. Regarding the most purchased product categories, the Portuguese products most purchased by consumers in Portugal are: wine, olive oil, bread, fruits, vegetables, cheese, rice, furniture and footwear. The study carried out by IAPMEI in 2014, states that 87.6% of consumers are globally satisfied with the Portuguese products they buy. The results derive from a total of 1301 valid responses, 52.5% of which were women; 18.6% of the Norte Litoral region, 11.7% of Grande Porto, 10.7% of the Interior Norte and Centro, 14.4% of the Centro Litoral, 29% of Lisbon and 15.7% of the South and Islands. 88% of Portuguese who purchase products with the national brand, make this decision because "it helps to keep jobs in Portugal" and "it helps Portugal to have a stronger economy". In the case of food products, 80% of respondents favour Portuguese products for the taste and quality of the product. National consumers tend to favour products with the Portuguese brand for reasons of ethnocentrism, accessibility and quality in purchases. Consequently, this decision presents an improvement in the quality of life of the population (e.g. service and product quality), but also of the national producers and professionals of the companies (e.g. due to working conditions and job maintenance).

Conclusions

The present case study showed the challenge to understand the role of social marketing strategies, such as is the case of the strategies implemented in the "Portugal Sou Eu" Program. In specific, the authors intended to understand the extent to which the «Portugal Sou Eu» Program aims to boost and enhance Portugal's offer with remarkable national incorporation (i.e. national added value and the promotion of informed consumption, through an active and national production with an impact on the population's quality of life). Through the data collection, the coordinating entity has shown that it is developing a dissemination work in order to reach the largest number of consumers leading them to join, even registering an increase in the purchase of Portuguese products frequently between 2014 and 2017, through a study. According to the Portuguese Ministry of Economy, this means that it has not yet been reflected in the attitudes of Portuguese consumers, in order to make them prioritize the consumption of products with "Portugal Sou Eu" seal at the moment of choice.

In summary, through the study performed, it is possible to realize that the attachment theory can be further developed in strategic terms to provide greater attraction by the public (i.e. citizens) and, consequently, the loyalty of national products (thus providing progress in quality of life). Decision makers and government forces should develop the attachment theory among the population (e.g. particularly the year 2020 was influenced by the Covid-19 pandemic and this event could provide greater bonds of affection with national and territorial brands). This program needs greater investment by public authorities in order to reach as many consumers as possible, making them more aware of the importance of valuing national production. Further recognition of this program is crucial, for example, including the appointed ambassadors. Their recognition and public exposure should be enjoyed through publications on their social networks about the program "Portugal Sou Eu", for example. Four out of five Portuguese consumers who purchase products with the national brand, make this decision because "it helps to keep jobs in Portugal" and "it helps Portugal to have a stronger economy". In the case of food products, 80% of respondents favour Portuguese products for the taste and quality of the product. National consumers tend to favour products with the Portuguese brand for reasons of ethnocentrism, accessibility and quality in purchases. Consequently, this decision presents an improvement in the quality of life of the population (considering the quality presented), but also of the national producers and professionals of the companies (due to working conditions and job maintenance). Therefore, it is important to highlight the attachment theory as an element that may cause changes in the population's consumption habits (and, consequently, in the citizens' quality of life). The attachment theory emphasizes an affective bond between people and specific places, brands or certain products.

The "Portugal Sou Eu" Program seeks to stimulate national production and encourage informed consumption of products and services, with the fundamental contribution of participating establishments, which actively contribute to add value to the national economy and generate employment: (1) to consumers: Dissemination of "Portugal Sou Eu" to consumers, with a special focus on the youngest, through communication and information campaigns that allow consumers to recognize the "Portugal Sou Eu" Seal as an unambiguous way of identifying the national origin of products and services, enabling informed choice and consumption and sustainable loyalty to the Portugal brand; (2) with companies: Promotion of "Portugal Sou Eu" among national entrepreneurs, especially SMEs, and awareness of the competitive advantage that the brand represents, promoting the adhesion and qualification of products and services and maximizing the range of products and services subject to certification and cooperation between participating companies through the "Portugal Sou Eu" Business Network; (3) with institutions and institutional buyers: Stimulating platforms that contribute to the meeting of supply and demand and that encourage interaction between national companies, especially SMEs, in order to enhance the establishment of integrated supply chains that to meet the needs of the national market; (4) Strategic partnerships that stimulate existing networks and opportunities: Celebration of strategic cooperation protocols with entities of recognized merit in the respective area of operation, with prestigious brands already rooted in national society and easily recognized by the consumer, or with networks of associates widely disseminated throughout the country and with a wide reach, in order to speed up the leverage of the "Portugal Sou Eu" brand and to foster mutual synergies.

Discussion Questions

Question 1. How can the valorization of national products or/and services can affect the society in general and, QoL in particular?

Question 2. What can social marketing do to change the disposition of consumers, in relation to the consumption of national products?

Question 3. What do you think about the communication carried out by the program "Portugal Sou Eu"?

Teaching Notes

Question 1. How can the valorization of national products and services affect the society and the quality of life?

The valorization of national products or/and services can affect the society in general and, also, the quality of life (QoL) of citizens and consumers. This valorization can lead to a greater promotion of conscious consumption and to foment the competitiveness of Portuguese companies, creating, this way, a sustainable economics. Enhancing the national supply, there is will be possible to the national companies to increase their export potential. National brands sometimes represent a strong identity, cultural and symbolic component that provides bonds of a psychological nature and can contribute to the higher quality of life for citizens. For example, the year 2020 was strongly marked by the Covid-19 pandemic. This event has allowed a greater communication effort by the territories to promote national brands and local values/culture, providing good feelings to the community (e.g. "buy what is ours", "visit our country"). The decision presents an improvement in the quality of life of the population (e.g. service and product quality), but also of the national producers and professionals of the companies (e.g. due to working conditions and job maintenance).

Question 2. What can strategic marketing do to change the disposition of consumers, in relation to the consumption of national products?

Strategic marketing can appeal to the Portuguese's sense of responsibility, leading them to change behaviors and, thus, making them more willing to consume national products. The social marketing and strategy decision must be based on demonstrating the benefits for the country in choosing products from the Portuguese brands adhering to the program. Particularly, in a pandemic context (i.e. 2020), citizens' predisposition to purchase national products and services is evident, since there is a greater distance between the community. Policy makers may, in these specific contexts, develop campaigns to promote and communicate national products and foster greater bonds of affection with the community.

Question 3. What do you think about the communication carried out by the program "Portugal Sou Eu"?

Through the collection and analysis of data, throughout the research, it was possible to realize that the communication and promotion of the program "Portugal Sou Eu" was not yet effective, because, in some cases, there is even a lack of knowledge about its existence. It is important to develop the "Portugal Sou Eu" Program in different communication channels and to diversify the communication tools through digital marketing and social networks. Initiatives should be proposed to accelerate the "Portugal Sou Eu" Program in the pandemic and post-pandemic contexts.

References

Aaker DA, Joachimsthaler E (2012) Brand leadership. Simon and Schuster

Boateng H, Kosiba JP, Adam DR, Ofori KS, Okoe AF (2020) Examining brand loyalty from an attachment theory perspective. Mark Intell Plan

Ghodeswar BM (2008) Building brand identity in competitive markets: a conceptual model. J Prod Brand Manag 17(1):4–12

Hidalgo MC, Hernandez B (2001) Place attachment: conceptual and empirical questions. J Environ Psychol 21(3):273–281

IAPMEI (2014). https://www.iapmei.pt/getattachment/PRODUTOS-E-SERVICOS/Qualificacao-Certificacao/Portugal-Sou-Eu/Forum-PSE_PortugalidadeCege_ISEG_Final.pdf.aspx

IAPMEI (2020). https://www.iapmei.pt/PRODUTOS-E-SERVICOS/Qualificacao-Certificacao/Portugal-Sou-Eu.aspx

Keller, K. L. (2013). Building, measuring, and managing brand equity

Lee N, Kotler P (2020) Social marketing: behavior change for social good. Sage

Malär L, Krohmer H, Hoyer WD, Nyffenegger B (2011) Emotional brand attachment and brand personality: the relative importance of the actual and the ideal self. J Mark 75(4):35–52

Quintela D (2020) Do projeto Marca Portugal ao portugal Sou Eu: que políticas públicas para a Marca Portugal. Sociologia, Problemas e Práticas

Scannell L, Gifford R (2010) Defining place attachment: a tripartite organizing framework. J Environ Psychol 30(1):1–10

Tonon G (2015) Relevance of the use of qualitative methods in the study of quality of life. In: Qualitative studies in quality of life. Springer, Cham, pp 3–21

References

Correction to: An Original Social Marketing Campaign to “Try Vegan”: Effectiveness and Impact on Quality of Life

Estela M. Diaz, Nora Lado, and David F. Martín-García

Correction to: Chaper 12 in: M. M. Galan-Ladero, R. G. Rivera (eds.), *Applied Social Marketing and Quality of Life*, Applying Quality of Life Research, https://doi.org/10.1007/978-3-030-83286-5_12

The name and affiliation of the author David F. Martin were corrected to David F. Martín-García, ICADE, Faculty of Economics and Business Administration, Department of Marketing, Madrid, Spain.

On page 205, in the 5th line of the abstract the phrase ‘more than 900,000’ was changed to ‘more than 1,400,000’.

On page 210, the second paragraph ‘In 6 years, since it was launched, Veganuary have gotten to be present in 192 countries around the world and have obtained an exponential growth of participation, with more than 400,000 participants in the last year and 900,000 people in total. Additionally, more than 600 brands, restaurants, and supermarkets sponsored the campaign, and launched more than 1200 new vegan products and menus in the UK market alone’. was changed to ‘In 7 years, since it was launched, Veganuary has gotten to be present in 192 countries around the world and has obtained an exponential growth of participation, with almost 600,000 participants in the last year and more than 1,400,000 people in total. Additionally, more than 600 brands, restaurants, and supermarkets sponsored the campaign, and launched more than 1200 new vegan products and menus in the UK market alone.’

The original chapter was revised.

The updated version of this chapter can be found at
https://doi.org/10.1007/978-3-030-83286-5_12

M. M. Galan-Ladero, R. G. Rivera (eds.), *Applied Social Marketing and Quality of Life*, Applying Quality of Life Research,
https://doi.org/10.1007/978-3-030-83286-5_27

The manufacturer's authorised representative in the EU is Springer Nature Customer Service Centre GmbH, Europaplatz 3, 69115 Heidelberg, Germany. If you have any concerns regarding our products, please contact ProductSafety@springernature.com

Printed and bound by CPI Group (UK) Ltd, Croydon, CR0 4YY
28/09/2026
02224065-0006